Elusive Peace

I. WILLIAM ZARTMAN
Editor

Elusive Peace

Negotiating an End to Civil Wars

THE BROOKINGS INSTITUTION
Washington, D.C.

About Brookings

The Brookings Institution is a private nonprofit organization devoted to research, education, and publication on important issues of domestic and foreign policy. Its principal purpose is to bring knowledge to bear on current and emerging policy problems. The Institution was founded on December 8, 1927, to merge the activities of the Institute for Government Research, founded in 1916, the Institute of Economics, founded in 1922, and the Robert Brookings Graduate School of Economics, founded in 1924. The Institution maintains a position of neutrality on issues of public policy. Interpretations or conclusions in Brookings publications should be understood to be solely those of the authors.

Library of Congress Cataloging-in-Publication data:

Elusive peace : negotiating an end to civil wars / I. William Zartman, ed.
   p.   cm.
Includes bibliographical references and index.
ISBN 0-8157-9704-4 (cl : alk. paper). — ISBN 0-8157-9703-6
(pa: alk. paper)
   1. History, Modern—20th century.   2. Civil war.   3. Conflict
management.   4. Mediation, International.   5. Peace.   I. Zartman,
I. William.
D421.E58 1995
909.82—dc20
                                       95-7653
                                        CIP

9 8 7 6 5 4 3 2 1

The paper used in this publication meets the minimum requirements of the American National Standard for Information Sciences—Permanence of Paper for Printed Library Materials, ANSI Z39.48-1984.

Typeset in Times Roman

Composition by Alpha Technologies/mps, Inc.
Charlotte Hall, Maryland

Printed by R. R. Donnelley and Sons, Co.
Harrisonburg, Virginia

To Olusegun Obasanjo

Acknowledgments

I AM MOST PLEASED to acknowledge the support of the John D. and Catherine T. MacArthur Foundation and the Carnegie Corporation for this project. I also thank Theresa Taylor Simmons for her fine assistance in the preparation of the many versions of this manuscript, and I am grateful for the patience and cooperation of my far-flung contributors during this book's long gestation. During this period, I have been largely responsible for updating and extending the analyses presented in chapters 3, 9, and 10.

Finally, I wish to acknowledge the inspiration and experience gained through collaboration with one of Africa's finest leaders, General and former President Olusegun Obasanjo, whose great work in search of elusive peace through the African Leadership Forum has been interrupted by fraudulent charges of sedition by Nigeria's current rulers. This book is dedicated to him, to his work, and to the hopes of his liberation and the continuation of his efforts for peace and good governance.

Contents

Part One

NEGOTIATING
INTERNAL CONFLICTS:
INTRODUCTION

CHAPTER ONE

Dynamics and Constraints in Negotiations in Internal Conflicts

I. William Zartman

INTERNAL CONFLICTS—civil wars—are the most difficult of conflicts to negotiate. Only a quarter to a third of modern civil wars (including anticolonial wars) have found their way to negotiation, whereas more than half of modern interstate wars have done so.[1] About two-thirds of the internal conflicts have ended in the surrender or elimination of one of the parties involved; fewer than a quarter of the international conflicts have so ended. Yet in internal conflicts more than in interstate wars, defeat of the rebellion often merely drives the cause underground, to emerge at a later time. On the other hand, in principle, negotiation is the best policy for both parties in an internal conflict. It is the government's job to be responsive to the grievances of its people; it is the insurgents' purpose to draw attention to their grievances and gain redress. Negotiation is the natural meeting point of these needs, an extension of the "normal politics" that should characterize a well-functioning polity. Yet internal conflict works against its own best outcome.

The challenge confronted in this book is to explain why internal conflict is so obdurately resistant to negotiations and then to turn that explanation on its head to find ways to bring about successful negotiations. Structurally, internal conflict is marked by asymmetry, a characteristic generally considered unconducive to negotiation, and attempts to redress asymmetry only

3

further complicate negotiation dynamics. Contextually, internal conflict and the parties to it are both subject to evolutions and life cycles that impose their own dynamics in competition, as it were, with the requirement of negotiation, thus often prolonging and complicating the conflict beyond the interests of the parties. Tactically, these conditions make it particularly difficult to get internal negotiations started, and require special devices, artifices, and attitudes often available only through mediation; yet mediation is an intrusion especially difficult to legitimate in internal conflict.

To understand internal negotiations, the normal purview of negotiation theory must be expanded. Negotiation theory must be further developed, tested against situations of internal conflict, and refined accordingly, so that deductive guides to the potentialities for negotiation can be established. More case studies are needed in order to generate insights and observations that can be used inductively to produce applicable concepts and theory.[2] That is one task of the analyses in this book. The major parameters and characteristics of internal conflict negotiations are set out in this introductory chapter.

Symbolic of the complexities of internal negotiations is the ambiguity of the subject itself. Few internal wars are purely internal, although the post–World War II rebellion in the Philippines, various guerrilla rebellions in the Andean countries, and to some extent the Basque insurrection in Spain are relatively autonomous and self-sufficient. Nothing else seems to distinguish these purely internal rebellions from the larger number of other internal wars that have a substantial and often dominant international dimension. Conflict of the latter kind has its subdivisions: internal rebellions that necessarily mirror regional conflicts because of transnational populations and interests, as in the Horn of Africa, Central America, and Southeast Asia; internal conflicts in which the overarching state identity breaks down and the component pieces draw in external support from their "brothers" in neighboring states, as in Sri Lanka, Cyprus, Kashmir, Lebanon, Afghanistan, and Northern Ireland; internal conflicts in which the search for external sources of power has turned into proxy wars for distant powers, as in Angola, Mozambique, former Yugoslavia, and Afghanistan; and a residual group of internal conflicts in which one or both parties have enjoyed sanctuary or support, or both, from outside, as in South Africa, Rwanda, Biafra, Mozambique, Sudan, and the Basque territory. As will be seen, the external dimension has profound effects on both the intractability and the mediation of internal conflicts. Regionalized, exploded, proxy, and supported conflicts are nonetheless internal in their cause and core. Former

U.S. assistant secretary of state Chester Crocker has made the insightful tactical observation that the external dimension must be resolved and removed before the parties can resolve the core internal conflict.[3] Yet even when reduced to its purely internal dimensions, the conflict remains intractable, as Angola and Afghanistan testify.

No less ambiguity exists concerning an appropriate name for the parties to a conflict, even the parties to the core dispute. "Government" is relatively uncontested as the name for one side, although the legitimacy implied by the term is often a major point of issue in the conflict. However, the other party can take on many names, some of which it rejects because of their implications. "Insurgents" is used in the analyses in this book, as are "rebels" and "opposition." One characteristic ties these and other terms together, however. This study is about negotiations between government and an opposition that contests the government's legitimate monopoly on violence and uses violent means to press its demands and to contest government authority. Thus it is not about just any internal conflicts and negotiations between government and opposition, many of which are at the core of normal politics or the business of authoritatively handling grievances and demands.[4]

Neither side, by any name, is a monolith. Beyond the pluralism of each side's external supports is the pluralism of its internal composition. Although there can be many sources of internal pluralism, the basic source is the tactical matter of conflict and negotiation: elements within both sides fall out over the tactical question—the necessity of violence and the advisability of compromise. Such divisions play an important role in the internal dynamics of the rebellion, as each side seeks to preserve its unity, establish valid spokespersons, and deliver on military and diplomatic promises. Like external support, internal pluralism can inhibit negotiation, although its role and influence can be turned positive under certain conditions.

Internal conflicts begin with the inability or unwillingness of the government to handle grievances to the satisfaction of the aggrieved; that is, they begin with the breakdown of normal politics. Internal conflicts are about many different things in different cases, but all aggravated grievances can be subsumed under two related categories—neglect and discrimination, or a distributional element and an identity element. Without distributional deprivation, identity remains a positive factor and not a motivation for conflict; without an identity element, distributional inequities remain unfocused and nonmobilizing. The mix of the two elements may vary, situating the conflict toward one end of the spectrum or the other, but that appears to have little effect on its course or tractability.

Thus in the Basque and Afghan conflicts the identity element has been much stronger than the distributional element. Basques have rallied around the chance to be themselves and not Spaniards, and Afghans rallied first around the possibility of being themselves and not communists and then around the need to be Tajiks, Pushtus, or true Muslims; they have not mobilized around any real deprivation (except that of political position) as Basques or as anticommunists or ethnoreligious zealots. At the other extreme, the Colombian, Philippine, Mozambican, and Angolan conflicts arose to protest national distribution policies, in favor of the rich in Colombia and the Philippines and in favor of a bungled, destructive communist effort to restructure society in Mozambique and Angola. Even in these conflicts there has been an identity element, the Colombian and Philippine rebels finding their identity in ideology, and the National Union for the Total Independence of Angola (UNITA) and Mozambican National Resistance (RENAMO) movements developing an ethnic concentration. The basic causes of the other conflicts studied in this book have all combined the elements of deprivation and discrimination: rebels in Sri Lanka, Sudan, Ethiopia, Lebanon, and South Africa (and eventually in Afghanistan and Mozambique) revolted because they felt they were being discriminated against *as* Tamils, southern Sudanese, Eritreans, Muslims, Blacks, Tajiks, and Ndaos. The conflicts in South Africa and Sudan stand as extreme examples of a zero-sum identity conflict; there (even objectively) whites and Arabs have each felt that their own identity depended upon a denial of identity rights to the other.

The outcome sought by the rebellion as a corrective to discriminatory neglect is of two major kinds, sometimes sharper in definition than in reality. In one, the contest of government authority seeks to replace the incumbents and establish a new central government. In the other, the contest is over government control of or policies for a group or a region of the country, and demands are made for some form of local self-determination ranging from autonomy to secession. Internal conflicts in Lebanon, Colombia, Peru, the Philippines, Afghanistan, Angola, Mozambique, South Africa, Rwanda, Burundi, and Ethiopia are conflicts over central authority, even though in many cases the rebels have a particular ethnic or regional base.[5] Conflicts in Eritrea, Cyprus, Sri Lanka, the Basque territory, Kashmir, Kurdistan, and Sudan are regional, although a number of them also have centralist implications.[6]

Centralist and regional protests have different goals and hence are satisfied by different outcomes, but they are so similar in many ways and one is so often a stage successive to the other that they can be considered together. At some point in the breakdown of normal politics, some of the aggrieved may become convinced that government cannot or should not rule the country; others may become convinced that although the government may still rule the country it cannot or should not rule the aggrieved party's group or region of the country. The fork in the road between those two conclusions is clear but not irrevocable, and conflicts sometimes shift from one path to the other, and even back again, as events in Sri Lanka, Sudan, and Ethiopia have shown. Conflicts also change in intensity and in the demands made on each party. By keeping in mind these distinctions and commonalities, an investigation can be made that fine-tunes concepts of internal negotiation and may generate better ways of conducting international relations where internal conflicts continue to affect international peace and security.

This chapter pursues its analysis of internal conflict and negotiation along three dimensions—the structural, the dynamic, and the tactical—that are also used in the subsequent case studies. It begins by analyzing a characteristic structure of imbalance and corresponding structural ways of getting out of the situation of asymmetry. A rebellion is then placed within its own evolutionary context, and further opportunities and constraints imposed by that evolution are identified. The inquiry then examines appropriate processes and behaviors inherent in negotiations—particularly mediated negotiations—as they can be pursued within the structural and contextual constraints.

Structures of Conflict

The most striking characteristic of internal conflict is its asymmetry: one party (government) is strong and the other (insurgents) is weak. This is true until tables are finally turned at the end (if they can be), and it is true not only in regard to the military components of power but also in regard to less tangible components such as legitimacy. Thus a rebellion is a dual protracted struggle, striving for both ends and means: a struggle for attention, redress, and legitimacy, inseparably interwoven with a struggle for the power to pursue those ends. Furthermore, only the first part of the struggle—the struggle for ends—is against the government; the other part is a struggle against "nature" or against the general domestic and international environment within which the conflict takes place.

The government has legitimacy, sovereignty, allies, armies, and access to resources. The insurgents have to fight for all of these. Moreover, the government determines and has the right to determine the rules of the game for the rebellion's struggle. If the rebellion's cause is one of regional rights, government sets both the conditions for petition and expectation and for its own response. If the rebellion's cause is a contest for national leadership, government sets the rules for conducting that competition and then runs in its own race. It is both participant and umpire. The rebellion is only petitioner and contestor, two positions of inferiority. Even when the rebellion builds up strength—with recognition, supporters, guerrillas, and resources—and the government loses its monopoly on these, the rebellion is only (with rare and extreme exceptions) approaching equality, and the tables have not yet really turned.

Negotiations under conditions of asymmetry (asymmetrical negotiations) are a paradox, because one of the basic findings about the negotiation process is that it functions best under conditions of equality, and indeed only takes place when the parties have some form of a mutual veto over outcomes.[7] That alone explains why so few internal wars are settled by negotiation. Asymmetry means that the most propitious conditions for resolving conflict are difficult to obtain. Numerous studies have shown that a mutually hurting stalemate defines the moment as ripe for resolution: both sides are locked in a situation from which they cannot escalate the conflict with their available means and at an acceptable cost.[8] Such a stalemate provides a window of opportunity that is narrow and highly conditional; it depends on perceived rather than objective reality, on a stalemate that affects both sides, and on a discomfort (preferably increasing) felt by both parties. Although the pain does not have to be equal or the stalemate exactly balanced, the asymmetry of internal conflict rarely produces the stalemate needed for negotiation.

Studies of asymmetrical negotiations without exception have focused on various ways in which the weaker party improves its outcome by reducing the asymmetry.[9] Yet generally in the cases covered by such studies there is a basic equivalence between the parties themselves, even if their power differs. Whether as states, individuals, or groups, the parties have existence outside of the conflict: they have other interests than the conflict, and the cost-benefit questions underlying the dynamics of their relationship (conflictual or negotiatory) revolve about how much of a larger pool of power and interests to devote to the particular conflict.[10] The asymmetry in these cases is thus basically different from the asymmetry found in internal conflicts and negotiations. In internal conflicts and negotiations, one party—the rebels—is totally fixed on the conflict, which involves its very existence, whereas the other—the government—has many interests. For government, the rebellion is only a worrisome distraction from the pursuit of other goals.

Thus rebels redress asymmetry by opposing the government's capabilities with their own commitment. To overcome their weakness in means, rebels overinvest in their attachment to ends. Initially, the insurgent party is willing to compete and to petition within the government-established rules, facing other competitors and petitioners on equal footing. But when the insurgents enter into rebellion, reject the rules and the government's right to impose them, and oppose the government itself, they take on a total and exclusive commitment to rebellion. They have no reason to exist outside the conflict; the rebel has nothing to do but rebel. The government, on the other hand, is distracted by many other considerations. Existence is not its only issue, and probably not its issue at all, except possibly at the conflict's end. At that point, the rebellion has either been repressed or has succeeded in imposing total commitment on the government as well, creating the ultimate zero-sum conflict. That is one of the dimensions of Henry A. Kissinger's statement that "the guerrilla wins if he does not lose; the conventional army loses if it does not win.[11] Because existence is the rebellion's only issue—hence its commitment—not losing preserves its existence and makes it win. The government has specific functions to perform, including maintenance of security, and it loses if it does not perform them properly, even if its existence is not threatened directly thereby. The rebels thrive on desperation because it reinforces their single-minded commitment. Commitment does not overcome a lack of resources, but it does change the calculations of the conflict.

This asymmetrical situation can be related to negotiation by dividing the motivations (ends) of the rebellion into two components: grievances and commitment. The protest begins with grievances, and its spokespersons need to build commitment to its cause. As long as redress of grievances and commitment to the cause are in balance, or the first exceeds the second as a motivator, negotiations are possible. But when commitment to continuing the rebellion exceeds grievances as a motivation, it becomes an end in itself. Even when the government accedes to the demand to negotiate, a rebellion can be so high on commitment that it throws away its chance to negotiate and compromise, as happened in the conflicts in Sri Lanka, the Basque homeland, Eritrea, and the Western Sahara, among others (see chapters 2, 3, and 5).[12] Reduction of grievances is sometimes even regarded by rebels as the government's way of deterring the militants from devotion to the cause; negotiation thus becomes correspondingly difficult, if not impossible. Rebellion becomes a way of life in a culture of violence.

Negotiation becomes difficult in that situation for at least four other reasons as well. First, there is no room for compromise on the part of the rebels. Recognition is both the top and the bottom line. Whether as a regional secession movement or as a national contestant for central power, the rebellion seeks recognition, and once this has been achieved only operational details remain to be negotiated. Second, there is no room for trade-offs, which are the components of bargains. The rebels' issue and commitment are integral and indivisible and the insurgents have little to give up but their rebellion. So the most important deal is made in the agreement to negotiate, leaving only details to trade off when negotiations begin.

Third, the issue of valid spokespersons, usually a precondition for negotiations, becomes the major issue in the conflict.[13] Once it has been decided, the core of the negotiation has been achieved. The government contests the rebel leader as a spokesperson for anyone, because to recognize that leader's position is to accede to the rebels' principle demand. The insurgents contest the government's right to speak for the country and want the government to step down from its superior position to one of equality, because the government's ability to speak for the nation is what the rebellion is all about.

Fourth, stalemate is a stable, viable, bearable compromise rather than a constraining burden that forces both sides to negotiation. Particularly in a regional protest, stalemate often means unrecognized partition of the country: the rebellion's complaint of regional neglect is formalized in the extreme as the insurgents keep government forces out of the region or liberated territory and consolidate their demands for regional autonomy. Even in a centralist conflict there are often liberated zones and territorial divisions, as in the conflicts in Lebanon, Angola, Mozambique, and Afghanistan (see chapters 6, 8, 9, and 10). The government maintains its claim of sovereignty over the region, keeps its army in operational training, and enjoys a mobilizing issue around a national cause. In a reverse of the usual situation, nonnegotiation is compromise and negotiation is a zero-sum victory for one side. These implications explain why negotiation in an asymmetrical internal conflict is so difficult.[14]

For negotiation to take place, exceptions to or ways around these inhibitions must be found. Typically, governments and insurgents alike try to play on the element of cost to make the stalemate hurt and force the other side to change its policy. But the stakes remain unequal: insurgents seek to make the government negotiate (implying, first, recognition), whereas the government seeks to make the insurgents surrender. Thus the asymmetries in power and commitment become a trap for their respective parties, preventing the negotiations that the parties seek to end the conflict.

There is also asymmetry in outcomes. In the cases referred to above that ended in surrender or in elimination, it was usually the rebellion that surrendered or was eliminated. Or at least apparently so, because where the rebellion had an ethnoregional base it simply slipped back into the recesses of subnational consciousness, to arise again at a later moment of breakdown in normal politics, either through new grievances or a new time of government weakness. If surrender or elimination are the most frequent outcomes, the government asks itself, Why bother to deal with the cause of the conflict, when the insurgency appears to be coming under control? And the insurgents, particularly when rebuffed, ask themselves, Why trust the government, when our strongest need is to keep our own belief in our identity alive? Government prevails, but the struggle continues and negotiation suffers, each side being a victim of its own part of the asymmetry.

Power asymmetry, compensating commitment by the rebels, and narrowed possibilities for negotiation are the structural characteristics of internal conflict and negotiation. They combine so clearly to indicate protracted and insoluble struggle that a search by the parties for a structural change in the situation is inevitable. The government seeks to turn asymmetry into escalation, to destroy the rebellion and break its commitment, and force the rebels to sue for peace. The insurgents usually seek to break out of their asymmetry by linking up with an external host state and neighbor, thus internationalizing the conflict.

In so doing the insurgents radically change the structure of the conflict from a doubly asymmetrical dyad to a wobbly triad of great complexity. The host state to the insurgents and the home state to the conflict have their own relations independent of the conflict, and they use the insurgency as a bargaining chip or a means to pressure one another. The government of the home state may have an interest in winning the rebels away from the host state or in making a deal with the host on the backs of the rebels. The host state has an interest in protecting but also in using and controlling the insurgency, and the insurgents as guests are both prisoners and occupiers of the neighbor-host. The insurgency has to be careful not to be sold out by a host acting as mediator or captured by a host serving as sanctuary. Under the conditions of such a triad, the chances for negotiation are actually worsened, as the conflict serves the purposes of all involved. If the home state also has an external patron and if other outside states become involved, the basic triad is made all the more complex, as conflicts in Eritrea, Angola, the Western Sahara, and Cyprus show. Someone can always be found to support a faction on one side or the other that seeks to escalate the conflict and avoid negotiation, thereby further reducing the meager chances of settlement.

Furthermore, governments are typically faced with questions about their relations to an insurgent-supporting neighbor (as seen in Lebanon, Afghanistan, Sudan, Ethiopia, Angola, Mozambique, and Sri Lanka): Is it better to seek an accommodation with the neighbor and undercut the insurgency, or to seek an accommodation with the insurgency by wooing it away from the neighbor? Similarly, the neighbor frequently hesitates between actions to change the government next door and support for the rebellion, implying different criteria for judging conflict resolution and conducting negotiations. On the other hand, the bilateral asymmetry can be attacked (or reinforced) through coalition politics, as in Colombia, Lebanon, Sudan, and South Africa.

Dynamics of Protest and Resolution

Beyond structural impositions lie the long-term dynamics of internal conflicts that further influence the chances of negotiation. Internal conflict is a moving target. Its nature changes over time as it passes through identifiable stages. As a result, outcomes that would have satisfied the protest and been possible for the government at one time no longer can resolve the conflict at other times.[15] The rules and expectations governing relations between the parties shift, and along with them the range of possible and resolving outcomes.

As the conflict evolves, the protest component of the dispute and the conflict management (resolving) component take their own separate directions. The protest component has its own evolution or dynamic as the rebellion seeks to develop attention, legitimacy, and power, and particularly as it seeks to consolidate its supporters and keep their commitment through lean times. If the rebellion goes on long enough these issues become the subject of intergenerational conflict over both tactics and succession, causing incumbents to act preemptively against rivals and heirs. Such motivations become more powerful determinants of the rebellion's tactics than do considerations of conflict and conflict resolution. In the final analysis, the question of appropriate tactics—the tactical question—becomes nearly as strong as the matter of commitment in redressing the structural asymmetry.

The resolving component of the conflict also has its own evolution, in which the actions of rebels and government join to bring the cause to the current agenda and then in various ways to put forward and eliminate potential solutions until an outcome is reached. The dynamics therefore involve a process of breaking down a previously accepted regime or set of rules and behaviors governing a particular situation, and by elimination finding the appropriate (resolving) successor regime. Just as the protest component involves more—and often more important—considerations than protest alone (notably the imperatives of consolidating support), so the resolving component involves more than simply identifying and imposing a solution (notably the elimination of inadequate proposals from either side).

Three elements in the conflict affect its dynamics and govern the possibilities of successful negotiation: the insurgents' needs and the phases of rebellion, the government's agendas, and structural relations between the two sides. The dynamics of each element are independent of each other; each has to be in the right phase for conditions to be supportive of negotiations. Such a multivariate determination of appropriate conditions further underlines the difficulty of resolving internal conflict.

Needs and Phases of Insurgency

The needs of the insurgents and phases of the rebellion affect the chances of negotiation by imposing agendas that may or may not be compatible with negotiation, and by affecting the choice of spokesperson for the rebellion.[16] Internal conflicts run through four phases, essentially distinguished by the mix of politics and violence (again, the tactical question) that characterizes them: articulation, mobilization, insurgency, and warfare.[17] The first phase is one of cultural protest led by groups of educated elites petitioning the government for political reform with political means. Such groups express many different and specific grievances and expect redress. The second phase—where this study begins—involves the formation of a single movement led by charismatic organizers who seek to unite the disparate groups and force the attention of the government to the grievances by means of coercive civil action. The third or insurgent phase turns from political to violent means of pressure through a mass movement with a more ideological and action-oriented leadership that contests the ability and legitimacy of the government to meet its demands. In the fourth phase direct military confrontation is used to overthrow the government or to secede from the state, with a leadership drawn from the field. Although these phases are sequential, the sequence is not unidirectional; the conflict can move back as well as forward and many of its dynamics have to do with conflicting attempts by the parties to push it in one direction or the other.

Not only do different notions of legitimacy, different sources of means, and different sources of leadership characterize each phase, but each also operates under different organizational imperatives. In the first phase of the protest, several organizations present different types of demands, representing different parts of the disaffected population. As the dissidence continues and moves from the articulation to the mobilization phase, it is under pressure to bring this diversity under one roof so that it can exert maximum pressure on the government and assert its legitimacy and representativeness on behalf of the protest. It is in the mobilization phase that the consolidating nationalist message comes out as an ideologically motivating and uniting factor. But as the conflict goes on without resolution the unity of the movement is likely to come under severe strains, primarily over tactical questions, and to require additional consolidating efforts if it is not to fall apart into factions. Some dissidents will challenge the policies of the movement's leaders as inadequate and offer their own prescriptions. Failure to resolve conflict also encourages dreamers who focus on pure and total (but currently unattainable) victory and therefore create more pluralism, as can be seen in splits within South Africa and the Angolan, Afghan, and Zimbabwean protest movements (see chapters 7, 8, and 11).[18] Only when one of the new factions makes progress again in furthering its cause does it have a claim on the dissidents' exclusive allegiance. Yet that moment is unstable and ambiguous, because the movement needs solidarity in order to compel the government to provide it with some success, and it needs success to attract solidarity. These needs and pressures tend to keep the conflict in the mobilization and insurgency phases, where it is not ready for resolution.

Paradoxically, another moment when dissidents' unity is threatened occurs toward the end of the conflict. The closer the protest moves toward success, the greater its need and effort to maintain unity, and the greater the temptation for rivals and subgroups to cut loose and try to make a deal with the government on their own. In so doing they both benefit from the nearness of the final goal and assist in its attainment. But that assistance is not unambiguous: such sprinters seek to get the benefits of group effort for themselves by offering a slightly better deal to the government. If they succeed and pull the majority of the movement with them, they have provided a better mutually satisfactory outcome for the two sides, as happened in the Addis Ababa agreement in the Sudanese conflict in 1972, the Lancaster House agreement to the Zimbabwean conflict in 1979, and the African National Congress (ANC) agreement in South Africa in 1993–94 (see chapters 4 and 7 and note 18 in this chapter). If they fail and are swept aside, they may well have helped clear the way for a more lasting solution by eliminating an option that seemed attractive to some, as in the Zimbabwe internal settlement. But they may also have so split and enfeebled the protest that the conflict is again thrown back into the mobilization phase and a potentially appropriate moment for resolution is lost, as has happened on several occasions in the Sudanese and Eritrean struggles.

The implications of the four phases engage both insurgent goals and leadership. In regard to goals, beyond the articulation phase and possibly short of the warfare phase, the middle two phases are not particularly helpful for negotiation.[19] In the mobilization phase, the leadership is too preoccupied with solidarity to be able to engage in problem solving.[20] In the insurgency or guerrilla phase, clandestinity, splintered organization, and ideological confrontation all work against negotiation.[21] This is not to say that negotiation is impossible during these phases of the conflict, but that it is extremely hard to achieve and has formidable indications arrayed against it. When negotiation again becomes possible during the final phase, it is on a completely new basis. Specific grievances are left behind; the focus is now on status—secession, autonomy, or a new political system. Legitimacy and equality are the new conditions. Mutually hurting stalemate now defines the ripe moment, but outright victory of one side or the other is more common.

As to leadership, different types of leaders qualify as valid spokespersons according to the phase of the conflict. Solidarity makers,[22] mobilizers, hard-liners,[23] and confrontation specialists are the types of leaders called for in the four phases, respectively; problem solvers, conciliators, softliners, and dealers are not needed. However, impending leadership rivalries that develop as the conflict tends toward (but has not yet arrived at) a new phase may provide strong incentives for accommodation among incumbent leaders. Drawing on examples from national liberation struggles, one incentive for the Aix-les-Bains agreements on Morocco in 1955,[24] the Evian agreements on Algeria in 1962,[25] and the Lancaster House agreements on Zimbabwe in 1979 was the concern of nationalist leaders that a prolonged war would result in their replacement by a younger, more radical group and the recognition by the other side that such a leadership change would result in a less attractive solution and in renewed violence before agreement would be possible. More recently the South African government of F. W. de Klerk was moved by the hope that Nelson Mandela and his generation of leaders would be susceptible to the same concerns, and that hope paid off. This realization on both sides, which creates a common interest in agreement between the two leaderships, is a matter of perception and therefore needs to be encouraged by the side that arrives at the conclusion first, as well as by mediators.

Government's Agendas

Much less clear than the needs and phases of the insurgency are the phases in the attention of the government, because government is preoccupied with and determined by many things other than the rebellion. The whole point of the protest at the beginning is to get the demand or grievance that needs attention and resolution on the government's agenda. Continuation of the protest indicates the insufficiency of the government's response. The government is most likely to consider the opposition as a group to be contested rather than a legitimate, demand-bearing group. Governments change, but for many reasons of which the rebellion is only one. A government coming to power by normal paths of succession is unlikely to be any more or any less willing to negotiate than its predecessor. If the predecessor was heading toward negotiation, the successor is likely to be susceptible to appeals for continuation, all other things being similar; but if the predecessor was hostile to negotiations there is no reason to expect a different attitude from the successor, and indeed continued refusal may be taken as a symbol of continuity as other policies are changed. The overthrow of a government charged with unsuccessful inflexibility toward the rebels generally brings a government ready to negotiate. The overthrow of a government charged with weakness toward the rebellion—unsuccessful flexibility—is not conducive to negotiations. In sum, not all leadership changes are propitious for negotiations, but those that are should be seized upon with

. vigor by the rebellion or the government because the window of opportunity is usually narrow.

Examples can be given of the effects of leadership changes on negotiation. In Sudan the arrival to power of Gaafar el-Nimeiri (in 1969), Sawar el-Dahab (1985), and Sadiq el-Mahdi (1986) produced propitious moments for negotiations by providing a valid government spokesperson with some interest in negotiation. Only el-Nimeiri carried the moment to fruition, because at the time domestic support made an agreement with the rebels and an end to the rebellion politically useful. In Colombia the successive governments of Presidents Julio Cesar Turbay, Belisario Betancur, Virgilio Barco, and César Gaviria each moved negotiations with the various rebel groups forward toward the same goal while criticizing and altering his predecessor's tactics. On the other hand, the coup by Hassan el-Bashir (1989) in Sudan was a reaction to rumors of flexibility on the part of el-Mahdi and was most discouraging for any negotiation. On assuming office President Corazon Aquino in the Philippines began negotiations, eventually unsuccessful, with communist and Muslim rebellions. When the succession of F. W. de Klerk to P. W. Botha in the presidency of South Africa's National Party and then of South Africa itself, both in 1989, broke the logjam in the contradictions of obdurate apartheid, the African National Congress accepted the opportunity to negotiate in 1990, much as the passing of Leonid Brezhnev in the Soviet Union opened the possibility for Mikhail Gorbachev to negotiate in Afghanistan. It was the passing of General Francisco Franco in 1975 in Spain that removed much of the meaning from the Basque revolt and eventually opened the way to negotiations in 1989, albeit unsuccessfully.

Relations between the Two Sides

Under the pressures of conflicting dynamics, it is most difficult to define and to find the appropriate moment for negotiations to manage the dispute. It is generally true that it is better for government to negotiate with internal dissidents early rather than late and that internal rebellions not satisfied early only get worse. The analyses in this study address the internal situation once that truth has been ignored. In seeking a way out, some moments are more propitious and some tactics more effective than others for negotiation. The cases examined are eloquent about the importance and need to take advantage of ripe moments.

Ripe moments are composed of a structural element, a party element, and a potential alternative outcome—that is, a mutually hurting stalemate, the presence of valid spokespersons, and a formula for a way out.[26] Although stalemate has generally been the key component of ripeness, the characteristic asymmetry of internal conflict makes it hard to obtain and raises the importance of the agenda dynamics of the parties as a significant component.

Negotiations take place when both parties lose faith in their chances of winning and see an opportunity for cutting losses and achieving satisfaction through accommodation. The characteristic power asymmetry eliminates the possibility of obtaining a clear stalemate that is seen as a painful deadlock between two equal and checking powers, reinforced by an impending catastrophe. In the absence of power equality, the softer notion of a perceived stalemate as a no-win situation for both sides is the best that can be produced. Yet even under this softer notion of stalemate a hard goal must be met—replacement of a mentality focused on winning with one that is willing to trade in conflict for lessened goals. Negotiation offers the way to an alternative somewhere between unattainable triumph and unlikely annihilation, and that is a rather muddy field to play on. Yet this was the situation that preceded the Addis Ababa agreements on the southern Sudanese conflict in 1972, the Chadian defections of the mid-1980s,[27] and the Angolan and Mozambican attempts at final negotiations in the beginning of the 1990s (see chapters 4, 8, and 9).

Some kind of turning point in perceptions is needed to turn a soft stalemate into a search for alternatives.[28] The sources of such a turning point can be multiple: an inconclusive victory, an inconclusive defeat, a bloody standoff that suddenly brings costs home, a loss of foreign support or an increase in foreign pressure, a shift of fortunes that weakens the stronger side or strengthens the weaker, all accompanied by a new perception of the possibility of a negotiated solution. That turning point was provided by international economic sanctions in 1986 in South Africa, a costly and inconclusive battle at Mavinga in 1990 in Angola, a drought in the late 1980s in Mozambique, and the election of Aquino in 1986 in the Philippines. As essential elements, turning points must incorporate both a newly perceived stick and a newly perceived carrot—a worsening of the current situation or prospects, and a brightening of future possibilities under negotiation. In sum, a perception of unpromising ambiguity is traded for a perception of promising ambiguity. In a situation of continuing uncertainties, parties negotiate when they change their estimates of future potentialities.

Because of the inherent softness of perceived stalemate, turning points are likely to be transient and uncertain, a matter of interpretation at best. Their delicacy is reinforced by the likelihood that they may be reached at different moments by different parties and for different reasons.[29] To expect a single, simultaneous change of heart on the part of two (or more) parties for the same reason would be to look for an identity of perceptions that is unrealistic and unattainable under conditions of asymmetry. Yet such moments have existed in the past, as between South Africans and Angolans in 1987 in Namibia, between government and rebels in Sudan in 1971, between FRELIMO and RENAMO in Mozambique in 1991, and among Lebanese factions in 1989. As all examples indicate, however, coordinated perception of a turning point in a disparate context suggests a necessary role for a third party mediator, if only to hold one side's changed perception in place while the other side develops its own change of heart.

Escalations and attempted escalations in conflict also have a role in producing a turning point. Escalation is a significant change in the nature of the conflict in the direction of increased violence as distinct from a gradual intensification of conflict with no definable change in its nature. Stalemate is produced when the parties see conceivable escalation as unlikely to bring about the desired results. But some escalations can be helpful in defining ripe moments and in creating them. Potential escalations can serve as warnings that reinforce stalemates and foster negotiations. Like other deterrents, however, escalations become the subject of credibility contests the more they are brandished. Thus as a threatening riser on the stairway of conflict, escalation can be an alternative that makes negotiation appear more attractive, with best effects if pursued early. But once the escalation has taken place, negotiation becomes much more difficult until both sides have adjusted to the new situation and found a new stalemate.

As much as the elusive stalemate, it is the parties' agenda dynamics that relate to the turning point of perception and the broader determination of the ripe moment. Negotiations require recognized leaders on each side who are capable of making and holding an agreement and also capable of talking both forward to each other and backward to their followers. For the insurgents this means that spokespersons must be in tune with the shifts in the evolution of the insurgent movement so that they are not turning right when the movement is turning left. As seen, negotiations are most likely at the ends of the spectrum of conflict: before mobilization of the dissidents becomes a major imperative, or after it has taken place and provided a solid base for strong leadership. Negotiation is also most promising after an appropriate leadership change in government.

Narrower conditions may also create a turning point of perception, as when the stakes shift from societal to personal fortunes and insurgents are saved from elimination and commitment by cooptation into government (as happened partially in the Western Sahara in 1989); or when power can be so divided that the victory of one party does not mean the defeat of the other (as occurred under the Addis Ababa agreement on the Sudan in 1972); or when the warring parties can bury their conflict in an agreement to share power to the exclusion of a threatening new force (as in the case of Colombia in 1958). All three examples represent most unusual moments in the history of internal conflicts that are not easy to replicate.

Tactics of Mediation

Internal conflicts are marked by intensity and commitment that, more than in many cases of international conflict, so lock the parties into opposition and hostilities that they cannot reach a turning point of perception and find a way out by themselves. They are unable to communicate with each other, unable to think of a solution that could be attractive to the other side as well as themselves, unable to conceive of any side payments or enticements to turn the zero-sum conflict into a positive-sum solution, and unable to turn from commitment and a winning mentality to problem solving and solutions to grievances. Thus civil wars, more than many external conflicts, need a mediator. Yet mediation is difficult, because the mediator necessarily interferes in the internal affairs of the government and encourages the commitment of the insurgents. The hardest problem for would-be mediators in the conflicts in Chad, Sudan, Angola, Sri Lanka, the Philippines, Spain, and Ethiopia, not to speak of South Africa, has been to achieve standing in a dispute in which the government can brush off their offers as unnecessary and intrusive. All of the internal conflicts examined in this study, however, except for those in the Philippines and South Africa, have seen the involvement of a mediator.

Because of the structural asymmetry of internal conflicts, mediators must combine the most intrusive of the three mediation roles—manipulation—with the other two—communication and formulation.[30] As communicators, mediators merely carry messages, overcoming the procedural communications gap between parties; as formulators, mediators put forward their own ideas about possible outcomes, overcoming the substantive communications gap; but as manipulators mediators are involved in sharpening the stalemate and sweetening the proposed outcome. The most important key to obtaining welcome is leverage, which comes in three forms: it is achieved either by the provision of side payments that turn the zero-sum game positive, or by the delivery of each side's agreement to an outcome that the other side can find attractive, or by a threat to end the mediation process through withdrawal ("a pox on both your houses") or taking sides ("a pox on one of your houses"). Beyond such leverage the mediator has no power. The success of mediation depends on persuading the parties to change their perceptions of the value of current situations and future outcomes—that is, to see a stalemate and reach a turning point.

The most prominent candidate for the role of mediator is a third party host or even distant patron of the insurgency, under special conditions.[31] The host state has no reason to negotiate and usually has other extraneous (state-to-state) reasons not to negotiate unless it too perceives itself in a hurting stalemate (as did Iran in 1972 in regard to the Kurdish rebellion in Iraq,[32] India in 1987 during the Tamil rebellion in Sri Lanka, Ethiopia in 1971 during the southern Sudanese rebellion, Syria in 1989 in the Lebanese conflict, Pakistan in Afghanistan in 1992 and 1993, and both Malawi and Zimbabwe in Mozambique in 1989). A host not hurting has no interest in ending support for a rebellion, because a nonburdensome rebellion is not the worst and may be the best of neighbor relations. For such triangulation to turn from a negative effect to a positive effect for negotiation, the entire conflict must escalate to the point where it is no longer useful and begins to hurt the host-neighbor. Of the three sets of parties, it is usually the external host and supporter who cracks first, although even that takes time. Only then can the host envisage a helpful role in negotiations—that of a mediator, through which the host-neighbor helps to find a solution and then delivers the agreement of the rebellion to which it has given support and sanctuary. Mediators need not be impartial, but they must deliver the side to which they are perceived as close; they must not be perceived as selling a proposed agreement that is biased in their friends' favor.

The eventual key to the effectiveness of mediators and negotiators is an outcome that returns the conflict to normal politics. In this respect, too, civil wars differ from many other conflicts. Internal conflict cannot be resolved by some wise judgment on an outstanding issue, such as the location of a boundary, the exchange of disarmament quotas, or the terms of a peace treaty. Rather, the outcome must provide for the integration of the insurgency into a new body politic and for mechanisms that allow the conflict to shift from violence back to politics. Generally this involves creating a new political system in which the parties to the conflict feel they have a stake, thus in a very positive sense coopting all parties—government and rebels— in a new creation. There is a danger to that cooptation; it can be used by opponents to discredit the negotiating leadership, but that merely strengthens the notion that a stable outcome must be a joint creation with benefits for both sides to hold them to the agreement.

Some parts of each side will be left out. The most important tactical judgment concerns the size of the excluded segments. If the array of parties involved is considered to represent a spectrum of groups holding different attitudes toward the issue of negotiations and negotiability, then some kinds of coalition analysis can be applied.[33] A coalition of parties interested in negotiations must be big enough to settle the substantive issues and carry the remaining members of the spectrum. Parties on the extremes will try to delegitimize this activity and upset the negotiations, both by trying to maintain dominance on their respective sides and trying to discredit or eliminate the negotiating middle. Opponents of negotiation try to restore commitment and return the conflict to its dyadic state; proponents of negotiation try to carve out a problem-solving coalition in the middle.

If that middle coalition is too small, its efforts will fail and it will be discredited—an important consideration since legitimacy is a crucial ingredient in the structures of asymmetry. In Sri Lanka, Spain, Lebanon, and the Philippines rebellion occurred because the moderates were perceived as too completely coopted into a system of inadequate normal politics, leaving representation of the aggrieved to the radicals, who set about using violence to attack government and to build commitment. Tactics of coalition-building are most effective if they reach out to the middle of the *other* side, isolating the irrecuperables but presenting a significant number of the rebellion's mainstream with an offer both attractive and resolving. That is what Nelson Mandela and F. W. de Klerk did in South Africa in negotiating with each other rather than with representatives of the moderate fringes, such as a Progressive Party leader on the white side or an Inkatha Freedom Party leader on the black side.

Many attempts at negotiations fail, at least in the early stages, because parties persist in talking to unrepresentative counterparts who cannot speak for large groups of followers or carry out an agreement if it were reached, as happened in the internal settlement in Zimbabwe in 1978. The requirements of legitimate leadership have a number of implications. First, because leadership is a prized political good, there will be serious infighting within the parties—particularly among the insurgents—to capture the position of valid spokesperson. Such infighting is neither a sign of immature instability nor the work of government agents, but a natural consequence of the struggle and a requisite for negotiation. Second, the spokesperson or ''spokesgroup'' must represent the mainstream of each side; this is particularly important for the insurgency. Dealing with a negotiator who represents only the willing fringe closest to the government will not produce agreements that will be obeyed and end the rebellion. Third, although negotiations must have mainstream leaders, mainstream leaders may not be able to negotiate. In principle, negotiations will be most difficult as long as a leadership struggle is going on, because an opponent can always tar a leader with claims of softness implied by negotiation, as happened in Angola in the 1980s and in South Africa in the 1990s. By the same token, it is difficult for the other party to intrude in the leadership struggle of its opponent with offers to negotiate with a particular candidate, because such a move could immediately brand an individual as the enemy's candidate and so delegitimize the candidate. Thus the proper policy of the other side during its opponent's leadership struggle is not to pick and favor candidates, but to keep the issue of negotiation present and active for eventual use once the leadership has been consolidated.

Nevertheless, there is often temptation for one side to play politics within the other side on the negotiation issue—an option usually more conceivable for the government than for the rebels. This can take one of three forms. One side may be tempted to divide the other and make a separate peace with factions, winning away pieces; such tactics can be useful in isolating either the radicals of a movement who may have been preventing a solution, or a leader in chief whose personality would be indigestible in a new government-opposition coalition. Or one side may be tempted to seek out a third force to negotiate with in order to get around the obduracy of the rebellion's leaders, on the assumption that a third force might not only be able to come to an agreement but be able to end the rebellion by doing so. Or one side may be tempted to make an agreement with a moderate fringe of the rebellion and make common cause with those with whom it could work. Examples of the first form are found in conflicts in Chad and South Africa; of the second form, in el-Nimeiri's undoing of the Addis Ababa agreements on Sudan at the beginning of the 1980s; and of the third form, in the internal settlements in Zimbabwe in 1978 and with the legal (nonviolent) Basque parties (see chapter 3). Few such attempts (in

Spain, South Africa, and Chad in part) have been successful. Partial solutions of this kind must provide benefits for the rebels that are at least as great as the benefits that might have been negotiated with a mainstream leader. Yet the leader who achieves a partial solution will have a much harder time delivering adherence to the agreement by followers—without which the agreement is pointless. Governments sometimes confuse payoffs to the representatives of a faction with payoffs to the rebellion; only in those rare cases in which there is an established patron-client structure and there are strong vertical divisions within the rebellion are such partial solutions conceivable, as in Chad.

In the long run, all solutions are only experiments. Because solution does not mean a definitive settlement of specific issues (however prominent specific grievances may be among the causes of the conflict) but rather a restoration of normal politics, and because settlement does not mean elimination of the parties but rather their incorporation as actors in a new regime, rebels will bury their guns (figuratively, but sometimes literally) until they see how the new system works. Most of the conflicts studied in this book are ongoing because a solution had been negotiated which soon proved unsatisfactory in addressing the causes of the rebellion. Although some experiments may hold, others may fail because they do not address the causal problem at all (as in the 1978 internal settlement in Zimbabwe), because they contain mechanisms that can be used to undo the agreement itself (as in the 1972 Addis Ababa agreement in Sudan), or because they give rise to the conflict in a new form as a result of their success (as in the case of the 1958 National Front in Colombia) (see chapters 4 and 11).

Studies of Cases

The cases examined in the following chapters have been chosen to cover different forms of internal conflict in which attempts have been made to achieve solutions through negotiations, but without complete success. They are therefore cases of current and ongoing interest, both for their intrinsic importance to unfolding events and for the lessons they can provide about partial success and failure in handling internal conflict. In a few of these cases violent conflict has been transformed into political conflict on the way to a return to normal politics. In Eritrea this has been accomplished by military victory; in Lebanon by imposition of an external patron; in Mozambique by patience and ripeness; and in South Africa by wisdom and skill in conducting successful negotiations. These cases permit some evaluation of purported solutions and of the processes by which they were attained, and they can be compared with other cases in which negotiations have not succeeded.

The cases examined fall into three categories of internal conflict. In the first, the conflict is based on rebellions whose cause is regional autonomy or secession. Solutions must be found through a formula that meets both the regional insurgents' demands for self-determination and self-government and the national government's demands for national integrity. Such conflicts are found in Sri Lanka, the Basque territory in Spain, and initially in Sudan and Ethiopia. These regional cases shade into a second category in which regional minorities rebelling against the government are so discouraged in their struggle or so alienated that they become a majority calling for the overthrow of the nation's central institutions. The conflict in Sudan teeters on the edge of this category, to which the conflicts in Ethiopia and Lebanon already belong. In the third category, the largest, are cases in which the conflict is over central power and the rebels are ideologically or socioeconomically motivated; ethnic minorities come into play only incidentally. In such situations negotiations will find success only through a solution of power-sharing between groups presently monopolizing power and those presently excluded. The conflicts in Angola, Mozambique, Afghanistan, the Philippines, and Colombia are such cases. Although the categories of conflict are conceptually different, they do shade into one another, and there is often debate as to which category is appropriate for a specific conflict. This uncertainty can add to the problems of negotiation.

In considering specific cases of internal conflict, many questions are suggested by the conceptual framework outlined in this chapter: How can asymmetry be overcome to catch the elusive peace? Are there propitious conditions for internal negotiations, and if so what are their characteristics? Can those ripe moments be developed as well as seized? How can the parties restore—or create—normal politics? What is needed to break down the stalemate to negotiation? What distractions are likely to occur, and how may they be handled so as not to derail negotiations? What is the relation of cease-fire to agreement? Are there roles for third parties? What gives potential mediators entry, standing, and leverage?

Each of the following chapters identifies its own key to understanding both the conflict analyzed and its possible resolution, and proposes the elements necessary to end the conflict. The keys are based on and related to the concepts developed in this introduction. The lessons learned should be relevant to understanding specific cases of internal conflict as well as internal conflict in general for some time to come. The insights developed in this book are offered as a guide in the search for solutions to these and other cases of internal conflict.

Notes

1. Paul R. Pillar, *Negotiating Peace: War Termination as a Bargaining Process* (Princeton University Press, 1983); Stephen John Stedman, *Peacemaking in Civil War: International Mediation in Zimbabwe, 1974–1980* (Boulder, Colo.: Lynne Rienner, 1990).

2. See Pillar, *Negotiating Peace*; Stedman, *Peacemaking in Civil War.*

3. Chester A. Crocker, *High Noon in Southern Africa: Making Peace in a Rough Neighborhood* (W. W. Norton, 1992).

4. See I. William Zartman, ed., *Governance as Conflict Management: Politics in West Africa* (Brookings, 1995).

5. On the conflict between Tutsis and Hutus in Rwanda and Burundi, see René Lemarchand, *Burundi: Ethnocide as Discourse and Practice* (Cambridge University Press, 1994); René Lemarchand, *Rwanda and Burundi* (New York: Praeger, 1970); and Filip Reyntiens, *L'Afrique des grands lacs en crise* (Paris: Karthala, 1994).

6. On the conflict between Cypriot Greeks and Turks, see Richard N. Haass, *Conflicts Unending: The United States and Regional Disputes* (Yale University Press, 1990), chapter 3. On the conflict between Muslims and Hindus in Kashmir, see Haass, *Conflicts Unending*, chapter 4; Thomas Perry Thornton, "The Indo-Pakistan Conflict: Tashkent," in Saadia Touval and I. William Zartman, eds., *International Mediation in Theory and Practice* (Boulder, Colo.: Westview Press, 1985), pp. 141–74. On the conflict between Kurds and their neighbors, see Edmund Ghareeb, *The Kurdish Question in Iraq* (Syracuse University Press, 1981).

7. Jeffrey Z. Rubin and Bert R. Brown, *The Social Psychology of Bargaining and Negotiation* (Academic Press, 1975), pp. 199, 214–21; I. William Zartman and Maureen R. Berman, *The Practical Negotiator* (Yale University Press, 1982), pp. 57–62; Jeffrey Z. Rubin and I. William Zartman, eds., *Power and Asymmetry in International Negotiations* (Newbury Park, Calif.: Sage, 1995); Christopher R. Mitchell, "Classifying Conflicts: Asymmetry and Resolution," *Annals of the American Academy of Political and Social Science,* vol. 518 (November 1991), pp. 23–39; and "Asymmetry and Tactics of Resolution," in I. William Zartman and Victor Kremenyuk, eds., *Cooperative Security: Reducing Third World Wars* (Syracuse University Press, 1995), pp. 29–61.

8. See I. William Zartman, "The Strategy of Preventive Diplomacy in Third World Conflicts," in Alexander George, ed., *Managing U.S.–Soviet Rivalry: Problems of*

Crisis Prevention (Boulder, Colo.: Westview, 1983), pp. 341–63; I. William Zartman, *Ripe for Resolution: Conflict and Intervention in Africa*, 2d ed. (Oxford University Press, 1989); Touval and Zartman, eds., *International Mediation in Theory and Practice*; Haass, *Conflicts Unending*; Louis Kriesberg and Stuart J. Thorson, eds., *Timing the De-escalation of International Conflicts* (Syracuse University Press, 1991); Crocker, *High Noon in Southern Africa.*

9. See I. William Zartman, *The Politics of Trade Negotiations between Africa and the European Economic Community: The Weak Confront the Strong* (Princeton University Press, 1971); Morton Deutsch, *The Resolution of Conflict: Constructive and Destructive Processes* (Yale University Press, 1973), pp. 351–400; Glenn H. Snyder and Paul Diesing, *Conflict Among Nations: Bargaining, Decision Making, and System Structure in International Crises* (Princeton University Press, 1977), pp. 254–62; Rubin and Brown, *Social Psychology of Bargaining*, n. 3; P. Terrence Hopmann, "Asymmetrical Bargaining in the Conference on Security and Cooperation in Europe," *International Organization*, vol. 32, no. 1 (1978) pp. 141–77; Vinod Aggarwal and Pierre Allan, "Evolution in Bargaining Theories: Toward an Integrated Approach to Explain Strategies of the Weak," paper presented to the American Political Science Association, 1983; Rubin and Brown, *Social Psychology*, pp. 382–86; I. William Zartman, ed., *Positive Sum: Improving North-South Negotiations* (New Brunswick, N.J.: Transaction Books, 1987), pp. 278–301; Rubin and Zartman, eds., *Power and Asymmetry.*

10. Andrew Mack, "Why Big Nations Lose Small Wars: The Politics of Asymmetric Conflict," *World Politics*, vol. 27 (January 1975), pp. 175–200; Thazha V. Paul, *Asymmetric Conflicts: War Initiation by Weaker Parties* (Cambridge University Press, 1994).

11. Henry A. Kissinger, "The Viet Nam Negotiations," *Foreign Affairs*, vol. 47, no. 2 (January 1969), p. 214.

12. On the conflict between Morocco and the Sahrawi nationalists over the Western Sahara, see John Damis, *Conflict in Northwest Africa* (Stanford: Hoover Institute, 1983); Zartman, *Ripe for Revolution*, chapter 2.

13. Janice Gross Stein, ed., *Getting to the Table: The Processes of International Prenegotiation* (Johns Hopkins University Press, 1989).

14. For further development of this issue, see I. William Zartman, "The Unfinished Agenda: Negotiating Internal Conflicts," in Roy Licklider, ed., *Stopping the Killing: How Civil Wars End* (New York University Press, 1993), pp. 20–35.

15. Edward E. Rice, *Wars of the Third Kind: Conflict in Underdeveloped Countries* (University of California Press, 1988); Donald L. Horowitz, "Making Moderation Pay: The Comparative Politics of Ethnic Conflict Management," in Joseph V. Montville, ed., *Conflict and Peacemaking in Multiethnic Societies* (Lexington, Mass.: Lexington Books, 1989), pp. 451–75; Michael Lund, *Preventive Diplomacy* (Washington: U.S. Institute for Peace, 1994); and Jeffrey Rubin, Dean Pruitt, and Sung Hee Kim, *Social Conflict*, 2d ed. (McGraw Hill, 1994).

16. See I. William Zartman, "Negotiations and Pre-Negotiations in Ethnic Conflict: The Beginning, the Middle and the Ends," in Montville, ed., *Conflict and Peacemaking*, pp. 511–33.

17. Charles A. Micaud, Leon Carl Brown, and Clement Henry Moore, *Tunisia: The Politics of Modernization* (Praeger, 1964); William B. Quandt, *Revolution and Political Leadership: Algeria 1954–1968* (MIT Press, 1969); and I. William Zartman, ed., *Elites in the Middle East* (Praeger, 1980).

18. Richard Gibson, *African Liberation Movements: Contemporary Struggles Against White Minority Rule* (Oxford University Press for the Institute of Race Relations, 1972). On the Zimbabwean struggle for independence, see Stedman, *Peacemaking in Civil War*; and Jeffrey Davidow, *A Peace in Southern Africa* (Boulder, Colo.: Westview Press, 1994).

19. Some unusual explanatory evidence for this pattern comes from social psychology. Paul Swingle, reviewing experiments that used prisoner's dilemma games and chicken dilemma games to test the effects of punishment on negotiation, found that cooperation increases as violence and punishment increase or decrease. Negotiation was difficult at mid-levels of violence and punishment, where escalation was still possible and threats evoked counterthreats; at high levels threats induced cooperation, and at low levels cooperation induced cooperation. See Paul Swingle, "Dangerous Games," in Paul Swingle, ed., *The Structure of Conflict* (Academic Press,1970), pp. 235–76. I am grateful to Bertram Spector for the reference. These findings confirm the thinking behind the concept of mutually hurting stalemate, because in the middle stages of internal conflict there is potentially plenty of room to escalate and little pressure to stalemate.

20. Herbert Feith, *The Decline of Constitutional Democracy in Indonesia* (Cornell University Press, 1962).

21. Quandt, *Revolution and Political Leadership*, n. 17.

22. Feith, *Decline of Constitutional Democracy in Indonesia*.

23. Snyder and Diesing, *Conflict Among Nations*, pp. 297–309.

24. On the Aix-les-Bains agreements, see Stephane Bernard, *Le conflit franco-morocain*, vol. 1 (Brussels: Université Libre, 1963), chapters 7, 8.

25. On the Evian accords, see I. William Zartman, "Les relations entre la France et l'Algérie depuis Evian," *Revue française de science politique*, vol. 14, no. 6 (December 1964), pp. 1087–1113.

26. Zartman, *Ripe for Resolution*, pp. 134–69.

27. On the Chad rebellion, see William Foltz, "Reconstructing the State of Chad," in I. William Zartman, ed., *Collapsed States: The Disintegration and Restoration of Legitimate Authority* (Lynne Rienner, 1995).

28. For a further investigation of the notion of hurting stalemates, see Fen Osler Hampson and Brian S. Mandell, eds., "Managing Regional Conflict," special issue of the *International Journal*, vol. 45, no. 2 (Spring 1990).

29. Stedman, *Peacemaking in Civil War*; Dean G. Pruitt and Paul V. Olczak, "Beyond Hope: Approaches to Resolving Seemingly Intractable Conflict," in Barbara Benedict Bunker, Jeffrey Z. Rubin, and others, *Conflict, Cooperation and Justice: Essays Inspired by the Work of Morton Deutsch* (San Francisco: Jossey-Bass, 1995).

30. For a discussion of these roles and other aspects of mediation, see Kenneth Kressell, Dean G. Pruitt, and others, *Mediation Research* (San Francisco: Jossey-Bass, 1989); Christopher R. Mitchell and Keith Webb, eds., *New Approaches to International*

Mediation (New York: Greenwood Press, 1988); and Touval and Zartman, eds., *International Mediation in Theory and Practice.*

31. For further development of this idea, see I. William Zartman, "Internationalization of Communal Strife: Temptations and Opportunities of Triangulation," in Manus I. Midlarsky, ed., *The Internationalization of Communal Strife* (New York: Routledge, 1993), pp. 27–42.

32. On the Kurdish rebellion and the 1972 negotiations, see Diane Lieb, "Iran and Iraq at Algiers," in Touval and Zartman, eds., *International Mediation in Theory and Practice*, pp. 67–90.

33. See Christopher Dupont, "Coalition Theory: Using Power to Build Cooperation, in I. William Zartman, ed., *International Multilateral Negotiation: Approaches to the Management of Complexity* (San Francisco: Jossey-Bass, 1994), pp. 148–77; William Riker, *The Theory of Political Coalitions* (Yale University Press, 1962); P. Bennett, "Nash Bargaining Solutions of Multiparty Bargaining Problems," in M. J. Humber, ed., *The Logic of Multiparty Systems* (Dordrecht, The Netherlands: Nijhoff, 1987).

Part Two

REGIONAL CONFLICTS

IN REGIONAL conflicts a new regime of self-government is sought for part of a nation, rather than for the entire state. That demand can be situated anywhere along the spectrum from local home rule to secession, and it usually slides back and forth along the spectrum during the conflict. There is a clear midpoint in that spectrum that can serve as the soft but salient basis of a resolving formula—a formula characterized by a procedural element of self-determination, most legitimately expressed in a referendum, and by a substantive element of regional autonomy.[1]

There are many obstacles to this outcome as a solution, however. Rebels can fixate their commitment on the sharper and equally salient goal of secession; they can doubt government's sincerity about living up to autonomy agreements, particularly if there has been bad faith in the past; some token sort of autonomy may already be in place, devaluing the promise of the solution. Governments are wary of a risky vote of self-determination, which could bring some surprises; they are also wary of real autonomy, although the record of such exemplary cases as Italy shows that autonomy lowers—not raises—risk of secession.

Another salient, but less soft, formula is federation, but federation is awkward when only one region is involved in rebellion. The Ethiopian-Eritrean federation of 1952–62 suffered from this imbalance, and a federation of Basque lands and Spain or the five autonomous regions and Italy would make little sense (see chapters 5 and 3). In the end, there are few salient solutions other than those found at the soft midpoint and the extremes of the spectrum. An additional characteristic of the soft solution of autonomy is simultaneously disadvantageous and advantageous: much of its actual form depends on the details, thus allowing flexible bargaining but also letting broad decisions hang on small straws in a suspicious atmosphere.[2]

The four cases presented in this section cover the spectrum of regional conflicts and attempts at their resolution. The Eritrean case marks one salient solution—secession, won by war and sanctified by a rather pro forma referendum. In the case of Sri Lanka, the Tamil region also demands independence, in part because autonomy and compensatory arrangements of the past have been scuttled by the government, and in part because the rebellion has become polarized in the hands of extremists for whom commitment to the total goal and violent means is the mark of their authority (see chapter 2). The complex slide of demands in the southern Sudanese rebellion—from federation to autonomy to revolution and toward secession—chronicles the wrenching debate among people who want to be Sudanese and southern (non-Muslim) at the same time, and are told by the government that those two qualities are incompatible and that the identity of the north can only be fully realized by a denial of the identity of the south (see chapter 4). The struggle of the Basques to ''guarantee [their] survival as a nation'' has been above all an ideologized and generational struggle against the Franco state in Spain;[3] that struggle has been largely undercut by the creation of an autonomous Basque region following Franco's death, yet a terrorist minority still demands self-determination, losing its followers but not its victims as a result.

All of these regional rebellions took on a new life under a new generation of leaders, who rebelled as much against the moderation of their elders as against the unresponsiveness of government. Whether government became more liberal (as in Spain) or more repressive (as in Sudan and Ethiopia) or just fumbled (as in Sri Lanka) made little difference to the leadership, although a liberal response did undercut the followership in Spain. None of the rebellions has won much sympathy from the followers of government in the rest of the country; indeed, the Eritrean rebellion was able to accomplish its goals only because it fostered the overthrow of the Ethiopian government by an ethnic rebellion led by Tigreans in 1990.

If the insurgents in the Basque, Sudanese, and Sri Lankan rebellions were able to impose negotiations on the government, with varying degrees of success, it was because they could raise the costs of not negotiating for the government and at the same time realized that they could not achieve their ultimate goals at an acceptable cost to themselves—in other words, a mutually hurting stalemate existed, although, in some cases it was short-lived. Yet in all three cases the negotiations failed, because the government saw the cost of concessions as being greater than the cost of continuing conflict. That perception was mirrored by the rebellions. The mediators, who might have brought those two perceptions into harmony, were worn out by their previous failures.

1. On saliency, see Thomas C. Schelling, *The Strategy of Conflict* (Harvard University Press, 1960).
2. On the atmospherics of bargaining at the detail stage, see I. William Zartman and Maureen Berman, *The Practical Negotiator* (Yale University Press, 1982).
3. Carmelo Landa, sole member of the Basque coalition Herri Batasuna in the European Parliament, quoted in Alan Riding, "Basque Peace Hopes Rise as Separatists Wane," *New York Times*, January 28, 1994.

CHAPTER TWO

Sri Lanka: Negotiations in a Secessionist Conflict

Howard Wriggins

THIS CHAPTER examines the protracted negotiations that began in 1977 between the government of Sri Lanka and spokespersons for Sri Lanka's Tamil minority, who originally sought at a minimum decentralization of the country's overly centralized government. A simple two-party negotiation became more complex as sympathetic Tamils in southern India supported the Tamil movement in Sri Lanka with money and arms. The government of India itself became directly involved in two ways: it became a mediator between the government of Sri Lanka and the Tamil insurgents, and a provider of arms, safe houses, training camps, and logistical support to various Tamil factions.

Four years of intensifying conflict produced a war of secession. In July 1987 President J. R. Jayewardene of Sri Lanka and Prime Minister Rajiv Gandhi of India signed the India–Sri Lanka Accord, which provided for the end of hostilities and the entry into Sri Lanka of an Indian peacekeeping force to protect the guerrilla fighters while they laid down their arms. However, because the accord had been arranged without the direct involvement of the leader of the most militant Tamil faction and provided less than independence, the guerrilla movement turned on the Indian peacekeepers and the conflict was resumed. After a year and a half of costly but indecisive warfare, the Indian army was told by Jayewardene's successor, Ransinghe Premadasa, to go home. The conflict has continued between the government of Sri Lanka and the most dogged of the militants.

To understand the development of the spiraling hostilities, mutual distrust, and growing violence in Sri Lanka, it is important to examine the
background to the Tamils' ethnosecessionist struggle and to trace over time
the negotiating exchanges between the principal protagonists as they sought
a negotiating formula to delimit the issues and exchanged offers and coun-
teroffers on details; the shifting balance of capability on the ground as the
struggle escalated; changes in the negotiating participants; and changes in
the government's position and the issues at stake as successive offers were
rejected by the most militant Tamil factions.

Background

Sri Lanka is a multiethnic island state off the south coast of India, the
size of West Virginia, with a population of some 15 million people. Sinhalese make up 74 percent of the population. Indigenous Tamils represent
some 13 percent of the total; they are concentrated largely in the Northern
and Eastern Provinces, although a third of them have lived for generations
in the cities and market towns of the south. A second Tamil-speaking
community are descendants of laborers brought to the island by the British
in the nineteenth century to work on the tea estates in the central highlands;
these Tamils have not been particularly active politically. A Muslim community, often called Moors, account for another 7 percent.[1]

Sri Lanka never went through the nation-building experience of a protracted
struggle for independence. At the time of independence spokespersons for the
69 percent Sinhalese majority, the 11 percent indigenous Tamil minority, and
the 6 percent Moorish minority together shaped a constitutional bargain that
provided for a democratic parliamentary system with substantial safeguards for
the rights of the minorities.[2] Since independence was established in 1948 there
have been nine parliamentary and three presidential elections.

Ever since the coming of independence, however, the relative political
and cultural standing of the Sinhalese and Tamil communities has been a
source of contention. Sinhalese zealots have maintained that Tamils have
been overrepresented in Parliament, in the bureaucracy, and in university
placements. As Sinhalese saw it in the early 1950s, though they were a
substantial majority of the population, more than 40 percent of the workers
in the clerical service and one third of all university graduates were Sri
Lankan Tamils.[3] Tamils have argued that democratic government by the
majority Sinhalese has systematically undercut their opportunities, that

over the years virtual second-class citizenship has been imposed on them, and that their personal security has become increasingly threatened.[4]

From 1956 onward an action-reaction dynamic between the Sinhalese and Tamil communities gained momentum. In such conflicted situations, reciprocal perceptions and mutual and escalating fears become crucial to an understanding of events.[5] At stake was the nature of the Sri Lankan state. The Sinhalese majority favored a centralized, unitary state of the kind inherited from the British; the Tamils sought a more decentralized state that would permit them to manage their own affairs, especially in the Jaffna peninsula where they were concentrated. That normal politics could not meet Tamil needs was demonstrated over and over again, most particularly in 1958 and 1969 when carefully negotiated agreements on decentralization between government and Tamil spokespersons were abandoned under pressure from Sinhalese protesters.

Linguistic and cultural nationalism intensified this issue. Politics within the Sinhalese community focused increasingly on Buddhist symbols and on legislation defining Sinhalese as the island's official language, reflecting an exclusivist conception of the Sri Lankan polity. This focus reinforced Tamil suspicions that the original constitutional bargain was being revised to their growing and ineradicable disadvantage.[6] Tamil defensive anxieties intensified their calls for a federal structure and devolution of centralization, which in turn intensified Sinhalese fears that the indigenous Tamil minority really wanted to join with the 55 million Tamil-speaking people in southern India. It was as if the majority community had a sharp sense of inferiority, its own Sinhalese Buddhist identity being perceived as under growing threat in a region believed to be dominated by the large Tamil community in India, only 25 miles across the Palk Strait.

Underlying sociodynamic factors having little to do with intercommunal relations were also at work. From 1956 on educational policy had set Tamil and Sinhalese youths on separate educational tracks, each to be taught in its indigenous language, so that communication between them became more and more difficult. A rapidly growing population and an expanding school system were producing graduates at a rate far faster than the economy was producing jobs, intensifying a sense of rivalry between these asymmetrical communities. Within the two communities competing political leaders, each seeking to win a political following at the expense of local rivals, intensified communal consciousness and exaggerated popular fears of the evil intentions of the other community. Moreover, the Tamil community was itself divided structurally between the numerically dominant Vellala (farmer) and the contesting Karaiyar (fishermen) communities, the latter rallying lower castes resentful of "Vellala domination."[7] Ironically, large-scale government investment in the settlement of hitherto uninhabited land, instead of easing population pressures, produced in effect apples of discord between the Sinhalese and Tamil communities, each holding that the other was getting an unfair share of scarce status- and wealth-giving land. Thus there were a number of intractable local forces at work to impede a negotiated resolution of Sinhalese and Tamil differences.

Before the 1977 election that brought J. R. Jayewardene's government to power in a sweeping victory for the United National Party, Tamil youths, based mainly in the Jaffna area of northern Sri Lanka, had become embittered and demanded the creation of an independent state in the northern and eastern parts of the country, to be called Tamil Eelam. The United National Party's election manifesto promised to deal with specific Tamil grievances while reaffirming the government's commitment to a unitary governmental structure.

On coming to power one of Jayewardene's first moves was to rescind the orders regarding university entrance that had been promulgated by the previous government, and which Tamil youths considered particularly discriminatory. And very early in Jayewardene's administration the Tamil language was given a substantially higher constitutional status than before. But these measures proved insufficient to soften the demands of Tamil youths for Tamil Eelam. The analysis in this chapter turns now to negotiations between the Jayewardene government and elected Tamil members of Parliament about what additional grievances should and could be corrected and how that should be done.

Two-Party Negotiations, 1978–82

From 1978 to 1982 principal negotiations focused on defining the structure and powers of proposed district development councils as a way of meeting Tamil demands for greater decentralization. At the outset the negotiating parties were the Tamil United Liberation Front (TULF), then occupying eighteen seats in Parliament and designated the official opposition, and President J. R. Jayewardene, whose United National Party (UNP) held a three-fifths majority in Parliament. There was little trust between the two sides.

In the 1977 elections the Tamil United Liberation Front had won overwhelmingly in Tamil-speaking areas on a platform demanding secession of those areas. Although publicly sounding sympathetic to the more intransigent Tamil youths, TULF leaders privately reassured the government that they were moderates ready to negotiate a resolution of Tamil grievances short of independence.

Jayewardene stood head and shoulders above all the other members of his United National Party. He held that Sri Lanka was overly centralized. However, the UNP had influential members whose views differed little from those of the rival Sri Lanka Freedom Party (SLFP), long an advocate of Sinhalese Buddhist interests at the expense of Tamil concerns. Because many Sinhalese saw any devolution from centralization as the first step toward partitioning the island, Jayewardene was reluctant to promptly offer the Tamil United Liberation Front the extensive devolution it demanded out of fear that to do so would split his party and strengthen the SLFP, which was ready to exploit any concessions he might make to the Tamils. Nor could Jayewardene entirely discount Tamil spokespersons who publicly held that proposals that fell short of independence were nevertheless significant first steps.

Moreover, there were other priority items on the government's agenda: introducing a new presidential constitution, and accelerating construction of a huge irrigation and hydroelectric system while foreign donors were in a generous mood. In addition, economic policy had to be liberalized to open up what had been a stagnant, semisocialist, and administratively controlled economy. Thus the Jayewardene government, caught in the middle between militant Tamil and Sinhalese zealots, proceeded slowly in responding to reiterated Tamil demands. These demands were now and again emphasized by acts of violence in the northern and eastern provinces.

The government possessed official authority and an army of some 13,000 men, although the army was without combat experience and at least at the outset was ill-disciplined. The army was almost exclusively Sinhalese, recruitment of Tamils having been sharply reduced by the preceding Bandaranaike government. There were some 14,000 police.

The Tamil youths at first seemed to be no match for government forces. However, they quickly learned the arts of guerrilla warfare, in part from the Palestine Liberation Organization in Lebanon, but also in training camps organized in India. They early demonstrated unusual resolve when arrested, committing suicide by biting into cyanide capsules rather than reveal the movement's secrets.

In 1978 the government and the Tamil insurgents had differing perceptions of the value of time in resolving the conflict. The government at first
was in no hurry. The number of committed activists, limited to the north,
was thought to be in the low hundreds. Internal rivalries had always plagued
Tamil politics, and some leaders of the United National Party hoped these
divisions might solve the insurgent problem with only a modestly increased
presence of the national army and police in the Jaffna area. However, the
elected leaders of the Tamil United Liberation Front, who were mainly
legally oriented, feared that unless there was more rapid progress in resolving Tamil grievances through negotiation they would be thrust aside by the
more violent Tamil factions.

The Negotiating Issues and Process

The first issues to be negotiated concerned the structure and powers of
proposed district development councils. Jayewardene saw districts as the
smallest administrative entities (apart from villages) and therefore the least
risky as focuses of decentralization. The more articulate Tamils wanted to
ensure that such councils could cooperate with one another in the northern
and eastern provinces, and even amalgamate if they wished. But to the
Sinhalese that raised the specter of secession, the development they most
feared.

The powers to be enjoyed by each council were subject to detailed
bargaining. Recruitment of local police and their deployment, as well as
taxation, education, economic planning, land allocation to farmers, and
water management had to be defined. Tamil spokespersons sought as much
discretion and as many resources as possible for the councils; the government appeared to be as parsimonious as possible.

Haggling over each of these details was often protracted. But as it turned
out, none of the government's cabinet ministers were persuaded that they
should sacrifice such centralized political resources as allocations, hirings,
and policy decisions to novel district entities. The government was too
preoccupied with other issues, and too reluctant to risk the Sinhalese backlash, to bear down heavily on the reluctant ministers.

As to the negotiating process, at first Jayewardene met informally with
spokespersons for the Tamil United Liberation Front, seeking to craft an
agreed upon formula for a settlement and negotiate specific details. For
nearly two years distrust between Jayewardene and the Tamil leaders
remained high and Jaywardene moved cautiously, fearful of precipitating a

backlash of Sinhalese opposition to any form of decentralization. Not until mid-1979, two years after Jayewardene's election, was a commission appointed to specify details of the structures, responsibilities, and powers for the proposed new district development councils the parties had been discussing. The commission's report of February 1980 became the basis for instructions to the legal draftsman, and by August 1980 Parliament had passed the necessary legislation authorizing creation of the councils.[8]

Tamil critics thought the process unduly tardy, which only confirmed their suspicions that the Jayewardene government, like its predecessors, was not serious about resolving Tamil grievances. Nevertheless, it was a real achievement to have parliamentary approval for such devolution as the district councils after two previous efforts at decentralization had fallen before Sinhalese popular opposition.

Time, however, was not on the side of moderates either among the Tamils or in the government. What might have been accepted by Tamil activists as satisfactory a year or two earlier came to be seen in the end as niggardly—too little, too late. Nevertheless, despite violent opposition from the most militant Tamils in the Northern and Eastern Provinces, the first elections for the district development councils were held throughout the island in June 1981.

Unfortunately, implementation of the district development councils was hampered when budgetary controls required by the World Bank and International Monetary Fund (IMF) in 1980–81 to curtail runaway expenditures had unforeseen political consequences. Inflation in Sri Lanka was then running at 30 to 35 percent; under the required controls and budget cutbacks most ministries' budgets were cut by 25 percent. Any allocations for new expenditures, including those for district development councils, were out of the question. Thus the councils did not receive the funds proponents had expected, and more Tamils were persuaded that the government was not serious about instituting the councils, even though it had agreed to them. There is no assurance that, had the district development councils been generously financed at that politically sensitive moment, events would have turned out differently; but an opportunity may well have been missed.

The Changing Security Context

During the year and a half of negotiations on the district development councils events on the ground did not stand still. The Tamil militants improved their ability to disrupt governance in the north and east. Their coordinated skills in ambushing police and armed forces, assassinating chosen personalities, robbing banks, and performing demonstrative violence were all improving. The evidence of the government's reluctance (or inability) to meet Tamil grievances through negotiation only strengthened the militants' conviction that the central government could not be serious in responding to their concerns. And unfortunately for the future, the moderates of the Tamil United Liberation Front who had staked their positions on those negotiations were discredited by the insufficient results achieved.

In view of bitter criticism of even the modest concessions negotiated, voiced by influential Sinhalese members of his own party, by the opposition Sri Lanka Freedom Party, and by Buddhist priests, Jayewardene could see the difficulties he would face if he moved at a faster pace. Moreover, the government's efforts to restore order in the north, to protect the safety of those Tamils who opposed Eelam (at the outset there were many), and to raise the costs to the militants of their activities, were often counterproductive. The language barrier left the Sinhalese troops in Tamil areas isolated, nervous, and ill-informed, and it was difficult for the troops to distinguish between Tamil militants and Tamils who opposed the militants. Militant attacks on the troops sometimes led to random, exaggerated responses, which increasingly overstepped the bounds of traditional legal restraints.[9]

Multiple Negotiations after 1983

In June 1983 massive anti-Tamil riots in Colombo, precipitated by Sinhalese who were enraged by Tamil ambushes of government troops in Jaffna, intensified a cycle of violence. The riots sharply radicalized more of the Tamil community, and led the government to pass a sixth amendment to the constitution, which required all members of Parliament to take an oath to defend the unitary constitution. In the late 1950s a similar requirement had calmed a Tamil independence movement in southern India; but in Sri Lanka in 1983 all parliamentary representatives of the Tamil United Liberation Front felt compelled to resign their seats, leaving Tamils without elected spokespersons in Parliament.

Furthermore, the riots induced thousands of Tamils to flee to Madras, where India's highly competitive parties outdid each other in dramatizing support for their beleaguered kin across the Palk Strait.[10]

These events provided Indian prime minister Indira Gandhi with an ideal opportunity to involve herself more actively in Sri Lanka's affairs as she sought to shore up her faltering political support in India by backing causes that attracted Madras politicians. The events also strengthened the solidarity and determination of the more radical Tamil militants. TULF leaders had no option but to demand a more ambitious focus for devolution—in this case, provincial councils—which inevitably intensified the anxieties of the Sinhalese.

Madras politicians and elements of the Indian government had already been helping Sri Lankan Tamils by providing sanctuaries and communications, and by turning a blind eye to fund raising and arms smuggling. Now support from the neighboring capital, New Delhi, became public and far more active. Worried Sinhalese feared a reprise of a role the Indian army had played in the 1971 breakup of Pakistan—a result that Tamil spokespersons in Madras and Jaffna eagerly demanded.

In Sri Lanka militant Tamils, disappointed by the results of the 1979–82 negotiations and aggrieved by the 1983 riots, were encouraged by India's support to oppose any government offers. At the same time, the activities of the security forces and of militant Sinhalese supporters of the government intensified the worst fears of the Tamils and sharpened their suspicions of the government.

Mediation by India, 1983–84

The 1983 anti-Tamil riots induced India to undertake a series of mediation efforts in the Sri Lankan conflict despite its involvement in the conflict.[11] A close foreign policy adviser to Mrs. Gandhi, a distinguished Tamil Brahmin, paid a number of diplomatic visits to Sri Lanka. He helped the Tamil militants to moderate their more extreme constitutional demands, and induced the Sri Lankan government to offer more effective forms of devolution. But he made little real progress in closing the distance between the two sides.

Four months after the riots, when the Commonwealth heads of government met in New Delhi, Jayewardene and Mrs. Gandhi had an inconspicuous opportunity to consider the mediator's ideas. These were detailed in a document known as Annexure C, which spelled out principles for devolving local police, land distribution, and other powers, and for the creation of an overarching council to encompass both the Northern and Eastern Provinces.[12]

However, the negotiating space was delimited by contradictory interests. From the Sri Lankan government's point of view, the larger the entity (such as an overarching council) permitted, and the more extensive the powers to be devolved, the more likely that entity would become the base for an even more determined secessionist movement. (For that reason the government's initiative of 1979–82 had specified limited powers assigned to the smaller entities, the administrative districts.) From the Tamil perspective, the more powers that were devolved, and the larger the entity, the more the Tamils would be able to protect their own interests; for those committed to achieving Eelam, that arrangement could be seen as a major stride toward independence.

The mediator's bona fides were weakened by India's contribution to the militants' firepower and resolve and by the visible (but denied) support of the militants by India's intelligence service.[13] On Jayewardene's return to Colombo, his cabinet colleagues vehemently rejected Annexure C as totally unacceptable.

The All Parties Conference

Adopting another expedient than third-party mediation, early in 1984 the Sri Lankan president called the meeting known as the All Parties Conference. Participants in this search for a Sri Lankan consensus reflected a broad spectrum of Sri Lankan opinion, including Sinhalese opposition parties, Buddhist priests, Christian spokespersons, as well as others. Jayewardene may have hoped that new coalitions might strengthen his hand against the inflexible members of both his own party and the opposition. Meanwhile, inconspicuous government discussions with Tamil United Liberation Front representatives, without either party having to make a negotiating first move, could continue. Although former prime minister Sirima Bandaranaike took her Sri Lanka Freedom Party out of the conference after one month, the conference continued to convene off and on during the year. In the end, although discussions had brought to the surface all possible alternative modes of decentralization, differences among the participants remained as wide as ever.

The government security services and the militants used the time gained through such protracted negotiations to strengthen their respective military positions. Tamil military units were becoming larger; their training in India by retired Tamil-speaking officers, and supplies from India and Singapore, made them more effective. Fearing revenge from the militant Liberation Tigers of Tamil Eelam (LTTE, or Tamil Tigers), fewer Tamils dared voice dissent from the rejectionist position insisted upon by the Tigers.[14]

Realistic members of the government were becoming more impressed by the difficulties of achieving an outcome acceptable to the bulk of the Sinhalese. Six years into his regime, Jayewardene's political room for concession was more limited than it had been in the early years of his government. However, during 1983 and 1984, with better equipment; with assistance from Pakistan, Israel, and China; and with more serious training and experience for its forces, the government stepped up its military activity against the militants. But deadlock continued. The guerrillas could not defeat the government, and the government could not reestablish order in areas the militants claimed as theirs.

Meetings Brokered by India, 1985

When Rajiv Gandhi succeeded Indira Gandhi as prime minister, India's policy became more neutral for a time. Rajiv Gandhi saw the inconsistency between India's meddling in Sri Lanka while objecting to Pakistan's meddling in the Punjab and Kashmir. He feared that Tamil Eelam in Sri Lanka might reawaken Indian Tamil secessionist sentiments that had so marked southern India in the 1950s. He also needed a foreign policy victory after a series of by-election defeats. At the same time, his concern for the opinion of his Tamil constituency in Tamilnadu led him to press for maximum Tamil autonomy within a unitary Sri Lanka.

In an effort to break the deadlock between the Tamil secessionists and the Sri Lankan government, Rajiv Gandhi brokered two consultations in the summer of 1985 in Thimpu, Bhutan, which for the first time brought the Sri Lankan government and all the Tamil factions, including the Tamil Tigers, to the table together. Thus with the support of the neighbor-host even the intransigent Tamil Tigers gained the hard-won right to negotiate directly with the government. The government proposed a three-month cease-fire and hoped that, far from the press, the parties could engage in serious convergence bargaining about the specifics of a provincial council formula. However, the Tamil Tigers raised the ante, now insisting that Sri Lanka's Northern and Eastern provinces be merged and that the Tamil community be recognized as a separate nationality possessing a right to a Tamil homeland.

The desire to consolidate the two provinces, which had been a sticking point for many years, was important to the Tamils for a number of reasons. Tamils looking ahead could imagine that some day the magnificent harbor of Trincomalee, in Eastern Province, could be a free-trade industrial zone, the center of a thriving regional economy comparable to Hong Kong; or that it could be a potential naval base leasable to an external power for a stiff annual rental. If the two provinces were linked, Tamils would clearly have majority control in the region. For precisely the same reasons the government, fearing the worst, was firmly opposed to linking the two provinces; it saw a demand as presaging the very partition of the island that it so opposed. Moreover, the population of Eastern Province was mixed, divided about equally among Tamils, Sinhalese, and Muslims. The Muslims were strongly opposed to linking the two provinces because they were unwilling to be dominated by Jaffna Tamils, even though they, too, were Tamil-speakers.

The issue of a Tamil homeland had other significance. Historically, land has long been a prime value in Sri Lanka, the source of social standing and of income. As the population more than doubled over the past thirty years, spokespersons for both Sinhalese and Tamil communities have stressed a growing sense of landlessness. Ironically, as large government and foreign resources were being devoted to expanding irrigation systems, the newly irrigated acres became apples of discord between what had become two jealous communities. For some Tamils, to declare a Tamil homeland was merely one way of confirming the Tamil claim to a meaningful share of the lands to be allocated in the future. To many Sinhalese, such a claim was seen mainly as a step toward Tamil independence.

Despite controversy at the Thimpu meetings, however, some progress was made. Through further negotiations between the Sri Lankan government and the Indian government, a formula for a settlement of the conflict was worked out that seemed reasonable to most Tamil groups and to some members of the government, and that the Indians seemed ready to support. A Draft Framework of Accord and Understanding set out some general principles and considerable detail. It provided for one provincial council in each province, devolution of certain law and order functions, land allocation, education, and cultural affairs, among other things.[15]

On the other hand, it was clear that the more extreme among the militants remained committed to their separatist goal of independence. Indian officials remained skeptical that unless subjected to sustained Indian pressure, the Sri Lankan government would be unwilling to accord enough autonomy to reassure the Tamils.

Each side stepped up its efforts to bring pressure to bear upon the other. Colombo had nearly doubled the size of its forces to some 37,600 as it made use of foreign military assistance; its equipment became more sophisticated, its troops more disciplined.[16] The militant groups continued to harass the government's troops, destroy government property such as buses and police stations, rob banks, and engage in demonstrative and selective violence to show how widespread and dedicated were their cadres. Either out of sympathy or fear, the Tamil populace was unwilling to provide evidence to help the government identify or locate those responsible.

Over time the militants had mined roads in key spots in Jaffna and Eastern Province and improved the defenses of their principal headquarters. Thousands of Tamil civilians had fled abroad. Hundreds had been jailed, and perhaps thousands had been killed either by the army or by militants retaliating against individual Tamils suspected of giving information to the government or supporting the wrong militant faction. Hundreds of troops had been killed. There was damage in many of the Tamil areas. In Jaffna the militants had established the rudiments of a parallel administration. Thus a stalemate persisted, but at a higher level of destruction. It was approaching a mutually hurting stalemate that might presage compromise (see chapter 1), but was not yet sufficiently severe to induce either party to concede enough to conclude a negotiated settlement.[17]

Private Conversations and Internal Party Negotiations, 1985–86

At the end of 1985 there were private conversations between the Sri Lankan government and the more moderate TULF spokespersons, who now pressed for a federal solution to end the conflict.[18] Both sides lacked confidence in the bona fides of new proposals under which the Eastern province would be split into three ethnicly homogenous districts. There were Tamils who feared that Jayewardene was really negotiating in an effort to divide the militants, to impress Rajiv Gandhi, or even to impress the Paris consortium of aid donors. The government, for its part, was unclear just what portion of the militant movement the TULF spokespersons represented.

Moreover, the influence of the Tamil United Liberation Front negotiators had been severely eroded since the Sixth Amendment had led them to resign their parliamentary seats. Even though the Tamil Tigers continued to insist that only full independence would do, TULF spokespersons felt compelled to argue there could be no solution if the Tamil Tigers were not included in the negotiations. The long period of trial and error had not yet produced a mutually acceptable formula.

None of the principal parties to the conflict was a unitary negotiating partner. Internal negotiations within each party prevented the more flexible negotiators from reaching a compromise solution. Whenever the government made a concession that the Tamil United Liberation Front found attractive, the Tamil Tigers would promptly reject it as not good enough. Similarly, whenever the TULF made a concession that interested Jayewardene, hard-liners in the cabinet would say no so vehemently that the president would back away from the offer.

At the same time, the Tamil militants were turning violence against each other. As they consolidated their hold in Northern Province, the Tamil Tigers liquidated rival leaders in bloody shoot-outs in Madras and Jaffna. They had become stronger and more ruthless than their most enthusiastic Indian supporters had ever envisaged. Moreover, it had become clear that their leaders conceived of government as dictatorial personal rule by their infallible leader, V. Prabakharan; coercion and brutality were its hallmarks.

Indian efforts at mediation continued, with increased Indian pressure brought to bear on the Sri Lankan government. Jayewardene called a new all-parties conference, seeking to evoke a consensus on the proposals first given shape as the Draft Framework of Accord and Understanding; through inconspicuous negotiations between Indian representatives, moderate Tamils, and the Sri Lankan government, these had been subsequently modified in ways favorable to the Tamils.

Meetings Brokered by India, 1986

In December 1986, on the occasion of (but not as part of) a meeting of the South Asia Association for Regional Cooperation in Bangalore, India, Jayewardene and Rajiv Gandhi negotiated further details of the draft framework to make it more acceptable to most Tamil militants. By taking the Tamil Tiger leaders into custody and temporarily confiscating their weapons and communications equipment, India made it clear that the militants could no longer count on full Indian support. But there was a question as to whether the Indians could still exert a decisive influence over this increasingly powerful Tamil faction.

In consultations it was proposed that the provincial councils for the Northern and Eastern provinces have a number of institutional linkages. Prabakharan, the unquestioned leader of the Tamil Tigers, was offered the chief ministership of the Northern Province, which he promptly rejected.[19] The revised proposals seemed to Indian negotiators, and to all the other

Tamil militant groups, to be reasonable and the most they could expect. Nevertheless, because the Tamil Tigers remained unbending on behalf of full independence, had the most guns, and were the most skilled at intimidating their Tamil opponents, Prabakharan's rejection had to stand.

Somewhat later Jayewardene agreed to accept the merging of the two provinces if a referendum following elections approved such a move. In return, the government of India agreed that should the time come it would insist that the militants accept the proposal that had been worked out between the two governments.

On his return to Jaffna, Prabakharan began to take over the role of government—controlling traffic, issuing automobile licenses, and opening secretariats, for example. These activities suggested to the Sri Lankan government that time was pressing hard.

A Hurting Stalemate

Following the year of protracted negotiations that had ended in the Tamil Tigers' continued refusal to compromise on secession, military activity intensified once again. The government's forces struck vigorously at Tamil Tiger strongholds in the Northern Province; Tiger forces retreated to the Jaffna peninsula. A government blockade prevented shipments of fuel to Jaffna in the hope that civilian opposition to the militants' rejectionist policy would undermine its position.

In the short run government troops did better than expected. Other aspects of the government's bargaining position were worsening, however, and time was working against the government. The cost of the better military effort had risen sharply and by 1987 represented nearly 8.9 percent of GDP.[20] The International Institute for Strategic Studies (IISS) estimated there were then more than 5,000 full-time Tamil activists and some 8,000 Tamil reserves.[21] Tourists were no longer coming to Sri Lanka; foreign investment had stopped. Foreign donors were cutting their assistance and urging a political settlement as they saw resources going into the protracted civil war. In April 1987, pressured by India, the government offered the rebels a new month-long truce, on condition the Bangalore proposals be accepted by the militants. The Tamil Tigers dramatized their rejection of the offer by bombing Colombo's central bus station and killing a busload of Buddhist priests elsewhere.

In May the government began a major military penetration of the Jaffna peninsula designed to cut off Jaffna from its principal sources of supply from the sea and to overwhelm the militant leaders' villages on the north-east coast. To the surprise of many the campaign succeeded militarily, although there were considerable civilian casualties and the Tamil Tiger leadership escaped. There were those in Colombo, including President Jayewardene, who now called on the forces to take Jaffna, to finally bring a stop to the Tamil Tiger insurgency once and for all.[22]

The Mediator Intervenes

The government of India actively intervened to deter such a move. It warned Sri Lanka's minister of national security not to attack Jaffna. Madras politicians provided more than U.S. $2.5 million to the Tamil militants. When a flotilla of Red Cross fishing boats loaded with civilian relief supplies was turned back by the Sri Lankan navy, Indian Air Force planes, accompanied by jet fighters, dropped relief supplies. India would permit neither a frontal attack on Jaffna nor a protracted blockade of the Jaffna peninsula. Yet without some form of decisive action the stalemate could go on indefinitely, a prospect the Sri Lankan government could not bear.[23] Moreover, India's intrusion into Sri Lanka's air space provoked intense public anger and fears that India would interfere as it had in Bangladesh in 1971.[24]

Among the Sinhalese there was growing anger at India and mounting resentment at the government's inability to bring the conflict to an end. The Janata Vimukhti Peramuna (JVP), a radical group that had attempted a coup in 1971 against the Bandaranaike government, reemerged. Strongly Sinhalese and xenophobic, the group found a ready response in the growing anti-Indian sentiment. Once more it engaged in demonstrative violence, threatening government supporters, detonating occasional bombs, and demanding radical change. Just as the Tamil militants had learned some lessons from the abortive JVP coup in 1971, it appeared that the JVP was learning some tactical lessons from the Tamil Tigers.[25]

The Indo–Sri Lanka Accord and Its Aftermath

In the face of these mounting pressures, in late July 1987 Rajiv Gandhi and Jayewardene signed the India–Sri Lanka Agreement to establish peace and normalcy in Sri Lanka. Both leaders worked with small groups of advisers, the usual bureaucratic specialists being held on the sidelines.

Gandhi proposed that if Jayewardene could confirm his acceptance of the agreements tentatively negotiated between them at Bangalore and modified since then in quiet negotiations, he would be willing to assist President Jayewardene in implementing the agreements. The accord called for a cease-fire, to be effective within forty-eight hours of the signing, with a surrender of the Tamil militants' arms and a withdrawal of government troops in Jaffna to barracks within seventy-two hours. As a fundamental part of a political solution the government was ready to acknowledge principles it had hitherto rejected: that Sri Lanka was a multi-ethnic society, that Tamil as well as English would be recognized as an official language, and that the Northern and Eastern provinces were areas that had traditionally been inhabited by Tamil-speaking people as well as other groups.

In a reversal of previous positions, the Sri Lankan government confirmed its willingness to establish a single provincial regional council to encompass both provinces, and accepted a jointure of the Northern and Eastern provinces. It further promised that elections would be held in the combined provinces under Sri Lankan supervision, with Indian assistance, by the end of the year. For its part, the government of India agreed to send to Sri Lanka an Indian peacekeeping force of some 3,000 men to protect the Tamil militants from the Sri Lankan army. Hoping to mollify the Sinhalese and those Muslims who lived in the Eastern Province, Jayewardene proposed that a continuation of the jointure of the two provinces be contingent on the results of a referendum, to be held within a year of the signing of the accord. He also insisted that to prevent further assistance to the Tamils from southern India there be joint Sri Lankan–Indian naval patrols of the Palk Strait, and that the government of India, if requested by Sri Lanka, would "afford military assistance to implement these proposals."[26]

Indian officials agreed to underwrite the accord. But they also insisted that in return the Sri Lankan government should satisfy some of India's foreign policy concerns—issues dealt with in an annex to the accord. Those issues revealed India's anxiety about how its small neighbor might adversely affect India's security through Sri Lankan relations with the United States.

By agreeing to invite the Indian peacekeeping force, Jayewardene and his associates believed they had ensured that India would become part of the solution rather than being part of the problem. Rather than supporting the militants, India would now assist the government in disarming them and in overseeing the local elections that were to be the first step in a return to normal democratic practice in the north.

However, neither the Sri Lankan nor the Indian governments could deliver their followers. Leaders on both sides had miscalculated. Jayewardene underestimated the anger his move would generate among the Sinhalese. For him to accept the presence of Indian troops in Sri Lanka was to touch an acutely sensitive Sinhalese nerve, evoking historic memories of Chola invasions and conquest during the tenth century and provoking intense public hostility. Indian officials misread reports of Tamil Tiger readiness to accept the accord's proposals and exaggerated the power of the Indian government to impose the agreement on the militant movement it had encouraged. The partial mediator had not been able to deliver the side it had supported from the beginning.

The Mediator Attacked

Within six weeks the Liberation Tigers of Tamil Eelam attacked the Indian peacekeeping force. In order to live up to its commitment to implement the accord, the Indian force had to take Jaffna. It did so with a severe loss of life among both troops and civilians, and with much damage to houses and official buildings.

Rarely in the history of interstate mediation has the mediator been attacked by one of the parties to a negotiation.[27] It is also remarkable that in this case the attacking party was a guerrilla movement that took on part of the world's fourth largest army—an army belonging to the government that had provided critical assistance to the militants in the first place. In the course of the subsequent conflict between the Indian peacekeeping force and the Liberation Tigers of Tamil Eelam, the Indian force swelled to at least 60,000 men.

This chapter does not examine that conflict in detail, nor does it examine closely what happened after India's forces withdrew in the summer of 1989.[28] At first the peacekeeping force drove the Tamil Tigers out of Jaffna and most of the Northern Province. But in the process so much damage was done and so many innocent civilians were killed that the Indian peacekeepers, originally welcomed as a harbinger of peace by most Tamils who were not with the militants, were soon seen as a destructive, occupying force.

Although the Indian force pressed the Tamil Tigers very hard and drove the insurgents into the jungle, it was never able (or perhaps was never willing) to seize Prabakharan or eliminate the top rebel cadres. As a result, when in 1989–90 the Indian force was told to leave Sri Lanka by President Ransinghe Premadasa, Jayewardene's successor, it was the Liberation Tigers of Tamil Ealam who asserted control over the Jaffna peninsula, much of Northern Province, and parts of Eastern Province. While the Indian peacekeeping force was still in Sri Lanka, the Sri Lankan government opened negotiations with the Tamil Tigers. These negotiations lasted nearly a year and a half; in the end the government offered the insurgents virtually everything they asked for except de jure independence. This offer too the insurgents eventually rejected, shortly after the Indian departure.

The Struggle Continues

In June 1990 the Tamil Tiger leadership abruptly broke off negotiations with the government and seized and killed more than 150 policemen who had specific orders not to resist capture. The struggle was thus resumed at the militants' initiative, and Premadasa's extended patience was shown to have been misguided.

The government's forces rolled back the area under Tamil Tiger control to the Jaffna peninsula, although occasionally the insurgents claimed credit for a demonstrative assassination or bombing in the south. The unusual geography of the Jaffna peninsula made decisive military action against an entrenched guerrilla force there very difficult. Yet the guerrilla forces could not defeat the government troops. The prospect therefore was—and is—for a sustained stalemate, with continuing though sporadic violence and no agreement.

Unless there is a change in the Tamil Tiger leadership, the militants are likely to agree to nothing but full independence. But given India's massive intervention and Sri Lanka's historical concern over the 70 million Tamils in southern India, no Sri Lankan government is likely to agree to that demand for independence. Despite repeated efforts, the government has been unable to dislodge the militants from effective control over the Jaffna peninsula. Trincomalee and much of Eastern Province remain largely under government control during the day, but at night the Tamil Tigers have wide scope for actions. It is likely there will be periodic instances of demonstrative violence there, emblematic of continued militant aspirations.

After the leadership of the Janata Vimukti Peramuna was captured by the government near Kandy, and its cadres were eliminated, life returned to a more normal tempo in the rest of the country. Economic activity picked up, local elections resumed, and provincial elections began. President Premadasa's executive energies and imperious ways suggested that he was pushing the executive presidency to its authoritarian limits. In the spring of

1993 a promising potential opposition leader was assassinated by an unknown hand; scarcely a week later Premadasa was killed by a suicide
bomber, as Rajiv Gandhi had been more than a year earlier. To everyone's
relief, Prime Minister Dingiri Banda Wijetunga succeeded to the presidency as the constitutional process required. Large popular turnouts in a
number of provincial and local elections since then suggest that outside the
Jaffna peninsula and parts of Eastern Province, at least, familiar orderly and
competitive politics have returned.

Sporadic efforts by the Tamil Tigers to disrupt continued. Some ten days
before a new presidential election called for November 1994, the prospective next leader of the governing United National Party was the victim of a
suicide bomber. However, the election proceeded without major incident.
President Wijetunga of the UNP lost, after his party had been in control for
seventeen years. He was replaced by Chandrika Kumaratunga, the daughter
of former prime minister Sirima Banderanaike. A voter turnout estimated at
70 percent further confirmed that politics outside the Tamil areas had
returned to Sri Lanka's norm.

In January 1995 the government and the Tamil Tigers agreed to a
three-month truce, in part to permit Tamil Catholics to participate in an
unprecedented visit to Colombo by the pope, then on an extensive visit to
Asia. Despite four rounds of negotiations, the truce was broken in April.
There had been truces before, but this time, given battle fatigue all around
and with a new government in Colombo, many hoped the outcome would
be different.

Conclusions

The analysis in this chapter, focusing principally on the negotiations
among the governments of Sri Lanka and India and spokespersons for the
Sri Lankan Tamils from the late 1970s to 1987, leads to a number of
conclusions.

As Zartman's model suggests (see chapter 1), an originally weak and
fragmented minority group facing a well-established, popularly elected
government was able to call up sufficient resources of dedication, commitment, and a sense of unjust grievance to challenge that government. The
minority used tactics of protracted guerrilla warfare and intimidation (even
elimination) of its opponents, and crucial support from abroad (ethnic kin
living next door, the large neighboring government, and a prosperous

refugee community abroad) to bring about, at least temporarily, virtual independence.

Efforts by the Sri Lankan government to negotiate with the more moderate members of the minority were sufficiently promising at the beginning to persuade the government and the moderate Tamil leaders to hope that negotiation could resolve the conflict. But because the concessions eventually gained through prolonged negotiations were perceived by the minority as reluctantly offered and niggardly in extent, and fell far short of what the more militant factions of the minority demanded, the moderate Tamil negotiators were gradually discredited in the eyes of the more impatient, largely younger members of the minority.

The prolonged, violent, and indecisive struggle between the guerrillas and the government produced polarization within both parties. Among the minority Tamils this led the more radical, violent, and lower-caste militant leaders to gain strength at the expense of the parliamentarians. Among the Sinhalese majority the moderates had less and less influence, until a change of government in the fall of 1994 produced a cabinet willing to reopen discussions.

The government's efforts to repress the secessionist movement were impeded by the lack of discipline among the troops, especially at the beginning, and by the difficulty the troops faced in discriminating between the radical Tamil secessionists and those Tamils willing to settle for a negotiated degree of autonomy. Moreover, the government was unable to evoke sufficient consensus among the Sinhalese factions to help reassure the Tamils that their interests would be protected in the kind of unitary government being offered.

Once the large neighbor became deeply involved as an active supporter of the militant Tamil factions, the capacity of the secessionists to disrupt the public peace and order greatly improved. The Tamils were then also less ready to make concessions toward accepting the government's successive offers, and the extreme faction became even less willing to settle for any arrangement other than full independence.

A near-total lack of trust further complicated negotiations. The government doubted the bona fides of even those Tamils who seemed ready to negotiate a compromise; the radical secessionists distrusted those moderate Tamils for being too soft. Both groups of Tamils distrusted the government's offers because they had been let down so often in the past. The one feared that the government was trying to divide the Tamils; the other feared that any relaxation of hostilities would reopen differences among the Tamils and that any steps toward accommodation might be the prelude to attempts to liquidate them. The majority Sinhalese community was beset by the looming shadow of India's 60 million Tamils, whose leaders often unwittingly intensified Sinhalese anxieties. Only the death of Rajiv Gandhi at the hands of the Liberation Tigers of Tamil Eelam turned South Indian Tamils against the Tamil Tigers and other Sri Lankan militants.

The character of the mediator played a critical role. India's size, its capacity to intimidate both parties, its special ethnic connection with the secessionist minority, its domestic political vulnerability to the secessionists' ethnic kin in Madras, and the claims of its foreign policy agenda profoundly influenced its perception of a desirable outcome. These considerations also affected how it played its cards.

The mutually hurtful stalemate became acute enough to induce the Sri Lankan government to invite in the Indian peacekeeping force. But the stalemate did not hurt enough to induce the majority to grant independence to the minority, or to induce the strongest secessionist faction to accept any of the numerous proposals that progressively went further and further toward meeting its demands, short of secession.

It would seem that only a sharp political change within the most extreme Tamil faction, and renewed readiness by the government to parley, can lead to a negotiated outcome in Sri Lanka.

Notes

1. See K. M. deSilva, *Managing Ethnic Tensions in Multi-Ethnic Societies—Sri Lanka 1880–1985* (Lanham, Md.: University Press of America, 1986).

2. For background, see H. Wriggins, *Ceylon, Dilemmas of a New Nation* (Princeton University Press, 1960), pp. 79–104; Michael Roberts, *Collective Identities, National-isms and Protest in Modern Sri Lanka* (Colombo, Sri Lanka: Marga Institute, 1979).

3. C. R. deSilva, *Sri Lanka: A History* (New Delhi: Vikas, 1987), p. 239.

4. For details of a communal outbreak following the general election of 1977, see Government of Sri Lanka, *Report of the Presidential Commission of Inquiry into the Incidents which Took Place between 13th August and 15th September, 1977*, Sessional Paper No. 7) (known as the Sansoni Commission Report) (Colombo, 1980).

5. Benedict R. O'G. Anderson, *Imagined Communities: Reflections on the Origin and Spread of Nationalism* (London: Verso, 1983); Robert N. Kearney, *Communalism and Language in the Politics of Ceylon* (Duke University Press, 1967).

6. See Wriggins, *Ceylon*, pp. 169–211. See also Satchi Ponnambalam, *Sri Lanka: The National Question and the Tamil Liberation Struggle* (London: Tamil Information Center and Zed Books, 1983).

7. Dagmar Hellman-Rajanayagam, "The Jaffna Social System: Continuity and Change Under Conditions of War," paper read at the Association of Asian Studies meeting, Boston, March 1994. For detail on developments within the Jaffna peninsula, see Rajan Hoole, Daya Somasundaram, K. Sritharan, and Rajani Thiranagama, *The Broken Palmyra: The Tamil Crisis in Sri Lanka—An Inside Account* (Claremont, Calif.: Sri Lanka Studies Institute, 1990).

8. For details, see K. M. deSilva and H. Wriggins, *J. R. Jayewardene of Sri Lanka: A Political Biography*, vol. 2 (London: Leo-Cooper, 1994), pp. 436–41; A. J. Wilson, *The Break-Up of Sri Lanka: The Sinhalese-Tamil Conflict* (University of Hawaii Press, 1988), pp. 140–55.

9. See K. M. deSilva, *Regional Powers and Small State Security: India and Sri Lanka, 1977–1990* (Washington: Woodrow Wilson Center and The Johns Hopkins University Press, forthcoming); Wilson, *Break-Up of Sri Lanka*; Sinha Ratnatunga, *Politics of Terrorism: The Sri Lanka Experience* (Belconnen, Australia: International Fellowship for Social and Economic Development, 1988). See also Barnett R. Rubin, *Cycles of Violence: Human Rights in Sri Lanka since the Indo-Sri Lanka Agreement* (Washington: Asia Watch, 1987).

10. For a theoretical discussion of such problems, see Myron Weiner, "The Macedonian Syndrome: An Historical Model of International Relations and Political Development," *World Politics*, vol. 23, no. 4 (July 1971), pp. 665–85.

11. For discussion of the "partial mediator," see Saadia Touval, *The Peace Brokers: Mediators in the Arab-Israeli Conflict, 1948–1979* (Princeton University Press, 1982), pp. 3–23; Saadia Touval and I. William Zartman, *International Mediation in Theory and Practice* (Boulder, Colo.: Westview Press, 1985), pp. 7–17 and 251–69.

12. For details on the negotiations that led to the drafting of Annexure C, see Sinha Ratnatunga, *Politics of Terrorism*, pp. 322–29.

13. For details of India's active support of the militants, see "Ominous Presence in Tamil Nadu," *India Today*, March 31, 1984, pp. 88–94; Anthony Mascarenhas, "Tamil Fighters Prepare for War," *Sunday Times* (London), April 1, 1984, p. 9; "Colombo Rides the Tiger," *South* (London), no. 53 (March 1985), pp. 13–15; and Edgar O'Balance, *The Cyanide War: Tamil Insurrection in Sri Lanka—1973–88* (London: Brassey, 1989), especially pp. 14–15, 38.

14. Formed in the mid-1970s, the Liberation Tigers of Tamil Eelam were the most violent of the militants. Their leader, V. Prabhakaran, claimed personal responsibility for the assassination of the mayor of Jaffna, defeated all rivals within the LTTE, and overcame other militant groups to dominate the Jaffna peninsula. For a discussion of typical stages of an insurgency, see Edward E. Rice, *Wars of the Third Kind* (University of California Press, 1988).

15. For details, see *Draft Proposals—30.8.85 to 19.12.86* (Colombo: Government of Sri Lanka, n.d.).

16. See International Institute for Strategic Studies (IISS), *Military Balance 1985–86* (London, 1985), p. 134.

17. I. William Zartman, *Ripe for Resolution: Conflict and Intervention in Africa* (Oxford University Press, 1989), pp. 255–88.

18. A long history has colored any mention of a federal solution. For many years Tamil politicians competed against each other with federalist slogans. For Sinhalese, the

unitary principle reflects the Sinhalese Buddhist concept that the whole island has a special Buddhist destiny derived from the Buddha himself.

19. The government of India was obviously recommending for Sri Lanka a policy that in northeastern India had successfully coopted a number of secessionist leaders and led them to desist from secession. See K. M. deSilva, "The Making of the Indo–Sri Lanka Accord," in K. M. deSilva and S. W. R. Samarasinghe, eds., *Peace Accords and Ethnic Conflict* (New York: Pinter, 1993), pp. 112–55.

20. International Institute for Strategic Studies, *Military Balance 1988–89* (London, 1988), p. 177. The distortion brought about by these events is clear when it is considered that the IISS reported that in 1980 defense represented only 0.7 percent of GNP. See IISS, *Military Balance, 1982–83* (London, 1982), p. 93.

21. IISS, *Military Balance: 1984–85; 1985–86;* and *1986–87*, p. 169.

22. See deSilva and Wriggins, *Jayewardene of Sri Lanka*, pp. 630–31.

23. DeSilva and Wriggins, *Jayewardene of Sri Lanka*, pp. 631–32.

24. In 1970–71, Pakistan's Bengali population rose in protest against an army crackdown, and several millions fled to West Bengal. Indian prime minister Indira Gandhi's intelligence organization trained and supplied a Bengali separatist movement, and eventually Indian "volunteers" and units of the Indian army entered East Pakistan and defeated Pakistani army units sent to repress the separatist movement. Bangladesh independence was soon declared, with India's enthusiastic support. See Pran Chopra, *India's Second Liberation* (MIT Press, 1974).

25. Rohan Gunaratna, *Sri Lanka: A Lost Revolution? The Inside Story of the JVP* (Colombo: Institute of Fundamental Studies, 1990).

26. For the text of the accord, see deSilva, *Regional Power*; and Ratnatunga, *Politics of Terrorism*.

27. A number of mediators have been assassinated by one or the other parties opposed to a settlement the mediator was proposing. Count Folke Bernadotte, the United Nations mediator in 1948 following the first Israeli-Arab war, is a prominent example.

28. For a detailed account of the conflict, see O'Balance, *The Cyanide War*.

I am indebted to K. M. deSilva's paper "India in Sri Lanka Relations, 1983–1991" (Occasional Paper 45, Woodrow Wilson Center, February 1992) for a most useful and detailed chronology of events in Sri Lanka as well as for many other points. I also acknowledge my use of Bruce Matthews, "Sri Lanka: An End to the Violence?" *Current Affairs Bulletin* (Sydney, Australia), vol. 65, no. 6 (November 1988), pp. 11–17; R. R. Premdas and S. W. R. de A. Samarasinghe, "Sri Lanka's Ethnic Conflict: The Indo-Lanka Peace Accord," *Asian Survey*, vol. 28 (June 1988), pp. 676–90; P. Venkateshwar Rao, "Ethnic Conflict in Sri Lanka: India's Role and Perception," *Asian Survey*, vol. 28 (April 1988), pp. 419–36. Interviews with President J. R. Jayewardene, his ministers, and officials between 1977 and 1993, and with Appapillai Amirthalingam and his colleagues in the Tamil United Liberation Front from 1977 on, provided indispensable background.

CHAPTER THREE

Negotiations for Basque Self-Determination in Spain

Robert P. Clark

ON APRIL 4, 1989, the Basque insurgent organization Euskadi ta As-
katasuna (Basque Homeland and Freedom, commonly known as ETA)
announced the end of a cease-fire it had declared three months earlier in its
ongoing conflict with the Spanish state.[1] The absence of any bloodshed
over the following few days—despite a number of bombs placed alongside
railroad tracks and in other public places—gave hope that ETA would not
immediately resume its violent attacks. This hope was shattered only a
week later when a member of the Spanish Guardia Civil was shot to death
in his car in Bilbao.[2] By the end of the year there had been nineteen more
killings, an estimated total by 1990 of around 800 victims of ETA violence
over the course of the conflict, in addition to an endless string of kidnap-
pings and bombings of public and state property.

The violence in April was even more tragic in that it signaled the failure
of a three-month-long attempt to negotiate an end to the internal conflict
between ETA and the Spanish state—a war that had been going on since the
founding of ETA in 1959 to achieve self-determination for the Basque
homeland and ''guarantee the survival of the [Basque] nation.''[3] Although
the negotiators, meeting in Algeria, had come closer to an agreement than
at any time in the past, the collapse of the talks should have been no
surprise. Attempts to negotiate a cease-fire with ETA had been going on
since the day Spanish General Francisco Franco was buried in November
1975; at least twenty and probably closer to thirty attempts had been made

59

by the end of the 1980s.[4] Some were abortive and failed to lead even to preliminary contacts; some consisted of little more than a single contact lasting several hours; others extended over periods of three or more months and involved many meetings of perhaps half a dozen negotiators. All these efforts had one thing in common: failure.

Yet in the 1990s the conflict took a different turn. On one hand, ETA was shaken by the arrest of its main leaders in 1992 and 1993; on the other, it was outflanked by the rise of a broadly based peace movement in the Basque country (similar to movements that have arisen in Northern Ireland), which isolated the Basque nationalist insurgents and gave organized expression to a public exhausted by violence. This development made possible a two-track negotiation strategy that analysts had long advocated to separate Basques' grievances from their political aims and commitments.

It is easy to discard some of the more frequently heard reasons why negotiations between the Basques and the Spanish state have failed. Lack of communication channels is not the problem; all parties involved (and they are numerous) know each other very well and are in frequent contact with one another whenever it suits their purposes. There is also clear evidence that both ETA and the Spanish government want the violence to end. With many of its key leaders either in French jails or in distant exile, and with 500 of its rank and file members in Spanish prisons, ETA itself is reaching the point of exhaustion, both materially and psychologically. For its own reasons the Spanish government would have liked to bring the conflict to a close before 1992, the year when Spain was very much in the international eye because of the Olympic Games held in Barcelona and the celebration of the 500th anniversary of the discovery of America. Nearly all Basque parties and government agencies stand to gain significantly from a cessation of violence. (However, a mutually hurting stalemate has yet to be perceived by the parties to the conflict.)[5] Outside support for the insurgents is also not a factor: more than other such conflicts, ETA's struggle is almost completely self-contained and independent of outside assistance. Public opinion too supports a negotiated settlement. In Spain generally, a clear majority favors a negotiated end to the struggle, and in the Basque country itself, where the majority of ETA's attacks occur, three-fourths of the population advocates a negotiated settlement—and the support is growing.[6]

How then can the many frustrated attempts to negotiate an end to this insurgency, and the shift in its course in the 1990s, be explained? In order to understand better why the negotiations have failed, and in the process to improve understanding of the obstacles and opportunities for negotiation between the insurgents and the Spanish state generally, a detailed study of more than ten years of efforts to negotiate with ETA was undertaken. This chapter reports the findings of that study.

The obstacles to success in the Basque negotiations can be clustered into three sets: the context-related, the violence-related, and the issue-related. The first of these involves the cultural and social context in which negotiations take place, and the ways in which that context intrudes into and frames the negotiations. Contextual obstacles include commitment of the participants, institutional complexity, and the need for mediation. A second set of obstacles has to do with the linkages between the cessation of violence and the conduct of negotiations. Although superficially these obstacles may appear to be nothing more than a problem of timing, in fact the difficulties are much more deeply rooted in the nature of the armed struggle and the importance to it of the tactical question of violence or compromise. A third set involves the nature of the negotiation itself, particularly the topics to be allowed on the agenda. At stake is the distinction between grievances and political issues, and the question of who has the legitimate right to bargain in which policy area. This chapter treats each of the three sets, concluding with discussion of a two-track negotiation strategy for removing the obstacles—a strategy that has gradually achieved some currency in the Basque conflict.[7]

The literature on negotiation with insurgents is scant, because writers on this issue have long assumed that such negotiations are a bad idea. The reasoning behind that assumption is well known: negotiations give insurgents legitimacy; insurgents are intransigent extremists and their demands are nonnegotiable; insurgents want a cease-fire only to gain time to recover from government antiterrorist measures and get ready to strike again.

This chapter—and this book—are based on the opposite premise: that there are many good reasons why a negotiated settlement should be attempted. Insurgent groups are not monoliths; negotiations should help discover which factions within a rebellion favor a settlement and which do not, and help separate the former from the latter. Negotiations should also uncover which of the insurgents' demands are amenable to bargaining and what they can be bargained for, as well as which demands are truly nonnegotiable. A negotiated truce or cease-fire will help reduce the level of anger so common in internal conflicts, and help build an atmosphere of trust and goodwill essential to resolution of the differences between warring parties. If a stalemate arises because the insurgents are so strongly supported by their home population that the government cannot suppress them or win over the bystanders, as has been the case with the Basque insurgents, negotiations become the only realistic way out of violence. In other words, negotiation may be the best solution to insurgency, not because it is such a good solution but because all the others are so bad.

Context, Commitment, and Mediation

Because the parties in conflict in Spain—ETA, the government of the Basque autonomous region,[8] and the Spanish national government—have been engaged in numerous negotiation attempts over many years, it seems likely that they would have learned what they need to know about the political, cultural, and social contexts within which such negotiations take place. Nevertheless, an outside observer can identify several obstacles to negotiation at the contextual level whose importance the negotiating parties seem to have overlooked.[9]

The first such obstacle is the extremely complex institutional milieu within which the parties operate. The conflict is not just between ETA and the Spanish state; many contending political forces and groups are involved, with constantly shifting agendas and priorities. As many as two dozen identifiable groups have a stake in negotiations with ETA; many of them can affect the outcome of negotiations in ways consonant with their own interests. These groups fit into one of four categories: ETA itself, with all of its factions, members in prison or in exile, and their families; other Basque groups, including the Basque autonomous regional government and the political parties and media associated with it; the Spanish government and its associated political parties and media; and international groups, including governments of other nations (neighboring France, which also has a Basque population, and Algeria) and organizations such as Amnesty International and Interpol.

The complexity of this universe of interested parties provides a daunting environment within which to negotiate. Most of these groups have multiple priorities; a settlement with ETA is an important goal for them, but not an imperative one, and the cessation of violence is not the most important objective of any of the parties.[10] The aim of ETA is to achieve self-determination for its region, and that is the purpose of its insurgency. The aim of the Spanish government is to bring the rebellion under control, and its varied means are subservient to that goal.

Most of the other interested groups want an end to the violence, but on their own terms. The parties to the conflict want a settlement that will benefit them politically, and will trade off the suspension of violence for the achievement of their goals. There is tension between the Basque autonomous regional government and the Spanish government over which of them should take the lead in conducting negotiations; moreover, on more than one occasion each has kept its negotiating initiatives secret from the other. Within each of these governments there is also tension among the various ministries, such as Interior and Justice, as each tries to advance its own bureaucratic goals.[11] The history of ETA itself is littered with internal divisions, many of which have turned on tactical questions about negotiations. There is also tension between the goals and priorities of the leaders and the rank-and-file members of all parties. Leaders on both sides appear reluctant to move too fast toward negotiation lest they appear too conciliatory toward their enemies—again, the tactical question. Under these circumstances, coalitions in support of negotiations are extraordinarily difficult to produce and easy to break apart. Yet leaders must continue to try to assemble such coalitions because no single political force controls all the economic, political, and legal resources necessary to secure a settlement.

Coalitions must also be formed to support negotiations because there are committed key actors on all sides of the dispute strongly opposed to a negotiated settlement. Antitruce elements have been able to frustrate negotiations, usually by withdrawing their support or by carrying out disruptive violence at strategic moments. For example, the assassination of Bilbao journalist José María Portell in June 1978 took place just as he was about to arrange negotiations between a faction of ETA and the Spanish government. His death not only ended this initiative, but set in motion a major increase in antiterrorist activity that made it impossible for several years to suggest publicly the option of negotiations. Similar actions and reactions happened at least half a dozen times throughout the 1980s. It is tempting to lay the blame for such acts of sabotage at the feet of ETA or one of its antinegotiation factions, but in most instances it is not possible to discover who actually committed an act, much less the motives for doing so.

The troubled course of attempted negotiations on the Basque problem suggests ways around the obstacles of context and commitment. Keeping initial meetings general and limited to preliminary administrative and technical questions such as site, participants, agenda, and procedural rules enables talks to get started.[12] Once talks have begun, participants must not reject out of hand any agenda item. Placing an item on the agenda is not necessarily a commitment to action on that item, one way or another; nor does it necessarily confer legitimacy on that demand if the contending parties do not wish to do so. Parties trying to arrange a cease-fire must identify and gain the support of those who favor negotiations. At the same time, pro-truce elements must identify those who oppose negotiations and defuse their opposition by refusing to state beforehand that a disruptive act will be taken as a reason to suspend the talks. By announcing that an armed attack will cause the talks to be suspended, the antitruce forces are given the power to block negotiations simply by committing that act. Governments must also recognize that for insurgents the tactical question of a negotiated settlement is not a simple matter of disagreement among friends; it can be a life and death issue. At least two ETA leaders (as well as a non-ETA leader of the Basque left) who favored negotiations have been killed; a third survived an attack that killed his wife; a fourth died in an automobile accident under mysterious circumstances. It is probable that their deaths had something to do with their position on negotiations—the tactical question referred to in chapter 1.

If the parties cannot find their own way around the obstacles of context and commitment, they will need help from a third party, and the lack of skilled mediators can be an additional obstacle to the successful conduct of negotiations. As already observed, in the Basque case a scarcity of lines of communication is not a problem: ETA leaders know how to reach their opposite numbers in the government and vice versa. But trust and confidence are the principal elements in short supply, and intermediaries trusted by all the parties to the struggle are few in number. Moreover, the mediators must have physical and political courage. At least two men who tried to act as intermediaries in the Basque struggle—Portell (in 1978) and Santiago Brouard (in 1984)—were killed in the midst of their negotiations by persons still unknown. Moreover, acting as a mediator with terrorists is technically a violation of Spain's antiterrorist laws, and at least one person who attempted mediation in a hostage case was arrested and charged with complicity in the kidnapping. Thus it is essential that the mediators be protected, both physically and legally, throughout any negotiation effort.

How the parties use the mediators can also be an obstacle. Both ETA and the Spanish government have been deeply suspicious of anyone who might offer services as a mediator, believing (perhaps with justification) that the intermediary was trying to capitalize on the strategic position between the two sides. One person who performed mediation service a number of times indicated that he would not do so again unless requested to in writing by both parties, so if the mediation failed they could not repudiate him or deny that he was acting at their request.[13]

The kinds of persons dispatched by the Spanish government as envoys to talk with ETA have affected negotiations. ETA has said repeatedly that it wants to talk with representatives of Spain's political sectors, not those who represent the police agencies of the government. Yet with the exception of meetings in Algeria in late 1987 and early 1988, the Spanish government has sent only Interior ministry and senior police officials. This might have been overlooked had not several of the government's most frequently used envoys had reputations as torturers of arrested Basques. Some meetings have even been held at which the torturer and his victims confronted each other across the bargaining table. Productive talks cannot be expected to take place under such circumstances.

The conduct of fruitful negotiations requires self-control and responsible reporting from the press in its coverage of negotiations. But in Spain and its Basque region there are few news media that can be considered neutral or disinterested. Many newspapers and news magazines are connected to a specific party (or even a faction within a party) or ideology, and try to advance their group's perceptions of an event. Television is even less well suited for reporting negotiations because it is a state monopoly (although the addition of several private broadcasting companies may diversify the industry). There is a regional television station in the Basque country, but it too is state owned and operated. The press cannot be kept completely out of negotiations, however, because newspapers are used frequently as conduits of information among parties who are not in direct contact with each other. Moreover, the role of the press in such delicate matters in a more or less open society is always sensitive. Although there are positive benefits to keeping negotiations out of the public eye, at least at the beginning, the parties in the Basque dispute—especially ETA—have been slow to recognize this. There is some evidence that there was greater secrecy during the third round of negotiations between ETA and the government in Algeria early in 1989, even though the eventual collapse of the talks stemmed from press reports of what were essentially two different versions—those of ETA and the Spanish government—of what had been agreed to.

Violence as an Obstacle

On more than one occasion, talks between ETA and the government have broken down because of disagreement about the linkage between a cease-fire and the negotiation process. At stake in such situations is the timing of a cease-fire—that is, whether it should take effect before, during, or after resolution of the issues. From the beginning the Spanish government has insisted that violence must be halted before negotiations could begin and that there would have to be ironclad guarantees that the violence would not resume as long as the talks were under way—a position that could be described as "first truce, then talks." Regardless of what kind of regime has ruled the state, or the personalities involved, the Spanish government's position has always been clear; it would not sit across the table from ETA while killing was going on. ETA's position on this issue, on the other hand, has undergone substantial change over the years and cannot be easily or simply characterized.[14]

From the mid-1960s until 1974, during its mobilization and consolidation phase, ETA operated from the strategic premise of revolutionary war; violence had a key role to play in attaining the final objectives of the struggle—an independent, reunified, socialist, and Basque-speaking homeland. Its leaders knew that ETA was too weak to confront the Spanish military directly; but by applying an "action-repression spiral theory" they believed that violence could be used to provoke Madrid into destabilizing repression, leading to increased turmoil and finally civil war that would foster commitment and unite support. This position could be described as "first final victory, then a cease-fire."

ETA's first real experience with the revolutionary war strategy, in 1968, was so damaging, however, that it reassessed the wisdom of that approach. The result was the adoption, by 1974 (just before the death of Franco), of a two-stage strategy. The first stage would culminate in an autonomy, which, although substantial, would fall short of independence; the final goal of independence would be achieved only at the second stage. Although it was implicit in this strategy that the potential for armed struggle would be maintained during both stages, it gradually became ETA policy to reduce violence during the second stage, after the first-stage goals had been achieved. This approach could be called "first autonomy, then consideration of a truce."

By February 1978 the two-stage strategy had evolved into the negotiating posture that ETA was to maintain for a decade. The end of the first stage would be signaled by achievement of a set of five demands, known as the KAS Alternative (after a coalition of ETA-related groups[15]): amnesty for all prisoners and exiles; legalization of all parties; withdrawal of all Spanish law enforcement agencies from the Basque country; improvement of working and living conditions of the workers; and an autonomy statute that promised (among other things) official status for the Basque language, an autonomous police force, and the right of self-determination. Violence would continue until these five demands were achieved, at which time there would be a cease-fire; in other words, "first autonomy (the KAS Alternative), then truce." However, ETA would continue to exist even after these demands were met, and would retain its right to resume violence in pursuit of its second-stage goal.

Until ETA issued a truce proposal on January 28, 1988, its position was that the cessation of violence was the objective of negotiations, not a precondition for them, as the Spanish government insisted. In contrast, the January 28 communique was widely interpreted as an offer of a sixty-day cease-fire to take effect the moment talks began. Instead of waiting until the KAS Alternative had been achieved, ETA was willing to cease violence as soon as the Spanish government agreed to begin political negotiations. This position might be characterized as "truce and talks together." The government, however, still wanted a cessation of violence as well as a guarantee of no future violence before coming to the negotiating table. Because ETA was unwilling to yield on that point, talks were broken off. ETA then adjusted its position on the cease-fire question once more. ETA's January 1989 statement declared a cease-fire would be in effect before political negotiations had begun, as long as the Spanish government would meet with ETA and accept openly that political negotiations would eventually be undertaken. This position could be characterized as "truce when talks are promised." The 1989 talks collapsed at least in part because the government was unwilling to accept this condition.

The next ETA proposal came in July 1992, just before the Olympic Games were to be held in Barcelona. At that time ETA offered a two-month truce if the government would agree to "official contacts" in a mutually acceptable neutral country, to be followed by "political conversations." The proposal avoided the word negotiations, which the government had always rejected. The government rejected this proposal too, citing the Algerian experience in 1989. The truce was observed by ETA nonetheless for sixty-eight days, making the proposal a "truce in the hope of talks." In June 1993, on the eve of Spanish elections, ETA simply called for talks with the new government, and then three weeks later set off bombs (killing seven in Madrid) when the proposal was ignored.

It is clear that over the years ETA has changed its position on the linkage between a truce and a settlement, each time coming closer to the position

held by the Spanish government. But the debate over technical preconditions will continue to complicate negotiations until all the parties recognize
that negotiations serve to resolve conflicts, not simply to confirm prior
resolutions. Negotiations must precede, not follow, the termination of the
conflict. Thus ETA's insistence on acceptance of the KAS Alternative or of
political negotiations before a cease-fire, like the Spanish government's
insistence on a cessation of violence before talks can begin, are both
unrealistic and unreasonable. The principal problem here is the continuation of violence while negotiations are going on. ETA leaders must know
that it is impossible for their adversaries to enter into negotiations while
provocative violent attacks are still being launched; on the other hand, by
making a cessation of violence an absolute precondition to beginning
negotiations, the Spanish government has—wittingly or not—played into
the hands of persons within ETA and elsewhere who do not want negotiation to proceed.

A major problem is that both sides want to negotiate from a position of
strength, and neither wants to be seen as seeking peace from a position of
weakness. Many Basques believe that the Spanish government uses an
incorrect psychological approach in frequently claiming that ETA is growing weaker and will be forced to sue for a cease-fire. With such public
claims, Spanish officials provoke ETA into acts of violence to prove that
the organization is still strong and committed and that it enters into negotiations from strength, not weakness.[16] That ETA's violent attacks are especially dramatic and timed for maximum disruption magnifies their harmful
impact on the dynamics of negotiation.

The very nature of internal conflict makes it impossible for the rebellion
to renounce the use of force before securing its aims. As numerous ETA
strategists have pointed out, the only thing they have to offer at the bargaining table is their ability to turn off the violence. If they have already played
that card before the game begins, they remove from the government any
incentive to negotiate in good faith. Therefore, as long as ETA exists the
threat of violence will loom over the bargaining table, no matter what verbal
promises there may be between the two sides.

ETA suffered setbacks in the early 1990s that overshadowed the truce
issue and put negotiations on hold. In March 1992, in February 1993, and
again in June 1994, as a result of greater intra-European cooperation, the
French police arrested a number of ETA's top leaders who were using
France as a sanctuary and sentenced them to prison terms. The arrests did
not prevent—and may have prompted—ETA's new proposals in 1992 and

1993 and the subsequent terrorist acts, but they hardened the Spanish government's opposition to any talks. Among Basques, the continuing acts of terror also weakened support for ETA's tactics and goals, without, however, weakening commitment to Basque identity and to a nonviolent approach to achieving a status somewhere between present autonomy and self-determination. More important, the use of force has weakened its own legitimacy as a weapon and therefore its effectiveness as a pressure for negotiation. As ETA moved out of the Franco era and increased its interest in negotiation, the Spanish government lost whatever little interest it had in the negotiating process as it saw support for ETA's violent pressure tactics waning.

Issues as Obstacles

The distinction between negotiations over political issues and grievances was first suggested in 1981 by the Basque socialist and former ETA leader Mario Onaindia.[17] At the time, Onaindia and Juan Maria Bandres had just begun negotiations that led to the dissolution of ETA (political-military, or p-m) and the freeing or return of some 200 prisoners and exiles—one of the few instances of successful negotiations on record between ETA and the Spanish government. The success of this negotiation effort lay not only in the skill and persistence of the two Basques and in the flexibility of the Spanish interior minister, Juan José Roson, but also in the separation of the agenda into two sets of issues: those that were "technical" and open for discussion and those that were "political" and could not yet be placed on the agenda. A schematic comparison of the negotiating positions of the two parties as of 1989 suggests some of the differences between the two sets of issues (see table 3-1). The differences become clearer in examining this two-track approach as a way to overcome issues as obstacles to negotiations.

A two-track strategy for dealing with ETA's demands has been recognized and discussed in Spain since at least 1984. The earliest public reference to such an approach was made in August 1984 by the Spanish government's director of state security, Rafael Vera, who commented that political negotiations, although unthinkable with ETA directly, could be conducted with the political party that had close ties to ETA, Herri Batasuna (Popular Unity, or HB).[18] In August 1985 the president of the Basque autonomous government, José Antonio Ardanza, was quoted as rejecting political nego-

Table 3-1. *Negotiating Positions of the Spanish Government and ETA,*
1989, on ETA Demands in the KAS Alternative

KAS Alternative	Government position	ETA position
Immediate unconditional amnesty	Selective amnesty	Immediate, unconditional amnesty
Legalization of all parties	Not an issue: achieved before 1989	Not an issue: achieved before 1989
Withdrawal of all Spanish police and Guardia Civil	Phased reduction of forces after a cease-fire	Phased total withdrawal
Regional autonomy statute, including:	Under statute in effect in 1989, existing institutions are acceptable	Statute in effect in 1989 not legitimate, fails to meet demands
Basque self-determination	Not possible	Essential
Navarra integration into Basque country	Navarrese to decide	Process negotiable
Euskera to be official language	Basque issue	Co-official status, in effect, is acceptable
Basque control over police, army	Irrelevant	Phased total withdrawal

tiations with ETA but admitting the possibility of such negotiations with
"forces that have shown that they represent a portion of the {Basque}
electorate."[19] In December 1986 Herri Batasuna leader Inaki Esnaola was
reported as declaring that "we have never said that negotiations with ETA
are the only channel. We have defended them because no one offered
others, but if now new channels are opened, in HB we would study them."[20]
There is ample evidence that by the summer of 1987 a two-track approach
was being actively considered in key Spanish government circles.[21]

The two-track strategy first appeared in actual negotiations in talks in
Algeria in November 1987 between the Spanish government's representative, Julen Elgorriaga, and ETA's spokesman, Antxon Etxebeste. According to an interview with Elgorriaga, "when Antxon understood that the
government would never negotiate with ETA on political questions, which
in a democracy is the responsibility of the political parties, he asked what I
thought about the PSOE (the Spanish Socialist Workers' Party, the governing party) talking directly to HB. I answered that that might be acceptable,
that that was what we were trying to do, to talk and stop the killing, and that
where you discussed political questions was in the parliament."[22]

That exchange suggests that a two-track approach offers a way around
the unwillingness or inability of Spanish officials to negotiate political
issues directly with ETA terrorists. This is important because in ETA's

view for violence to end certain political questions (such as the Basque right of self-determination and the relationship of the neighboring province of Navarra to the Basque autonomous community) must be addressed. But the Spanish government has been willing to discuss only nonpolitical grievances, such as amnesty for ETA members and police practices directly with ETA. Moreover, not only would most Spanish political leaders oppose direct negotiations on political issues, but many Basques would object as well. The Basque leaders who have opted to work through the democratic parliamentary system would feel betrayed by any substantial deal struck directly with ETA on which they were not consulted. This problem could be met by the two-track approach—the use of two negotiating channels. On one track, the Spanish government could talk directly to ETA about technical issues; on the other, political issues could be addressed in a forum at which ETA was not physically present but where its interests would be safeguarded. Presumably activity on the two tracks would overlap in time; negotiations on both sets of issues would be going on at the same time.

The potential for success of the two-track approach lies in the separation of the negotiations into two venues, two agendas, and two negotiating bodies. Such a division makes it possible for parties in conflict to negotiate with one another without actually appearing to do so. One negotiation arena (track one) is set aside for issues that can plausibly be characterized as narrowly technical or that concern specific grievances, for the handling of which institutional mechanisms and procedures already exist. Amnesty for convicted insurgents is an example of one such issue. Because constitutional and statutory arrangements already sanction the discussion of this kind of issue, governments can engage in direct negotiations with insurgents without jeopardizing their own legitimacy. The other negotiation arena (track two) can thus be set aside for political negotiations concerning issues that cannot be encompassed within existing institutions. These issues challenge the legitimacy of existing constitutional arrangements, so they must be discussed among the widest possible array of political groups, including parties and other interested groups. It is significant that insurgents themselves are not present at these second-track negotiations; because their presence would imply recognition, the insurgents are represented by intermediaries who enjoy the confidence of the rebels but who are also regarded as legitimate participants in civil society.

First-track negotiations generally deal with such technical issues and grievances as public order, law enforcement, security, and the administration of justice. In the Basque case, the Spanish government would participate in track-one talks through representatives of the affected ministries, particularly the Justice ministry (because the prison system would be involved) and the Interior ministry (because the roles of the national police and the Guardia Civil would be involved). However, ETA has made it clear that at two-track talks it wants people present who can speak for, and make commitments for, the country's political leadership. ETA wants the Spanish government to recognize that violence in the Basque country is not a police question but a political one. In view of the sensitivity of such discussions, most observers agree that talks between ETA and the Spanish government should be held at a site outside Spain, but still relatively accessible. Algeria was a suitable location for earlier talks, but the parties lost interest in returning there and the Algerian government officially withdrew its offer to mediate the dispute. Other European countries, such as Belgium, might pick up the role. In June 1989 Venezuelan president Carlos Andres Pérez offered his good offices as an intermediary and his country as a possible venue for resumed negotiations.

In track-one talks, the first major issue to be discussed would be amnesty. As it has previously, ETA seeks an amnesty declaration by King Juan Carlos that is immediate, unconditional, and total; that is, it wants amnesty automatically for all ETA members, whether in prison serving sentences or awaiting trial (estimated at about 500 individuals), at large in Spain or in exile in France or elsewhere. It also demands that amnesty be extended to all ETA members regardless of the nature of their alleged crimes, and that ETA members not be required to do anything to obtain this pardon, either beforehand or subsequently.

The Spanish government, on the other hand, seeks to make amnesty conditional and partial, to be handed out on a case-by-case basis. Moreover, ETA members would be required to request amnesty and to sign a statement affirming their intention to live within the laws of Spain. Not all crimes would be covered by the pardon. Many Spanish leaders would not be willing to pardon those ETA members (about 150 persons) convicted of so-called blood crimes. Such persons might be granted some sort of "covered amnesty" or "amnistía encubierta" under which they would be released from prison on the condition that they leave Spain for a long period.

Other first-track negotiations would involve measures to ensure the cessation of all acts of violence in Spain related to ETA's struggle. A number of questions must be addressed. For example, would an agreement restrain acts of police violence (such as torture in prisons and local police stations) just as it would prohibit armed attacks by ETA? Exactly what acts of violence would be off limits? Would an agreement prevent ETA from collecting funds or from carrying on propaganda activities? What would happen if provocative acts were to occur while track-two negotiations were being held? Given the hatred built up over the years between ETA and the Spanish police and Guardia Civil, violent incidents are likely to erupt more or less spontaneously; would they be allowed to interrupt the negotiation process, or would the participants agree that some threshold of violence would have to be crossed before talks were suspended? Other sensitive questions would involve ETA's weapons. Some Spanish officials have declared that ETA must turn in all of its weapons as a guarantee not to undertake further armed attacks (as happened in the Mozambique conflict). Apart from the obvious difficulty of policing such a step, it seems highly unlikely that ETA would agree to disarming, at least during the early stages of negotiations. Finally, would there have to be a guarantor of the provisions of an agreement? In ETA's truce communique of January 28, 1988, Algeria was proposed as a guarantor of the negotiation process, but the Spanish government rejected that suggestion, declaring that the issues were an internal Spanish matter and that intervention by other governments would not be welcome.

In the Basque case the naming of the negotiating team for track-two talks might be formalized during track-one talks, but it seems likely that there would already be substantial agreement on participants before negotiations on track-one issues were held. As noted, the key to the success of track-two negotiations (and indeed of the two-track approach in general) is ETA's willingness to let the more controversial political issues be settled in a forum at which ETA is not actually present. The formula that would make this possible is the participation of representatives of the Basque National Liberation Movement (Movimiento de Liberaçíon Nacional Vasco, or MLNV), an organization that includes the political coalition Herri Batasuna.[23] Presumably ETA has complete confidence in the HB leaders, and because HB is a legitimate political party that customarily wins between 15 and 20 percent of the vote in elections in the Basque country, the Spanish government could claim that the sensitive political issues were not being discussed with a so-called terrorist group but rather with a bona fide representative of a sizable segment of the Basque population.

Other participants in track-two negotiations would depend on the exact agenda and the nature of subsequent ratification of agreements. At some point other Basque political parties and the Basque government would have to be involved, and eventually the Basque parliament would be asked to ratify an accord. The role of the Basque parliament could prove difficult because Herri Batasuna and ETA do not accept its legitimacy, and the Navarrese do not accept its authority over them. Nevertheless, for all the other Basque parties it is essential that their parliament be centrally involved in the negotiations, especially when the time comes to produce workable solutions to various political issues. If the status of Navarra is to be discussed, Navarrese representatives must be present, and the Navarrese parliament and the people of Navarra must be amply consulted. The Spanish government might be represented by government officials or by representatives of the governing party. Most interested parties would probably insist that the talks be held in the Basque country to symbolize that Basque issues were being settled locally by local authorities. Ideally, the meetings to negotiate would not be kept secret, but the press would be excluded and would be informed periodically through briefings about the course of negotiations.

An agenda for track-two negotiations would be difficult to work out because some of the most sensitive questions in Basque-Spanish relations would be treated. ETA has announced many times that the sole basis for negotiations must be the KAS Alternative (see table 3-1). The first of the KAS Alternatives, amnesty, would be dealt with in track-one negotiations. But because the second item—party legalization—has already been achieved; the fourth item—improved working conditions—is vague and ambiguous; and the fifth item—statutory autonomy—already exists in part, track-two negotiations would probably boil down to three major issues. These are the withdrawal of Spanish law enforcement authorities from the Basque country, the status of Navarra, and the right of the Basque people to self-determination. It remains to be seen exactly how a formula could be drawn up that would satisfy all parties on these three sensitive issues; but by separating them from other issues by putting them on the second track, and by involving negotiating parties other than ETA in their solution, the two-track approach offers a procedural solution to the nonnegotiable character of the substantive political questions.

In the 1990s events appear to have jumped over such potential negotiations into a different two-track approach. Herri Batasuna has generally maintained its electoral support, but the population of the Basque region, in demonstrations and political statements, has come out openly in growing numbers against the use of violence to press the issue of special status. The action-repression spiral has not provided the amount of committed support that would allow the insurgent movement to emerge from its consolidation phase, and the loss of French sanctuary after the entry of Spain into the European Union made the ETA leadership—of the generation of the 1960s—vulnerable to control and arrest. Sporadic terrorist acts have become increasingly counterproductive, and the Spanish government has indicated willingness to talk only on track-one issues, and that after an ETA renunciation of violence.[24] A mutually hurting stalemate has never set in, and the Basque question in the 1990s seems relegated to track-one negotiations on technical issues and grievances, within the existing framework of the Basque autonomous region.

Notes

1. This chapter draws on material from Robert P. Clark, *Negotiating with ETA: Obstacles to Peace in the Basque Country, 1975–1988* (University of Nevada Press, 1990). (Copyright 1990, University of Nevada Press, and used by permission.)

2. *Diario Vasco* (San Sebastían), 5 and 13 April, 1989.

3. Carmelo Landa, sole member of the Basque coalition Herri Batasuna in the European Parliament, quoted in *New York Times,* January 28, 1994.

4. For a history of the Basque rebellion, see Cyrus Ernesto Zirakzadeh, *A Rebellious People: Basques, Protests and Politics* (University of Nevada Press, 1991).

5. See Pedro Ibarra Guell, *La evoluctíon estratégica de ETA: de la "guerra revolucionaria" (1963) a la negociacíon (1987)* (Donostia, Spain: Kriselu, 1987), pp. 180–83.

6. The results of public opinion surveys published in *Deia* (Bilbao, October 17, 1987. Many other surveys reveal similar findings: see, for example, *Euskadi 1988* (San Sebastían: EGIN, 1988), p. 157, for the results of three polls taken in late 1987 and early 1988; and Alan Riding, "Basque Peace Hopes Rise as Separatists Wane," *New York Times,* January, 28, 1994, p. A3.

7. There may also be cultural factors that affect Basque-Spanish relations, or that impede the ability of one or the other culture to engage in the bargaining and compromise necessary to conduct negotiations to end internal conflict. I leave to anthropologists the discovery and explanation of these obstacles, if indeed they exist. See the provocative study by Joseba Zulaika, *Basque Violence: Metaphor and Sacrament* (University of Nevada Press, 1988); and David Laitin, "National Revivals," Working Paper 1993/49 (Madrid: Instituto Juan March de Estudios e Investigacíones, 1993).

8. Under provisions of the 1978 constitution, Spain is divided into a number of autonomous regions, of which the Basque country is one of the original (along with Catalonia and Galicia). See Juan Linz, "Spanish Democracy and the 'Estado de las Autonomías,' " in Robert A. Goldwin, A. Kaufman, and W. A. Schambra, eds., *Forging Unity Out of Diversity* (Washington: American Enterprise Institute, 1989), pp. 260–303.

9. This section is adapted from Robert Clark, "Obstacles to Negotiating a Ceasefire with Insurgents: The ETA Case," *TVI Research*, vol. 7, no. 1 (1986), pp. 11–12.

10. Clark, *Negotiating with ETA*, p. 4.

11. See Graham T. Allison, *Essence of Decision: Explaining the Cuban Missile Crisis* (Boston: Little, Brown, 1971).

12. See Janice Gross Stein, ed. *Getting to the Table: The Processes of International Prenegotiation* (Johns Hopkins University Press, 1989).

13. Xabier Arzalluz, interview by Robert P. Clark, Bilbao, July 26, 1988.

14. See Ibarra Guell, *Evolucíon estratégica de ETA*.

15. KAS is the acronym for the Koordinadora Abertzale Sozialista (Patriotic Socialist Coordinating Council), formed in the mid-1970s. See Robert P. Clark, *The Basque Insurgents: ETA, 1952–1980* (University of Wisconsin Press, 1984), p. 86.

16. Gorka Aguirre, interview by Robert P. Clark, Bilbao, July 26, 1988.

17. Patxo Unzueta, "El díalogo y la negociacíon con ETA," *El pais* (Madrid), August 31, 1987, p. 9.

18. *Tiempo* (Madrid), September 3, 1984; *Deia*, August 30, 1984.

19. Patxo Unzueta, *Sociedad vasca y politica nacionalista* (Madrid: Edicíones El Pais, 1987), p. 133.

20. *Tiempo* (Madrid), September 21, 1987. An interview by Robert P. Clark with Inaki Esnaola, San Sebastián, August 3, 1988, confirmed this position, although not the exact quote.

21. Joseba Azkarraga, interview by Robert P. Clark, *Vitoria*, July 14, 1988. See also, *Deia*, August 23, 1987.

22. *Diario Vasco*, February 7, 1988.

23. Ibarra Guell, *Evolucíon estratégica de ETA*, pp. 14–144.

24. For an interesting comparison of violent and nonviolent protests, see Laitin, "National Revivals."

CHAPTER FOUR

Negotiating a Hidden Agenda: Sudan's Conflict of Identities

Francis Mading Deng

THE CIVIL WAR that has raged intermittently in Sudan for nearly four decades has evolved into a conflict over national identity that is becoming increasingly polarized, seemingly irreconcilable, and therefore difficult to negotiate. As a result, although there is much talk about talking and some agreement on the issues to be discussed, there is a tendency to focus on process and to avoid discussing the substantive issues involved. If raised, substantive issues reveal cleavages that are exceptionally difficult to bridge. The implications for the resolution or management of the conflict are considerable, but largely obscure and ambiguous. Identity issues become divisive, but are shrewdly evaded or glossed over in political debate. Thus there are almost as many Sudanese who acknowledge that there is a national identity crisis as there are who deny there is such a problem.

The thrust of I. William Zartman's argument in chapter 1 about internal conflict in general is most pertinent to Sudan: "It is the government's job to be responsive to the grievances of its people; it is the insurgents' purpose to draw attention to their grievances and gain redress. Negotiation is the natural meeting point of these needs, an extension of the 'normal politics' that should characterize a well-functioning polity. Yet internal conflict works against its own best outcome." What distinguishes the Sudanese situation from the general challenge of governance implied by normal politics is that the crisis of national identity separates the people of the South from the government. In political terms, they are not "its people";

they do not see the government as theirs; they see the government as unresponsive to their needs; the task of the insurgents as they see it is to restructure the country's identity and its leadership or fall back on secession.

The Identity Factor

Despite the controversy on the issue, there now appears to be a consensus that a major factor in the Sudanese conflict has to do with identity. On virtually every agenda suggested for negotiations, open-ended dialogue, or talks on a constitution, the issue of national identity has figured prominently. Sometimes it is phrased as a problem of competing nationalities or as a conflict among such identity factors as race, culture, language, or religion. It is often posed as a question of whether the country is Arab, African, Afro-Arab, or Arab-African. From a religious perspective, the critical question is whether the country is to be considered Islamic and governed by Sharia law, or secular, with constitutional guarantees of religious freedom and equality.

The conventional emphasis on the racial and cultural differences between the North and the South reflects an exaggeration that has been recognized and modified, yet nevertheless also reflects the divergence of self-perceptions, if not the objective realities, in the identities of the two sets of peoples. It is the projection of these self-perceptions to the collective level that generates the crisis of national identity. The renowned Sudanese writer el-Tayeb Salih, a Nubian from the northern region, posed the crisis in terms of the layers of civilizations the country had experienced and the implications of those layers for contemporary Sudanese identity: "The Sudan," he observed, "was Pharaonic, heathen, Christian and then it became Muslim. . . . The main issue is . . . identity. Who are we? We may claim that we are something, but sociologically or historically we may be something else."[1] Similarly, Mansour Khalid, a scholar with a distinguished record of public service, has written that "Sudan's crisis is, first and foremost, a crisis of self-identification: What is Sudan? And taking into consideration all the inhabitants of the country, what makes them Sudanese? It is this question, more than any other, that has perturbed political relations among the Sudanese people and influenced their growth as a nation.[2] And Martin Daly, a historian, has observed, "The civil war that has been under way since 1983, no less than that which lasted from 1955 to

1972, has as one of its principal causes fundamentally opposing views of what it means or should mean to be a Sudanese. These form bases for historical visions that are incompatible. . . . [M]uch more is seen to be at stake than constitutional formulas and degrees of power-sharing. Resolution of the conflict may therefore involve a major change in the social and political structure of the Sudan, and may in turn influence national politics and nation-building elsewhere in the region.''[3]

In reaction to the northern Sudanese identification of the country with "Arabism," southern Sudanese put forward an equal and even greater claim to the identity of the nation, endorsing secularism as the best means of ensuring religious freedom and equality, placing Christianity and traditional beliefs on a par with Islam, and advocating a foreign policy based on those domestic adjustments. The controversy is not merely one of semantics regarding inconsequential labels of self-identification, for there is much substantive content to the competing notions of national identity. They have implications not only for domestic policies on education, public information, cultural development, and the role of religion in public life but also for strategic international relations, especially as they reflect linkages with the internal elements of identity and the interests and aspirations of the people involved.

Evolution of the North-South Dichotomy

Today's southern Sudan People's Liberation Movement (SPLM) and northern Revolution for National Salvation (which seized power on June 30, 1989) are the culminations of contrasting historical processes. Arabization and Islamization in the North were brought about through stratifying and discriminating processes that favored the Arabs, their religion, and their culture over the African race, religions, and cultures. These assimilationist forces were successfully resisted in the South, which remained indigenously African until the advent of Christianity and Western influence.

Although the roots of Arabization go back to early penetration by Arab traders who settled among the indigenous northern population, the process intensified after the advent of Islam in the seventh century. Arabs of the Muslim empire invaded the Sudan, established remote controls over the country, opened channels of communication with the Arab world, guaranteed freedom of movement for Arabs, and protected their trade and settlements, but otherwise left the Sudanese in peace and virtually independent.

Although the Arab settlers were traders and not rulers, their privileged position, their more cosmopolitan and universalizing religious culture, and their superior material wealth, combined with the liberal assimilationist Arab Islamic tradition, opened gates to universal brotherhood and made them an appealing class for intermarriage with leading Sudanese families. As Arabs did not come with their wives and as Islam did not permit the marriage of Muslim women to non-Muslims, intermarriage was one-sided. The children identified with the male line, and in the course of time the Arab element predominated. As Yusuf Fadl Hasan has pointed out, the pre-Islamic system was not so much overthrown as turned inside out.[4] Yet even today parts of the North, especially in the west and the east, have not been much affected by Arabization, and a number of ethnic groups (including some among the riverain tribes of central Sudan) have retained their indigenous languages and customs.

Arab migration to and settlement in the South was discouraged by natural barriers, climatic conditions, and the resistance of the warrior Nilotic tribes. The few Arab adventurers who engaged in slave raids there were not interested in Arabizing and Islamizing the southerners, as to do so would have taken the southerners from the *dar el-harb* (land of war) category and placed them in the *dar el-Islam* (land of Islam) category, thereby protecting them from slavery. Nineteenth-century Turko-Egyptian and Mahdist raids in the south aggravated southern apprehension about waves of invasion from the north. With the Anglo-Egyptian reconquest of Sudan in 1899 and the formation of condominium rule dominated by the British, with the Egyptians in a subordinate posture, law and order eventually prevailed, but the gulf between the South and the North was reinforced. That gulf was extended into the modern context through Britain's infamous separatist Southern Policy, which was reversed in favor of unqualified unity only nine years before independence.

After 1956, post-colonial governments aimed at unifying the country through a centralized system, supplemented by assimilationist policies. The South, on the other hand, wanted the dualism of the country maintained through a federal system, which was initially demanded through constitutional channels. When that was rejected and repressed, southern demand escalated in the 1960s to a separatist armed rebellion. But the South also began to challenge the northern view of national identity as Arab and Islamic, turning southern grievances into a commitment to fundamentally restructuring the national identity. That challenge was more recently picked up, expanded, and consolidated by the Sudan People's Liberation Movement and its army (SPLA), under the leadership of John Garang de Mabior. As the divisive symbols of Arabism and Africanism have become challenged by some, they have become exalted by others, upheld with pride, and reinforced. The result is that the gap dividing the people of Sudan has narrowed and widened at the same time.

The dualism in Sudan has evolved through three parallel phases in both North and South; these could be characterized as traditional, transitional, and modern, even though they overlap or coexist. In the North, the tribal structures of indigenous Sudanese or Arab societies have been transcended, though not obliterated, by sectarian Islam and the broader concept of Arabism, which though objectively cultural, is subjectively perceived as also racial. As a result of this "conservative" blend of tradition and sectarian Islam, several movements have appeared that represent a modernizing reaction, among them the Communist Party, the wider Democratic Front, the Republican Brotherhood, and the Muslim Brotherhood. The Muslim Brotherhood broadened its political net in the 1960s under the banner of the Islamic Charter Front, and more recently reorganized politically into the National Islamic Front. The National Islamic Front is now widely recognized as the brain trust behind the Revolution for National Salvation, the fundamentalist military regime that took control of Sudan on June 30, 1989. For that regime, a politicized Islam offers the symbol and the model of identity for nation-building.

In the South, tribal structures have been transcended by, though not obliterated by, the Christian, mostly missionary-educated, westernized secular elite that has assumed political leadership in the modern context. The Sudan People's Liberation Movement and its army represent the most modern phase in the evolution of the South's symbols and models of identity for nation-building.

In both North and South there are forces in the center with a range of conservative and liberal dispositions. They include professional associations, trade unions, farmers' associations, women's and youth organizations, and student unions. Although they have periodically played key roles in instigating popular uprisings against military dictatorships, they have never offered a sustainable political role at the center. An exception has been the short-lived influence of the National Alliance for National Salvation during the 1984–85 transitional period from military rule to parliamentary democracy.

Negotiating Identity

Throughout the history of North-South relations, negotiations have centered on how to manage the politics of the dualistic identity of the country.
The options within the unitary framework have ranged from a call for some
form of recognition of the dualism to various forms of integration and
assimilation. The North backed integration and assimilation, and has more
recently been willing to accommodate various forms of diversity and decentralization; the South has shifted from a call for secession, which was
not negotiable to the North, to the postulation of a "new Sudan" in which
the inequities of race, culture, language, religion, and gender would be
eliminated. This ideal would require a major restructuring of national
identity and its power base and is therefore not acceptable to the leaders and
the beneficiaries of the status quo.

In regard to internal conflicts generally, Donald Rothchild has observed that among factors not easily amenable to negotiation are "a fear
of restratification and the loss of political dominance; an assertion of
group worth and place; the existence of negative remembrances and
images; the determination to resist a controlling group's effort to spread
its language, culture or religion; and evidences of a sense of superiority
on the part of a politically or economically dominant minority. . . .
Where ruling state elites and their constituents fear the consequences of
a fundamental reordering of regime procedures or where political minorities remain deeply anxious over their subordination or their cultural or
physical survival, ethnic conflicts are likely to be intense and, in some
cases, highly destructive of lives and property. Adopting an 'essential-
ist' perception regarding their ethnic adversaries . . . allows little scope
for negotiated, mutual gains outcomes."[5]

Several negotiations in the history of Sudanese North-South relations
illustrate the range of outcomes that have been envisaged in negotiating
identity and the manner in which positions have evolved toward even more
difficult options. Among these events are the Juba Conference of 1947, the
Round Table Conference of 1965, and the Addis Ababa Talks of 1972.

The Juba Conference

The first major forum in which northerners and southerners sat together
to negotiate a common future was the Juba Conference of June 1947, during
the colonial period. The issue there was whether the South was prepared to

join the process of political development in the North by sending representatives to the national Legislative Assembly, about to be formed, or would
prefer first to have an advisory council of the kind that had preceded
establishment of an assembly in the North. The British, as the dominant
partner in the condominium rule, had already decided on Sudanese unity;
and at issue at the Juba Conference was agreement on transitional measures
that would accelerate political and economic development in the South so
that when independence came southerners would be able to hold their own
in equal partnership with the northerners.

Only a year before the shift toward unity the colonial government had
envisaged several options for the South. The approved policy then was "to
act upon the facts that the peoples of the southern Sudan are distinctively
African and Negroid" and that the duty of the government was to push
ahead as fast as it could with their economic and educational development
on African lines of progress, and not upon the Middle Eastern and Arab
lines of progress that are suitable for the northern Sudan.[6] Changing conditions, and in particular the pressures mounting in the North and in Egypt for
acceleration of the process leading to independence of the Sudan as a
geographical whole, necessitated the change of policy. The new policy was
to recognize "that geography and economics combine (so far as can be
foreseen at the present time) to render them [the African and Negroid
peoples of the South] inextricably bound for future development to the
Middle-Eastern and Arabized Northern Sudan; and therefore to ensure
that they shall, by educational and economic development, be equipped to
stand up for themselves in the future as socially and economically the
equals of their partners of the Northern Sudan in the Sudan of the future."[7]

The initial reaction among southerners to the question of joining the
national Legislative Assembly (and among some even to the already decided issue of unity) was to accept the principle, but allow time for learning
the art and skill of government and observing the attitude of the northerners
before making up their minds. However, on the second day of the Juba
Conference a number of southerners, mostly the civil servants, reversed
their position in favor of immediate participation in the Legislative Assembly. A prominent spokesman of the South, Clement Mboro (an administra-
tor who later became a leading figure in the southern movement), stated that
"since the conference of the day before he had fundamentally changed his
mind and now considered that the best way in which the Southerners could
protect themselves would be to go to Khartoum now to legislate together
with the Northerners. . . . In spite of their backwardness . . . southerners

must defend themselves and speak and think for themselves."[8] James Tembura "agreed emphatically with . . . Clement Mboro," and when asked by the conference chairman why he had changed his mind, Tembura replied "that Judge Shingeiti had said that if [southerners did not participate immediately] they would have no say in the future Government of the Sudan, and he had thought this over very carefully the previous night after considering what had been said during the day."[9] When Governor Richard Owen asked Clement Mboro what his safeguard would be if, in spite of southern objections, the Legislative Assembly passed a law against the interests of the southerners, Mboro replied that the government would protect the southerners.

Most of the tribal chiefs insisted that a change of position would be a violation of the mandate they had received from their people. According to chief Cir Rehan, "what they had said yesterday [on the first day of the conference] was not their own opinion only but that of their people. They had agreed to join the North in a government for the whole Sudan only if they were given time. Was he to go back and tell his people that the Northerners insisted on their coming in at once or not at all? He did not feel that it showed a brotherly feeling to try to force them."[10] It is clear that at the Juba Conference southerners did not match their northern counterparts and the British in education, experience, sophistication, or administrative status. The tribal chiefs, whose source of power and knowledge of public affairs was rooted in a cultural and political framework as representatives of their people, demonstrated an autonomous decisionmaking attitude that was firmer and more grounded than that of the more vulnerable southern civil servants. This made it easier for northerners to outmaneuver southerners. But, as Mansour Khalid has observed, "successful as their manipulations were, [the northerners] seemingly failed to perceive southern fears in their real perspective, possibly with the only exception of Ibrahim Bedri. The North may have won a battle at Juba but certainly not the war."[11]

Bedri observed at the Juba Conference that the self-perception by southerners that they were disadvantaged was a factor that northerners should consider: "When a man thinks he is backward it is difficult to persuade him that he is not. . . . The northern Sudanese must appreciate this difficulty."[12] Bedri later presented a foresighted note to the 1951 Constitutional Amendment Committee that was set up to examine the situation and to recommend steps to prepare for self-government; he wrote:

> When I say the South I do not mean the inhabitants of the three Southern Provinces alone, but also those of the Southern Fung, Blue Nile Province, as well as some of the inhabitants of Darfur and of the Nuba Mountains of Kordofan . . .

all of these people neither profess Islam nor speak Arabic . . . there are no traditional, religious, linguistic or cultural ties between them and the Northerners; the only tie is a territorial one which can be traced back to the Egyptian Conquest in 1820.

Such expressions as "Our brothers in the Southern part of the Valley" . . . which are being used to demonstrate our goodwill towards people who until recently were raided by our fathers, who enslaved them and sold them as animals, . . . are not sufficient to make the people of the South forget their past sufferings and change their attitude towards us and Egypt, simply because we have secured their freedom in the constitution. . . . What safeguards have we made for the continuance of stability, the securing of freedom and the right of self-determination for such people?[13]

Events moved rapidly after the changes in the southern policy and the convening of the Juba Conference. The Legislative Assembly opened in December 1948, and was followed several years later by formation of the Constitutional Amendment Committee. The only southern representative on the committee advocated federation, but was overruled. A proposed provision for a draft constitution would have empowered the governor-general to protect "the interests of the people of the southern Sudan." Another provision proposed the establishment of a ministry for southern affairs, with a council of advisers selected in consultation with the governor of the southern provinces. The protective clause was later watered down by the Legislative Assembly to a provision giving the governor-general responsibility for ensuring fair and equitable treatment of all the inhabitants of the various provinces of the Sudan; the proposal for a separate ministry was rejected by the assembly.

In 1953 northern parties agreed with Egypt and Britain, the condominium powers, on a transitional period of Sudanese self-government that would lead to self-determination in three years. The South was not represented at those negotiations. Britain and Egypt were not only partners, but competitors for alliance with Sudanese political parties; in the negotiations both were therefore interested in winning over the northern parties. During the accelerated march to independence, "the British Civil Secretary [Sir James Robertson] was preoccupied with how to win the northern Sudanese intelligentsia away from the Egyptian government in the contest between the two condominium powers. . . . Robertson believed that safeguards for the South were bound to drive northern Sudanese political leaders over to Egypt which was craftily championing the northern Sudanese case for unconditional unity of the two regions of the Sudan."[14] The self-government statute that resulted from the trilateral negotiations between the

North, Egypt, and Britain did not contain any safeguards for the South. When in December 1955 southern representatives in the Legislative Assembly postulated federation as a condition for supporting a motion for independence, northern politicians once again manipulated their vote with a promise that was, in retrospect, never intended to be kept.[15]

In September 1956 the Legislative Assembly appointed a committee to draft a national constitution. Only three of its forty-six members were southerners. When they reiterated the southern call for a federal constitution, they were outvoted. In despair, the southerners walked out of the committee and boycotted the rest of its work. A southern observer has written that "Southern calls for a federal system of government were subsequently outlawed. By the end of 1958 Southerners either went to jail or chose a life in exile for supporting federal principles. In only a decade since the Juba Conference, Mohamed Saleh Shingetti, who had become Speaker of the Constituent Assembly of 1958, had already forgotten the graphic warnings of Chief Lolik Lado" that "a hurried union might result in an unhappy home, likely to break up in a violent divorce." By 1958, "the hurried marriage was already in trouble."[16]

The Round Table Conference

The 1965 Round Table Conference on the Southern Problem convened by the Transitional Government of Sirr el-Khatim el-Khalifa, which had taken power from the military rule of General Ibrahim Abboud in 1964, was the second occasion when representatives of the two regions met to discuss their mutual concerns. In 1965 there was more symmetry in the representation of the two regions and in the level of sophistication than there had been at the Juba Conference. The southern problem and the military role of the Southern Sudanese Liberation Movement (SSLM), the forerunner of the SPLM, had been significant factors in the overthrow of the military government, and northerners were prepared to give the South its due. But what the South stood for proved to be unpalatable for the North.

The South presented a long list of grievances attributed to northern mistreatment and historic animosities, and proposed federalism, self-determination, or outright separation as remedies. Aggrey Jaden of the Sudan African National Union (SANU) articulated the extremist southern view when he said to the conference, after pointing out that Sudan fell sharply into a "hybrid Arab race" in the North and an "African" group in the South, "With this real division, there are in fact two Sudans and the most important thing is that there can never be a basis of unity between the two. There is nothing in common between the various sections of the community; no body of shared beliefs, no identity of interests, no local signs of unity and above all, the Sudan has failed to compose a single community. The Northern Sudanese claim for unity is based on historical accident and imposed political domination over the Southern Sudan.''[17]

Jaden's view was widely shared by many southerners at the time. During the Round Table Conference a southern newspaper wrote in an editorial: "There is little in common between the North and the South except our mother the Nile and the accident of common colonial masters. . . . It was the belief of the southerners that Sudan was a multi-racial and multi-national state and it should have developed as such. . . . Unfortunately, the experiment of co-existence between the Arabs and the Africans has failed."[18]

At the conference the North asserted its Arab-Islamic identity and agenda. Ismail el-Azhari, National Unionist Front prime minister and later the first "permanent" president of the Sovereignty Commission of Five (the collective head of state), said that ''We are proud of our Arab origin, of our Arabism and of being Moslems. The Arabs came to this continent, as pioneers, to disseminate a genuine culture, and promote sound principles which have shed enlightenment and civilization throughout Africa at a time when Europe was plunged into the abyss of darkness, ignorance and doctrinal and scholarly backwardness. It is our ancestors who held the torch high and led the caravan of liberation and advancement; and it is they who provided a superior melting-pot for Greek, Persian and Indian culture, giving them the chance to react with all that was noble in Arab culture, and handing them back to the rest of the world as a guide to those who wished to extend the frontiers of learning.[19]

The northern parties suggested a measure of "regional government," which the southerners dismissed as equivalent to an "unconditional unity." The southerners made their own suggestions for a relationship tantamount to a loose federation or confederation. Despite these disagreements, the conference adopted many resolutions for bettering the situation in the South, but, unable to reach a unanimous resolution, appointed a twelve-man committee to dwell on the issue of the constitutional and administrative setup that would protect the special interest of the South, as well as the general interest of the Sudan.[20] That committee eventually reached agreement on a number of issues, among them the transfer of some central powers to the regions, the preservation and development of southern languages, the establishment of regional legislative bodies and a national development committee with regional branches, the adoption of a parliamentary system of government, and the selection of a technical committee to recommend financial arrangements for the proposed system.[21] But in the course of debate and informal exchange of views it became clear that there were fundamental differences, reflecting the conflicting values between North and South, "on which a nation-state could stand or disintegrate."[22]

About two months after the 1965 conference, the pendulum had already swung back to the dark past of North-South relations. The idealism of the northern Sudanese intelligentsia, who then held the reins of power, soon brought back parliamentary democracy, and elections in 1965 brought back sectarian political parties. The premiership went to Mohamed Ahmed Mahgoub, who announced a new southern policy on June 26, 1965: the government would "face the southern Problem which was inherited from the imperialists by adopting a clear and firm policy which will affirm the unity of the country and the prosperity of the people without discrimination. We will not permit any foreign intervention and will liquidate terrorist organizations and unlawful blocks by making a full seizure of arms. Security forces will be fully empowered to deal with whoever attempts to endanger the security of the people or obstruct their progress."[23]

The instant reaction of the southern Sudanese was expressed in an editorial in *The Vigilant*, the only southern mouthpiece: "We deeply regret to tell the Prime Minister that the chances of permanent solution of the southern Problem by military force are extremely remote."[24]

The issue of an appropriate constitutional system for the country was considered by a national committee formed in 1968, at a time when, as Abel Alier explained,

> The fever for an Islamic constitution was high. The sectarian based parties, the Umma, NUP [National Unionist Party] and PDP [People's Democratic Party] had found a formidable challenger in the ICF [Islamic Charter Front] under whose influence the old parties in the North, except the Communist Party, were pushed to come up with proposals for some form of Islamic constitution. Even leaders like the late Ismail El Azhari and the late Mohamed Ahmed Mahgoub, who had long looked for a secular state, were impelled to support the demand. Southern representatives, of whom I was the spokesman in the constitutional draft committee, pressed strenuously but in vain for a secular constitution. . . . The argument in favor of an Islamic constitution was that the majority of the people of the North are Moslems. One of the dangers of this proposal is that it be countered by raising the issue of race. . . . The imposition of religious uniformity invites a response of race as a countervailing force.[25]

With such sharp disagreements in the twelve-man committee and in the national constitution committee, "southern representatives said enough was enough. In December 1968 we [southern representatives] packed our bags and left the committee. A boycott of a constitution draft committee had been reached for a second time in ten years."[26]

The Addis Ababa Talks

Hope for a more lasting reconciliation between the South and the North came on May 25, 1969, when young officers under the leadership of Major Gaafar el-Nimeiri seized power and announced socialism for the whole country. In a statement issued on June 9, 1969, they declared a policy of granting autonomy to the South. They started out in alliance with the Communist Party, and when there was opposition from the Ansar—the religious-political Mahdist sect—the government clamped down on the Mahdist opposition. A ministry for southern affairs was set up under a southern minister, Joseph Garang, an avowed communist who believed that "the cause of the southern problem is the inequality which exists between North and South by reason of an uneven economic, social and cultural development. All the ills in South-North situations spring from this situation."[27] For Garang the solution was development and the elimination of economic and social disparity.[28] The implementation of autonomy was impeded partly because of Garang's preference for practical developmental steps to a constitutional settlement and partly because of the ambivalence of the North about the proposed arrangement.

A period of tension and uncertainty between the communists and the government was ended by an abortive coup by the communists inside the regime on July 19, 1971. Nimeiri returned to power after three days of apparent communist success. Those found responsible, including Joseph Garang, were convicted and executed. Abel Alier, who had played a significant role in southern politics and in whom southerners within the country and without had great confidence, replaced Garang as minister for southern affairs. Southern apprehensions about and mistrust of the Communist Party showed in the South's stand behind Nimeiri; in a statement on the Nimeiri regime's southern policy, the communists had accused the regime of embracing separatist elements. Soon after, when Nimeiri was overwhelmingly elected president of the Democratic Republic of Sudan in a plebiscite, Alier became one of two vice presidents, while continuing as the minister for southern affairs.

Alier persuaded Nimeiri to hold talks with the southern rebels, a strategy Joseph Garang had opposed. Both sides saw a golden chance for a settlement and worked diligently to make the talks a success. Delicate negotiations followed, in which the World Council of Churches and the All-African Council of Churches played pivotal roles, eventually ending in the Addis Ababa Agreement of February 1972 and enactment into law of the Southern Provinces Regional Self-Government Act of 1972.[29] When the law came into force on March 3, 1972, President Nimeiri explained:

> The 9th of June Declaration, issued when the Revolution was only a month old, offered regional autonomy to the South within the Unified Sudan. . . . But the treachery of those entrusted with the implementation of the policy in the South, as well as their "comrades" in the North, has impeded the progress of the regional autonomy plan. Those people, well-known to you, have used their official positions to further their selfish partisan interests; obstructing in the process of revolutionary policies towards the South. The sabotage acquired such dimensions that our southern brothers started to doubt the sincerity of our intentions and thought we were just feeding them with promises. But the revolutionary tide that swept the country after the failure of the perfidious Communist coup and which accompanied the plebiscite campaign, has opened new avenues for the country. A settlement preserving the unity of the country and satisfying the aspirations of the South, has become possible.[30]

It is instructive to examine these negotiations and the roles of the persons and parties involved, as well as the consequences of the settlement.

Although the domestic circumstances were opportune in 1971 and the new regime expressed its desire to end the conflict shortly after it came to power, there were irreconcilable differences within the Nimeiri government on the issue of negotiating with the rebels. It was only when Nimeiri's needs dictated reaching out for the South that he disregarded those differences and proceeded with negotiations. He had alienated both the right and the left and was building on the support of the center, which his key advisers suggested could include the South as the strongest alternative political and military power base. Nimeiri was persuaded of this against the opinion of his military advisers and senior officers, some of whom resigned in protest from the Revolution Command Council, the top executive authority of the regime. Those officers argued that it would be disgraceful for the military to negotiate with the rebels. President Nimeiri, who was well known for his decisiveness, argued that as the leader of the revolution any disgrace or dishonor for the military would first and foremost fall on him, a risk he was prepared to take.[31]

The regional and international circumstances favored Nimeiri's position. By his heroic victory against the communists he had endeared himself to the West, with which Sudan had broken relations after the Six-Day War of 1967 in the Middle East. With a foreign minister bent on normalizing relations with the West, an international and mostly western community desiring to assist a peaceful Sudan, and the new policy of the government attracting significant numbers of returnees in the South, there was much to gain and little to lose in ending the conflict. Alier himself had gone to Europe to meet with international governmental and private organizations, including the church organizations, to solicit assistance. A UN conference only a week before the Addis Ababa Agreement was reached resulted in pledges for assistance, which created a favorable international climate for peace in the country.

But perhaps most critical to the negotiations was the role of Abel Alier, a southerner whose modesty, loyalty, and commitment to a peaceful resolution of the conflict had been tested. Unlike the ideologically committed marxist Joseph Garang, Alier appeared to be almost a pacifist, a man who had considerable respect and trust across the political spectrum. After the execution of Garang, Alier emerged as his obvious successor and alternative, in whom Nimeiri and the North placed their trust—a trust enhanced by a compensatory zest as a result of not having heeded Alier's counsel in the first place. But Alier was by no means a northern stooge or puppet. He had been a prominent member of the Southern Front, which advocated self-determination for the South, had resigned his position as a judge to participate in the Round Table Conference, and had been the southern spokesman on the committee for drafting a constitution in 1968. That he was chosen by Nimeiri to lead the mediation team reflects both the effectiveness of authoritarian leadership in the negotiation process and—in view of the eventual fate of the Addis Ababa Agreement—the weakness and unsustainability of such narrowly based settlements, as will be seen below.

Alier's leadership of the Sudanese government's mediation team almost made the Addis Ababa negotiations a South-South dialogue. Such an imbalance was avoided only by his sensitivity and evenhandedness. As Alier has written, "I had not recommended any Southerner for the delegation, aware that even one or two more might make the talks appear one-sided, merely talks between Southerners. Indeed my leadership of the delegation was later criticized on these grounds. It was said that the Sudan government delegation was a Northern delegation whose leadership should have been Northern Sudanese."[32] This is an important insight because it reflects the narrow base of the peace initiative and process. Alier himself has intimated that "the government had only gradually been reconciled to this initiative through a series of proposals and declarations."[33] Alier has testified that the Sudanese government's delegation worked as a team, with the northern Sudanese maintaining their freedom to meet and plan alone, particularly in regard to the serious issue of security: "[W]hat they did was quite legitimate and necessary. They represented the North and in that capacity were entitled to discuss the subject without me. It was acceptable to me that they took this secret initiative, although I was aware of their meeting since it took place in the room next door to mine. . . . The SSLM [Southern Sudanese Liberation Movement] considered me a government man and as such spokesman for the North. That too was acceptable; this is how I wished it to be."[34]

Alier's role comprised an unusual blend of representation, negotiating positions, and perspectives on issues. When these were combined with the moderating role of the respected Burgess Carr of the All-African Council of Churches (supposedly in his individual capacity); the observer's standpoint of Ambassador Mohamed Sahnoun of Algeria, who was deputy secretary-general of political affairs of the Organization of African Unity; the towering moral influence of host Emperor Haile Selassie of Ethiopia; and the presence of representatives from several African countries, there was a convergence of compelling circumstances and of layered mediators. This accounted both for the negotiations' remarkable success and for the paradoxically feeble foundations of the agreement, which later made it possible for Nimeiri to dismantle the agreement unilaterally.

As calculated, the Addis Ababa Agreement provided Nimeiri with a solid southern base of support. That base proved most valuable in 1976 in confronting an attempted invasion by opposition groups in exile supported by Libya. But the attempt itself indicated the vulnerability of the regime to extremist elements in the North. Nimeiri tried later to pacify these elements, not only through a policy of "national reconciliation," which incorporated the opposition groups into the government, but also by extending the system of regionalism to the North. By doing so he unwittingly began to undo the arrangement with the South, which eventually provoked the resumption of hostilities.

Nimeiri revealed the asymmetrical character of his agreement with the South and the potential for unilateral abrogation of the agreement when he told a technical committee that was considering the application of regionalism to the North that he could not understand the fear of separation resulting from a regional arrangement. Invoking the name of God to tell the truth, he said that when the leaders of the revolution accepted the Addis Ababa Agreement their secret plan was to have the southern rebels surrender their arms and then, within two or three years, to tear up the agreement and continue with the revolutionary agenda without a military threat from the South. To their surprise, Nimeiri continued, regionalism had worked so well that they wanted to apply it to the whole country. The fear that such an arrangement might lead to fragmentation and possible disintegration of the country was therefore unjustified.[35]

When the threat from sectarian political parties and the Muslim fundamentalists proved sufficiently serious, Nimeiri decided to reverse his southern policy in the belief that the northern opposition groups were more dangerous than the South, and that the southern potential to rebel had been effectively and decisively neutralized. However, his policies of Islamization, division of the South, and manipulation of oil reserves and water resources, as well as his attempt to move southern troops to the North to undercut the capability for a potential rebellion, all combined to trigger the resumption of hostilities.

Although Nimeiri's pragmatic, short-term calculations are obvious, Alier's standpoint is more problematic. He clearly desired peace with justice for the South and honor for the North and had worked quietly and with perseverance for those objectives. He was not exactly a third party, for he was involved emotionally and politically as a leading member of the Southern Front that called for self-determination, and was viewed by most northerners as a separatist. A moderate in personality and disposition, he could not be accused of being a stooge, nor could he be classified as a member of the "willing fringe closest to the government" or of "unrepresentative counterparts who [can] neither speak for large groups of followers nor carry out an agreement if it were reached" (see chapter 1). Alier belonged somewhere in the uncharted middle; he was perhaps too honest for the calculating Nimeiri and too moderate for the extremist, suspicious South, both of whom constrained his effectiveness in the long run. The question arises: How valuable or useful are people like Alier who can bring other people together by being sensitive to many different points of view, but can be undercut in the long run by less scrupulous manipulators who have a far less flexible agenda?

Perhaps the most significant question to arise from the Sudanese experience centers on the dilemma of whether to deal with dictators who are decisive and practical in acting to end a conflict but who are unlikely to secure the broad-based support needed to sustain a settlement, or to embark on a democratic process that is more unlikely to bring about a workable consensus but can sustain any solution reached through consensus. This dilemma remains a major puzzle in the cause of peace in Sudan.

Dynamics and Prospects

Several of the dynamics discussed by Zartman in chapter 1 figure in the evolution of the Sudanese conflict, among them the shifts from grievances to commitment and from debate to mediation in the peace process, as well as the impact of these shifts on the positions of the parties and the prospects for peace.

From Grievances to Commitment

Perhaps the most important shift that the Sudan People's Liberation Movement and the Sudan People's Liberation Army have generated is in the South's self-perception: instead of perceiving themselves as a disadvantaged racial or ethnic minority aspiring for federalism, content with autonomy or threatening separatism, southerners have a more confident self-image that enables them to postulate restructuring national power to create a "new Sudan" in which race, culture, religion, and gender would not determine status or participation in political and economic life, and in which southerners could become part of an African or non-Arab majority that would play a more pivotal role in shaping the identity of the nation.

In Zartman's terms this means that the conflict has evolved from grievances that could be (and were temporarily) met through an autonomous arrangement to a more ambitious commitment to the goal of redefining and restructuring the state. When this commitment was combined with the formidable force commanded by the SPLM and SPLA, which with the support of Mengistu's Ethiopia in the 1980s (see chapter 5) virtually liberated all of the South except the major towns, the asymmetry of the internal conflict in one sense was replaced by a form of conceptual, psychological, political, and even military balance of power. This shift was further accentuated by the emergence of the SPLM as the North's most effective ally in forcing undesired governments out of office, however the North may have perceived the movement. The SPLM was pivotal in overthrowing Nimeiri in 1985, and was actively courted a decade later by the opposition groups, including the traditional political parties, in their campaign to overthrow General Hassan el-Bashir. Although that alliance of basically incompatible partners has not been durable beyond the short-term objective of changing the government in Khartoum, it has added to the legitimacy of the Sudan People's Liberation Movement and its army at the national level.

Although such symmetry should make negotiating on an equitable basis easier and a settlement more feasible, the substantive factors involved have shifted from distributive issues that are negotiable to nonnegotiable demands for restructuring power. According to Rothchild, "distributive issues between different ethnic interests that share a sense of common destiny normally are policy questions with tangible referents, goods, jobs, taxes, roads, schools—and frequently amenable to political solutions."[36] By demanding the redefinition of the nation, the SPLM has gone beyond asking for fairness in the distribution of goods to contest the soul or the heart of the nation; that contest has zero-sum implications.

With the intensification of the conflict after 1989 by the Islamic alliance of General el-Bashir and the National Islamic Front, which has pursued jihad with a vengeance, and the loss of support for the southern rebel movement that had been provided by Ethiopia under Mengistu Haile Mariam, the military situation in the field has been significantly reversed over the last several years. This turn of events, combined with internal differences within the leadership of the SPLM-SPLA—instigated or at least exploited by the government—has led to a reconsideration of the policy position of the movement. By the mid-1990s the factionalized SPLM-SPLA had offered the government options that ranged from the old objective of restructuring the country into a new Sudan to a confederal arrangement and to outright partition.

From Debate to Mediation

Efforts made in the peace process since Nimeiri's overthrow can be classified into three main strands: direct negotiations between the parties (whether on their own initiative or through mediators), third-party mediation, and scholarly and intellectual dialogue involving both neutral resource persons and participants who represent or reflect the positions of the parties.

The outcomes of and meetings for direct negotiation have so far included, in chronological order, the Koka Dam Declaration of March 24, 1986; the Sadiq-Garang talks of July 31, 1986; the Harare (Zimbabwe) meeting of March 20–22, 1988, which was under the auspices of the Global

Inter-Action Council of Former Heads of State and Government; the Mirghani-Garang Agreement of November 16, 1988; two meetings between the SPLM-SPLA and el-Bashir's Revolution for National Salvation, the first in Addis Ababa on August 19–20, 1989, and the second in Nairobi (Kenya) on December 1–5, 1989, under the auspices of former U.S. president Jimmy Carter; and several meetings mediated by Nigeria and then, through 1994 and awaiting revival, by the Inter-Governmental Authority on Drought and Desertification (IGADD). As implied, only the Koka Dam Declaration and the Mirghani-Garang Agreement represented successful negotiations. Even those successes were only partial. For one thing, the agreements were merely procedural, aimed at facilitating progress toward a constitutional conference, and did not provide a comprehensive settlement of substantive issues. For another, the agreements were not comprehensive as to representation; on the contrary, they excluded some pivotal factions. As happened with the Addis Ababa Agreement, which eventually suffered from reliance on Nimeiri alone, such partial agreements are likely to meet with opposition from excluded factions—especially the seasoned political parties in the North that are now banned by the Islamic dictatorship of General el-Bashir. If a settlement is envisaged that calls for the unity of the country, the inclusion or exclusion of all major political forces could be critical to the prospects of long-term success.

Third-party mediators have been Sudanese politicians, African leaders, international personalities, and church representatives, each with their own advantages and disadvantages. In regard to advantages, Sudanese and (to a lesser degree) African mediators are likely to have insight into the complexities and sensitivities of the Sudanese situation, the issues involved, and the positions of the parties. They are also likely to be less inhibited in raising issues, probing, and combining those mediators' functions defined by Zartman as manipulation, communication, and formulation. However, because they are closer to the Sudanese parties than other mediators, they are also likely to be suspected of partiality. But perhaps their biggest disadvantage is that for the most part they have lacked leverage—in Zartman's terms, "the most important key to obtaining welcome," which can take the form of side payments that turn a zero-sum game positive, or the delivery of one side's possible agreement to an outcome that the other side can find attractive, or a threat to end mediation through withdrawal or by taking sides. In this respect, the position of IGADD mediators has been exceptional as it has carried with it significant potential for at least two of the three elements of leverage. Of all efforts to mediate the Sudanese conflict, only the IGADD mediation now appears promising, although success is uncertain.

International mediators have just the reverse advantages and disadvantages. Generally, the distance of such mediators from the parties involved facilitates impartiality and neutrality. They are also likely to command resources that they can use as a carrot or a stick—as leverage. But for the same reasons of distance and leverage, they are likely to be less informed about the complexities of the conflict and the parties' positions, are susceptible to suspicion of external interference, and could be viewed as serving strategic foreign interests.

Scholarly and intellectual forums have provided excellent opportunities for in-depth, uninhibited discussions with a minimum fear of any accusations from the parties. With respect to Sudan, such forums have included a workshop convened by the Woodrow Wilson International Center for Scholars in 1987 and a follow-up symposium organized by the Center for International Development, in Bergen, Norway, in 1988. Both forums focused on the prospects for peace in Sudan.[37] Such forums come closest to exploring the true nature of the conflict in great depth. But their contribution remains largely of paper value, for the benefit of scholars and intellectuals.

By implication some complementary combination of the three mediation channels discussed here might prove effective in promoting conflict resolution in Sudan.

Positions of the Parties

In the Sudanese conflict a crucial point of focus has continued to be the perspectives of the parties and the issues on which they differ. From the point of view of the Sudan People's Liberation Movement and the Sudan People's Liberation Army, as well as of the South in general, the history of South-North relations has demonstrated that the wielders of power at the center and northerners in general are not going to heed the message of southern grievances unless and until that message is clearly conveyed on the battlefield. But southerners, to avoid sounding arrogant with military power and to win sympathy and political support, recognize that they must play up their commitment to a negotiated settlement as a matter of principle.

From the standpoint of the successive governments in Khartoum, any significant success by the SPLM-SPLA in achieving its declared objectives—whether through military or political means—would threaten the status quo that underlies the dominance of the Arab Muslim North. Except by rare statesmanship, it is difficult for any government leader to make major concessions voluntarily. On the other hand, compromising from a strong military and political vantage point would mean less radical change in the status quo—change that the system could absorb without danger of self-destruction. But as has been the case with the SPLM-SPLA, governments have generally tended to raise their peace banners in order to moderate their predispositions toward the military advantage they need to combine compromise with survival.

Comparable factors have been at work with respect to the issue of unity and separation. With the prolongation and intensification of the conflict, the forces of unity and separatism have both been paradoxically strengthened. There is little doubt that separatism has deep-rooted sympathy, if not open support, in southern circles. On the other hand, the leaders of the SPLM-SPLA have consistently stood for the unity of the country, although their commitment now appears to be increasingly tactical. Participants in the movement realize that the overwhelming majority of southerners would prefer separation if it were achievable. But in the view of movement leaders, fighting for equality and the elimination of all forms of discrimination is more likely to ensure the liberation of the South than openly fighting for secession, which—until Eritrea achieved independence from Ethiopia—was most likely to be opposed not only nationally but also regionally and internationally. The regional and international atmosphere of the 1990s is less hostile to making a justified exception to the preservation of state borders, a factor that has undoubtedly influenced the southern call for self-determination.

The North, too, has become less certain about the value of unity under the existing conditions of chronic military confrontation and their political, economic, and moral impact on the nation as a whole. There is reason to believe that the desire of some northern Sudanese to disengage even to the point of discarding the South is genuine. However, this option is often expressed in terms of letting the South go as an act of despair, as though the decision rests solely with the North; the underlying assumption is that southerners would want to secede if they could and would be delighted to be "released." Such an assumption means that the declared policy of the SPLM-SPLA in favor of unity has never been believed or taken seriously by most northerners. How seriously that policy was ever intended to be remains a debatable issue even among the southerners.

Stalemate and Prospects for Peace

It is now widely recognized that the Sudanese conflict is stalemated, in the sense that despite the military advantage of the government neither party can exact a decisive victory and impose its vision for the nation on the other. More than a million people are estimated to have been killed or to have died as a result of war-related conditions since the outbreak of hostilities in 1955. It is estimated that in 1988 alone as many as 260,000 people (some allege as many as 500,000 people) died in the South as a result of the use of food as a weapon; close to a half-million southerners were reported to have fled to neighboring countries; and an estimated two million people moved to the North, where they lived under appalling social conditions and even physical insecurity.[38] Yet the stalemate is still not mutually hurting because national leaders do not identify with the civilian victims of the war. With escalating environmental degradation contributing to recurrent drought and famine throughout the country, it can be seen that the magnitude of the human tragedy is increasing just as national capacity is diminishing. Economically, not only is the conflict costing the country $1 million a day (without adding in the cost to the SPLM-SPLA), but it has brought to a halt major development projects, among them the exploitation of discovered oil reserves and the completion of the Jonglei Canal that was to drain the Sudd region to provide water for irrigation and retrieve the swampy lands for agriculture. On top of all that, Sudan is burdened with a foreign debt of 12 billion U.S. dollars. Yet apparently the level of the hurt has not induced the parties to seek a settlement in earnest.

This raises the question of when a conflict becomes mutually hurting: Is it when a nation bleeds to a dangerous point, or when the leaders themselves feel a threat to their political survival? Nimeiri's Sudan was not bleeding to death when he negotiated the Addis Ababa Agreement, but he was feeling himself and his regime severely threatened by the opposition forces. The Sudan of the post-Nimeiri regime is a nation at the brink of total collapse, but the leaders themselves have apparently not felt the personal threat of imminent demise. The SPLM-SPLA on the other hand, finding dignity in the commitment to self-liberation through a protracted armed struggle, are not about to make another compromise that would retain the conventional equations of the power structure in the country, as happened under the Addis Ababa Agreement.

If the objective of conflict resolution is to return the conflict to normal politics, as Zartman has posited, it is fair to say that such a state of normalcy has hardly ever existed in the history of North-South relations in Sudan, except under the separatist policies of the British. The pessimistic assessment that the dismal record of North-South relations suggests is implicit in the subtitle of Abel Alier's recent book, *Southern Sudan: Too Many Agreements Dishonored*. A significant part of the book is Alier's statement of options:

> Federal systems were evolved to cater [to] the needs of heterogeneous groups with various religious beliefs, nationalities and historical backgrounds. Options which would be available within the unity frame of reference range from administrative decentralization[,] which was tried in the northern Sudan in 1980, regional autonomy[,] which was tried in the southern Sudan from 1972 to 1983[,] and federation[,] which was partially tried in the form of regional autonomy, to confederation[,] which has not been tried.
>
> The second option is one which splits the nation-state into two or more sovereign entities. . . . That could only be obtained either in the battlefield or by a violent and reactionary revolution in the northern Sudan determined to adopt a theocratic system of government and an all-out Arab nationalism making no provision for African nationality.[39]

The ambivalences of perpetrating the war while yearning for peace, or upholding the principle of national unity while contemplating separation, emanate from hidden agendas related to the cleavages that divide Sudan, the parties' perceptions of the cleavages, and the seeming conviction that the cleavages are unbridgeable and therefore undiscussable—or, if discussed, unresolvable. The issues involved are essentially those of competing identities and the alternative visions they offer the nation. Are the issues of Sudanese identity unresolvable within the framework of unity, or are there alternative bases for reconceptualizing the country's self-perception to be more collectively and equitably accommodating? That is the question that the Sudanese and all those concerned with the welfare and future of the country must confront and address realistically, courageously, and creatively. Negotiating hidden agendas will never end the chronic conflict between the North and the South. Candor and honesty must now be the values that guide genuine negotiations and third-party mediation.

Notes

1. Quoted in Constance E. G. Berkley, *The Roots of Consciousness Molding the Art of El Tayeb Salih: A Contemporary Sudanese Writer* (Ann Arbor, Mich: University Microfilm International, 1985), pp. xxviii.

2. Mansour Khalid, *The Government They Deserve: The Role of the Elite in Sudan's Political Evolution* (London and New York: Kegan Paul International, 1990), p. 4.

3. Martin W. Daly, "Islam, Secularism, and Ethnic Identity in the Sudan," in Gustavo Benavides and Martin W. Daly, eds., *Religion and Political Power* (State University of New York, 1989), p. 83.

4. Yusuf Fadl Hasan, *The Arabs and the Sudan: From the Seventh to the Early Sixteenth Century* (Edinburgh University Press, 1967), p. 90.

5. Donald Rothchild, "An Interactive Model for State-Ethnic Relations," in Francis Mading Deng and I. William Zartman, eds., *Conflict Resolution in Africa* (Brookings, 1991), p. 194.

6. "1946 Memorandum on Southern Policy" concerning Khartoum Secret Dispatch, no. 89, August 4, 1945, in Mohamed Omer Beshir, *The Southern Sudan: Background to Conflict* (London: C. Hurst and Co., 1968), appendix 2, p. 120.

7. "Proceedings of the Juba Conference on the Political Development of the Southern Sudan, June 1947," Beshir, *Southern Sudan*, appendix 9, p. 137.

8. "Proceedings of the Juba Conference," in Beshir, *Southern Sudan*, appendix 9, pp. 146–47.

9. "Proceedings of the Juba Conference," in Beshir, *Southern Sudan*, p. 147.

10. "Proceedings of the Juba Conference," in Beshir, *Southern Sudan*, p. 147.

11. Khalid, *The Government They Deserve*, pp. 94–95. Bedri was a particularly liberal northerner who had served as an adminstrator in the South.

12. "Proceedings of the Juba Conference," in Beshir, *Southern Sudan*, p. 143.

13. Quoted in Khalid, *The Government They Deserve*, pp. 451–52.

14. Abel Alier, *Southern Sudan: Too Many Agreements Dishonored* (Exeter: Ithaca Press, 1990), pp. 21–22.

15. Mohamed Ahmed Mahgoub, *Democracy on Trial: Reflections on Arab and African Politics* (London: Andre Deutsch, 1974), p. 57.

16. Alier, *Southern Sudan*, pp. 20, 23.

17. Quoted in Francis Mading Deng, *Dynamics of Identification: A Basis for National Integration in the Sudan* (Khartoum University Press, 1973), p. 41.

18. Deng, *Dynamics of Identification*, p. 41.

19. Quoted in Deng, *Dynamics of Identification*, p. 74.

20. On the conference and the southern problem, see Mohamed Omer Beshir, *The Southern Sudan: From Conflict to Peace* (London: C. Hurst and Co., 1975), p. 13. Beshir was secretary to the conference.

21. Some issues were left unresolved, among them whether the national parliament would be empowered to override regional legislatures or not, the effect of a state of emergency on the regional powers and institutions, the nature of financial relations between the regions and the center, and the degree to which regional governments would assume charge of security.

22. Alier, *Southern Sudan*, p. 36.

23. *The Vigilant*, June 27, 1965.

24. *The Vigilant*, June 27, 1965.

25. Alier, *Southern Sudan*, pp. 38–39.

26. Alier, *Southern Sudan*, pp. 38–39.

27. Quoted in Deng, *Dynamics of Identification*, p. 76.

28. Joseph Garang's commitment to development as the real solution is obvious in this passage from an address he made at the British House of Commons on April 16, 1970, to a group of parliamentarians, pressmen, trade-union leaders, and writers: "As for the problem of our rebels in the forest or in Uganda, and who are threatening to start trouble, and who have been making contacts with certain foreign organizations and governments, all that we say unto them is this: We will construct, you destroy; We will build schools, you burn them down; We will build hospitals, you destroy them; We will build roads, you burn and break bridges. It shall be the people of the South to decide for themselves: who is building and who is destroying. In the end, it is they who will determine who shall be the political leaders: those who are destroying or those who are building." Quoted in Deng, *Dynamics of Identification*, n. 22, p. 83.

Garang later became critical of the government because his line of approach was not followed with the speed he had desired. In a press conference in Khartoum in April 1970, he stated, "It is true that we declared a sound policy for the South. But what matters is the implementation of that policy. What is important is what every ministry did to execute its part of the plans and projects. Action is not going on with the required speed. . . . The real danger to the revolution will come from the South." Quoted in Deng, *Dynamics of Identification*, n. 22, p. 84.

29. For the details of the peace process leading to the Addis Ababa accord, see Hizkias Assefa, *Mediation of Civil Wars: Approaches and Strategies—the Sudan Conflict* (Boulder, Colo.: Westview Press, 1987); see also Alier, *Southern Sudan*, chapters 4–8.

30. Quoted in Deng, *Dynamics of Identification*, p. 77.

31. The most authentic source on this is Nimeiri himself in a conversation with the author, held in Khartoum in the 1970s when the author was minister of state for foreign affairs.

32. Alier, *Southern Sudan*, p. 95.

33. Alier, *Southern Sudan*, p. 95.

34. Alier, *Southern Sudan*, pp. 106–07.

35. Witnessed by the author, who participated in the meeting.

36. Rothchild, "An Interactive Model for State-Ethnic Relations," p. 196.

37. See Francis M. Deng and Prosser Gifford, eds., *The Search for Peace and Unity in the Sudan* (Washington: Wilson Center Press, 1987); Abdel Ghaffar, M. Ahmed, and Gunmar M. Sorbo, eds., *Management of the Crisis in the Sudan: Proceedings of the Bergen Forum, 23–24 February, 1989* (Bergen, Norway: Centre for Development Studies, University of Bergen, 1989).

38. Francis M. Deng and Larry Minear, *The Challenges of Famine Relief: Emergency Operations in the Sudan* (Brookings, 1992).

39. Alier, *Southern Sudan*, p. 277.

CHAPTER FIVE

Eritrea and Ethiopia: Negotiations in a Transitional Conflict

Marina Ottaway

FOR ALMOST thirty years various liberation movements in Eritrea, most important among them the Eritrean People's Liberation Front (EPLF), fought against the Ethiopian government in an attempt to gain independence for the former Italian colony. Eritrea had been reintegrated into Ethiopia in 1952. Neither the imperial regime of Haile Selassie nor the ruthless Marxist-Leninist government of Colonel Mengistu Haile Mariam succeeded in quelling the uprising, but victory also eluded the insurgents for a very long time. The stalemate was finally broken in May 1991; the decisive factor was the sudden upsurge of the Tigrean People's Liberation Front (TPLF) and of the broader multiethnic coalition it controlled, the Ethiopian People's Revolutionary Democratic Front (EPRDF). With the insurgents closing in on Addis Ababa, Mengistu—whose demoralized army had stopped fighting—fled the country on May 21. A few days later a new, powerless caretaker Ethiopian government met in London with representatives of the EPLF, the EPRDF, and the Oromo Liberation Front (OLF). With United States Assistant Secretary of State Herman Cohen acting as mediator, the caretaker government reluctantly agreed to give up the fight, allowing EPRDF troops to enter Addis Ababa unopposed. Power was transferred to the EPRDF.

The defeat of the Mengistu regime signaled the beginning of Eritrean independence. After two years of de facto self-government, with no interference from the Ethiopian government in Addis Ababa, the Eritrean People's Liberation Front organized a referendum in April 1993. The following month Eritrea became formally independent, obtaining immediate recognition from the international community.

The long struggle for Eritrean independence had thus come to an end not through negotiations, but through a clear military victory. There were numerous attempts at negotiations, but they all failed. A major reason for the failure was the changing nature of the conflict. What had started in the 1960s as a bilateral confrontation between the Ethiopian government and the Eritrean nationalists turned by the late 1980s into a much broader struggle in which the Tigrean People's Liberation Front figured prominently. This transformation frustrated the success of the most serious negotiations to take place in almost three decades of war. With the bilateral conflict hopelessly stalemated, in 1989 the Ethiopian government and the EPLF accepted an invitation by former U.S. president Jimmy Carter to mediate the conflict. Official talks were held in September in Atlanta and in November in Nairobi, but they made slow progress on form and none on substance, and were finally called off by the Eritrean People's Liberation Front in the spring of 1990.

The failure of the talks in 1989 was also a result of a shift in the character of the conflict. The negotiations had started at an unpromising time, prompted not by favorable conditions but by the humanitarian concerns of the mediator. From a political point of view the intervention came either too late or too early. By the time the talks had started it was too late to tackle the Eritrean conflict as a bilateral one; but the new, multilateral conflict was still too undefined, the relations among the parties were too unclear, and the hopes of the TPLF for a military victory were too high for an attempt at mediation to succeed. The conflict was in a transitional stage, and as a result the negotiations failed.

This chapter discusses the special problems of negotiations in a transitional conflict. It focuses mainly on the now-concluded Ethiopian-Eritrean conflict, but also shows how the same problems became manifest again in early 1994 as the new Ethiopian government and new nationalist opposition groups sought negotiations to prevent a renewed cycle of violence. The transitional nature of the new conflicts was to become a central issue.

The Eritrean Problem

The problem of Eritrea was created by Italian colonialism. The territory became an Italian colony in 1890. Italian hopes of further expansion were dashed in 1896 by an Ethiopian victory at Adowa. That defeat gave Eritrea its present borders. Beyond these basic points, interpretations of the Eritrean problem by Eritreans and Ethiopians have always diverged sharply.

To the Addis Ababa government, the area colonized by Italy was an integral part of the Ethiopian empire. To the Eritrean nationalists, it had been a territory with a history separate from Ethiopia's since the decline of the Axumite kingdom after the sixth century A.D. Both positions were absurd. The Ethiopian empire never had fixed boundaries, and many parts of Eritrea had only loose and intermittent connections with the center. It is not a foregone conclusion that, but for Italian intervention, the entire territory known as Eritrea would have ended up within the boundaries of Ethiopia. But the Eritrean contention that ties between Ethiopia and Eritrea were severed many centuries ago is quickly belied by the language, religion, and other cultural traits shared by the highland populations north and south of the Ethio-Eritrean boundary line.

The Ethiopian position on Eritrea remained unchanged from the collapse of the Italian empire in 1941 to 1991: Eritrea was part of Ethiopia. The Eritrean position, if anything, hardened. The Eritrean People's Liberation Front originally claimed that Eritrea had the right to self-determination because it had been a colony, but later argued that in any case Eritrea had nothing in common with Ethiopia.[1] On a continent where efforts to reconstruct the past—and occasionally to invent one of dubious authenticity—abound, Eritrea represented the paradoxical case of a territory denying parts of its recorded history and culture because they did not fit present political requirements.

Both the Ethiopian government and the Eritrean nationalists found it convenient to consider the problem of Eritrea unique. Indeed, when the conflict started in 1961, in the context of a seemingly stable empire, this was not an unrealistic point of view. But the overthrow of Emperor Haile Selassie in 1974 set in motion a process of change, which centered in the 1970s on the transformation of the socioeconomic system, and in the 1980s on relations among the component parts of the old empire. The "problem of the nationalities" flared up, but so did old rivalries and ambitions, above all the historic competition for control over the empire between Amharas and Tigreans. In this second period the Eritrean problem appeared not unique, but part of the overall process of remolding Ethiopia from empire into state.

The Old Conflict

After 1941 the conflicting claims of the emperor and the Eritrean nationalists delayed a decision on the future of the colony until 1952. The United Nations, responsible for the former Italian colonies, finally compromised by giving Eritrea to Ethiopia, but in the context of a federal structure under which Eritrea had its own elected parliament and executive. This arrangement did not fit at all with Emperor Haile Selassie's views, and in 1962 he succeeded in causing the Eritrean parliament to vote for the complete reincorporation of Eritrea into Ethiopia. The vote probably did not reflect the real sentiment of the parliament—it was called in the absence of many representatives certain to oppose reintegration—but a strong unionist current nonetheless existed in Eritrea at the time.

An armed conflict between Eritrean nationalists and the government had started a year before the dissolution of the federation. It escalated slowly through the 1960s, then much more rapidly after Haile Selassie's overthrow. Between 1978 and 1990 the conflict was effectively stalemated, though neither side gave up the hope of breaking the impasse. Two major factors sustained the conflict for such a duration, preventing serious negotiations: first, the Eritrean nationalists, like all liberation movements, could only survive by fighting, and second, rapid political change in the rest of Ethiopia after 1974 gave hope to each party in turn that the stalemate could be broken and victory achieved.

Initially the imperial government believed it could defeat the new nationalist movement easily. This conviction was strengthened by a schism in the Eritrean ranks, with the new Eritrean People's Liberation Front splitting off from the original Eritrean Liberation Front (ELF).[2] The Eritrean Liberation Front was seen as rural-, lowland-, and Muslim-oriented. The Eritrean People's Liberation Front had its roots originally among urban, better educated, and Christian highland Eritreans—the population that had given some support to the emperor in the past. Nevertheless, in the short run the split within the nationalist ranks was good for the central government, for the two movements were soon fighting as much against each other as against the imperial army.

In the early years the nationalists did not score major victories, but they could find encouragement in their growing ranks. After 1974 they began to see the possibility of a quick military victory. The crumbling of the imperial regime and the apparent disarray of the Derg, the military committee that replaced Haile Selassie, led the Eritrean movements to the conclusion that it was time to strike. An attack on Asmara in January 1975 marked the beginning of a crescendo of military activity, which culminated in a near victory in 1977, at a time when the Ethiopian army was also fighting against the Somalis in the Ogaden. The government was forced to abandon most garrisons (in the end it only controlled four towns) and the nationalists began again to close in on Asmara.[3] Victory appeared near, but in the end the insurgents failed. A major reason was the incapacity of the EPLF and the ELF to set aside their differences and make a final joint effort.

After 1978 it was the turn of the Ethiopian government to believe again in the possibility of a military victory. Large supplies of Soviet arms allowed the government to increase the size and strength of the military.[4] Somalia had been defeated in 1978 after the initial success, and 15,000 Cuban troops were helping to protect that border.[5] The government was also slowly making progress in reorganizing the country internally, creating a political party and thus establishing more effective control in most areas.

In 1982 the government was confident enough of its new position to launch the so-called Red Star campaign in Eritrea. Initially conceived as a "multifaceted approach to the Eritrean problem, including recognition of the guerrilla movements, a search for a non-military solution, and attention to the economic and social problems of the region," the campaign eventually degenerated into a purely military exercise that failed to break the stalemate.[6]

Despite the 1982 failure the government still believed that it could settle the Eritrean problem on its own terms through a new territorial arrangement created by the constitution of 1987.[7] Largely inspired by the Soviet model, the constitution envisaged the division of Ethiopia into regions and subregions, some of them autonomous. Eritrea was divided into two autonomous regions, Eritrea and Asab. The new Eritrea in turn was divided into three subregions. The government's ploy was simple enough. It hoped to separate from Eritrea most of the coast and especially the port of Asab, which serves Addis Ababa. The new Asab region corresponded roughly to the territory occupied by the Afars; the government hoped the Afars would welcome the creation of their own autonomous region and strive to keep the Eritrean People's Liberation Front from operating there. The division of the rest of Eritrea into three subregions was based on the hope of playing the Eritrean Liberation Front, which was stronger in the lowlands, against the more dangerous EPLF, which dominated the highlands. The Ethiopian government had repeated contacts with the ELF during this period.

The government's hope that the constitution would provide a solution to the Eritrean problem proved illusory. The Eritrean People's Liberation Front, on the other hand, again started hoping that a military victory was possible. Inside Eritrea, the movement was well organized and strong, encountering little competition. The ELF still existed, and endless factional struggles were creating new splinter groups, but none had a significant guerrilla force. An increasingly strong Tigrean People's Liberation Front had the Ethiopian army tied down in combat even before it reached Eritrea. There were also clear signs of disarray inside the Ethiopian army. The strength of the Addis Ababa regime ultimately resided in Mengistu's ability to keep the allegiance of the military; this was still true after the launching of a political party in 1984.[8]

The Rise of the TPLF

The transformation of the Tigrean People's Liberation Front during the 1980s from one of many liberation movements of marginal importance opposing the Addis Ababa regime into a major player in the politics of Ethiopia made it much more difficult to separate the Eritrean problem from that of the overall transformation of the Ethiopian empire.

The Tigrean People's Liberation Front was formed after 1974 with the encouragement and direct support of the Eritrean People's Liberation Front, which aimed at creating a buffer between Eritrea and the Ethiopian army. The ploy worked well. There was no shortage of grievances in the province of Tigrai for the TPLF to draw upon because the region, historically part of the empire's core, had turned into an economic and political backwater. Tigrai had enjoyed a brief period of renewed importance in the late nineteenth century when a "revival of international commerce and arms trade in the Red Sea" gave it enough of an advantage for a Tigrean to become emperor as Yohannes IV.[9] But Yohannes died in 1889 fighting invading Mahdists from neighboring Sudan. His Amhara successor, Menelik II, embarked on a program of conquest that moved the geographic and economic center of the Ethiopian empire to the south, leaving Tigrai politically marginal. Tigrai was also an impoverished region, overpopulated, badly eroded, and vulnerable to drought and famine. But Tigreans never quite accepted the authority of Addis Ababa, and Haile Selassie managed the problem only by allowing descendants of Yohannes to act as governors of the province.

Like all other major opposition groups in the country, the Tigrean People's Liberation Front was led by young, educated, and extremely ideological and contentious individuals who had honed their political skills in the struggles of the student movement.[10] The organization was characterized by a mixture of hard-line Marxist ideology and intense greater Tigrean nationalism. Although the TPLF in theory was a front representing a wide spectrum of ideological trends, its core was the League of Tigrean Communists, a faction that called itself pro-Albanian to show its ideological purity and its rejection of the revisionist trends evident in China and the Soviet Union.

But the Tigrean People's Liberation Front was also intensely chauvinistic—its detractors said imperialistic. Maps of Tigrai appearing in TPLF publications depicted a region with much-enlarged boundaries, extending all the way to the Sudanese border, which strongly suggested the existence of an element of Tigrean imperialism within the movement. Furthermore, the TPLF fought fiercely not only against the Ethiopian army but also against other movements operating in Tigrai.[11] The TPLF grew slowly initially. It had its strongest impact in rural areas, but the towns and main roads of Tigrai remained in government hands.

All this changed suddenly in 1988 as a result of the collapse of the Ethiopian military. In April of that year government troops suffered a major defeat at Afabet, in Eritrea, after an officers' mutiny left the garrison there bereft of leadership.[12] The defeat at Afabet signaled the beginning of the army's disintegration. Purges followed the defeat and more purges took place after an attempted coup in May 1989. The morale and the fighting capability of the government troops in Eritrea and Tigrai diminished rapidly as a result.[13] Entire garrisons surrendered to the EPLF and TPLF.

The first beneficiary of the disintegration of the Ethiopian army was the Tigrean People's Liberation Front. By late 1989 it had wrested virtually all Tigrean towns from Ethiopian control, and it had pushed well south into Welo province and even beyond into northern Shewa province. Fighting there was carried out not by the TPLF proper but by the Ethiopian People's Democratic Movement (EPDM), a predominately Amhara organization set up by the TPLF and controlled by it.

Success affected the TPLF's goals.[14] The front was not a secessionist movement, but had fought originally for regional autonomy. With success, however, came the ambition of replacing the central government with one in which the Tigrean People's Liberation Front would play a major role.[15] This broader plan was manifested in the formulation of the EPDM and later of the Ethiopian People's Revolutionary Democratic Front, an umbrella organization that originally included the TPLF and the EPDM and later other ethnic movements created by the TPLF. By setting up and controlling these organizations, the Tigrean People's Liberation Front gained the ability to operate outside of Tigrai province without creating resentment and opposition among non-Tigreans.[16]

The internal collapse of the Ethiopian army, coupled with the Tigrean offensive, broke the stalemate that had been developing during the 1980s. The possibility of an insurgent military victory became real once again. Yet it was at this moment that the Eritrean People's Liberation Front agreed to enter into negotiations with the government, with former U.S. president Jimmy Carter as mediator. The Tigrean People's Liberation Front in turn rushed to set up its own negotiating process, opening talks with the government in Rome under Italian government auspices. This paradox can only be understood by taking into consideration the impact of the rise of the TPLF on the conflict in Eritrea.

The New Conflict

The establishment of the Tigrean People's Liberation Front was encouraged by the Eritrean People's Liberation Front, but sudden success made the Tigrean movement potentially threatening. Officially, the Eritreans denied that this was the case; they argued that the TPLF recognized the Eritrean right to self-determination, and that far from being a problem, the success of the TPLF would hasten Eritrean independence.

There are reasons to doubt that the relationship between the two movements was so simple. The Tigrean People's Liberation Front was bound either to claim a central role in a new government coalition or to rule an autonomous Tigrai if the Mengistu regime collapsed. In either case, the independence of Eritrea would limit Tigrean power. It would leave Ethiopia a much weakened and landlocked country, and it would thwart greater Tigrean nationalism by making many Tigrinya-speaking people into Eritrean citizens.

Recognition of the Eritrean right to self-determination in itself was no proof that the TPLF would not try to raise obstacles to Eritrean secession.

The Ethiopian political culture is marked by a passion for duplicity and double meanings—"wax and gold," to use the Ethiopian expression.[17] Since the beginning of the revolution there had been no genuine political alliance between any two liberation movements in Ethiopia. In the mid-1970s the All-Ethiopian Socialist Movement (MEISON) supported the Derg but used the relationship to try to build a political organization capable of overthrowing the military.[18] In 1978 an alliance of Marxist-Leninist organizations cooperated with the military council in trying to form a new party; this time the alliance collapsed because each movement was doing its Machiavellian best to undercut the others.[19] The EPLF and the ELF tried to negotiate a unification agreement in late 1975 and failed; a new splinter group was formed instead. The list could continue.

The ambiguity of the relationship between the Eritrean People's Liberation Front and the Tigrean People's Liberation Front was confirmed in 1989 when the two movements entered into separate negotiations with the government. The EPLF participated in the Atlanta talks at a time the TPLF was scoring significant military victories, suggesting that it was not confident that the ascendancy of the Tigreans guaranteed Eritrean independence. The Tigreans responded by immediately initiating a separate negotiating process, suggesting that the TPLF did not want a special solution for Eritrea and did not trust the Eritreans not to enter into an agreement with the government detrimental to the Tigreans.

The Tigrean People's Liberation Front acknowledged that relations among the various movements fighting against the Ethiopian government were difficult. In late 1989 the organization's secretary-general admitted that the opposition to the Ethiopian government was divided and that "armed clashes" between the movements could not be ruled out after the fall of the Mengistu regime.[20]

All of these factors suggest that in 1990 the Eritrean conflict was no longer simply a bilateral one between the Ethiopian government and the EPLF; nor was it a three-way conflict between the government, the EPLF, and the TPLF. Rather, it was a conflict pitting the government against a loose alliance of movements, of which the Eritrean People's Liberation Front and the Tigrean People's Liberation Front were by far the most important.

Attempts at Conflict Resolution

After 1974 the military regime made numerous attempts to settle the Eritrean conflict, with and without the intervention of third parties. The attempt took place a few days before the formal deposition of Emperor Haile Selassie in September 1974. General Aman Michael Andom, then defense minister, led a delegation to Eritrea with the message that all problems would be solved in the new Ethiopia; however, he offered no concrete proposal. As Derg chairman, he later opposed sending more troops to the region. Aman's position on Eritrea was one of the factors leading to his dismissal and to his death while resisting arrest on November 23. Troops were dispatched to Eritrea within hours of his death.

In January 1975 the Derg sent envoys to Eritrea to open a dialogue with the Eritrean Liberation Front and the Eritrean People's Liberation Front through town elders. As Aman had, these envoys only brought a vague message of goodwill, not specific plans. The Eritrean nationalists responded with a major attack on Asmara.

The pattern thus established was never modified. Numerous contacts between the insurgents and the government took place in the following years, always in the absence of an agenda or concrete proposals. The Nine-Point Policy of April 1976, to which the Derg subscribed until its demise, was a model of vagueness and ambiguity. It recognized "the right of any nationality existing in Ethiopia to self-determination," but also defended "the unity of Ethiopian nationalities . . . based on the common struggle against feudalism, bureaucratic capitalism, imperialism and reactionary forces."[21] Eritrea, however, was not recognized as a "nationality." Under the policy the military committee offered to negotiate with "the progressive groups and organizations in Eritrea which are not in collusion with feudalists, reactionary forces in the neighborhood, and imperialists," but it also stated that the purpose of negotiations was to "promote the unity of the oppressed classes of Ethiopia."[22] At that time, the Derg was hoping to make a deal with the Eritrean People's Liberation Front—the progressive Marxist-Leninist movement—that would exclude the Eritrean Liberation Front and thus weaken the Eritrean ranks. Not surprisingly, contacts with Eritrean nationalists in the months after the policy was issued achieved nothing.

Third-party attempts at conflict resolution did not add concreteness to the discussion. In March 1977 the Soviets and Cubans proposed a grand scheme to solve all conflicts in the Horn of Africa at one stroke, suggesting the formation of a federation that would include Ethiopia, Eritrea, Somalia, and the People's Democratic Republic of Yemen. The proposal was immediately rejected by all sides. After the acute phase of the conflict in Eritrea was over in 1978, East Germany offered its services as a mediator, but the EPLF became convinced that the East German representatives were supporting the Ethiopian position. The Italian Communist Party tried to facilitate talks between the government and the Eritrean Liberation Front, even after the ELF had ceased to be a fighting force within Eritrea. In the meantime, bilateral contacts between the government and the Eritrean People's Liberation Front continued; according to the Eritreans there were ten encounters between 1982 and 1985, all of them desultory.

Against this background of peacemaking without concrete proposals, the Atlanta talks of September 1989 and the Nairobi talks of November 1989 represented a real turning point in the history of the Eritrean conflict. The Eritrean People's Liberation Front and the government admitted openly that they were talking, and worked to establish an agenda with the help of Jimmy Carter—an impartial and experienced mediator. Had the Eritrean conflict still been the old one there might have been a chance of success. But the situation was in transition, and the conditions for solving the new conflict were not even remotely present.

Negotiating in a Transitional Conflict

In chapter 1 and elsewhere, I. William Zartman has singled out four major factors that create favorable conditions for negotiations: a mutually hurting stalemate, a deadline, valid spokespersons, and a vision of an acceptable compromise.[23] These factors are considered here in turn as they apply in the Eritrean conflict.

In 1990, with the new conflict under way, there was less of a mutually hurting stalemate than had existed two or three years earlier when the old, bilateral Ethio-Eritrean conflict had reached a dead end. In the old conflict both sides had tried repeatedly to launch major, decisive offensives, and both had failed to break the stalemate. The level of fighting remained high even between major offensives, with severe casualties, significant loss of materiel, and increasing impoverishment of the civilian population. But the new conflict, in which the Tigrean People's Liberation Front figured prominently, could not be considered stalemated. On the contrary, the government was losing the war.

In neither the old nor the new conflict was there a deadline that gave all parties a sense of urgency. In 1990 the TPLF was a relatively new movement, with time apparently on its side. The government did face a deadline—the arms supply agreement with the Soviet Union would expire at the end of 1990, and Moscow had stated officially that it would not renew the agreement on the same generous terms. However, it was unclear whether the Ethiopian government took Moscow's threat seriously. Although undoubtedly there were frictions between Moscow and Addis Ababa, the Soviets' behavior in Afghanistan and Angola suggested that they remained reluctant to abandon their clients.[24]

The Eritrean People's Liberation Front had reasons to hasten into an agreement with the government, but it also had reasons to postpone negotiations. The growing power of the Tigrean People's Liberation Front suggested that it might be better to reach an agreement with the weakened Mengistu regime soon rather than with a strong TPLF later. On the other hand, even in early 1990 the government appeared so close to collapse as to make negotiations pointless. This seems to have been the conclusion reached by EPLF leaders in the spring of 1990.

Thus there was no clear deadline concerning either the old or the new conflict. There were some time pressures, particularly for the parties to the old conflict, but they were both ambiguous and asymmetrical and therefore not likely to facilitate negotiations.

The existence of valid spokespersons was not a problem in the old conflict. The Eritrean People's Liberation Front was a formally constituted organization, with a structure remarkably similar to that of the Ethiopian government.[25] In preparations for the Atlanta conference in 1989 there was no argument over who had the right to represent either side. Although the government still maintained contacts with the Eritrean Liberation Front, it accepted the EPLF as the negotiating partner for Eritreans.

In the case of the new conflict, the situation was different and questions of representation arose on all sides. Who would negotiate with the government and the Eritreans? Certainly the EPLF and the TPLF would be represented, but would they have equal weight? Would the Ethiopian People's Democratic Movement or the Ethiopian People's Revolutionary Democratic Front be recognized as organizations separate from the TPLF? Would a voice be given to groups that had participated very little in the fighting but had also sought independence or autonomy for their respective territories, such as the Oromo Liberation Front or the Afar Liberation Front? Would competing factions in the various movements be represented? The insurgents' alliance was too loose, its goals too uncertain, and many of the organizations too divided or too shadowy for common representatives to be accepted easily by all. At the time of the Atlanta talks there were no undisputed spokespersons for any sides in the new conflict.

The concept of compromise was absent in both the old and new conflicts. In the early 1990s the Eritrean People's Liberation Front and the government had not changed their positions for three decades. The Tigrean People's Liberation Front and other groups had vague and changing goals, but these were becoming more ambitious rather than more moderate. Under such conditions a mediator would have an impossible task. The parties to the conflict needed more than technical advice on how to craft a mutually acceptable compromise; they needed to be convinced that the purpose of negotiating was to reach a compromise rather than to win the surrender of the other side. But the very concept of compromise seems to be alien to the Ethiopian political culture. At best, compromise is seen as a temporary solution until victory becomes possible—Haile Selassie, for example, accepted the federal compromise in Eritrea until he found means to dismantle it.

Conclusions

The Carter initiative of 1989 took place at the time the old conflict between the Eritrean People's Liberation Front and Ethiopia was turning into a new and broader conflict in which the Tigrean People's Liberation Front figured prominently, making conditions more unfavorable to talks and compromise. The major obstacle to the success of the negotiations appeared to be the transitional nature of the conflict. But there were other, more idiosyncratic obstacles. Among them was the absence of a political culture of compromise, which affected equally the old and the new conflicts. Other obstacles, in particular the absence of a mutually hurting stalemate and the absence of valid spokespersons, were clearly related to the transitional phase the conflict had entered in 1989.

A transitional conflict is by definition not stalemated. What makes it transitional is precisely that new elements have been added, and that the balance of forces among the parties has been altered as a result. In Ethiopia in 1990, the enhanced role of the Tigrean People's Liberation Front and the collapse of the Ethiopian military broke the stalemate reached by the government and the Eritrean People's Liberation Front. With the TPLF controlling virtually the entire Tigrai region and pushing far south toward Addis Ababa, and with the port of Massawa having fallen to the EPLF, a military defeat of the government side was no long an impossibility, as events were later to prove.

The absence of valid spokespersons also appears inevitable in a transitional conflict because the importance of the various parties changes, and so do relations among them. Both the EPLF and the TPLF were highly structured and hierarchical organizations. Taken individually, both had valid spokespersons. But the relations between the two organizations changed as the Tigreans became more successful militarily and spawned new groups such as the Ethiopian People's Democratic Movement, with the result that nobody could really speak for that loose alliance of changing groups. It is not surprising that the 1989–90 negotiations should have been undertaken separately by the EPLF and the TPLF.

The case discussed in this chapter thus suggests that in a transitional conflict certain basic conditions are inherently unfavorable to negotiations. After Eritrean independence, a new Carter initiative to promote negotiations between the government of President Meles Zenawi of Ethiopia, dominated by the TPLF, and ethnic opposition movements fighting against it raises the question of whether different circumstances might facilitate negotiations. New elections and a new constitution providing a procedure for exercising the right of self-determination contributed new ingredients to the situation and a softer conflict, but not an immediate result.

The defeat of Mengistu did not mark the end of conflict in Ethiopia. Unable to challenge the Eritrean People's Liberation Front, the new government accepted the independence of Eritrea. However, it continued to challenge and try to contain other nationalist groups operating in Ethiopia. Originally allies of the Tigrean People's Liberation Front in the common purpose of defeating Mengistu, these organizations had developed an increasingly adversarial relation with the new government, accusing it of imposing Tigrean rule on the country and of denying other ethnic groups the same right to self-determination that the TPLF had sought for its own people. The largest and most vocal of these nationalist organizations was the Oromo Liberation Front.

Aware that it could not simply repress ethnic nationalism—Mengistu had tried to do that and failed—the TPLF-dominated government tried to contain it by setting up separate political organizations for all the major, and many minor, ethnic groups in the country, all controlled through the Ethiopian People's Revolutionary Democratic Front. The EPDM was the first of these groups. It was followed by a series of ethnically defined "people's democratic organizations" operating in the different regions, such as the Oromo People's Democratic Organization. Far from making the country's new leadership more acceptable, the creation of these TPLF-controlled ethnic organizations increased the determination of the independent ethnic movements opposing the government.

In July 1991, shortly after the overthrow of Mengistu, a compromise was negotiated among all pro- and anti-EPRDF organizations. A conference in Addis Ababa resulted in the creation of a council of representatives and a government of national reconciliation that included all groups. But the allocation of seats in the council left the Ethiopian People's Revolutionary Democratic Front in control, with the Oromo Liberation Front a distant and very dissatisfied second. The compromise did not last, and a crisis occurred in June 1992 when elections for regional and local councils were held. The election process degenerated quickly. The government closed down most offices of those parties not aligned with the EPRDF (although those parties were officially part of the government) and kept them from registering their candidates. The results were that the major independent parties withdrew from the elections, which turned into a virtually single-party exercise, and that fighting between the army and the OLF militias resumed. The government coalition narrowed to the EPRDF and ethnic parties aligned with it.

The narrowing of the new regime's political base, coupled with mounting dissatisfaction on the part of the non-Tigrean population, convinced former president Carter that the country faced a renewed cycle of conflict unless the opposition parties were brought back into the political process. He thus attempted to launch negotiations between the government and the opposition in January 1994.

The conflict Carter undertook to negotiate was once again a transitional one. Only one side to the conflict was clearly defined—the Meles government. Defining the other side was much more complex. There were questions about which opposition groups commanded enough support to be included, and which were simply exiled paper organizations. And there were questions about whether the major opposition groups were willing to band together and enter into bilateral negotiations with the government. The OLF, the most important of the opposition groups, appeared uncertain whether it wanted to work together with the smaller groups or break ranks and define a separate role for itself. The rebellion was still in its mobilization or consolidation phase.

The goals of the various parties to the conflict were also somewhat fluid. Theoretically committed to multiparty democracy and blaming their opponents for making democracy impossible, all parties, including the EPRDF, were obviously intent on maximizing their power, but uncertain about how best to do that.

Although the situation had some similarities to that of 1989, in that the sides were not clearly defined and the goals remained uncertain, there were also major differences. Although the Eritrean People's Liberation Front and the Tigrean People's Liberation Front in 1989–90 could hope for an outright victory, neither the government nor the opposition could hope for victory in 1994. Also, in that year the costs of refusing to negotiate were potentially high for both sides, because the government risked losing United States support if it showed itself undemocratic and uncooperative, and the opposition, which had been unable to engage the government in a dialogue on its own, needed outside help to get back into the negotiating process.

Under these conditions the transitional nature of the conflict in 1994 might prove to be an asset, allowing the mediator to rely on the process of negotiation to mold the identity of the participants and the nature of their goals in such a way that compromise could become possible. But if the attempt at promoting negotiations were to fail in this very early phase of a transitional conflict, a long period of escalating strife is likely before the opponents emerge from the consolidation phase, develop a perception of stalemate, and go back to the negotiating table.

Notes

1. For example, some Eritreans argued that the Tigrinya language should be written in the Latin alphabet rather than in the alphabet it shares with Amharic, in order to emphasize that Tigrinya is not an Ethiopian language. But Tigrinya is spoken in both Eritrea and the Tigrai region of Ethiopia, and its alphabet is not borrowed from Amharic, but derived from Ge'ez, the ancient language from which both Amharic and Tigrinya derive.

2. See John Markakis, *National and Class Conflict in the Horn of Africa* (Cambridge University Press, 1987), especially pp. 104–45.

3. In early 1978 only Asmara, Barentu, and the port cities of Massawa and Asab remained firmly in government hands. See Markakis, *National and Class Conflict*, p. 245.

4. Between 1977 and 1987 the Soviet Union delivered more than $8 billion worth of military equipment to Ethiopia. See U.S. Arms Control and Disarmament Agency, *World Military Expenditures and Arms Transfers, 1988* (1991), ACDA publication 131 (1989), pp. 84, 111.

5. Cuban troops never fought in Eritrea, theoretically refusing to take sides in an internal conflict and to go against the Eritrean nationalists they had supported in the days of Haile Selassie. Cuban troops on the Ogaden front, however, freed Ethiopian troops for use in Eritrea. Cuban troops withdrew completely from Ethiopia in 1989.

6. Dawit Wolde Giorgis, "The Power of Decision-Making in Post-Revolutionary Ethiopia," in Marina Ottaway, ed., *The Political Economy of Ethiopia* (Praeger, 1990),

p. 66. Dawit does not explain what recognizing the liberation movements meant, or what kind of political solution the government had in mind.

7. On the constitution of 1987, see Edmond J. Keller, *Revolutionary Ethiopia: From Empire to Republic* (Indiana University Press, 1988), p. 239–43; Bereket Habte Selassie, "Empire and Constitutional Engineering: The PDRE in Historical Perspective," in Ottaway, ed., *Political Economy of Ethiopia,* pp. 115–36.

8. On the Workers' Party of Ethiopia, see Christopher S. Clapham, *Transformation and Continuity in Revolutionary Ethiopia* (Cambridge University Press, 1988), pp. 65–100.

9. Haggai Erlich, *Ethiopia and the Challenge of Independence* (Boulder, Colo.: Lynne Rienner, 1986), p.19.

10. On the TPLF's link with the student movement, see the transcript of the broadcast of the Voice of Tigray Revolution, October 21, 1989, in Federal Broadcasting Information Service, *Sub-Saharan Africa,* October 24, 1989.

11. See Markakis, *National and Class Conflict,* p. 254 ff.

12. See "Ethiopia: A Battle Lost, a War in Stalemates," *Africa Confidential,* vol. 29 (April 29, 1988), pp. 1–3.

13. See "Ethiopia: A Blow-by-Blow Account," *Africa Confidential,* vol. 30 (May 26, 1989), pp. 1–3.

14. On the TPLF, see Markakis, *National and Class Conflict,* pp. 253–58; Clapham, *Transformation and Continuity,* p. 204–14.

15. A TPLF statement of June 13, 1989, issued in London, summarizes a TPLF peace proposal. The major point is the "establishment of a provisional government constituted from all political organizations, for a transitional period, until a constitution has been adopted by the people and a democratic government has been elected." Thus the TPLF sought a role in the central government.

16. On the beginning of the EPDM and EPRDF, see "Ethiopia: Mengistu Survives by His Fingertips," *Africa Confidential,* vol. 30 (November 3, 1989), pp. 1–3.

17. This cultural trait is analyzed at length in Donald N. Levine, *Wax and Gold: Tradition and Innovation in Ethiopian Culture* (University of Chicago Press, 1965).

18. On the Derg-MEISON relationship, see Marina Ottaway and David Ottaway, *Ethiopia: Empire in Revolution* (New York: Africana, 1978). pp. 122–23 and 187–89.

19. See Negussay Ayele, "The Ethiopian Revolution: Political Aspects of the Transition from PMAC to PDRE," in Ottaway, ed., *Political Economy of Ethiopia,* pp. 11–29.

20. See Agence France Presse, "TPLF Leader Holds London News Conference," in Federal Broadcast Information Service, *Sub-Saharan Africa,* November 28, 1989, p. 2.

21. *Ethiopian Herald,* May 18, 1976, April 21, 1976. See also Ottaway and Ottaway, *Ethiopia,* p. 158.

22. *Ethiopian Herald,* April 21, 1976.

23. I. William Zartman, "Negotiations in South Africa," *Washington Quarterly,* vol. 11 (Autumn 1988), pp. 141–58.

24. Weapon deliveries to Ethiopia increased substantially in January 1990. This may have simply been a long-scheduled delivery, but it did not help convey a sense of urgency. See also chapters 8 and 10.

25. See Clapham, *Transformation and Continuity* p. 213–14; Markakis, *National and Class Conflict,* p. 246–48.

Part Three

CENTRALIST CONFLICTS

CENTRALIST CONFLICTS seek a new system of government for the entire state. Their goal is generally more than a change of rulers; it is a revision of the whole structure and philosophy of the political system. Behind that goal usually lies a view that the system needs replacement because, by its nature, it excludes the people and the cause that the rebels represent. Sometimes this is a class- or ideologically related cause, as claimed by the rebels in the Philippines and Colombia. Sometimes it has an ethnic or religious base, as in South Africa, Lebanon, and Afghanistan, although there is often some class and ethnoreligious coincidence, as the rebellions in South Africa and Lebanon show. Even where the excluded are simply politically motivated, as in Angola and Mozambique, they may also represent ethnic or socioeconomic groups and grievances.

The danger is that victory for the rebellion may often carry with it the mirror image of the previous exclusions, triggering new repressions and exclusions. Thus a healthier solution in terms of the objective goals and grievances, as well as a positive-sum solution in terms of the parties to the conflict, comes through negotiation. The salient result is again a softer outcome than simply victory. It involves the design of a new, open, shared political system in which legitimacy, participation, and allocation are available to all. Often it is achieved through such a simple measure as removing the restraints of a previous pact, as has happened in South Africa, Colombia, and Lebanon, or of a previous winner-take-all contest, as happened in Angola and Mozambique. The simplicity of the remedy does not mean that the tasks of carrying it out, of disengaging competing commitments, and of designing a replacement system are also simple, but it does indicate that a conceptual target is present around which new commitments can crystallize. That is what happened to a great extent in Colombia and in South Africa (a conflict about as polarized, hostile, ideologized, committed, and dehumanizing as they come). Why has a solution been possible there and not elsewhere?

In South Africa the parties were frightened by the horror of a violent confrontation, shadows of which had already appeared over the land in the form of police oppression under the apartheid system and the terror involved in rivalries between the African National Congress and the Inkatha Freedom Party. Political—that is, negotiating—leaders still remained in charge; militant leaders had not yet taken over. In Lebanon, on the other extreme, political leaders were pushed aside by a new militant generation, whose life was tied to confrontation and violence; the parties could only be brought to agreement through the imposed authority of a mediator. In Afghanistan the war had removed the political leaders to begin with; the militant leadership scorned negotiation. In Angola and Mozambique the conflicts reinforced militant thinking, but in Mozambique political consolidation among the rebels and then a humbling drought brought both sides to a wary, fragile redefinition of the political system that turned the rebels legitimate and their conflict political. In Angola, even when the conflict was defined as political, the militant leaders remained in control and the conflict was still viewed in militant zero-sum terms; the election of 1992 was seen as only a battle in a renewed war. Where such militants have taken over, a mutually hurting stalemate defined as exhaustion is the only trigger to negotiation.

The conflicts in Angola and Mozambique, and to some extent those in Lebanon, the Philippines, and Afghanistan, have been postcolonial struggles among former allies to define the new independent political system. Perhaps even the conflicts in Colombia and South Africa could be defined in the same way. In all cases the political system had not yet settled into place (or, in the case of Colombia and South Africa, had done so prematurely and inadequately) and was in need of definition. In Colombia and the Philippines the conflicts have involved a legitimate government struggling with an insurgent problem, not unlike the regionalist conflicts discussed in part 2. In the other centralist cases the illegitimacy of the government has been a cause of the conflict. Yet only in Angola and Mozambique has mediation been accepted (mediation was marginal in Afghanistan and imposed in Lebanon). Where illegitimacy of the government is part of the problem conflict resolution depends not only on exhaustion but also on shifts in the balance of forces that allow parties with longer-range, cooperative, or coalitional interests to see an advantage in creating a new political system—or else that allow one side simply to win.

CHAPTER SIX

Internal Negotiations in a Centralist Conflict: Lebanon

Mary-Jane Deeb and Marius Deeb

THE LEBANESE CONFLICT has dragged on since 1975 and has gone through a number of phases, each with its own rationale and each incorporating different issues and at times different players. Throughout there have been attempts at different levels (both domestic and external) to find a solution to what is plaguing the country and eroding its political and social institutions. Three times only, however, have representatives of the domestic factions met together and come up with formulas that appeared to address everyone's concerns. This chapter examines these three attempts at internal negotiations within the framework of the government-insurgency conflict resolution process analyzed by I. William Zartman in chapter 1 in order to gain a better understanding of why the first two attempts failed and the third attempt basically succeeded. On a more theoretical level, the Lebanese case provides new insights into the process of internal multilateral negotiations, the structure of asymmetry, the ripe moment for negotiations, the role of external mediators, and the issue of valid spokespersons.

At issue in the Lebanese conflict has not been the identity of each party or group involved or the identity of the parties in relation to one another, but the amount of power that each group would hold in government (notably in Parliament) and the amount of territory it would control. It has therefore been a zero-sum, distributive conflict over the nature of the state. Also at issue has been the degree of support to be given to Palestinians on Lebanese soil. The previous arrangement for the distribution of power, established in

1943, had broken down because of demographic changes and because of growing Palestinian influence in Lebanon, both of which changed the balance of power in favor of the Muslim part of the population.

Structurally the Lebanese conflict is unique in that the government does not constitute an entity on its own and has not been a distinct actor in the negotiation process. Whereas the governments of South Africa, Sudan, and Sri Lanka can be considered primary actors in negotiations with distinct insurgency movements, the Lebanese government represents the whole spectrum of the nation's political views and opinions, and most leaders of the so-called rebellion are part of the political system. Furthermore, the separation of powers between the executive and the legislature is blurred, with roles and jurisdiction overlapping. Consequently negotiations have taken place in most cases between members of the executive and the legislature rather than between members of the government and parties to an insurrection.

The National Dialogue Committee and the Constitutional Document of 1976

The first attempt at resolving the conflict took place a few months after the conflict erupted. That attempt began with the formation of the National Dialogue Committee (NDC) on September 24, 1975, and ended with the promulgation of the Constitutional Document of February 14, 1976. There were few actors then, aligned primarily into two camps, as well as a small number of individuals representing a gamut of viewpoints that bridged the gap between the two sides. On one side stood the predominantly Muslim Lebanese National Movement (NM, or National Movement) in alliance with the Palestine Liberation Organization (PLO); on the other stood the Christian Lebanese Front (LF, or Lebanese Front).[1]

The National Dialogue Committee was composed of twenty members, equally divided between Muslims and Christians: four Shiites, four Sunnis, and two Druze on the Muslim side, and four Maronites, three Greek Orthodox, two Greek Catholics, and one Armenian on the Christian side.[2] They represented the most powerful Lebanese politicians and bloc leaders in Parliament. Out of the ten Christian members, five were members of Parliament and three were Cabinet ministers.[3] Only three were not prominent members of the political establishment *per se*, but two of these were proteges of leading politicians (and one member belonged to both the cabinet and Parliament).[4] On the Muslin side, five members only were part of the political system, but four of these were cabinet ministers and one was the prime minister. All five were also the most powerful traditional Muslim leaders in the country, representing the sectarian interests of their own communities.[5]

Two groups were not represented on the National Dialogue Committee: the Palestine Liberation Organization and the Movement of the Disinherited, a new Shiite movement headed by a charismatic cleric that would eventually emerge as a major force in the Lebanese conflict.[6] As a non-Lebanese group the PLO was not an acceptable partner to the negotiations, but its interests were represented by the members of the Muslim Lebanese National Movement. The Shiite cleric was still too unimportant to be recognized as an alternative to the traditional leaders of the Shiite community represented on the committee.

The issues that divided the committee participants were the Palestinian armed presence in Lebanon and the need for political reforms. The Christian Lebanese Front viewed the armed presence of the Palestinians on Lebanese territory as a threat to the sovereignty of Lebanon. Its members described the PLO as a state within the state, and accused the Palestinian leadership of not abiding by the Cairo Agreement and the Melkart Protocol that had defined and circumscribed their role in Lebanon.[7] The Palestinians were perceived as having altered the delicate balance of power between the various religious communities in Lebanon, to the detriment of the Christian community. The Lebanese Front's solution was to curb the power of the Palestinians and limit their presence to certain regions of Lebanon.

The Lebanese National Movement, on the other hand, took a very different stand. It considered the armed presence of the Palestinians in Lebanon irrelevant and claimed that the conflict was intra-Lebanese, stemming from an archaic political system based on a sectarian division of power that favored the Christian community. The National Movement demanded that major reforms be instituted that would curb the powers of the Christian president, increase the powers of the Sunni Muslim prime minister, and enlarge Parliament. Members of Parliament would be elected on a nonsectarian basis to secularize and modernize the system.[8]

Among the members of the National Dialogue Committee were three powerful politicians, a Maronite (Raymond Edde), a Sunni (Sa'ib Salam), and a Shiite (Kamil al-As'ad),[9] who took a halfway stand between the Lebanese Front and National Movement positions and attempted to find a compromise—namely, limiting Palestinian influence in Lebanon and introducing some reforms in the Lebanese political system. According to the theoretical model under consideration in this book, those three leaders could have bridged the gap between the two sides and created a coalition "to settle the substantive issues and carry the remaining members of the spectrum."[10] They were not able to achieve a broad coalition, however. Unlike the other members of the National Dialogue Committee they were unwilling to create their own militias and use force to push forward their ideas and programs for reform, although both the Lebanese Front and the National Movement were using their forces on the ground to increase their bargaining power at the negotiating table.

The mediator in this first attempt at resolving the conflict was Syria, through its envoys: Syrian foreign minister 'Abd al-Halim Khaddam and the Syrian chief of staff Hikmat Shihabi. Before the Lebanese conflict flared up the Syrian government of President Hafez el-Asad had had good relations with most parties to the conflict, including the PLO, the Christian president, and the leaders of the National Movement. Syria was therefore perceived as a valid mediator whose intentions were purely disinterested and were based on a desire to see law and order restored in Lebanon.

Syria invited itself in as a mediator from the earliest stage of the conflict. It was not a disinterested party, as later events would demonstrate, and had its own agenda in Lebanon. It moved quickly to preempt Arab mediation of the conflict and to take sole charge of the negotiations.[11] Syria pushed for a cease-fire, and was instrumental in the formation of the National Dialogue Committee. However, even before the committee met suspicions had emerged that Syria was not an even-handed mediator, but was backing the primarily Muslim National Movement. The reason for those suspicions was that a faction of the Palestine Liberation Organization—the Sa'iqa—was Syrian controlled, and that its leader was chair of the military department of the PLO. Furthermore, different factions within the National Movement had close ties to Syria, which was providing them with arms either directly or through the PLO.

The National Dialogue Committee met seven times. After each meeting violence escalated as each party attempted to strengthen its position and undermine that of the opposition. The fighting continued until the two sides reached a stalemate, with each side scoring some victories and suffering a high number of casualties and losses of territorial control. Syria was then able to get the parties together to agree, in February 1976, on the so-called Constitutional Document. That document strengthened the power of the Sunni Muslim prime minister, weakened that of the Maronite Christian president, reallocated power in Parliament by equalizing the number of

Christian and Muslim deputies, and called for Palestinians to abide by the Cairo and Melkart agreements between the Lebanese state and the Palestine Liberation Organization.[12]

The Constitutional Document was never implemented, because a new crisis took place immediately after the agreement was made, changing the balance of forces on the ground. An army insurrection, led by a junior officer with strong leanings toward the National Movement and the PLO, resulted in the disintegration of the army along sectarian lines. The National Movement and the Palestine Liberation Organization went on the offensive as they saw a chance to increase their power and their control over the state.

Syria, realizing that this was a golden opportunity to intervene, entered Lebanon militarily in April 1976, ostensibly on the side of the Christian Lebanese Front, to redress the balance and bring about a resolution to the conflict. It did not bother to implement the Constitutional Document it had sponsored. Syria had acted as host to the PLO leadership; it can therefore be viewed both as mediator and as a host-neighbor having to determine its relations with the Lebanese state, with the PLO, and with the various factions in the Lebanese conflict. But in a reversal of the model (see chapter 1), Syria's role as mediator preceded its actual participation in the conflict as a host-neighbor, thus paving the way for its increased involvement with and control over the actors and the state—which complicated the situation even further and escalated the violence.

The Geneva and Lausanne Conferences

By 1983 the structure of the conflict and many of the players had changed. Whereas in 1975–76 there had been little or no asymmetry in the negotiations, by 1983 the situation had become completely asymmetrical. Because in 1975 the political system had represented most of the warring factions, and because the National Movement and the Palestine Liberation Organization had prevailed on the president and the cabinet not to use the army to quell the fighting (on the premise that the army would disintegrate along sectarian lines if it were used), no group or faction had had a monopoly on force or legitimacy.

By 1983 Syria had become the dominant power in Lebanon, with 30,000 troops on Lebanese territory. Although the old Lebanese army had disintegrated after the rebellion of 1976, a new fledgling, American-trained national army was being built. Armed militias proliferated, but none had as many troops or was as well organized and well armed as the Syrian army. If all the men making up the militias fighting each other in Lebanon had been added together, they still would not have equaled in number the Syrian troops posted in Lebanon.

The actors in the second set of negotiations had also changed. The Shiite community was now being represented by both a traditional leader who was part of the political establishment and a new militia leader who challenged traditional authority and controlled the forces on the ground. Some of the middle-of-the-road, traditional leaders had gone into exile; others had lost their constituencies in a shuffle of alliances and the shift of power to those groups that controlled militias. New coalitions between leaders and factions had been created that were different from those that had existed during the first set of negotiations.

The official parties to the second set of negotiations included ten members—five Christians and five Muslims. All the Christians were Maronites: the Lebanese president, Amin Jumayyil; the president of the Lebanese Front, Camille Sham'un; the president of the Phalangist Party, Pierre Jumayyil; and the former president of Lebanon, Sulayman Franjiya, who had been president when the conflict started. The fifth Christian leader, Raymond Edde, had called for a compromise during the negotiations of 1975–76 and had since gone into exile in Paris, refusing to attend the negotiations at Lausanne and Geneva. The Muslim side included two former Sunni prime ministers, Sa'ib Salam and Rashid Karami; one Shiite who was a former Speaker of the House, 'Adil 'Usayran; the traditional head of the Druze militia, Walid Junblat; and the head of the Shiite militia, Nabih Birri. Except for Birri, all were part of the political establishment.

The issues had also changed. Israel had destroyed the Palestinian military infrastructure in Lebanon in 1982, and Palestinian leaders and their forces had been forced out of the country. The role of the Palestinians in Lebanon was thus no longer an issue in the negotiations. Instead, the Lebanese-Israeli security agreement of May 17, 1983, had become the principal issue of discussion, and political reform had been relegated to a secondary position in the negotiations.

Those who wanted to abrogate the agreement were Syria and its allies: the Druze leader, the leader of Shiite faction AMAL, the two Sunni leaders (one of whose constituency was in the Syrian controlled part of northern Lebanon), and the Maronite ex-president of Lebanon (who also represented part of northern Lebanon under Syrian control). The Lebanese president and the two other Christian leaders were in favor of the agreement.

The Geneva Conference was the result of an escalation of the fighting by the Syrian-supported factions of the Druze and non-PLO Palestinian forces who came from the Syrian controlled areas of Lebanon in the Biga' region. They attacked the Lebanese Forces, the principal Christian militia, in the area of Mount Lebanon, which was under Christian control. The army intervened to stop the advance and impose a cease-fire. The fighting reached a stalemate; all factions were ready for mediation.[13]

The mediator in the second set of negotiations was Saudi Arabia. It called first (in September 1983) for a cease-fire between the warring parties and Syria, which had been an active participant in the latest round of fighting. It then negotiated with Syria and the Lebanese factions to have a conference in Geneva, Switzerland, to seek agreement on the main issues that divided them. The Geneva Conference convened from October 31 to November 4, 1983. Syria was represented in Geneva by its foreign minister and was technically an observer. Nevertheless, Syria played an important role in the negotiations by ensuring that the five Muslim leaders and the Maronite leader Sulayman Franjiya, who was Syrian, under influence, toed the line and did not break away from the position Syria wanted them to hold.[14]

The Geneva Conference achieved very little except to recommend to the president of Lebanon that the Lebanese-Israeli Agreement be abrogated and that an end be put to Israeli occupation of Lebanese territory. Each participant presented a plan for Lebanese political reform to the secretariat of the conference, but those plans were not fully discussed.[15]

A second round of talks was held in Lausanne, Switzerland, four and a half months later, in March 1984. It was the result of a further escalation of the fighting by Druze and AMAL militias against the Lebanese army in West Beirut. The fighting was orchestrated by Syria, which financed its Druze and AMAL allies, gave them logistical support, and advised them on military strategy. The result was the disintegration of the army for the second time. Another result was abrogation of the Lebanese-Israeli Agreement, which had been the major demand of the Muslim participants at the conference in Geneva.[16]

The negotiations at the Geneva and Lausanne conferences differed from those of 1975–76 in a number of ways. In 1983 and 1984 asymmetrical relations with Syria determined the issues that were discussed, the escalation of the fighting, and the results of the conferences. Although Syria continued to pretend that it was a neutral mediator in the conflict, in 1983 it had thrown its weight behind the Shiite and Druze militias and put pressure on those leaders who represented the northern parts of Lebanon where Syrian troops were stationed. Consequently the agenda of the negotiations in Geneva reflected primarily Syrian concern about the Lebanese-Israeli Agreement rather than the Lebanese concern about political reforms. It is noteworthy that a number of the Muslim leaders who pushed for the abrogation of the Lebanese-Israeli Agreement in Geneva had supported the agreement when it was first reached in May 1983. Political reforms were never really discussed in the second set of negotiations.

In 1983–84 the mediator's power was also different from that held by Syria in the first round of negotiations in 1975–76. Saudi Arabia was not a host-neighbor to Lebanon or to any party in the conflict. It did not pursue its own agenda in Lebanon, and it did not invite itself to mediate the conflict. Its only motive was to secure a peace agreement among the warring factions. It had no power on the ground to implement the resolutions of any agreement. Saudi help was sought by all major Lebanese factions to the conflict precisely for those reasons, and also because Saudi Arabia had good relations with all parties concerned, as well as a tradition of mediating conflicts in the Arab world. It also helped the process along by generously subsidizing its mediating efforts and getting the support of Western powers.

The Lausanne Conference was merely a way of formalizing the redistribution of power on the ground. The Shiite and Druze militias were on the ascendancy. Syria, through them, had achieved its major aim (at that time) of abrogating the Lebanese-Israeli Agreement. The Lausanne Conference resulted in a cease-fire and called for the formation of a cabinet of national unity, which was created in April 1984. That cabinet included all the major participants of the Geneva and Lausanne conferences, including militia leaders—among them the Shiite AMAL leader, who now became part of the government. The inclusion of Syria's major allies in the cabinet—the prime minister himself and the Druze and the Shiite militia leaders—was a major victory for Syria. That victory opened the way toward Syria's ultimate goal: the expansion of Syrian forces over Lebanese territory. The expansion began in an incremental, protracted way in September 1985 and was completed in October 1990. Each step was legitimized by the Lebanese cabinet, and after 1989 by both the cabinet and the president.

The Ta'if Conference

In comparison to the other two attempts at resolving the Lebanese conflict, the Ta'if negotiations were structurally the least representative of the actual warring factions in Lebanon. Despite the fact that they included the largest number of Lebanese political figures, they did not include any of the major leaders of militias or parties actually involved in the fighting. To find a formula to end the conflict, thirty-one Muslim and thirty-one Christian deputies, or sixty-two out of the seventy-one surviving members of the 1972 Lebanese Parliament, convened at Ta'if in Saudi Arabia in September 1989. However, the interim prime minister and commander of the army, General Michel 'Awn, who had been battling Syrian and Syrian-backed forces for the previous six months, did not attend. Nor did the head of the Druze community and leader of the Druze militia, or the leaders of the two major Shiite militias, AMAL and Hizballah, all of whom had been involved in the latest round of fighting on Syria's side. Absent also from the negotiating table were the four external powers who were operating on Lebanese soil and whose ouster had been requested on a number of occasions: Syria, Israel, Iran (which supported some Shiite militias), and the Palestinians (both PLO and non-PLO).

The Ta'if meeting took place as a result of intensive fighting, which started in March 1989 and continued almost uninterruptedly for six months. By September 1989 the fighting reached a stalemate when the Syrians imposed a naval blockade on Christian ports. The Arab world, France, and the United States criticized Syria's action and called for a settlement of the dispute.[17]

The fighting was primarily between the forces of the Lebanese army, which were located in the Christian sector and were headed by the Christian commander of the army and interim prime minister Michel 'Awn, and the Syrian army and the Druze militia. The Lebanese Forces—the Christian militia—fought on the side of the army; some members of the Shiite militia of AMAL joined the Syrians and the Druze. The army attempted to close down illegal ports in Muslim areas, which resulted in Syrian intervention on behalf of the Druze leader. Commander Michel 'Awn of the Lebanese army then turned the confrontation into a war of liberation against the Syrians.

Throughout the fighting 'Awn requested that the Syrians and the Lebanese army form a security committee to supervise a cease-fire between the two sides. He suggested that Lebanese-Syrian talks should follow to negotiate a withdrawal of Syrian troops from Lebanon and to discuss Syrian security interests. Syria, however, insisted that the conflict was intra-Lebanese, that it was not a party to the conflict, and had nothing therefore to discuss or negotiate with the Lebanese. Syria refused to hold any talks or be a party to the negotiations in Ta'if, claiming that its role in Lebanon was only that of a mediator.

The role of mediator at Ta'if, however, was undertaken by a tripartite Arab committee composed of the foreign ministers of Saudi Arabia, Algeria, and Morocco, assisted by the Arab League's assistant secretary-general, Al-Akhdar al-Ibrahimi. The committee was formed as a result of a decision by Arab heads of state at the Arab summit meeting in Casablanca in May 1989 to find a solution to the Lebanese crisis. The legitimacy of the mediator, therefore, rested on its regional support and the backing of the League of Arab States. The mediator had little power, however, to help implement an agreement, and the Saudis' only carrot appears to have been significant financial inducements to all parties concerned.

Three major issues were debated at the Ta'if Conference: political reforms, based primarily on the Constitutional Document of 1976; the withdrawal of all foreign forces from Lebanese territory; and the election of a new president, as Lebanon's Parliament had not been able to meet to elect a president since the previous president's term had expired a year earlier.

The issue of political reforms presented few problems at the Ta'if negotiations. The parties agreed to expand the number of deputies in Parliament from 99 to 108, with equal representation for Christians and Muslims rather than the existing 6:5 ratio for the two communities. The powers of the Maronite Christian president would be curtailed, and he would no longer be able to appoint the Sunni prime minister, who would be elected by Parliament instead. That in turn would strengthen the prime minister, and consequently increase the power of the Sunni community. The term of the Shiite Speaker of the House would be extended from one to four years, thus enhancing the Speaker's powers and through him those of the Shiite community. The parties also agreed that all Lebanese and non-Lebanese militias should be disbanded and that their weapons be surrendered to the state.

The divisive issue at the Ta'if negotiations was the role of the Syrian military forces. All but one of the Muslim deputies were hesitant about calling for the withdrawal of Syrian forces. The Christian deputies were divided; the majority wanted Syrian forces to leave Lebanon, but seven others, whose constituencies in northern and eastern Lebanon were under Syrian control, were on the side of the Muslim deputies.

After protracted mediation by the members of the tripartite Arab committee, and intensive Saudi-Syrian discussions, an agreement was reached on the wording of an accord. The accord was signed by fifty-eight of the sixty-two deputies; three Muslims and one Christian abstained. The agreement stated that Syria would help the Lebanese state to "impose its author-ity over all Lebanese territory" within a period of two years, after which Syria would redeploy its troops to specified areas in Lebanon. A second stage of the negotiations would then begin between the Lebanese and Syrian governments concerning the phasing out of Syrian troops from Lebanon.[18] Those security measures would be undertaken, according to the agreement, only after the agreement had been ratified, a new president had been elected, a new government had been formed, and the political reforms agreed upon had been implemented.

Most of the Ta'if accord was implemented, but some of it was not. Two weeks after the accord was signed the parliamentarians elected a new president, Rene Mu'awwad, as a first step to resolving the conflict. The commander of the army, Michel 'Awn, refused to recognize him, claiming that Mu'awwad was Syria's candidate rather than that of the Lebanese. Twenty days later Mu'awwad was assassinated. The parliamentarians then elected another president, Ilyas al-Hirawi; he was also rejected by the army commander, who claimed that presidential elections could not be free in a country under occupation. The commander then called for the withdrawal of Syrian troops.

The standoff between the newly elected president and the commander of the army led to the breakdown of internal security. From January to May 1990 there was fighting between those Christian forces who supported the commander's view that Syria should withdraw before free presidential elections could take place and those Christian forces (the Lebanese Forces militia) who were more willing to accept the Ta'if accord. In August 1990 the Ta'if reforms were passed by the Chamber of Deputies, and on October 13, 1990, Syrian troops were asked by President al-Hirawi to dislodge General 'Awn, who was the interim prime minister, from his enclave in Ba'abda. The general took refuge in the French Embassy, and ultimately in France. General 'Awn's troops surrendered to the new commander of the Lebanese army, General Emile Lahhud.

Although the Ta'if accord ended the internal war in Lebanon, it failed to disarm Hizballah, a major Shiite militia, and failed to stop the contrived low-intensity conflict that Syria and Iran supported in southern Lebanon against Israel and the South Lebanon Army. The price the Lebanese paid for ending the internal war was the domination of Lebanon by Syria in both the domestic and foreign spheres. This price was clearly embodied in the Treaty of Brotherhood, Cooperation, and Coordination that was signed in May 1991 by the Syrian and the Lebanese presidents. The treaty called for joint Lebanese-Syrian government institutions in the areas of defense, internal security, and foreign policy. Furthermore, five years after the adoption of the reforms Syria still refused to redeploy its troops, as the Ta'if Accord had stipulated.

Theoretical Implications of the Lebanese Negotiations

The negotiations to end Lebanon's internal conflict, and the political and military context in which they developed, contribute further insight into the theoretical aspects of conflict resolution as set out by Zartman in chapter 1. This section analyzes the Lebanese situation in relation to asymmetry, the structure of negotiations, the mediator's role, and the ripe moment.

Triangulation and Problems of Asymmetry

Triangulation in the Lebanese case has been structurally different from the classic model's triad of government, opposition, and host-neighbor. Because of Lebanon's de facto lack of separation of powers between the executive and the legislature, the government initially included, either in the cabinet or in Parliament, all parties to the conflict. There was no real opposition outside the political system. Consequently negotiations on issues of political reform could take place among government leaders themselves.

The army, at the outset a national army, could not be used for or against any group because it was representative of all the religious communities in Lebanon. The conditions for asymmetry therefore did not exist at the start of the conflict, but were created along the way.

Because the army could not be used initially, Lebanese politicians created an alternative paramilitary structure of armed militias. The most powerful leaders in the cabinet and in Parliament thus became those with militias who fought their battles on the ground, taking over territory, expelling constituents from their homes, and creating new facts. Political leaders who had no militias lost their bargaining powers in negotiations. In the 1975–76 negotiations, the middle-of-the-road traditional leaders could not have their voices heard because they did not command armed power on the ground.

A second way of creating asymmetry where there is none is to form alliances with foreign paramilitary groups; in the Lebanese case the foreign group was the Palestine Liberation Organization. The Lebanese leaders who sought the military force of the PLO changed the balance of power of the various communities on the ground and increased their own bargaining power at the negotiating table.

But it was the Syrian military intervention in 1976 (after the first set of negotiations fell through) that created the real basis for asymmetrical relations in the conflict in Lebanon. Siding first with the Christian forces and against its erstwhile allies—the predominantly Muslim National Movement and the Palestine Liberation Organization—Syria managed to receive regional and international approval and consequently legitimacy for its intervention in the conflict.[19]

With the Syrian intervention in Lebanon the conflict became triangularized and asymmetrical. Syria's armed forces in Lebanon increased in number and spread out over Lebanon, extending its political and military control over 80 percent of the Lebanese territory by the time of the last set of negotiations in 1989. In the meantime, however, the PLO forces in Lebanon were destroyed by the Israelis and could no longer play a significant role in the Lebanese conflict. Militias on both the Christian and Muslim sides proliferated, at times enhancing the power of their leaders in the political system and at other times fighting among themselves and weakening their leaders—thus increasing Syria's hold over the country.

It can therefore be concluded that the negotiations that had the most likely chance to succeed were those of 1975–76, when little asymmetry existed in the relations among the parties concerned. As asymmetry set in and Syria became the major power in Lebanon, the issues at the negotiating table began to focus on Syria's own interests rather than on those of the Lebanese parties. By the time of the Ta'if negotiations political reforms were accepted easily by everyone, and the divisive issue was the withdrawal of Syrian forces.

Thus the buildup of asymmetrical relations through the creation of militias, alliances with paramilitary organizations, and acceptance of external military intervention, was counterproductive. It worsened the conflict, increased the number of players, undermined the power of moderate leaders, waylaid the original issues of the conflict, introduced new problems, and prolonged the conflict. The success of the third set of negotiations, however limited, was contingent on accepting the asymmetry as permanent. This led to the domination of Lebanon by Syria and therefore the loss of Lebanese independence.

For the host to overcome such an asymmetrical situation the occupying forces would have to be defeated by a more powerful internal or external army, or would have to withdraw voluntarily because of the political or economic cost of maintaining the occupation, or would have withdrawn because of a domestic crisis requiring their redeployment at home.

The Structure of Negotiations

In the Lebanese case the groups that sought political reforms were not outside the pale of government. They were therefore not the typical opposition fighting for recognition and legitimacy. They were simply demanding a greater share of power. Furthermore, they were used to negotiation and compromise; the viability of the state for thirty years had been based on negotiation and power-sharing arrangements. The ''most important deal'' (in Zartman's terms) therefore was not the ''agreement to negotiate.'' The conflict occurred when the traditional process of negotiation broke down and the parties decided to resort to force to press for changes in the status quo. The conflict worsened when external forces became involved on one side or another.

In terms of structure, the most important deal in the Lebanese conflict revolved around who was included in the negotiations and who was excluded or chose not to join the negotiations. In the first set of negotiations, in 1975–76, the most important leaders of the warring factions, except for the PLO, were present at the negotiating table. The Constitutional Document that was drawn up then remained through the years the most viable agreement, on the basis of which all subsequent accords were made.

The next two attempts at reconciliation, however, did not include all the major parties to the conflict. At the Geneva and Lausanne talks fewer leaders participated. Some of the moderate leaders did not attend; nor was the army represented. More significantly, Syria, which had been directly involved in the fighting on two occasions and had provided arms and logistical support to one of the factions, chose to be an observer. Syria controlled the agenda and manipulated the participants, but was never an actual party to the negotiations. The meetings therefore served only as a vehicle for Syria's demands, and not as a means to negotiate the problems that divided the Lebanese.

The last attempt at negotiations was the least representative of the three, as it gathered together a group of parliamentarians who had no real power on the ground and who could not implement the reforms they agreed upon.

The heads of the major militia groups and the commander of the army were not represented, nor was Syria, which again had been party to the fighting. There was very little chance that the proposals made could be implemented without the voluntary consent of those absent leaders and parties.

Theoretically it follows that no solution to a conflict is likely to be successful if all the major parties to the conflict are not directly involved in the negotiations. Nor are substitutes likely to succeed, however legitimate and representative they may be, because they do not have the real power to implement the agreements—unless agreement is imposed by an external power seeking domination of the conflicted nation.

The Mediator's Role

A number of attempts at resolving some issues in the conflict in Lebanon have involved external mediators. Examples include mediation by Arab states in October 1976 to create an Arab deterrent force to ensure that the Palestine Liberation Organization would abide by the Cairo Agreement and that Lebanon would return to the status quo antebellum, Saudi Arabia's successful mediation of the Syrian siege of a Christian town in eastern Lebanon in June 1981, and mediation by the United States to solve the Lebanese-Israeli conflict in southern Lebanon.

But there have been only the three attempts discussed in this paper to mediate the conflict internally among all major parties concerned. In the second attempt, in 1983–84, Saudi Arabia first played the role of mediator as communicator and then the role of mediator as formulator.[20] It was primarily as a facilitator that Saudi Arabia brought the parties together in Geneva and in Lausanne. It had legitimacy, had been sought by all parties concerned, and had no interest in the conflict except in helping the parties find a solution. But Saudi Arabia had no power to pressure the participants to come to an agreement, and could provide only financial inducements if they succeeded. During the negotiations the Saudis had observer status and were not directly involved in the bargaining process.

Similarly, during the third attempt at negotiation in 1989, the tripartite committee of Arab foreign ministers acted as communicators and formulators. They helped convince the parliamentarians to attend the meetings, provided a neutral area (Ta'if) where participants could meet without fear for their safety, and communicated with Syria to ensure its support of the arrangements. The committee also actively encouraged the parties to reach an agreement and to sign the Ta'if Accord. In terms of mediation theory, the foreign ministers were successful mediators.

Syria was the mediator in the 1975–76 meetings, but its role was that of mediator as manipulator.[21] It had the ''power, influence, and persuasion that can be brought to bear on the parties to move them to agreement.''[22] It was successful in getting the parties together and in pushing forward the most important of the accords that were signed by Lebanese parties, the Constitutional Document of 1976. And yet in the final analysis those accords appear to have failed as well.

It can be contended that some mediators initially or eventually become active participants in the conflict. They become mediators not always to find a solution to conflicts but to advance their own interests. This is the case especially when those mediators are neighboring states that are in a position to take advantage of a breakdown of law and order to extend their influence directly or indirectly over the various parties in the conflict. It is therefore in such a neighbor's interest that the conflict be prolonged and that the parties concerned seek its help and become dependent on its political, economic, or military support. It is also to the neighbor's advantage that negotiations take place, now and then, that are mediated by others, and that such negotiations fail so the parties have no alternative but to seek the neighbor's help again.

It is also in the interest of such would-be mediators that no party to the conflict wins politically or militarily over the other. That would make the role of mediator superfluous and undermine its influence in the conflicted country. Such mediators—they are usually mediator-manipulators—are seen shifting their support to whichever party appears to be losing power during the conflict or during the negotiation process.

The Ripe Moment

One of the major reasons for the failure of the first two sets of negotiations in the Lebanese case was that the basic elements of the ripe moment were not present. Ripe moments occur, according to Zartman, when three elements are present: a mutually hurting stalemate, a formula for a way out, and valid spokespersons. Only in the first (1975–76) and third (1989) sets of negotiations were there mutually hurting stalemates. In the second set (1983–84) the Christian forces only were hurting and the Syrian-backed opposition was winning; consequently the Geneva and Lausanne negotiations formalized the gains made on the ground by the winning forces rather than addressing the demands of all parties concerned.

The formula for a way out was found in only two of the three attempts at conflict resolution: the first set of talks yielded the Constitutional Document of 1976, and the third set resulted in the Ta'if Accord of 1989. Both agreements had well-formulated provisions that addressed the demands of all the factions. In the Lausanne and Geneva talks, however, the issue of political reforms was never seriously addressed, even though each member did submit a proposal for discussion.

It was only in the 1975–76 talks that all the valid spokespersons for the main parties to the conflict participated in the negotiations. In 1983–84 only a few were present, and at Ta'if in 1989 none of the valid spokespersons participated. According to theory, therefore, only the first set of negotiations, held when the Lebanese conflict was only a few months old, occurred at the ripe moment and consequently had any chance of succeeding. Yet it was the third set of negotiations that succeeded—because the participants had no choice but to accept the Ta'if Accord.

One of the major obstacles to the resolution of the Lebanese conflict has been the assassination of the principal valid spokespersons for each of the major communities in Lebanon. Those assassinations occurred when the leaders appeared to be ready for negotiation and reconciliation. The head of the Druze community and the founder of the National Movement, Kamal Junblat, was assassinated in March 1977. He was the principal force behind the movement for reform during the 1975–76 period. Although an ally of Syria at the outset, by 1976 he had become strongly opposed to its role in Lebanon. He was replaced by his only son, a weaker leader, who has been since then one of Syria's principal allies in Lebanon.

In 1978 Imam Musa al-Sadr, the head of the Shiite Movement of the Disinherited, which would later become the AMAL movement, disappeared in Libya, where he was presumably assassinated. He was a powerful leader who had mobilized a strong Shiite following. He represented an alternative to the traditional Shiite leadership. Although a reformist too, he was a conciliator and had strong ties with some leaders in the Christian community. He was eventually replaced, in 1980, by a Shiite lawyer who became the major supporter of Syria's role in Lebanon.

In 1982 a young charismatic Maronite leader, Bashir Jumayyil, who had been elected president of Lebanon, was assassinated before taking office. As he campaigned for the presidency during the previous year he had created a large following among all the communities in Lebanon. He had called for reconciliation and reforms and for the withdrawal of all foreign troops from Lebanon. He was replaced by his brother, who lacked his national appeal and did not force the issue of the withdrawal of Syrian troops as a first priority.

In 1987 the Sunni prime minister from northern Lebanon, Rashid Karami, was assassinated. Although a traditional ally of Syria for years, he had just signed a secret agreement with the Christian leadership to resolve the Lebanese conflict. He was a traditional politician belonging to one of the most important Sunni families in Lebanon. He was replaced by a weak Sunni leader, a university professor who had no political base and was dependent on Syria for his power. Although a moderate politically, he had no power to institute reforms.

In 1989 the mufti Hasan Khalid, the highest religious authority in the Sunni community, was assassinated. He had called for reconciliation and for negotiations with the Christian leadership, and had been publicly critical of the Syrian role in Lebanon. He had the respect of all the major communities, and although not a political leader, had enormous political influence in the country.

Finally, the Maronite president Rene Mu'awwad, elected in 1989 after the Ta'if agreement was reached, was assassinated. There had been hope that he would be able to implement the agreed-upon reforms and pull Lebanon out of its quagmire. He was a moderate leader who had the support of all communities in Lebanon. A Maronite businessman was elected to the presidency a few days later; he had no political base of his own and was known to have close links with the Syrian regime.

The assassination of those valid spokespersons who sought negotiations and reconciliation has prevented a real dialogue among the Lebanese parties and has made the implementation of reforms almost impossible unless they are imposed.

Prospects for Future Negotiations

The Lebanese case adds certain elements to the framework of negotiations discussed in this book. It raises the issue of the collapse of the central power: Under what conditions does a regime collapse? What kind of regimes collapse? How does one recognize the collapse of a regime?

Some political scientists would argue that Lebanon's political system collapsed for sixteen years because it was unable to perform such basic functions as defending the territorial integrity of the state, preserving law and order, and distributing basic services. The central government was always weak in Lebanon. That was its strength: the strength of the willow that could bend with the wind when the oak could only break. Had the government been strong and democratic there presumably would have been no conflict; but had the government been strong and authoritarian there would have been opposition to it, attempts to overthrow it, and then the scenario of the government in power versus the opposition out of power.

Also, the Lebanese political system has never performed its basic functions very well in times of peace, and has done a little worse in times of war. It has been a matter of degree. For instance, it has always been understood that Lebanon could not defend its borders—it is too small, too weak; it has relied on external protection for border defense. On the other hand, Lebanese politicians have always performed basic services for their constituents, and they continued to do so during the conflict, if less efficiently than before. But law and order did break down, and it was redress of that problem the Lebanese were demanding from the time the conflict began.

A second issue raised by the Lebanese case is the role of the mediator. Who is the "ideal" mediator—the formulator, the communicator, or the manipulator? In the Lebanese conflict Saudi Arabia was on two occasions the most disinterested of all mediators. It exerted tremendous effort, time, and money to bring the parties together to resolve the conflict. It communicated with all parties concerned, it assisted in finding a formula for reforms, and offered many carrots to urge the negotiations forward, but it did not have the power to implement the agreements until the parties themselves were willing to settle their differences at Ta'if.

In Lebanon the only mediator to have the power to implement agreements has been Syria, or the manipulator. Because of Syria's power, which is primarily military, negotiations have been successful only when Syrian domination became part of the agreement itself (as in the Ta'if Accord). Syrian interests are served by the perpetuation of the conflict in southern Lebanon, by keeping certain militias (such as Hizballah) armed, and by keeping Syrian troops in Lebanon rather than deploying them or withdrawing them completely. The presence of Syrian troops allows the Syrian regime to control Lebanon politically and economically.

In Lebanon Syria has carried out acts of terrorism, such as bombing foreign embassies and taking western hostages, to serve its foreign policy interests, while blaming such acts on the various factions in the conflict. Pretending to confront the Israeli threat in Lebanon by maintaining a low-intensity conflict on Lebanon's borders, Syria has been able to justify domestically a continued state of emergency and regionally the presence of 40,000 Syrian troops in Lebanon. Lebanon has also been an economic safety valve for the Syrians, who suffer severe shortages in their state-controlled socialist economy but can find what they need on the free-wheeling Lebanese market.

Thus a manipulator may not be the ideal mediator either, because in a worst-case scenario such as the Lebanese conflict its interests may be best served by perpetuating the conflict rather than resolving it, unless the dominance of the manipulator is accepted as an integral part of the solution. At worst the interests of the manipulator may come before those of the conflicting parties and add new pressures and demands to an overburdened agenda, thus hampering the process of conflict resolution rather than facilitating it. In Lebanon, for example, the withdrawal of Syrian troops became an added thorny issue in the third set of negotiations. The way the Ta'if Accord has been implemented shows clearly that to find solutions for Lebanon's unresolved problems future negotiations must be undertaken without the pressure of a mediator-manipulator.

The role of communicator has been played by all external powers involved in the Lebanese conflict. However, that role often becomes the tool of the formulator and the manipulator, so the content and form of communication may not necessarily serve the interests of the conflicting parties. The communicator as a mediator is consequently useful only if completely independent from the other two roles. The ideal mediator would combine the best characteristics of all three mediators: it would communicate effectively, formulate options that best serve the interests of the parties to the conflict, and have the means and power to implement any agreement reached.

Notes

1. See Marius Deeb, *The Lebanese Civil War* (New York: Praeger, 1980), pp. 21–121 and pp. xiii–xiv.

2. Deeb, *Lebanese Civil War*, p. 3; *Al-Nahar*, September 25, 1975, p. 1.

3. The most prominent Christian leaders on the National Dialogue Committee (NDC) were Camille Sham'un, Pierre Jumayyil, and Raymond Edde. Sham'un was at the time a member of Parliament and a cabinet minister; he had been the president of the Republic in 1952–58. On the ground Sham'un controlled through his party (the National Liberals' Party) the second-largest Christian militia. Pierre Jumayyil was a member of

Parliament and a former cabinet minister, who through his Phalangist Party controlled the most powerful Christian militia. Raymond Edde was then a member of Parliament and a former cabinet minister. He was the leader of the Christian National Bloc, having succeeded his father Emile Edde, who had been president of the Republic before 1943. Although Raymond Edde refused to form a militia, he had considerable political clout because of his independent character and charismatic personality. The two remaining Christian members of Parliament, who were also former cabinet ministers, were Rene Mu'awwad, an ally of President Sulayman Franjiya (who hailed from the same Zgharta region) and Khatchik Babikian, a prominent politician representing the Armenian Tashnaq Party. Ghassan Tuwaini, a publisher and a journalist, and Philip Taqla, who had frequently served as minister for foreign affairs, were members of the cabinet but had no power on the ground. See Deeb, *Lebanese Civil War*.

4. Only Raymond Rabbat, who was a prominent jurist, a former university professor, and an expert on constitutional law, did not belong to the political establishment. Ilyas Saba and 'Abbas Khalaf, who were former cabinet ministers, were respectively proteges of President Franjiya and the Druze chief and head of the National Movement, Kamal Junblat. See Deeb, *Lebanese Civil War*, pp. 78–84.

5. Three of the four Sunnis were prominent politicians: Rashid Karami was prime minister at the time, and was also a member of Parliament; Sa'ib Salam was a member of Parliament and a former prime minister; 'Abdallah al-Yafi was a former prime minister and a former member of Parliament. Najib Qaranuh, a physician by profession, was not a member of the political establishment but was a protege of Sa'ib Salam. The leading Shi'i traditional politician, Kamil al-As'ad, who was the Speaker of Parliament, was member of the NDC. But the remaining Shiite members, Rida Wahid, Hasan 'Awadah, and 'Asim Qansu, were not members of the political establishment. The first two were prominent civil servants but had no political clout. Qansu was a leader of the pro-Syrian Ba'th Party in Lebanon; he headed a militia and worked for Syrian intelligence services—that is, he was Syria's protege.

6. On AMAL (Afwaj al-muqawama al-lubnaniyya, or Group of the Lebanese Resistance) and its founder, Imam Musa al-Sadr, see Marious Deeb, *Militant Islamic Movements in Lebanon: Origins, Social Basis and Ideology*, (Washington: Center for Contemporary Arab Studies, Georgetown University, 1986); Marius Deeb, "Shia Movements in Lebanon: Their Formation, Ideology, Social Basis, and Links with Iran and Syria," *Third World Quarterly*, vol. 10 (April 1988), pp. 683–98; Augustus R. Norton, *AMAL and the Shi'a: Struggle for the Soul of Lebanon* (University of Texas Press, 1987); Fuad Ajami, *The Vanished Imam* (Cornell University Press, 1986).

7. For the views of the Lebanese Front, see Deeb, *Lebanese Civil War*, pp. 37, 41, 54. The Cairo Agreement was an agreement between the Lebanese government and the PLO. It was signed in Cairo in November 1969 to regulate the armed presence of the PLO in Lebanon, confining it to the Palestinian camps and other regions of southern Lebanon. The Melkart Protocol was an addendum to the Cairo agreement, signed in Beirut in May 1973.

8. Deeb, *Lebanese Civil War*, pp. 74–78.

9. Al-As'ad refused to attend the meetings because as the Speaker of the House he believed he, rather than Prime Minister Karami, should preside over the NDC. Deeb, *Lebanese Civil War*, p. 79.

10. See Chapter 1.

11. Deeb, *Lebanese Civil War,* pp. 106, 124–37.

12. Deeb, *Lebanese Civil War,* pp. 85–87.

13. Marius Deeb, "Lebanon's Continuing Conflict," *Current History* vol. 84 (January 1985), p. 34.

14. George Bashir, Philip Abi 'Aql, and Fawzi Mubarak, *Umara' al-Tawa'if min Geneva ila Lausanne* (Beirut: Fanfal-Tiba'a Press, 1984), pp. 41–116.

15. Bashir, 'Aql, and Mubarak, *Umara' al-Tawa'if,* pp. 114–16.

16. Bashir, 'Aql, and Mubarak, *Umara' al-Tawa'if,* pp. 139–41.

17. Foreign Broadcast Information Service (FBIS) *Daily Report: Near East and South Asia,* September 25, 1989, p.38.

18. FBIS, *Daily Report: Near East and South Asia,* October 23, 1989, p. 4.

19. Deeb, *Lebanese Civil War,* pp. 11, 17–19.

20. On a mediator's role and choice of method, see Saadia Touval and I. William Zartman, eds., *International Mediation in Theory and Practice* (Boulder, Colo.: Westview Press, 1985) pp. 10–14.

21. Touval and Zartman, *International Mediation*, pp. 12–13.

22. Touval and Zartman, *International Mediation,* p. 12.

CHAPTER SEVEN

Negotiating the
South African Conflict

I. William Zartman

NEITHER HISTORY nor analysis could have predicted a negotiated out-come to the internal conflict in South Africa. In history there is no precedent anywhere for successful negotiations allowing a poor majority to take over from or even to share power with a rich minority when majority and minority identify and are identified ascriptively. That only happens by revolution or by postcolonial replacement. From an analytic standpoint, all the reasons enumerated in chapter 1 for the difficulty of negotiating an internal conflict exist so strongly in South Africa as to make negotiation there appear impossible. For negotiation to succeed in South Africa an apparent sociopolitical miracle would be required.[1] If miracles are not part of social science analysis, at least unique events are. The crowning lesson from South Africa is that human events are not prisoners of history: unprec-edented events can take place. The South African case tells the conditions and processes necessary to make difficult internal negotiations succeed.

The South African conflict came to negotiation because of a mutually hurting stalemate—not a short-lived, sharply marked deadlock as in Angola in 1987 and 1990 (see chapter 8), but a gradual long-term realization by

I am grateful to Timothy Monahan for his help in the research for this chapter, to the MacArthur Foundation for its support, to the United States-South Africa Leadership Exchange Program (USSALEP) for its assistance, and to a large number of colleagues in South Africa for their aid in interviews and appointments.

both sides that the current course was a dead end, as in the conflicts in Colombia and Afghanistan (see chapters 10 and 11). After the mid-1980s the perception of asymmetry was slowly replaced by the realization of symmetry and the understanding that the white minority government could not control the black majority at acceptable cost just as the black majority could not overthrow the white government at acceptable cost. For the whites to preserve the status quo would have meant a retreat to the laager, and hence a destruction of the status quo; for the blacks to impose a new order would have required a bloodbath, and hence anarchy or costly disorder. As Joe Slovo, head of the South African Communist Party (SACP), put it, "neither side won the war. The National Party [NP] couldn't rule any longer, and we [the African National Congress, or ANC] couldn't seize power by force. So that means both sides have to compromise. That's the reality."[2]

But that is only half the picture. To the arising symmetry of power was opposed a symmetry of commitment. It would be a mistake to understand the remarkable volte-face in South African politics that occurred in 1990 as a conversion of either side to the views of the other. Each side maintained its vision of an acceptable outcome. To President F. W. de Klerk and his followers there were four aspects to the inadequacy of the old regime: the regime was no longer able to provide security and prosperity for the privileged minority; it was unable to contain and control the dispossessed majority; it had lost international legitimacy and brought pariah status on itself and its own banishment from the world community; and the cost for all these shortcomings was steadily mounting beyond the country's economic capacity.[3]

The failure of the old regime as a system of governance, however, does not mean that the party associated with it is about to disappear. It still has its own existence as a player and its own interests to defend as it embarks on a search for a replacement regime. Negotiation thus became a matter of identifying how much of the old order could be retained in the construction of a new regime, while recognizing that a new regime would not even have a chance of working if it were not determined with the participation of the formerly excluded majority. The whites led by de Klerk still wished to maintain their dominant position in society and their privileged way of life; the blacks led by ANC president Nelson Mandela wished to achieve majority rule and to buy into that way of life. What changed was their mutual appreciation of the means to that end. Each side realized that in a situation of symmetry it could not achieve its ends without the agreement of the other side, and thus that negotiation was the preferred means.

The new shared commitment to a negotiatory means implied a mutual understanding of reduced ends, but not a new shared commitment to the same outcome, until perhaps the very end. Thus each side played hard on the other's understanding of the new implications in order to force concessions on the outcome from the other side. As the talks continued they ran into crises over the way in which conflicting goals could be crammed into the same outcome. At each crisis the parties broke off the talks and postured in very real ways to remind one another of their ability to invoke a painful alternative. They then returned to the bargaining table and resumed negotiations. At each turn the governing National Party made most of the concessions on the distribution of power so as to remain part of the process after power changed hands in elections. The trade-off of power for position in the creation of a new political system is a classical bargaining strategy.

Crises, showdowns, ruptures, and reevaluations are normal events in negotiations,[4] but that does not make them any less real, dramatic, and critical. Outcomes can turn either way, depending on unpredictable elements such as the parties' evaluation of the stakes, their ability to bluff and force the other party, the real differences that separate their positions regardless of the acceptability of any alternatives, and the commitment of their spokespersons and their clienteles. In South Africa commitment has been particularly important. The ANC is a national liberation movement looking for a takeover of power, and if its spokespersons do not measure up to that image they face replacement.[5] The white majority has been trained to enjoy power, and if the National Party does not continue to exercise it voters can defect to other organizations that will defend laagers of their own. Thus equally as important as the horizontal negotiations—the "pact" between the African National Congress and the National Party that exchanges power for position[6]—are the ongoing vertical negotiations between these two elites and their followers. But there is one difference in their symmetry of commitment—the direction of change. In historic terms, the outcome moved from the National Party's position to the African National Congress's position, so the original asymmetry has been reversed. Destruction of incumbent authority, which is the ANC's alternative or security point, is a closer threat than maintenance of that authority, which is the NP's alternative point.

Unfortunately for the smoothness of the process, the ANC and the NP are not the only players in South Africa. As the conceptual framework in chapter 1 indicates, the closer the parties come to the resolution of their conflict, the greater the pressures for splits in the sides. Because the two major parties and their associates (such as the trade unions) are represented by spokespersons from the middle of the two sides rather than from their moderate fringes, the splits come from the edges of the two sides—the extremes and the bypassed moderates. Both fringes see the elite pact as a way to their own marginalization, and have tried either to undercut the elites and capture some of their masses or to derail the process that threatens their power, as spoilers. It is the ultimate curse inherited from the old regime of apartheid that the ability of such groups to do both will last long after the resolution of the conflict has been negotiated.

Confrontation over Competing Formulas and Regimes

The South African conflict arose from the whites' attempt to turn a long-implanted colonization into a bizarre caricature of itself. Just at the moment when other colonial regimes were gradually opening the doors of political participation and social equality to their subjects, leading to the eventual replacement of the regime, South Africa's white minority constitutionally turned the African majority into nonpersons, beyond the pale of political life. As the gap between the historic world trend and egregious South African practice grew more manifest, both through the increasing measures of apartheid and through the gradual awakening of African consciousness,[7] the conflict intensified. Perception of the gap was heightened by the open appearance of contradictions within the government position as white ruling society became more and more dependent on black urban labor, yet could not permit blacks to be part of urban society and got tied up in extraordinary legal contortions over the definition of a black.

Following the election of the Afrikaners' National Party to power in 1948 the debate on both sides of the color bar focused on the position of the majority in regard to government. The government's repression of the Defiance Campaign of 1952 against apartheid legislation led to the Congress of the People and its adoption of the Freedom Charter in 1956. In the ensuing Treason Trial, Nelson Mandela came out in favor of negotiations leading to gradual change and universal franchise. The Sharpeville demonstrations and massacre of 1960 marked a turning point that confirmed the conflict over means as well as that over ends, in the clash of the majority's nonviolent protest strategy and the government's violent repression. The All-African Conference before the declaration of the republic in May 1961 demanded a fully representative national convention to establish a union of all South Africans, and Mandela, writing to Prime Minister Hendrik Verwoerd, called for a national convention representative of all South Africans to draw up a nonracial and democratic constitution. In response, Mandela was charged at the Rivonia trial with plotting to overthrow the republic and was sentenced for life to the Robben Island prison. By the time of the trial, in 1963, the African National Congresses' position had evolved to encompass both nonviolent civil disobedience and violent sabotage to force government to convene a representative national convention to negotiate a new nonracial constitution.

The reform program of the National Party, initiated after the Soweto riots of 1976 but stepped up sharply after the accession of P. W. Botha as prime minister two years later, failed both to meet the majority expectations it had aroused and to consolidate the minority hold on the country. It was out of the gradual realization of this failure, on both sides, that stalemate arose. The constitutional reforms—known as dispensations in South Africa—of 1983, nearly a decade in preparation, created a tricameral parliament under a powerful state president, but locked blacks out of even the minimal participation newly opened to the coloureds and Asians. Rising pressure caused the government to cast about for ways out of its contradictions. Botha created a cabinet committee to draw up a plan for the constitutional future of urban blacks, whose permanent existence he acknowledged for the first time. Rural blacks had already been relegated to the "independence" of the homelands, which were achieving their formal status one by one over the period. Botha also authorized the first of an ongoing series of contacts with Mandela by Justice Minister Hendrik Coetsee, beginning in July 1984.[8]

On the majority side, expectations suddenly burst out of control in 1985 as the youth came to feel that they had nothing to gain from the current system and nothing to lose by taking matters into their own hands. Fed by the memories of the Black Consciousness movement and the heroes of 1976 who had joined ANC training camps abroad, they declared that liberation must precede education, launched school boycotts and community sit-ins, and created "liberated areas" in townships. The active wing of the majority finally adopted violence and self-organization and thus brought the stalemate of consolidation and violence into focus. The ensuing state of emergency crushed activities, dashed hopes, and led to the gradual awareness of a deadlock in which neither side saw an ability to prevail. Thus the first round of confrontation over the way to reform, fought over the competing formulas of dispensation and negotiation, ended in the rejection of dispensation as a formula for dealing with the crisis and moved toward a further definition of negotiation as a formula.

There then began the long process of opening negotiations about negotiations—deciding the conditions under which talks about the conditions under which talks about constitutional change would take place. Botha began discussions with Mandela in early 1985, offering release from prison if Mandela would live in Transkei and the African National Congress would unconditionally renounce violence. "The choice is his," declared Botha. "All that is requested of him is that he should unconditionally reject violence."[9] The government's strategy was to shift focus to the renunciation of violence by the protesters and to reduce the majority's position to that of a petitioner, in both cases seeking to destroy the stalemate by creating a situation of inequality between the two sides.

Mandela, in his first interview since the 1960s, declared that the ANC would call a truce in its armed struggle if the government "would legalize us, treat us like a political party and negotiate with us," and that "armed struggle was forced upon us by the government and if they want us to give it up, the ball is in their court." "Only free men can negotiate freely," he declared; "prisoners cannot enter into contracts."[10] As a result of the deadlock the African National Congress hardened its position and increased its commitment to pressure, emphasizing the need to seize power and rejecting negotiation. To the formula "Mandela in exchange for nonviolence," the ANC responded with "legality in exchange for nonviolence, but thanks for bringing up the release of Mandela," and Botha's gambit became an albatross. Although the government then continued to consider conciliatory moves, a series of events in the summer of 1985 made Botha stop dead in the water and instead deliver a finger-wagging display of belligerence in an important speech to a National Party congress in Durban in August, in which he wrapped reform in the political jargon of local Afrikaner politics.

In reaction to government's dropping the ball, the private community picked it up and ran with it intensely, for a while. Anglo-American Corporation chairman Gavin Reily, among others, declared that it was necessary for the government to enter into real negotiations with representatives of all groups for a new political system of genuine power sharing, and then led a group of businessmen to meet with African National Congress representatives in Zambia; on their return the group called for the abolition of apartheid, negotiations with "acknowledged black leaders," and the convocation of a national convention.[11] In November 1985 the government indicated to the ANC leadership that Mandela could be released to Zambia, but the ANC rejected the offer, instead calling on the government to create a "climate conducive to talks about talks" and specifying the necessary conditions—release of all political prisoners, lifting of the state of emergency, suspension of political trials, and acknowledgment of talks with the African National Congress.

A new government initiative, in February 1986, invited blacks to sit on a national statutory council under Botha's chairmanship; "my government and I," Botha stated, "are committed to power-sharing."[12] The offer was rejected because the state of emergency remained in effect. Secret talks with Mandela in Cape Town in July, by the ministers of justice and constitutional development, also came to naught. Both sides pulled back to their conditions. Again the private sector rushed in to fill the gap, putting pressure publicly and privately on the government. A meeting of African National Congress and Afrikaner Broederbond representatives on Long Island, New York, in June turned sour, but a similar meeting in Dakar, Senegal, sponsored by the Institute for Democratic Alternatives in South Africa (IDASA) was more productive, reinforcing the call for negotiations and underscoring the inherence of force to the politics of racial domination, and thus of counterforce to its removal.[13]

As a result, inching closer to the position of its opponents, the government published a bill in September 1986 that would give blacks who were "ordinarily resident" outside the homelands a chance to vote for a multiracial advisory council that would have an open agenda and constitutional drafting powers. At the same time the government was working on its own framework for constitutional change and negotiation. The framework was based on seven principles: equal participation by all citizens outside the independent homelands, no domination by any single group, maintenance of peace and stability throughout the negotiations, constitutional reform accompanied by social and economic reform, decentralization of decisionmaking, maintenance of Christian values and norms, and maintenance of a private enterprise economy. Reform took a new turn but reached a dead end in 1988 as the government pursued its aim of granting limited black participation rather than negotiating full and equal participation. Black township councils and coloured management committees were established in July and elections were held in October, but were boycotted by the electorate. Attention then returned to focus on the African National Congresses' preconditions for meaningful dialogue.

Annoyed with the slow pace of the release of political prisoners, which he insisted must precede his own release, Mandela drew up a political statement on appropriate measures for the government to take to prepare the country for dialogue. He also requested a meeting with Botha, which took place on July 6, 1989. Botha agreed to the release of historic ANC figures, including former general secretary Walter Sisulu, after the white elections of September had shown support for F. W. de Klerk as his successor. De Klerk's accession to National Party leadership in February 1989 and then to the state presidency in August was the occasion for further movement and clarification of the government position. He announced that whites would share limited power with the black majority in a ''new chapter'' in the nation's history, but invited the African National Congress to a ''process of dialogue and negotiation'' if it would endorse Mandela's statement by ''committing itself to the pursuit of peaceful solutions''—a watered-down version of the previous demand for unconditional renunciation of force.[14] The ANC responded with an endorsement by the Organization of African Unity (OAU) of its own framework for negotiations and elections leading to majority rule, ruling out mediated transitions such as that undertaken by the British at Lancaster House for Zimbabwe in 1979; according to an OAU declaration made at Harar, Ethiopia, the government would have to create a ''climate for negotiations'' by lifting the state of emergency, releasing political prisoners, legalizing political organizations, withdrawing troops from the townships, and ending political trials and executions.[15]

Immediately upon his election as state president, de Klerk began to take actions to answer the ANC's prenegotiation demands and other measures to create a climate for dialogue. After releasing the former African National Congress and Pan-Africanist Congress (PAC) leaders, he loosened restrictions on protests and authorized demonstrations, met with Archbishop Desmond Tutu and other antiapartheid clerics, ordered desegregation of beaches and four urban residential areas and announced imminent desegregation of other public places, limited the security forces' formerly dominant role in regional and local government, and moved responsibility for security from the State Security Council to his own cabinet.

As a result, the struggle to retain ''Mandela in exchange for non-violence'' and similar trade-offs was finally dropped and a deal put together on the basis of the ANC's formula, ''legality in exchange for non-violence'' (although neither element was fully achieved at first). De Klerk changed his offer, meeting only one condition fully—he lifted the ban on the African National Congress and other political parties on February 2,

1990—but did fulfill the others in large measure: the release of some prisoners (including Mandela) and the suspension of some provisions of the emergency. He agreed that "only a negotiated understanding among the representative leaders of the entire population is able to insure lasting peace. . . . The agenda is open and the overall aims . . . include: a new democratic constitution; universal franchise; no domination; equality before an independent judiciary; the protection of minorities as well as of individual rights; freedom of religion; a sound economy based on proven economic principles and private enterprise; dynamic programs directed at better education, health services, housing and social conditions for all."[16]

On the other side, neither the African National Congress nor Mandela renounced violence. "There are further steps as outlined in the Harar Declaration that have to be met before negotiations on the basic demands of our people can begin," Mandela announced upon his release from prison on February 11, 1990. "The people need to be consulted on who will negotiate and on the content of such negotiations. . . . The future of our country can only be determined by a body which is democratically elected on a nonracial basis."[17] Thus the imminent closure of one round of preconditions to negotiations opened a second round, over whether the installation of nonracial politics would precede or follow constitutional negotiations.

Up to the turning point of February 1990 much preliminary movement was achieved by tacit negotiations conducted through public pronouncements and pressures, involving alternative formulas and discrete concessions and punctuated at the end by a few face-to-face meetings. Nothing touched the basic issues, yet in maneuvering over some of the preconditions the two sides measured strength, converged stands, adumbrated formulas, validated spokespersons, defined processes, clarified goals, and positioned themselves for future negotiations on negotiations.

Talks about Talks

The negotiations comprising the second round were much more explicit and direct than those of the first round. They were structured about four full-scale meetings between Mandela and an ANC team and de Klerk and a government team on May 2–4, 1990, in Cape Town, on August 6, 1990, in Pretoria, and separate meetings on February 12 and 25–26, 1991, in Cape Town; a number of other meetings between the two leaders were held in between. These prenegotiations were talks about talks, designed to identify and eliminate the obstacles or preconditions to constitutional negotiations. The Groote Schuur Minute from the May 1990 session cited the identification of, release, and immunity for political prisoners as the main task of a working group of technicians; the government agreed to "review security legislation" and "work toward lifting the state of emergency" in exchange for an African National Congress (and government) pledge to "curb violence and intimidation."[18] The two elements of the agreement provided a balance of concessions and benefits between the two parties. The Pretoria Minute from the August 1990 session resolved the issue of political offenses, and committed the government to give immediate consideration to repeal of certain offensive provisions of the Internal Security Act and to "consider lifting the state of emergency in Natal" (the only province where it remained in effect) in exchange for ANC suspension of all armed actions. "Against this background," the minute declared, "the way [is] open to proceed towards negotiations on a new constitution."[19]

However, it took two more meetings, in February 1991, to put together refinements of the formula, which were embodied in the D. F. Malan Accord. At the first February meeting the government agreed not to demand the disbanding of the small guerrilla branch of the ANC, Umkonto we Sizwe (Spear of the Nation, or MK), which the ANC could not have accepted, and the African National Congress agreed not to activate the guerrilla group but to use organized political protests instead, which the government agreed to tolerate. With this agreement the way was clear for the government to proceed with the release of political prisoners and the return of exiles, as decided at the previous round, by the end of April.

The focus of the second February meeting was different: a leap was made over procedural and constitutional issues into substantive policy. The meeting dealt with education, which, with land policy, was the primary payoff issue of immediate concern to the ANC rank and file. Thus the meeting set up a study group to recommend policy on a matter whose solution would normally depend on prior constitutional reforms.

The events of February 1990 through February 1991 completed the bargain on the formula "legality in exchange for nonviolence" and the defeat of the counterformula "only Mandela in exchange for nonviolence," thereby opening up bargaining over several other procedural principles that would lead to negotiations.[20] The first procedural question was, Are negotiations to be interracial or nonracial? Interracial talks would represent a revolution *within* the apartheid regime because they would be the culmination of a separate-but-equal doctrine, restoring the long-denied second element. Nonracial talks would represent a revolution *of* the apartheid regime because racial categories would no longer be the basis of representation. But what would be the basis? It is hard to find alternative criteria that would not contain hidden racial filters. Direct at-large election would reflect the dominance of the black majority; smaller constituencies would reflect the racial balance of their populations as they are gerrymandered. Even a different, nongeographical basis such as corporatism would betray the pervasive imprint of the apartheid regime: most South African unions are black, most management is white. Political parties, the normal candidates for political representation, have tried to escape the confrontation by seeking to be nonracial, but the National Party has attracted only a few black (mainly coloured) members, the Inkatha Freedom Party (IFP) got little response to its multiracial appeal (prefaced in Zulu), and white members in the African National Congress have reflected only their position as the minority.

The second procedural question was, Shall the negotiations be hierarchical or equal? Or more specifically, Is the minority's representative a party among others or are the talks to be convened and presided over by the government? The first option, favored by the African National Congress, would see talks between the National Party and the ANC, and possibly other parties; the second, favored by the National Party, would see talks by the government with the ANC and others. Throughout 1990 it had never been clear whether it was the National Party or the government that confronted the ANC at Groote Schuur and Unity House (Pretoria), until the issue was finally resolved in favor of the first option at an NP "bush indaba" (country meeting) in January 1991. But the basic issue still was not settled, and the first round resolution by the beginning of 1991 gave rise to new and deeper, even substantive questions. Even if the negotiations were between two parties, were they to be over eventual joint participation in government or over the transfer of powers from one party to the other? And when would these various steps take place?

As time went on, it became evident to the majority that all talks were about the future and that in the meantime the National Party continued to rule as the government. At the first ANC national conference inside South Africa in thirty-two years, held at the beginning of July 1991, Mandela demanded the installation of an interim government of national unity immediately, before the creation of a constituent assembly or the promulgation of a new constitution. It has been noted that de Klerk's view of the outcome was a treaty, whereas Mandela's view was a surrender; in this difference lay the core of the crisis of 1992 and the basic issue of the constitutional negotiations. It was only at the very end that the multiparty notion of the negotiations was accepted, with only a few minor holdouts from the white right.

The third procedural question concerned the underlying nature of the final bargain: Was it to be a bilateral deal between two mainstream leaderships, or an all-inclusive consensus of all parties? Consensus is an optimum solution, but any internal negotiation reaches agreement at the price of some exclusion, the crucial wager being over whether enough of the moderate middle is included in the bargain to form a winning coalition (see chapter 1). It is in the interest of both negotiating parties to restrict participation to those susceptible of reaching an agreement, but it is also in the interest of each to bring in as many of their extremes as necessary to strengthen their bargaining positions. The popular image of an agreement among whites in South Africa was the pact, but that notion gave fuel to critics who portrayed the negotiations as a black and white elite bargain between Mandela and his followers and de Klerk and his followers. This was the cry of both the Pan-Africanist Congress on the left and the Inkatha Freedom Party on the right, who saw the emerging constitution as a deal to deprive them of their power and their principles. The ideal of consensus, which the major parties went to great lengths to achieve, proved in the endgame in 1994 to be a source of power for the last major holdout, the Inkatha Freedom Party.

The approach of final negotiations to end the internal conflict, which had for so long seemed merely a fantasy, opened up new forms of conflict within the majority that were related to the third procedural question. Before the ban on the ANC was lifted in February 1990, the largest legal organization and domestic spokesman within the majority was Inkatha, the Zulu association led by Chief Gatsha Buthelezi, chief minister to the Zulu king. But the absence of other legal organizations meant that the real size of Inkatha was uncertain. That uncertainty alone would have been enough to occasion tests of strength and outbreaks of violence. But unbanning propelled the ANC on the scene with such popularity that Inkatha began to lose members rapidly. In danger of losing its place at the table as well, just as negotiations finally became a possibility, and threatened by aggressive ANC recruiting, Inkatha, Buthelezi, local warlords, and neighborhood groups all reacted violently. In an attempt to bolster its position, on July 21, 1990, Inkatha declared itself a political party—the Inkatha Freedom Party—open to all and launched its own recruitment campaign beyond the province of Natal, where the Zulu territories are located. Other, related events took place: the South African Communist Party staged a reentry rally on July 29, and the ANC launched new sections, particularly in Cape Province, on August 4. (The African National Congress and its earlier breakaway, the Pan-Africanist Congress, had gotten used to their split, which began in 1959 over tactics.) But in the 1990s the ANC-Inkatha war escalated out of control as the two rivals positioned themselves first for negotiations and then, by the end of 1992, when the demands of the IFP's thin-skinned leader came to be recognized as imprecise and extravagant, for open civil war over whether elections for a transfer of power should be held at all.

In April 1991 the African National Congress demanded an end to the township violence and broke off negotiations. Again the private sector intervened, as business and church leaders worked for months to restore communications among the parties. Weakened by revelations of police complicity in IFP funding, the government addressed some of the ANC's concerns, and in mid-September the three parties met with other political and labor organizations in the company of religious and civic groups to sign a National Peace Accord on September 14, 1991.[21] Although the accord was designed to meet the causes of violence at multiple levels with a code of conduct for both political and security forces, and with national, regional, and local dispute resolution mechanisms, it took hold only slowly and suffered from a lack of means of enforcement. Government complicity in the violence merely hid in deeper levels of clandestinity,[22] and outbreaks of violence created their own self-perpetuating cycles of revenge.

Substantive Negotiations: CODESA

The signing of the National Peace Accord completed the removal of obstacles to substantive negotiations. These were undertaken at the Convention for a Democratic South Africa (CODESA) of nineteen political organizations, which met on December 20–21, 1991, and again (abortively) on May 15–16, 1992. Its first round produced a declaration of intent, an agreed list of constitutional principles, and five working groups that were to carve out the specifics.[23] The declaration began the process of finding a formula for agreement, with some specific trade-offs between the two main parties' positions clearly indicated (for example, it stated that "the electoral system will be based on the principle of equal franchise for adults and the principle of proportionality [proportional representation]''). But it only opened the basic questions of difference between the two sides, rather than producing a formula for agreement.

Negotiations continued in the working groups, gradually moving the two sides closer together. Bargaining went on over the new constitution, the interim arrangements, and the timetable for both—all separate elements but intimately related. The National Party's position, also subscribed to by most white liberals, was to retain a cooperative government of joint responsibility—power-sharing—as long as possible;[24] the constitution would protect group rights through such pluralist mechanisms as a bicameral legislature, proportional representation, and federal devolution of power to regional governments. The African National Congresses' position called for an all-parties conference to set up an immediate, short-lived interim government of national unity that would organize an early election for a constituent assembly, based on the principle of one-person, one-vote, to bring in a black majority and immediately write a constitution; the constitution would guarantee individual rights and provide for centralized government.[25]

National Party acceptance of CODESA as an all-party congress of nineteen political organizations was a major step toward the African National Congress, but the NP looked on CODESA itself, rather than some subsequently elected body, as the constituent assembly while the NP remained in power as the government. In January 1992 the National Party shifted its position to consider the CODESA-generated constitution provisional, but still hoped that these transitional arrangements would last for a while. In response the African National Congress called for an interim government of national unity to be appointed by mid-1992, and a constituent assembly to be elected by the end of that year. Facing the gap in their positions, the parties then took further steps toward each other. The African National Congress dropped its demand for an immediate interim government and substituted for it a transitional executive council (TEC), which would supervise existing institutions—National Party government, the NP-dominated Parliament, and the security forces. The council would also establish an independent media commission (IMC) to supervise the media and an independent election commission (IEC) to supervise elections for a constituent assembly within six months of its appointment. The newly elected assembly would be both a parliament and a drafting body, to produce a constitution by a two-thirds vote within nine months of its election. National Party acceptance of the principle of an elected constituent assembly was another enormous step, but the process of convergence then collapsed over the two-thirds figure, with the NP holding out for a three-quarters vote of approval.

While the working groups were carving out the specifics, both sides and all parties worked on their power relations. Their power came from two sources—the solidarity of support within the group each claimed to represent, and the means of pressure each could bring to bear on the others. The government set about to abolish the legal manifestations of the apartheid system and thus gain international support and lifting of the sanctions applied in the mid-1980s. The African National Congress and the Inkatha Freedom Party continued their bloody strife in an effort to damage each other as spokespersons for the black population. Confidence in both the ANC and NP began to slip among their constituents in early 1992 as the new process brought no quick benefits for the majority and specters of danger for the minority. As the two parties appeared to lose support, each took a tougher stance in order to strengthen its position among its followers and to gain a crucial edge over the opponent in a time of weakness, and each questioned whether the opponent was representative enough to merit concessions and to hold to a deal.

The weaker party of the moment appeared to be the National Party. It had been losing support in by-elections since the 1990 policy change, and suffered a particularly significant loss to the Conservative Party in Potchefstroom in February 1992. A flagging economy, rising domestic crime and violence, and a sudden drought contributed to the NP's weakened position, making it impossible for de Klerk either to drive a hard bargain or to stall in the negotiations at a crucial point. With his customary gambler's instinct, however, de Klerk called a referendum among the whites on "the reform process . . . and . . . a new constitution through negotiation" on March 17, 1992.[26] He won nearly 70 percent support in the referendum. The African National Congress had quietly endorsed the campaign for a yes vote. Although the results gave solid backing to negotiations to resolve the South African conflict, they also gave the National Party a strengthened position. At the CODESA meeting on May 15–16, 1992, the NP refused the ANC offer of 70 percent as the vote required for the constitution, as well as the ANC's demand for a limitation on the transition period, now doubled to eighteen months. In June, shaken by a particularly bloody outburst of Inkatha Freedom Party violence at Boipatong, which occurred with alleged police connivance, the African National Congress broke off the CODESA talks.[27]

The breakdown over a difference of five points on a figure was not frivolous. It had to do with an important issue in a process that was moving haltingly to a closure that pleased each side more in principle than in detail. The issue concerned the cohesion of the parties' support groups and the relation of solidarity making to problem solving in the final stages of the negotiations. Neither side was sure of the support it could count on in the negotiations and then translate into votes in the ensuing one-person, one-vote elections. The African National Congress was assured of most of the black votes (blacks were 75 percent of the population, although half were under voting age) but not sure of the other groups in an election; in the negotiations it was torn between the moderates (supporters of a pact) and radicals (expecting a takeover). The radicals included not only militants such as the returned exiles and the trade-union leaders, but also the mass of grass-roots followers in the townships. Thus the Boipatong incident provided a test for the party leadership, and the offer of 70 percent began to look like the highest level at which the hurdle could be placed with confidence. The National Party was heartened by the support shown for the negotiations in the referendum, but was also uncertain of how large a vote it could muster from white, coloured, and Asian voters in the elections. Thus even the 70 percent hurdle, which the NP finally accepted before the process was interrupted, may have been too low to live with.

The crisis and breakdown of negotiations in mid-1992 was another round of the rupture and reevaluation that characterizes such negotiations as they come closer to the point of agreement. At each crisis the parties return to the basic components of power and commitment, reaffirming their current positions on each count and reevaluating the projected outcome, its alternatives, and the chances of inflecting it in their favor. Each crisis too returned to the tactical question, allowing the more radical wing of leadership to try its hand at producing better results. In mid-1992 the African National Congress reactivated its source of power and commitment, calling a rolling mass action that included a general strike in Pretoria, but that ended tragically on September 7 at a march on Bisho, capital of the Ciskei homeland, at which a police confrontation killed some twenty-eight marchers.

The confrontation sobered the ANC moderates, discredited the radicals, and brought Mandela and de Klerk together again three weeks later to agree to a Record of Understanding that set up the formula for a final agreement.[28] Democratic elections would open an interim period of fixed duration, with an interim government of national unity and an interim parliament serving as constituent assembly; the assembly would be free to design a constitution, limited only by the principles adopted in the preelection negotiations. The African National Congress, adopting an idea launched by Communist Party leader Slovo, then dropped its goal of winner-take-all majority rule and in mid-November accepted the idea of power sharing with the National Party during and beyond the transitional period after the elections. By mid-February 1993 the two parties had begun to clothe this formula with details by agreeing to a multiparty transitional executive council (TEC) to oversee the current government up to elections, now scheduled for early 1994, and to a government of national unity (composed of parties winning more than 5 percent of the national vote) to share power for a five-year transition period after the elections. The formula had been established, combining early majority rule with guaranteed minority participation through the end of the decade.

The Record of Understanding also marked the final shift of the National Party into a wary pact with the African National Congress and away from its alliance with the Inkatha Freedom Party.[29] The kwaZulu-based IFP made its own alliance with white extremist groups, notably the Conservative Party, and with other homeland governments, notably with Ciskei and Bophuthatswana, first as the Concerned South Africans' Group (COSAG) and then as the Freedom Alliance. The alliance of the black and white right made common cause of an alternative formula of confederalism and opposition to the emerging NP-ANC agreement, and throughout 1993 sought to bargain an agreement on its own terms. The dominant alliance of the National Party and African National Congress worked hard to bring the spoilers back into the fold, as described below.

Cleared by the formula agreement, a third round of the Convention for a Democratic South Africa convened on March 5, 1993, although it was renamed the Multiparty Negotiating Forum because seven new parties now engaged (including the IFP, the Conservative Party, and the PAC) wanted to symbolize that their presence meant a new process was taking place. However, the IFP and the Conservatives, members of the Freedom Alliance, left the forum in July 1993 when April 27, 1994, was chosen as the date for elections. The remaining twenty-one parties forged ahead on further details, their momentum overcoming the serious shock posed by the assassination of Chris Hani, an African National Congress and Communist Party leader, by a Conservative Party sympathizer in April. At the same time that the election date was set, the ANC agreed that the forum could draft an interim constitution before the elections. Agreement was reached on the Transitional Executive Council in early September 1993. With twenty-one members, the council began supervising government activities in December as a multiracial "supergovernment," operating by consensus or qualified majority among equal members. Seven specialized committees of the TEC, as well as the Independent Elections Commission, the Independent Media Commission, and the Independent Broadcasting Authority went into operation at the same time. Power in the present, not just in determining the future, was finally in the majority's hands.

The process of actualizing the power shift moved another step on November 17, 1993, when the forum approved an interim constitution containing governing details and the immutable principles that would guide the definitive constitutional drafting by the constituent assembly to be elected. The interim constitution was approved a month later by the all-white parliament, thereby effectively ending that parliament's existence.[30] Under that constitution the constituent assembly would be composed of a national assembly of 400 members, half of them elected proportionally on the basis of party totals in the nine provinces and the other half allocated so that the total would be proportional to each party's national vote; and a 90-member Senate with equal delegations from each province, chosen proportionally by each provincial legislature. An executive president would be elected by the National Assembly; deputy presidents, having consultative but not veto powers, would be drawn from the top two parties and any other parties having more than 80 seats in the assembly. A cabinet would be chosen proportionally among all parties having more than 20 seats. The constituent assembly would vote in the new constitution by a two-thirds majority; a number of deadlock-breaking mechanisms would be provided. A bill of rights would give immutable protection to equality, liberty, and property, among other rights. Thus did the interim constitution flesh out the details of the initial formula agreed to a year earlier.

By the beginning of 1994 the evolving momentum toward completion was overtaken by a contrary dynamic operating on the negotiations. The race among the mainstream coalition to complete the details and meet the deadlines required by the election date was countered by an effort by the spoilers to use the date and deadlines to gain additional concessions and, indeed, to impose an alternative formula. It was more than kind tolerance that made the mainstream coalition—especially the African National Congress—take time out from the main race to try to mollify the spoilers. Although unable to argue its case successfully, the Freedom Alliance could threaten to disrupt the election—and hence the negotiation—results. It was generally admitted that elections in Natal could not be free and fair without IFP participation, that the holdout homelands were not just an embarrassing skeleton in apartheid's closet but also a potential barrier to full electoral participation, and that the Conservative Party's demand for a fully autonomous Volksstaat (autonomous Afrikaner homeland) could disrupt the vote and its results through violence and sabotage. Thus the final agreement that was settling into place between the two mainstream parties had to be reshaped again to try to ensure the participation of the spoilers.

African National Congress as well as National Party officials handled the Conservative Party by persuading General Constand Viljoen to form a version of the party (the Volksfront) that would participate in the elections in exchange for consideration of the demand for autonomy after the elections. This meant introducing amendments in mid-March 1994 to the constitution already passed by parliament in December 1993; the amendments provided for the constitutional possibility of creating a volksstaat and for strengthening the legal competence of the provinces.[31] The homelands were handled piecemeal. Ciskei was persuaded to return to the Multiparty Negotiating Forum in January 1994. The ANC increased grass-roots pressure on the rulers of Bophuthatswana to participate in the multiparty negotiations, thus turning the spoilers' deadline dynamics against the spoilers. The issue came to a major confrontation in mid-March when the Tswana chief fled the homeland, disorder broke out, a motley group of white extremists swarmed in to reoccupy the area, and the new Multiparty Defense Force ruthlessly defeated them. The Ciskei government was similarly overthrown a week later. The Bophuthatswana incident deflated both fears of and faith in the white right's capability to carry out effective violence.

As the negotiations moved to their denouement in the April 27 elections, the main effective holdout was Chief Buthelezi. Because the Zulu homeland and budget, and the chief minister's position, would cease to exist on the date of the election, Buthelezi's ploy was to turn the deadline against his opponents, removing it for himself by threatening to make that date a day of untenable violence for the country. In early March the National Party agreed to submit the federalism issue to international mediation. Former U.S. secretary of state Henry Kissinger and former British foreign minister Lord Carrington soon arrived as mediators. The ANC reserved its position on the arrangement. But when Buthelezi used the mediation procedure as a pretext to renew his demand for a postponement of the elections as a precondition to participation, the international team went home. After a bloody demonstration by Inkatha Freedom Party followers in downtown

Johannesburg at the end of March, the government responded by declaring a state of emergency for Natal, in an attempt to assure the conditions for elections by introducing troops to protect the right to vote. Buthelezi then agreed in early April to a four-party summit that put himself and his king, Goodwill Zwelithini, on the same level with Mandela and de Klerk, but the summit was unable to separate the king from the chief and win agreement to sovereign existence of the kwaZulu kingdom.

As the election deadline approached, it was then the turn of a Kenyan businessman, Washington Okumu, to step in and broker an agreement— only eleven days before the election. The agreement allowed the Inkatha Freedom Party to register to campaign after the deadline. Only after the election was it discovered that the deal was made possible by a last-minute bill, passed by the provincial parliament and approved by de Klerk, that placed the lands of kwaZulu—a third of Natal province—under the legal trusteeship of the king, a concession refused by Mandela the previous week.

The apartheid regime and the white government came to an end with the elections of April 26–29 (they were extended a day because of the inability to get balloting materials to all the polling places in time). The South African conflict was transformed not only in that violent means gave way to political means, but also in its very terms: an ascriptive minority subjection of an ascriptive majority gave way to a multiparty struggle over power, its use, and its beneficiaries. The Independent Election Commission judged the election to be "substantially free and fair" despite heavy-handed campaigning and confusion in Natal and some other places, and it was actually free and fair in enough places for that judgment to be accurate. As the votes were being counted the African National Congress was headed toward a majority of greater than two-thirds, with known ANC strongholds still to be counted, but the IEC stopped the trend and the ANC came in officially with 62.8 percent of the vote, thus calming fears on the issue that had broken down the CODESA meetings two years earlier. Mandela, the former life prisoner, was elected president. The National Party received 23.1 percent of the vote and an executive vice-presidency for de Klerk, as well as four ministries. The Inkatha Freedom Party received 6.7 percent, and Buthelezi became minister of home affairs.[32]

As in any internal conflict when the never-dreamed-of horizon of resolution is finally reached, in South Africa there proved to be many pits and boulders in the political terrain beyond the horizon. Reconstitution of the army, residues of violence, putting the federal principle into operation, restructuring housing and education, settling the historic land issue, and meeting the wild economic expectations of the masses of the majority (while keeping the loyalty and cooperation of the minority) remained for the new government to handle. During all this the new parliament was faced with the task of devising a final design for the exercise of power and a new structure of beneficiaries. But the unprecedented miracle of getting to that decisive point had been accomplished.

Conclusions

The South African conflict is resolved. The majority has taken over and is subject to its own internal rivalries and divisions; the whites become a faction and a coalition partner among others. To be sure, new or renewed conflicts appear, including those involving old relationships under new conditions, such as the fate of the Volksstaat and kwaZulu, or those reversing the previous relationship, such as the danger of majority exploitation of the minority. The working out of those conflicts, however, belongs in another chapter, and the need to analyze ongoing history should not blur the view that one chapter in South African history has ended. Three questions remain, in conclusion: What happened to produce the miracle? Why did it occur? What are its lessons?

What happened in South Africa was the epitome of a negotiating process that created a negotiating outcome, that is, that brought into being a new political system characterized by compromise and pluralistic participation, a culture of negotiation to replace the two authoritarian cultures of the Afrikaners and the traditional African societies. To the National Party's one-sided history of dominance through apartheid was opposed the African National Congress's one-sided hope of takeover as a national liberation movement; the resulting compromise was a cooperative system with a place for everyone and a need to continue working out stages and details by politics and negotiation. If this is a pact, as it was in some senses, that should not hide the reality of the sometimes bitter and disillusioned relations between de Klerk and Mandela, their hard-fought electoral campaign, the scathing African National Congress attacks on the National Party for its police and army connivance with the Inkatha Freedom Party, or the bloody toll of violence in the civil war between the ANC and the IFP, abetted by the NP. A successful conclusion does not imply a friendly process.

Indeed, it was the fear and presence of conflict that kept the negotiations on track. The rising violence showed that the unthinkable was at the doorstep, not just a vague potentiality. Inkatha violence kept the two mainstream parties together, but the two parties also used violence and breakdown to keep each other on track, flex their muscles, give their own hardliners an occasion to mark their mettle and its limits, and show off the strength of their power and commitment. Thus moments of breakdown were crucial to the dynamic of continuity. Such moments sometimes made it appear as if the parties were practicing the approach-avoidance so common to many types of negotiations.[33] In such behavior the parties return to their stalemate, unable to break the deadlock in positions and expectations, and able only to continue to inflict pain on each other. Eventually one side may appear to win, but the conflict is not ended; it merely smolders in the hearts of the vengeful. Such has been the story in Ireland, Yugoslavia, Ethiopia (see chapter 5), Sri Lanka (see chapter 2), and South Africa itself before the 1990s. In general in such situations the parties drop the behavior after a while, when they realize where it is going. The negotiating leadership is either replaced or changes its goals, going back to conflict, either open or sublimated, as an alternative. But in South Africa there is no alternative. Other processes are more distasteful, and other outcomes are no better. So the miracle seems to be explained.[34]

The points in the evolving events in South Africa—which happened at regular intervals—at which the parties broke off the negotiation process and reevaluated were real. Rationally, the parties may have seen that there were no alternatives, that a new regime would be preferable for each side to the old with its consequences, but it took a time of tension, anxiety, and suspense before they narrowed their differences and made another step of progress. In the process they created a new base, in both power and commitment, for the next round of negotiations. They developed new power relations and new expectations. Each measured the extent of the other side's concessions, not the distance from their original desires and initial demands, and each responded in kind. The National Party obviously made the largest concessions in creating a one-person, one-vote system and giving up power;[35] the African National Congress responded by letting the NP stay in the game after the elections, agreeing to a federal system, and ultimately agreeing to fall short of the magic 66 percent majority vote. At each step the process moved on, rectifying its aim, in a decision-expectation-adjustment or threshold-adjustment process.[36] This adjustment or rectification process was crucial to agreement in South Africa, and is crucial to internal negotiations in general. Unless commitment is worn down to some extent on both sides, the two (or more) ideal outcomes can never be brought into harmony.

But a peculiar characteristic of internal negotiations also warns that more permanent rupture remains an alternative to miracle until the final regime transformation is accomplished. That characteristic is the multilayered composition of the parties and their negotiations. Although international negotiations conducted among sovereign states may encounter problems of ratification, they generally do not involve societies in all their depth clashing in conflicts of power and expectations as they meet in negotiations. The peculiar characteristic means that the grass-roots mass as well as corporate groups at all levels can play a spoiler's role in internal negotiations. Necessary for support but not responsible for the process, such groups can veto convergence by simply insisting on their own interests, goals, visions, or commitments. Because of the real need for their support, spokespersons are obliged to meet the demands of such groups, or at least to take them into account. In South Africa, moreover, the official national-level negotiations were accompanied by myriad local negotiations involving civic organizations, local authorities, labor and management, and grass-roots dispute settlement groups, often focusing on detailed parts of the same subject but without adhering to a coherent relation with the national-level negotiations.[37] Such transitional disorder also contributes to the culture of negotiation, and attenuates the outcome's nature as an elite deal or pact.

In seeking the explanation and lessons behind the success in South Africa, it is nearly impossible to separate the situational from the behavioral aspects of the negotiations. After each crisis the parties came back, taking a new step toward each other, and they came back because each party appreciated the constraints and opportunities of the situation. To begin with, both sides came to realize that they were in a mutually hurting stalemate. De Klerk's four-point syllogism and Mandela's prison training reflected the understanding that neither the government's control nor the ANC's uprising was winning, and that winning—or at least avoiding losing—was only possible through agreement with, not the defeat of, the other party.[38] Furthermore, the stalemate in South Africa was not a comfortable resting place, as stalemate was in many internal conflicts; the insurgents did not hold a liberated territory, nor did they seek more international recognition. They had gone beyond the need to consolidate, and, fortuitously, the opponent had preserved a towering leader for them who came from the previous, nonguerrilla generation and was ready to reconcile.

In terms of the components of the stalemate, the characteristic imbalance had been rectified. The majority's impressive commitment had only grown with the years despite increasing powerlessness,[39] effectively neutralizing the power of the authoritarian government, which was dependent on labor from the townships it could not control. But the National Party's hope of retaining power by sharing it also increased its own commitment, and with it the threat of carrying that commitment into the laager, to destroy the house if it could not rule it. Thus by the beginning of the 1990s each side had its share of both power and commitment.

A number of events at the end of the 1980s contributed to locking this favorable structure into place. One was the collapse of the Soviet Union; white South Africa had long seen the USSR as the clear and present danger behind the African National Congress. Even in the 1994 electoral campaign a National Party theme designed to attract the maximum number of voters represented the ANC as a communist threat.[40] Although this made good campaign material, the collapse of the foreign ally meant that the African National Congress was a weaker and more manageable threat than before. Also contributing to lock the structure in place was the decade of negotiations over the independence of Namibia and the withdrawal of Cuban troops from Angola, which ended in 1988 in an agreement brokered by the United States but also by the Soviet Union.[41] This agreement also weakened the communist threat, but it gave South African blacks the final proof that the wave of history was at their door; it was made possible by the defeat of the military faction around P. W. Botha and the culmination of world pressure by the imposition of sanctions. Thus at the turn of the decade the National Party's weakening position was nonetheless at its strongest, and the African National Congress's strengthening position was seen as less threatening.

All of these favorable situational elements had to be exploited correctly by the negotiators themselves: ripe moments do not do anything; they must be seen, seized, and used. The step-break-gesture-step dance pattern was the key to making progress over four years in gluing the two one-sided positions together into an agreeable formula for a new political system. Perhaps the most important lesson of the process is that the middle elements—break and gesture—are normal and salutory; they should neither be overdone nor subject to overreaction. They also afford a healthy occasion for stocktaking, reevaluation, and readjustment, as well as a necessary occasion for gathering in the stragglers and consolidating support at each step.

In the regress of explanation it all comes down to individuals, and no account of the miracle should omit the chance of having the two Nobel Prize winners—Nelson Mandela, the consummate convincer, and F. W. de

Klerk, the skillful manipulator—as the heads of the mainstream parties. They were what they were by accidents of history; had each rationally chosen to be a particular person, Mandela would necessarily have chosen to be firmly conciliatory and reassuring in order to keep the whites from flocking to the extremes and upsetting the boat, and de Klerk would necessarily have chosen to cover his retreats with assertiveness to avoid both loss of his own constituency and a winner-take-all takeover by the majority. This is not to say that both of the figures did not make serious mistakes, even within their own characters. Mandela's failure to meet with Buthelezi in 1990 and de Klerk's implication in police connivance were notable errors that made the negotiation process more difficult. The ultimate misfit in the Great Men explanation of the history, however, is Buthelezi, whose thin-skinned prickliness went far beyond the objective deterioration of his power position, and whose lack of statesmanship cost the majority thousands of lives just short of the Promised Land.

Notes

1. See Catharine Drinker Bowen, *Miracle at Philadelphia: The Story of the Constitutional Convention, May to September 1787* (Boston: Little, Brown, 1966) for discussion of another such event; and Anthony Lewis, "Talking Peace: Miracle in South Africa?", *International Herald Tribune*, July 3, 1993, p. 7. For a sound analysis of the difficulties of the process, see Marina Ottaway, *South Africa: The Struggle for a New Order* (Brookings, 1993). See also "In Search of South African Analogies," *CSIS Africa Notes*, nos. 66 and 99 (Washington: Center for Strategic and International Studies, December 19, 1986, and June 30, 1989).

2. Quoted in Paul Taylor, "South African Communist Sparks an Explosive Debate," *Washington Post*, November 22, 1992, p. A32.

3. From interviews in South Africa.

4. Daniel Druckman, "Stages, Turning Points, and Crises: Negotiating Military Base Rights, Spain and the United States," *Journal of Conflict Resolution*, vol. 30 (June 1986), pp. 327–60. See also the following works on catastrophe theory and cusp catastrophes, which analyze the accumulating pressures that can turn events in unexpected directions; Rene Thom, *Structural Stability and Morphogenesis: An Outline of a General Theory of Models* (Reading, Mass.: W. A. Benjamin, 1975); C. A. Isnard and E. C. Zeeman, "Some Models from Catastrophe Theory in the Social Sciences," in Lyndhurst Collings, ed., *The Use of Models in the Social Sciences* (London: Tavistock, 1976), pp. 44–100; and S. Beer and John Casti, "Investment against Disaster in Large Organizations," RM-75-16 (Laxenburg, Austria: International Institute of Applied System Analysis, 1975).

5. Marina Ottaway, "Liberation Movements and Transition to Democracy: The Case of the ANC," *Journal of Modern African Studies*, vol. 29 (March, 1991), pp. 61–82.

6. On elite pacts in transitions to democracy, see Guillermo O'Donnell and Philippe Schmitter, eds., *Transitions from Authoritarian Rule* (The Johns Hopkins University Press, 1986), especially vol. 4, *Tentative Conclusions about Uncertain Democracies*.

7. For sensitive explanations of why the awakening took so long, see Mary Benson, *The African Patriots: The Story of the African National Congress of South Africa* (London: Faber and Faber, 1963); Millard Arnold, ed. *Steve Biko, Black Consciousness in South Africa* (Vintage, 1979); and on the other side, James A. Mitchener, *The Covenant* (Random House, 1980).

8. For a short survey and a full-length portrayal of the ensuing negotiations, see, respectively, Witney W. Schneidman, "Postapartheid South Africa: Steps Taken, the Path Ahead," *CSIS Africa Notes* 156 (Washington: Center for Strategic and International Studies, January 1994); David Ottaway, *Chained Together: Mandela, de Klerk, and the Struggle to Remake South Africa* (Times Books, 1993); and Timothy Sisk, *Democratization in South Africa: The Elusive Social Contract* (Princeton University Press, 1994).

9. Alan Cowell, "Pretoria Promises City Blacks a Say," *New York Times*, January 25, 1985, p. A2.

10. Alan Cowell, "Jailed South African Rebel Gives Terms," *New York Times*, January 26, 1985, p. A1; Alan Cowell, "South Africa Hints at Conditional Release," *New York Times*, February 1, 1985, p. A7.

11. Sheila Rule, "Business Leaders in Pretoria Urge End to Apartheid," *New York Times*, September 30, 1985, pp. A1, A10.

12. "Botha Woos South Africa's Blacks," *New York Times*, February 3, 1986, p. A2.

13. Richard Everett, "Breaking Out of the Cocoon," *Africa Report*, vol. 32 (September–October 1987), pp. 31–34.

14. "New Chapter on Apartheid Seen," *New York Times*, June 30, 1989, p. A7; "De Klerk Makes an Overture," *New York Times*, July 23, 1989, p. A4.

15. Mandela's revised "nonpaper" in December reiterated the same conditions. See "South Africa Rebels Blueprint Backed by Regional Leaders," *New York Times*, August 22, 1989, p. A8.

16. Christopher Wren, "South Africa's President Ends 30-Year Ban," *New York Times*, February 3, 1980, p. 1.

17. David Ottaway and Alistair Sparks, "South Africa Frees Mandela," *Washington Post*, February 12, 1990, p. 1.

18. "Countdown to Negotiations," *South Africa Foundation Review*, vol. 16 (July 1990), p. 2.

19. Tos Wentzel, "It's a Truce," *Argus*, August 7, 1990.

20. David Welsh, "F. W. de Klerk and Constitutional Change," *Issue*, vol. 19, no. 2 (1990), pp. 3–5.

21. "The National Peace Accord, 14 September 1991," *Notes and Documents* 23/91 (New York: UN Centre Against Apartheid, November 1991).

22. Amnesty International, "South Africa State of Fear, Security Force Complicity in Torture and Political Killings, 1990–1992" (New York: June 10, 1992).

23. "The Convention for a Democratic South Africa," *Notes and Documents* 1/92 (New York: UN Centre Against Apartheid, January 1992).

24. See, for example, Frederik van Zyl Slabbert, "South Africa in Transition: Pitfalls and Prospects" *CSIS Africa Notes* 133 (Washington: Center for Strategic and International Studies, February 1992); "After Apartheid; Power Sharing" and a summary of party positions in *South Africa Update* 3 (Washington: Embassy of South Africa, 1992). For the first constitutional draft of the National Party, see *Rapport* (Johannesburg), August 25, 1991, pp. 1–2.

25. African National Congress, National Executive Council statement, January 8, 1991; Christopher S. Wren, "Pretoria Drafts Charter Based on Universal Vote," *New York Times*, August 27, 1991, p. A14.

26. On power and positions in mid-1992, see Marina Ottaway, "South Africa after the Referendum," *CSIS Africa Notes* 135 (Washington: Center for Strategic and International Studies, April 1992).

27. For good analyses, see Timothy Sisk, "SA Talks Derailed, Will Find Another Track," *Washington Report on South Africa*, vol. 10 (July 28, 1992, pp. 42–45); "The Issue of Political Power behind the Deadlock at Codesa II" and other articles in *South Africa Foundation Review*, vol. 19 (June 1992), pp. 1–5; Bill Keller, "De Klerk and Mandela; Each Says, It's Your Move," *New York Times*, August 21, 1992, p. A8; and Marina Ottaway, "South Africa after the Referendum."

28. Edyth Bulbring and Sharon Chetty, "FW, Mandela Shake Hands and Get Talks Back on Track," *Sunday Times* (Johannesburg), September 27, 1992, pp. 1, 2. The Record of Understanding was actually negotiated by Roelof Meyer and Cyril Ramaphosa throughout the preceding weeks of September. On "balanced asymmetry," see Paul Taylor, "Hopes for Peace Emerge from Massacre in S. Africa," *Washington Post*, September 13, 1992, p. A25.

29. For a government-related view of the pact and its effect on other alliances, see *South Africa Foundation Review*, vol. 19 (March 1993).

30. For a summary, see Lawyers Committee for Civil Rights Under Law, "South Africa: The Countdown to Elections," special edition (Washington: February 14, 1994).

31. For several discussions of these moves, see *Negotiation News*, vol. 14 (March 15, 1994), published by the Institute for a Democratic Alternative in South Africa (IDASA).

32. Bill Keller, "De Klerk Concedes" *New York Times*, May 3, 1994, p. A1.

33. See I. William Zartman, *Ripe for Resolution: Conflict and Intervention in Africa* (Oxford University Press, 1989), pp. 49–51, 196–99.

34. Keller, "De Klerk and Mandela."

35. On concession-convergence bargaining, see Dean G. Pruitt, *Negotiation Behavior* (Academic Press, 1981).

36. See Alan Coddington, *Theories of the Bargaining Process* (London: Allen and Unwin, 1968); Daniel Druckman, "Social Psychology and International Negotiations: Processes and Influences," in Robert F. Kidd and Michael J. Saks, eds., *Advances in Applied Social Psychology*, vol. 2 (Hillsdale, N.J.: Lawrence Erlbaum Associates, 1983), pp. 51–81; and Druckman, "Stages, Turning Points, and Crises."

37. See I. William Zartman, "Local Negotiations," in Stephen John Stedman, ed., *South Africa: The Political Economy of Transformation* (Boulder, Colo.: Lynne Rienner, 1994), pp. 65–84.

38. On cutting losses versus winning gains, see Janice Gross Stein and Louis W. Pauly, eds., *Choosing to Cooperate: How States Avoid Loss* (Johns Hopkins University Press, 1993).

39. For an earlier account that seeks to explain the tenacious pacifism of the Africans, see Benson, *The African Patriots*.

40. See, for example, the televized debate between R. F. Botha and Thabo Mbeki, South African Broadcasting Corporation (SABC), March 28, 1994.

41. Zartman, *Ripe for Resolution*, pp. 170–254; Chester A. Crocker, *High Noon in South Africa: Making Peace in a Rough Neighborhood* (W. W. Norton, 1992).

CHAPTER EIGHT

Interstate and Intrastate Negotiations in Angola

Donald Rothchild and Caroline Hartzell

IN ANGOLA two types of conflict have existed concurrently: the interstate and the intrastate. The intrastate conflict has had personal, ideological, interethnic, and interregional dimensions. As a consequence of U.S. Assistant Secretary of State Chester A. Crocker's determined mediation efforts, backed by the Soviet Union, the interstate conflict was eventually settled in December 1988 by a tripartite agreement, which provided, among other things, for Namibia to move by stages to independence and for the redeployment and disengagement of Cuban troops from Angola. The intrastate conflict between the Angolan government, led by the Popular Movement for the Liberation of Angola (MPLA, or Popular Movement), and the insurgent movement, the National Union for the Total Independence of Angola (UNITA), continued until 1991, when a Portuguese-mediated effort, actively supported by the United States and the Soviet Union, resulted in the Bicesse Accords of May 1991. This agreement has proved difficult to implement, however, because UNITA leader Jonas Savimbi refused to accept the outcome of elections held in 1992 under the agreement. He also urged the United Nations to assume a more active role in the mediatory process.

This chapter examines the origins, tensions, and structural dimensions of the interstate and intrastate conflicts, and compares and contrasts the two different conflict management and mediation processes and their apparent consequences. Incentives influencing the preferences of the various actors, as well as the mediators' resources, abilities, and motivations, are also

175

examined and are linked to movement toward or away from settlement of each conflict situation.

The Preindependence Context and Colonial Mediation

What began in the early 1960s as a struggle by Angolan nationalist movements against the colonial power, Portugal, had become by the time of Angolan independence in 1975 a war with both interstate and intrastate dimensions. The three leading nationalist movements—the Popular Movement for the Liberation of Angola, the National Front for the Liberation of Angola (FNLA, or National Front), and the National Union for the Total Independence of Angola—although sharing the goal of liberating Angola from Portuguese colonial rule, had distinct ethnic roots, varying ideological inclinations, and different ties to external actors. All of these variables proved to be key factors influencing the course of the interstate conflict over a period of one and a half decades.

War in Angola was fought not just against Portugal but also among the three nationalist movements in their struggle for power. Two of the nationalist movements, the MPLA and the FNLA, were active in leading the Angolan insurgency against Portugal. They were joined by a third movement, UNITA, in 1966. The years between 1961 and 1974 saw the MPLA, FNLA, and UNITA contend for control over peoples and territory within Angola, as well as for international recognition by countries and multilateral organizations and the access to resources that often accompanied such recognition. Because it had the largest army at the time, the National Front appeared to be in the best position to challenge not only the Portuguese but also the MPLA and UNITA. However, the National Front was handicapped by its lack of experienced administrators, Holden Roberto's closely held and at times erratic leadership, and an overly strong identification with the political, economic, and social interests of the Bakongo people that made the movement less appealing to other ethnic and class interests in Angola.[1] The smaller size of the MPLA's armed forces limited its ability to challenge the FNLA militarily. This was partly compensated for by the Popular Movement's cohesive ideology, well-educated leadership, and class appeal, which cut across ethnic lines. However, internal struggles for control of the movement weakened it to such an extent that by 1972 it had become virtually defunct as a fighting force, both against the Portuguese and the other nationalist movements. The National Union, which had the smallest military force by far, engaged in survival politics. Under the charismatic leadership of Savimbi, it pursued a number of political strategies directed at gaining international legitimacy for UNITA and consolidating its power and influence.

Suffering as they did from military and internal weaknesses and unwilling to unify their forces, the three nationalist movements were unable to achieve major military successes against the Portuguese. The road to Angola's independence was cleared in April 1974 by a coup in Portugal itself; army officers in the Movement of the Armed Forces (MFA), demanding an end to Portugal's protracted and unwinnable wars in Africa, overthew the government, making possible Angola's move toward independence. In January 1975 Roberto met with Savimbi and Agostinho Neto, leader of the MPLA, first in Mombasa under the auspices of Kenyan president Jomo Kenyatta and then in Alvor, Portugal, under the auspices of the Portuguese.[2] The resulting Alvor Agreement provided for a tripartite transitional government in Angola, in which each nationalist movement would be represented; for integration of military forces; and for elections and Angolan independence, to begin on November 11, 1975.

The Alvor Agreement was undermined, however, when renewed fighting broke out among the three nationalist movements in March and continued despite mediation by Kenyatta at a meeting in June and pressure from an Organization of African Unity (OAU) summit meeting in July. Fighting for Luanda, the capital of Angola, became intense. On November 10—the day Portugal withdrew from Angola—forces of the Popular Movement for the Liberation of Angola, assisted by Cuban troops, decisively defeated the National Front's forces, which had been assisted by South African troops.[3] This military victory, in combination with the withdrawal of UNITA contingents to their heartland area in the south central part of Angola, left the MPLA free to proclaim an independent People's Republic of Angola on November 11, 1975.

From that moment on the conflict in Angola ceased to be a colonial one and became a civil conflict with important international dimensions. In this civil conflict the nationalist movements had linkages with external powers. Foremost among these were the United States and the Soviet Union, which were indirect intervenors and which made commitments of economic and military assistance to their local nationalist allies without sending combat troops to the area; and Cuba and South Africa, which were direct intervenors and which deployed regular combat troops in Angola.

Postindependence Incentives for Conflict

In the Angolan conflict different incentives motivated internal actors such as UNITA, the Popular Movement, and the National Front, and external actors such as the United States, the Soviet Union, South Africa, and Cuba. The varying ethnic, regional, class, and ideological bases on which the three nationalist movements rested imposed interests that the three movements sought to fulfill. Not all of those interests constituted long-term, nonnegotiable incentives for conflict. The three nationalist movements shared the goals of ending colonial rule, bringing economic development to Angola, and fostering pan-African unity. However, other incentives for conflict among the internal actors in Angola persisted after independence. One arose from the apparent incompatibility of the MPLA commitment to state and party hegemony with UNITA's declared preference for genuine power sharing. The Popular Movement, which has been in power since Angola gained independence in 1975, remained determined to adhere to Marxist-Leninist principles on the primacy of a centralized, one-party state. Savimbi, whose ideological inclinations have often been unclear over the years (and who might thus be said to provide a personalist or populist type of leadership for UNITA) called both for the elections that were promised under the Alvor Agreement and for genuine power-sharing between the MPLA and UNITA.

A related incentive for continuing conflict concerned Savimbi's role. Although UNITA and the MPLA agreed there should be a centralized (as opposed to a federal) solution in Angola, and the Popular Movement held that members of UNITA should be granted amnesty and integrated into Angolan politics, the MPLA also held that Savimbi was a "renegade" and "traitor" who should be excluded from the political process.[4]

Because of the nationalist movements' ties to organizations and sovereign countries outside of Angola, the incentives of the internal actors for engaging in conflict cannot be considered apart from the incentives of the external actors for becoming involved in Angola. Although external actors such as the United States, the Soviet Union, Cuba, and South Africa did not provide the initial incentives for conflict among the three nationalist movements, the financial, matériel, and troop assistance provided by external actors contributed to the internal actors' incentives for conflict.

Soviet intervention in Angola primarily took the form of financial, matériel, and training assistance for the Popular Movement for the Liberation of Angola. Ideology was one incentive contributing to the Soviet

Union's decision to intervene. The MPLA's Marxist roots probably attracted Soviet support for a regime with shared values. Furthermore, by aligning itself with such a radical third world regime as Angola's, the USSR could attempt to put to rest criticism that the Soviet-U.S. detente then in progress had led it to become a status quo power. Jiri Valenta has argued that "a tough stand" by the Soviets on Angola "could have been perceived by [Soviet president Leonid I.] Brezhnev and his supporters as a convenient demonstration to critics at home and abroad that detente [was] not a 'one-way street,' that the USSR [did] not 'betray' the revolutionary forces in the Third World."[5]

A second incentive for Soviet intervention in Angola was the USSR's desire to deny the United States and China the opportunity to expand their influence in southern Africa. A competition for influence in Africa had been undertaken by the Soviet Union and China in the late 1950s; China had increased its efforts in Africa once the Cultural Revolution came to an end in 1969. The possibility of a U.S.-Chinese condominium in southern Africa was a source of great Soviet anxiety. This fear was further fueled by U.S. and Chinese support for the same nationalist movement in Angola— the National Front—and by public references by U.S. Secretary of State Henry A. Kissinger to "parallel views" held by the United States and China on certain Angolan issues.[6]

U.S. intervention in Angola took the form of economic and military assistance, the latter funneled through Zaire, initially to the National Front and later to UNITA as well. The primary incentive for U.S. involvement was its desire to impede what was perceived as the expansion of Soviet power and influence into the area. Soviet actions in Angola were referred to by U.S. president Gerald Ford as "the Soviet-backed effort to take over the country by force."[7] Moreover, Kissinger was concerned that Soviet intervention in "Angola represent[ed] the first time since the aftermath of World War II that the Soviet Union ha[d] moved militarily at long distance to impose a regime of its choice"; he argued that under such circumstances the United States had to respond appropriately to the Soviet challenge.[8]

Another incentive to U.S. intervention was a desire to see the status quo maintained in Africa. The United States wanted not only to encourage political stability in southern Africa, but also to preserve the region's linkages to the international economic system. A study by the U.S. Congressional Research Service determined that "Kissinger . . . stressed the necessity of maintaining regional balances so that the larger global balance might be preserved."[9]

South African intervention involved not only the same kinds of assistance offered by the Soviet Union and the United States but also the use of South African combat forces in Angola in support of the National Front and UNITA. Security concerns were one incentive for South African involvement: South Africa was worried about challenges to its continued control of Namibia and about a total communist "onslaught" on the African continent.[10]

Domestic political pressures to take action against perceived Marxist threats to South Africa and Namibia constituted a second, related, incentive for South African intervention. Deon Geldenhuys has stated that the South African military, in conjunction with a few advisers close to Prime Minister B. J. Vorster, was the driving force behind South Africa's involvement in Angola.[11]

Cuba intervened in Angola in support of the Popular Movement for the Liberation of Angola. Cuba's primary contribution was combat troops, which engaged in fighting in Angola, although Cuba also provided training and military equipment. A major incentive for Cuban intervention appears to have been ideology. Under Fidel Castro's leadership revolutionary Cuba had long identified with what it considered to be progressive movements and third-world causes. Moreover, defense of the Cuban revolution was considered to be provided through international solidarity with developing and nonaligned countries. Thus Cuba set about fostering ties with nationalist movements like the MPLA primarily for ideological reasons.

A related incentive for Cuban intervention may have been Cuba's—and particularly Castro's—desire to be seen by other developing and nonaligned countries as a third-world leader. Castro's aspirations in that direction may have been threatened in the early 1970s by the growth of superpower detente and the spread of nationalism in the third world. Cuban ties to and dependency on the Soviet Union became increasingly clear in an era that saw other third-world countries advocating autonomy from both superpowers. Thus an effort to reclaim its status as a third-world leader may well have led Cuba to pursue an interventionist course in Angola.

Although Cuba may have wished to assert its autonomy vis-à-vis Moscow, turbulent Cuban-Soviet interactions throughout the 1960s may also have prompted Castro to try to put the relationship on firmer ground through Cuban intervention in Angola. Such an exercise would allow Cuba to prove its political worth to the Soviet Union as a third-world leader and to demonstrate Cuban military capabilities on behalf of a cause favored by the Soviets.

Military Climax and Stalemate

After Angola achieved independence in 1975 the country's new army, the Popular Armed Forces for the Liberation of Angola (FAPLA), bolstered by Cuban forces and Soviet-supplied military equipment, began the process of consolidating the government's control over the country. In doing so the Popular Armed Forces faced two major antagonists: UNITA, the government's main internal opponent, and South Africa, UNITA's powerful external host country. Clashes between the Popular Armed Forces and the South African Defense Forces (SADF) proved inconclusive, and by the mid-1980s a stalemate had developed. In this situation the relatively well-trained and well-equipped FAPLA army controlled the major cities and the oil-producing areas of Angola, but it lacked the ability to inflict a decisive defeat on the South African–backed UNITA insurgents.

If the stalemate on the ground was to be overcome, two basic choices faced the Angolan government and the Cubans on the one hand and UNITA and the South Africans on the other: either the two sides could fight on, with each side hoping to attain a military victory, or they could seek a political settlement through negotiations. Although some proposals were floated on the diplomatic front, movement toward a negotiated settlement could not progress far as long as the two sides believed in the possibility of a military victory. An armed engagement remained inevitable before any serious talks that might lead to a negotiated settlement.

The summer and fall of 1987 saw the Popular Armed Forces become involved in two major military encounters against UNITA and South African ground forces, in the towns of Mavinga and Cuito Cuanavale. Although in neither case was FAPLA able to inflict a decisive defeat, its emergence at this time as an effective fighting force able to stand up to South African forces signaled an important change in the balance of military forces in the region.

By the spring of 1988 the Cuban force, newly enlarged, went on the offensive in southern Angola, concentrating its attack on South African contingents there. Cuban troops clashed with South African forces on June 26 near the hydroelectric dam at Calueque, and Cuban-piloted MiG-23s bombed South African positions as well as the dam itself, killing a substantial number of white South Africans and shocking the dominant whites in the country into realizing that a protracted and costly war was looming. A change in the balance of forces in the area may best explain why a South African counterattack never materialized; Gillian Gunn has stated that "the

Angolan-Cuban forces now had a significant edge in the air war and could give the SADF a good run for its money on the ground.''[12] For the South Africans, as well as for the other intervenors and the MPLA regime, a point had now been reached at which the costs of the war exceeded its anticipated benefits. This stalemate contributed to a change of perceptions on all sides that raised a negotiated peace to the status of a preferred option.

Negotiation with Interstate Mediation

When the change in the balance of strategic forces and the war weariness of the MPLA regime and the direct and indirect intervenors were linked to a third factor—the increasing pragmatism in the relations between the two superpowers—movement toward mutual disengagement on the part of the direct intervenors became a serious possibility. The two indirect intervenors, the United States and the Soviet Union, became increasingly conscious of the opportunities for tacit cooperation on resolving regional conflict issues that the more pragmatic approach of Soviet general secretary Mikhail Gorbachev had created; thus they became more willing to explore initiatives aimed at a settlement. As the perceptions of the various parties changed in the summer of 1988, a move from a military deadlock toward a negotiated settlement became a realizable objective.

The Negotiation Process

The critical negotiations to end the stalemate and bring about a regional agreement stretched across eight months, beginning with prenegotiation talks in London in May 1988 and ending with the signing of accords on Namibia's independence and the withdrawal of Cuban troops on December 22, 1988. Negotiations proceeded through a number of rounds in accordance with well-established principles of third-party mediation.

Formal mediation began following separate discussions between U.S. officials and the South African authorities and between U.S. representatives and those of the Angolan regime (MPLA) and the Cuban government in early 1988. The formal mediatory process, presided over throughout the negotiations by U.S. assistant secretary of state Crocker and his American team, started with exploratory discussions among representatives of the Angolan, Cuban, and South African governments in London in May, at which an initial timetable for the withdrawal of Cuban forces from Angola was agreed upon. In follow-up sessions at Brazzaville and Cairo, the United States and the Soviet Union used their influence to press their respective allies to adopt conciliatory stances on such issues as the pace of Cuban troop withdrawal, external assistance to UNITA, and the inclusion of UNITA in Angola's ruling coalition. The extent of superpower influence on these partly autonomous actors must not be overstated, but it certainly facilitated the process of exchange between bitter rivals.

Negotiations among the three parties—the Angolan government, Cuba, and South Africa—then moved ahead through the following stages at meetings in New York, Geneva, Namibia, and Brazzaville: determination of principles for a peace settlement; announcement of a cease-fire and work on modalities for the cease-fire; attempts to narrow differences among the parties; tentative acceptance of a timetable for Cuban troop withdrawal; preliminary agreement on the withdrawal of Cuban troops from Angola and South African forces from Namibia; examination of the means of monitoring verification; approval of a provisional agreement and acceptance of terms for a political settlement; and signing of a formal agreement providing for Namibian independence and the withdrawal of Cuban forces.

Clearly, once all sides had come to recognize the hurtful stalemate and the costs of continuing the status quo, they were able to advance at a steady pace toward a peaceful settlement of some of their important differences, most notably the issues of Cuban troop withdrawal from Angola and a South African withdrawal from Namibia. One senior American official involved in the negotiations, when asked why compromise was possible at this juncture, cited "an element of exhaustion, mutual confidence and clearly the fact that the U.S. and the Soviets have made progress dealing with issues around the world" as key factors.[13] Such progress was also possible because changes in the incentives of the major actors moved their interests away from conflict and toward settlement.

Changing Incentives

Between 1975 and 1988 the different incentives that the United States, the Soviet Union, South Africa, and Cuba had for being engaged in the Angolan conflict continued to have a common denominator in the confrontation between East and West. But by 1988, as the cold war waned, the totalist perceptions that the East and West had of one another had eased and pragmatic views were gradually gaining ascendancy in the Soviet Union and the United States. For U.S. President Ronald Reagan the Soviet "evil empire'' had become a state with national interests, and in the USSR the ''new thinking'' of General Secretary Mikhail Gorbachev was encouraging Soviet leaders to reassess the costs of substantial involvement on the side of the MPLA in Angola and to consider experimenting with joint U.S.-Soviet problem-solving efforts for regional conflicts.[14] Although the direct intervenors, Cuba and South Africa, were slower to adjust to detente, changing regional and global imperatives left them with few alternatives over time. The result was a settlement enabling the Angolan government and the various direct and indirect intervenors to achieve at least some of their major objectives: the Angolan government brought an end to the internationalized dimensions of a destructive conflict; the Cubans emerged as champions of third-world causes; the South Africans secured a formal agreement on Cuban troop withdrawal and an informal agreement on the closing of African National Congress (ANC) training camps in Angola; the Soviets showed themselves to be supportive of African purposes at critical junctures; and the United States, with the agreement on Cuban withdrawal, promoted its larger security objectives for the region, and raised its prestige through its role as peacemaker. These results are examined in more detail below.

It is important also to take account of the changes taking place in the perceptions in Angolan government circles by 1988. MPLA authorities in Luanda, who had experienced decades of conflict with a colonial power, internal rivals, and external intervenors, had every reason to look positively on an end to the military struggle. The war against the insurgent movements and South African intervention was costly not only in terms of funding and supplying armed forces but also in terms of social and economic development. To deal with economic and social deterioration, Angolan government authorities began to see that it was necessary to overcome the military stalemate and begin the process of normalizing regional and extraregional relations.

Of the direct intervenors, Cuba had been the most determined proponent of a confrontational stance. When Cuba was able to alter the balance of forces in Angola in favor of Luanda, the shift enabled Castro to claim a victory and therefore to negotiate on disengagement without loss of face.[15] Having displayed ''a strong internationalist spirit'' and effectively championed the Marxist-Leninist revolutionary cause in Angola, the Cubans could rest content and avoid becoming further enmeshed in an extended war of attrition.[16] They were in a position to accept a negotiated settlement, especially one favored by their Soviet mentors.[17] Moreover, the alternative of continued conflict would likely have proved burdensome in terms of health hazards (particularly the threat of AIDS, or Acquired Immune Deficiency Syndrome), increasing battle casualties, and financial outlays (Angola would be unable to cover the costs of Cuban military activities because of a drop in world oil prices).

The other direct intervenor, South Africa, gradually altered its assessment of the external and internal Angolan contexts in 1987–88. The Soviets had come to appear less adventurous and less inclined by this time to expand their influence in southern Africa. Moreover, the Americans seemed more determined than ever to press South Africa to change its policies on Namibian independence and apartheid. The United States sought Namibian independence on terms that would produce a stable sub-regional environment, one in which the possibilities for Soviet influence would be minimized. To that end U.S. policymakers linked the goal of Namibian independence to a pullout of Cuban forces from Angola, and enacted legislation to impose economic sanctions on South Africa, threatening to tighten these laws if necessary. In the region, the easy military dominance that South African units had displayed in cross-border raids in the early 1980s had given way to a difficult and costly war of attrition with well-armed Cuban and Angolan government forces. Within South Africa, the seemingly endless involvement in Angola was beginning to have psychological and economic costs as well. The loss of military superiority held out the prospect of increasing white casualties and a lengthy military commitment with uncertain benefits. Moreover, the economy, averaging a growth rate of less than 2 percent a year, seemed stagnant, mired in heavy foreign debt, beset by rising inflation, and suffering a lack of investment capital. To reduce the diplomatic and economic pressures on their country and to regain legitimacy in the eyes of the world community, South African leaders reassessed their priorities and began to view a negotiated solution in Angola to be in their long-term interests.

Because the two indirect intervenors had been careful to avoid sending their own nationals into combat in Angola, it was less difficult for them to alter their priorities and to disengage than was the case with the direct intervenors. For the Reagan administration, initial U.S. goals with respect to the Angola-Namibia negotiations were clear: "to restore and advance U.S. influence in the region; to expand [U.S.] cooperative relations with African states; and to deny to the Soviet Union the opportunity to use its influence to exacerbate already dangerous situations in Angola, South Africa, and the other countries of the area."[18] Subsequently the withdrawal

of Cuban troops and an Angolan national reconciliation that would enable
UNITA to be included in the ruling coalition also became important aims of
the United States.

If U.S. incentives for becoming involved in the Angolan conflict remained reasonably constant between 1975 and 1988—the persistence of
these incentives explaining in part the United States' decision to resume
military assistance to UNITA in 1985—the same cannot be said of the
Soviet Union, whose incentives for Angolan involvement were not as
constant as those of the United States. Soviet strategic and economic
interests in Angola were limited, and with the emergence of Gorbachev as
general secretary in the mid-1980s there was growing recognition of the
costs to the Soviets of continuing superpower rivalries in third-world conflicts. Determined to achieve an arms accord and to pursue their domestic
developmental objectives, Soviet leaders deemphasized their roles as revolutionary leaders and opted for a more pragmatic vision of their relations
with Western countries, particularly the United States. The effect was to
place regional conflicts on a lower order of priorities, and make possible
tacit cooperation with U.S. negotiators on bringing about a mutually acceptable agreement providing for the disengagement of Cuban and South African forces in Angola.

Although the Cubans, South Africans, and Angolans displayed a degree
of war weariness by 1988, all had the will and the capacity to continue to
fight unless some face-saving alternative to stalemate surfaced. Such an
alternative emerged decisively during the 1988 negotiations in the form of
tacit cooperation on the part of the two superpowers. As indirect intervenors
for whom the conflict was less salient than it was for the other actors, the
United States and the USSR were able to exert influence over the Angolan
government and the two direct intervenors through the manipulation of
incentives.

It would be an overstatement to contend that the two indirect intervenors
controlled either the Angolan government or the two direct intervenors.
Because the Angolans, Cubans, and South Africans were in part autonomous state actors, the two indirect intervenors could only achieve their
purposes through quiet pressures and positive and negative incentives.
Castro, who received some $5 billion a year in economic subsidies from the
Soviets, as well as Soviet logistical support and matériel for his African
campaign, was described as "highly vulnerable to Soviet politico-economic
coercion."[19] Similarly, the MPLA regime was in no position to reject
Soviet preferences out of hand, having received billions of dollars in mili-

tary assistance from the USSR over the years. Thus the Soviets had considerable, but not unlimited, influence over the decisions of its Cuban and Angolan allies.

The Reagan administration exerted some leverage over the South African government, despite the efforts of the latter to insulate itself from American pressures. In line with its active mediatory role, which can be viewed as manipulative, the United States used its leverage to shape a negotiated outcome to the conflict that was at least minimally acceptable to South Africa's rulers. Determined to achieve a Namibian settlement before his eight-year term expired, Crocker increasingly acted to affect South African affairs, implementing the sanctions legislation mandated by Congress and bypassing the South African government to give support to local antiapartheid groups. In addition, he "repackaged" the long-standing strategy of linking Namibia's independence to a withdrawal of Cuban troops from Angola, formerly the object of scorn on the part of the African nationalist states in the region (the so-called Front Line States), so that Namibia would gain its independence before the full withdrawal of Cuban troops from Angola.[20]

Intrastate Conflict and African Mediation

With the signing of the tripartite Angola-Namibia accords in December 1988 and with redeployment and disengagement of Cuban and South African forces beginning, the stage was set for a concerted effort to resolve the long and destructive Angolan civil war. The conflict in the country's southeast had proved unwinnable, even when external forces had been involved in a major way. Now the internal opponents were left increasingly to their own devices, and a continuing struggle offered them little prospect of significant benefits. Thus the problem following the international settlement was how to overcome the political stalemate and begin the search for a peaceful solution.

Harsh rhetoric notwithstanding, a perceptible softening of government and insurgent positions on the issue of a political solution to their differences became apparent in early 1989. Low-level talks between the MPLA government and UNITA (the FNLA having ceased to play an active independent role in the early 1980s) took place in January, limited to a discussion of a government offer of amnesty for UNITA troops who laid down their arms. This proposal was rejected by UNITA's spokesperson. However, at the request of Ivory Coast President Félix Houphouët-Boigny, who was acting as an intermediary between the adversaries, Savimbi called off UNITA's planned rainy-season offensive. In March Savimbi extended the moratorium on offensive action, announced the release of MPLA prisoners, declared that he was willing to reopen the strategic Benguela Railway (which linked interior Angola and Zaire to the Atlantic Ocean) to nonmilitary traffic, and indicated that UNITA was prepared to forgo participation in a transitional government leading up to free elections. The regime responded with its own peace platform, essentially consisting of its program of amnesty for rank-and-file UNITA soldiers.

There then began an extended mediation process that would lead to a summit meeting of protagonists and facilitators at Gbadolite, Zaire, and to the Gbadolite Declaration of June 1989. According to Zairian president Mobutu Sese Seko, that process began with a series of meetings that culminated with a conference of regional African leaders in Luanda on May 16 and separate meetings that Mobutu held on two occasions with Savimbi and Angolan president Eduardo dos Santos.[21] The Luanda conference was significant because it identified national reconciliation in Angola as an objective and recognized Mobutu's legitimacy as mediator. At Luanda eight African heads of state—from Zaire, Congo, Gabon, Zimbabwe, Mozambique, Zambia, Sao Tomé and Principe, and Angola—endorsed a seven-point Angolan government peace plan. The peace plan, which emphasized a peace zone along the Benguela railroad, an end to foreign interference, cessation of support for UNITA, and implementation of amnesty by the government, made only limited concessions to the insurgent movement.

Before the Gbadolite summit, then, the Angolan government had made few concessions to UNITA's demands for power-sharing and an autonomous existence. It insisted upon Savimbi's temporary exile and the integration of UNITA's civilian and military components into the MPLA-led one-party state. Savimbi, for UNITA, called for multiparty elections and the possibility of coalition government. He denied seeking absolute power for himself, but only enactment of the Alvor Accord principles on a tripartite transition government of the MPLA, UNITA, and FNLA before open elections were held.[22] The gap between adversaries remained wide, with neither side capable of a military victory in 1989.

The Gbadolite Summit and Sequels

With the war proving costly and unwinnable and with some signs of conciliation in evidence, external facilitators found themselves in a favorable position to take the next step—the summit meeting at Mobutu's country residence in Gbadolite, Zaire. This necessarily involved a meeting between the two main antagonists, dos Santos and Savimbi, which was not easy to arrange. It has been reported that when dos Santos, just before his departure from Luanda, received a phone call from Mobutu informing him that Savimbi might be present at Gbadolite, dos Santos reacted angrily and sought to cancel his travel plans; at that point various African heads of state apparently interceded and persuaded dos Santos to reconsider and to attend the summit meeting.[23] Throughout the seven-hour, closed-door meeting the two adversaries were kept apart. During the day Mobutu met with first one and then the other, cajoling and pressuring them in order to extract agreement on a summit declaration.

Mobutu also put pressure on the adversaries to reach an agreement by assembling an impressive array of African leaders at Gbadolite. In all some twenty countries were represented at the summit, eighteen by their heads of state—among them General Moussa Traoré, then chair of the Organization of African Unity and president of Mali; President Kenneth Kaunda of Zambia, President Paul Biya of Cameroon, King Hassan II of Morocco, President Ibrahim Babangida of Nigeria, and President Robert Mugabe of Zimbabwe.

What emerged from this effort was not a carefully worked out settlement; rather, the summit at Gbadolite on June 22, 1989, represented an advance in a larger negotiating process. That Africans had taken the initiative and quickly produced results in the form of a communiqué setting out the principles of agreement was viewed as a heartening sign. The first direct encounter between dos Santos and Savimbi and a handshake between these adversaries signaled willingness to search for national reconciliation by political means. In providing the framework in which this handshake could take place, Africa's leaders were facilitating Savimbi's emergence from the shadows of unrespectability. That the Angolan government negotiated with UNITA's leader and accepted the larger principle of national reconciliation gave the insurgent movement a certain credibility, even legitimacy, that it had lacked previously.

At the substantive level there was confusion about a number of unwritten understandings arising from the day's long and turbulent negotiating session, but at least three principles were put forth in the text of the Gbadolite Declaration. These principles acknowledged a desire on the part of both sides to stop fighting and to move toward national reconciliation. That desire was given some substance by the proclamation of a cease-fire, which was to become effective on June 24, 1989, and by the formation of a commission to plan for national reconciliation under the mediation of President Mobutu.

Clearly the Gbadolite meeting left unresolved a number of issues important to the main adversaries. Over and above the fact that the points of agreement were not written down was the larger reality of profound differences in perceptions and interpretations on the part of the two adversaries. Dos Santos and his supporters came away from Gbadolite convinced that Savimbi had agreed to a voluntary and temporary exile and that UNITA's civilian and military elements would be integrated into the MPLA's party, bureaucratic, and military units. Savimbi dismissed talk of his exile, refused the proposed offer of amnesty, rejected the integration of UNITA into MPLA institutions, and demanded the establishment of a multiparty system and free, open elections. Savimbi was determined to preserve UNITA's separate identity and to compete with the MPLA for power at the political center of the country. The insurgents could not compromise on the issue of legitimacy; they could compromise only on operational details after recognition had been granted.

In a situation characterized by state softness; persistent party, ethnic, and regional conflict; and personal animosity, highly conflictive negotiations such as those at Gbadolite are likely to have symbolic rather than substantive results. Dos Santos felt compelled to go to the summit meeting to demonstrate his party's commitment to peace. Savimbi, for his part, was distrustful of the process from its inception and appeared to participate only to the extent that it advanced his interests. A highly personalistic leader, he looked upon himself as indistinguishable from UNITA, thus making somewhat academic claims that he had agreed to his own exile and the integration of UNITA into the MPLA-dominated state structure.[24] "If I leave Angola," he asked, "who is going to lead UNITA into this process of national reconciliation?"[25] Each leader sought peace, but only on his own terms.

Although the parties at Gbadolite had agreed in principle upon a cease-fire to become effective on June 24, they failed to establish mechanisms to determine the rules of permissible behavior and to resolve violations. Not surprisingly, therefore, the cease-fire never really took hold. At first the hostilities between the MPLA and UNITA forces were limited and strategic in nature; soon, however, they increased in intensity, culminating in heavy fighting around Mavinga in late December 1989 and early 1990.

Despite the continuing military engagements in the field, Mobutu pushed ahead resolutely with his mediatory initiative. Following the

Gbadolite summit a series of four inconclusive meetings were held in Kinshasa, Zaire, to work out a cease-fire agreement. In August 1989 a second regional summit was held, attended by the leaders of eight African states—Angola, Congo, Gabon, Mozambique, Sao Tomé and Principe, Zaire, Zambia, and Zimbabwe. This summit, which took place in Harare, Zimbabwe, reviewed the situation since the Gbadolite meeting and made recommendations on questions not dealt with at the earlier summit. It is significant that UNITA was not represented at Harare, no invitation having been issued to Savimbi. The five-hour meeting reportedly brought sharp differences into the open. The more radical frontline leaders were highly critical of the conservative Mobutu and his failure to secure agreement on the peace terms from dos Santos and Savimbi in writing. The final communiqué issued at Harare reflected the front-line presidents' dissatisfaction with Savimbi's behavior since Gbadolite and was specific in encouraging Savimbi's temporary and voluntary retirement from Angola and the integration of UNITA into the MPLA and its state institutions. As anticipated, Savimbi "violently" rejected the communiqué, and Radio UNITA warned darkly "about the plot being prepared against [UNITA] as an organization, its leader, and peace in Angola."[26]

On September 18, 1989, eight regional heads of state met at Kinshasa for another summit. Savimbi was invited to attend, but despite pressures from U.S. assistant secretary of state for African affairs Herman J. Cohen and others, he declined. Under these circumstances the conferees at Kinshasa could do little more than reaffirm their support for the Gbadolite Declaration and call upon Savimbi to sign a new draft statement on the implementation process. Savimbi refused and countered with his own plan, which proposed the creation of a multinational force to verify and guarantee a cease-fire, and which called for open elections.

As memories of the Gbadolite meeting dimmed, the adversaries appeared to become more preoccupied with the questions dividing them than with the urgent need to negotiate over outstanding issues.[27] Savimbi ruled out significant concessions on the issues of his own exile and the integration of UNITA into MPLA structures, and continued to demand multiparty elections and power-sharing. Dos Santos appeared to be equally unwavering on the reverse of these points. Moreover, as time wore on factionalism increased among MPLA officials, making new conciliatory gestures more difficult than before. One Zairian diplomat reported that dos Santos was under "tremendous pressure from hard-liners in the Government"; feeling "burned" by Savimbi in the past, these hard-liners reportedly saw little to gain from a new cease-fire agreement at that point and argued instead for a military solution to the problem of insurgency.[28] The negotiation process started at Gbadolite was being complicated by a combination of historical memories, personal antagonisms, developing schisms within one of the bargaining parties, and the nature of the stakes involved in the conflict.

Mobutu as Mediator

In a sense, Mobutu's credentials to act as a mediator were the source of his weakness. The Zairian government, which had recognized the Luanda regime and at the same time had friendly relations with UNITA (Zaire even served as a transshipment point for U.S. military supplies to UNITA) was in a favorable position to communicate with both sides. Not surprisingly, therefore, the eight heads of state at the Luanda meeting in May 1989 authorized Mobutu to begin a peace initiative at that time. Later, despite their irritation over his failure to secure an agreement in writing at Gbado-lite and the renewal of fighting, they reaffirmed their "total confidence" in Mobutu as mediator.[29]

At various points in the negotiations Mobutu's past seemed to stand in the way of his peacemaking venture. The frustrations on all sides of the continuing civil war were placed largely on the mediator's shoulders; his failure to secure a written and binding agreement on the modalities of the cease-fire and the terms of the peace were deemed responsible for the breakdown that followed. As Mobutu tried to respond to these charges by holding dos Santos to the Gbadolite Declaration while securing Savimbi's exile and UNITA's incorporation into the MPLA, he found himself unable to satisfy either side. The MPLA leadership showed increasing signs of dividing into pragmatists and hard-liners, and Savimbi not only rejected the Harare summit plan but questioned the impartiality of the mediator him-self.[30] The mediator, in brief, had facilitated the negotiating process but had also emerged as part of the larger problem of peace in Angola. In March 1990 President dos Santos, determined to see the stalled peace talks re-newed, told the Angolan legislature that he was keen to have Mobutu's role assumed by an alternate mediator.[31]

Roles of South Africa and the Superpowers

In explaining the lack of movement toward resolution of the Angolan conflict following the Gbadolite summit it is important to note the parts played, or not played, by the strongest military power in the region and the two superpowers. Under the terms of the Angola-Namibia accords of 1988, Cuban troops would be redeployed north of the fifteenth parallel by August 1, 1989, and north of the thirteenth parallel by October 31, 1989; all Cuban troops would be withdrawn from Angola by July 1, 1991. In addition, South Africa would cease supplying UNITA with weapons and confine its troops to the Walvis Bay area. With Cuba and South Africa disengaging, the internal adversaries were to be left on their own, save for the continuing shipments of Soviet and U.S. military equipment to their respective clients—and on a basis that substantially favored the MPLA.

Although the Cubans withdrew their troops from Angola as scheduled, the South Africans sent mixed signals regarding their intentions. On one hand, there was evidence of diplomatic initiatives by the South Africans in August and September 1989 to keep the Gbadolite peace process—and the Angola-Namibia accords—from foundering. Pressure was reportedly put on both the MPLA and UNITA to abide by the cease-fire.[32] Even so, a question remained as to how much leverage the South Africans possessed and how much pressure they were prepared to bring to bear.

In regard to the two superpowers, the same question of leverage and willingness to exert pressure was relevant. The United States and the Soviet Union contributed simultaneously to arming the combatants and to conflict management. During the Angola-Namibia talks there had been frequent references to Soviet-Cuban pressures on the dos Santos government to negotiate with UNITA. At the Gbadolite meeting in June 1989 various observers concluded that Soviet pressure was a significant factor in wringing concessions from a hesitant and reluctant dos Santos.[33] Although important, such subtle behind-the-scenes pressures by the Soviets were apparently not intense enough to bring about a change in Angolan government perceptions regarding the nature of its opponent and UNITA demands.

Similarly, U.S. involvement with and pressures on Savimbi's insurgent movement had not proved sufficient to bring about a major change in UNITA's perceptions of its opponent and the issues at hand. But in backing the African initiative at Gbadolite, the United States combined both negative and positive incentives to push the process ahead. By not recognizing the Angolan government and by continuing to give military aid to the insurgents (such aid increased to an estimated $50 million in 1989) the United States hoped to change MPLA preferences.[34] In using positive incentives to promote cooperation, the United States held out the prospect of normalizing relations with the Luanda regime once it had concluded an internal settlement with the insurgent movement, and gave "tacit assurances" that with national reconciliation it would consider ending military aid to UNITA.[35] With respect to the mediation effort itself, the United States exerted pressure on Savimbi to attend the Gbadolite meeting and subsequent summits. Despite these positive initiatives, however, Savimbi refused to attend the Kinshasa summit. Steadfast U.S. support of Savimbi gave the American team sufficient leverage to press for cooperation, but not enough to assure movement toward a compromise agreement.

Soft Stalemate and Further Mediation

With the Gbadolite process deadlocked and Mobutu unable to bring sufficient political and economic resources to bear on the disputing parties to come to a settlement, a new approach to negotiations became imperative. The two Angolan adversaries remained wary and distrustful of one another; enmeshed in a soft stalemate, neither could muster sufficient military capacity to eliminate its opposition or force its capitulation. Moreover, conditions for a sustained military effort were not encouraging: not only were Angolans weary of the protracted civil war, but their external supporters were disengaging. Cuban forces withdrew from Angola in advance of the schedule set out in the Angola-Namibia accords; South African assistance to UNITA, reportedly extended in a clandestine manner, was obviously diminutive in comparison with former levels; and the great powers, having made the shift from adversarial to cautiously cooperative relations, were now anxious to reduce their involvement in the internal Angolan war and to pursue new openings toward peace.

Recognizing that the Mobutu initiative had stalled and forthright about the need to regain momentum in the negotiations, Angolan president dos Santos thus called for a new third-party intermediary. Portugal, the former colonial power, rose to the occasion, and from mid-1990 onward chaired a series of talks between representatives of the Angolan government and UNITA. In December 1990 the Portuguese-initiated talks were given an important boost when U.S. secretary of state James A. Baker III met publicly with the Angolan foreign minister and Soviet foreign minister Eduard Shevardnadze conferred openly with UNITA's Savimbi. The United States and the Soviet Union then cosponsored a meeting in Washington, D.C., of the two Angolan rivals, the Portuguese intermediary, and the two great powers. With the Americans and the Soviets present, the two antagonists managed to work out what became known as the Washington Concepts Paper—the basic framework for serious negotiation sessions to follow. And whereas at Gbadolite the great powers had given general support to Mobutu's peace initiative but displayed little urgency over the proceedings, the United States and the USSR were now brought directly into the Portuguese negotiations as official observers. U.S. assistant secretary Cohen, commenting on active U.S. and Soviet involvement in the negotiating process, observed that "we both played a very important role in helping to bring about compromises under the overall jurisdiction of the Portuguese mediator."[36]

The Washington agreement on basic negotiating principles gave a new impetus to the flagging talks at Bicesse, Portugal. By the time the sixth round of talks had taken place on April 4, 1991, most major points of disagreement had been resolved and the negotiators were able to focus attention on the key remaining issues: formation of a unified national Angolan army, dates for a cease-fire and for multiparty elections, and international monitoring of the cease-fire. The election date proved to be the most contentious point. Whereas UNITA proposed that elections be held between nine and twelve months after the cease-fire, the Angolan government proposed a waiting period of three years. The Portuguese recommended a compromise period of eighteen months before elections were held. Although the MPLA then indicated willingness to accept a twenty-four-month period, UNITA representatives continued to insist on a twelve-month period.

Haggling over the major outstanding issues continued through the remainder of April, when to the surprise of many the conferees achieved a breakthrough to peace. On May 1, 1991, Lopo do Nascimento, representing the Angolan government, and Jeremias Chitunda of UNITA initialed the various documents making up a peace accord. Under the terms of these preliminary agreements a complex package of provisions was settled upon, including a cease-fire, to come into force on May 15; UNITA's recognition of the Angolan government and President dos Santos until general elections were held; UNITA's right to take part in political activities in a multiparty democracy; free and fair elections under the supervision of international observers; consultation among all Angolan political forces to determine the specific timetable for elections, tentatively set for late 1992; and, once the cease-fire came into effect, creation of a single national military force, to be made up of the current Angolan government air force and navy and an army evenly divided between government and UNITA troops.[37] These prelimi-

nary accords were vague, however, about the framework for decentralization, leaving such matters as the structure of regional and local governments
to be decided upon after the elections. It was significant that the great
powers that had helped to overcome impediments to a negotiated settlement
now agreed to take part in the implementation process.

Implementation of the Bicesse Accords has proved to be most difficult.
During the negotiations in Portugal both sides agreed to maintain the
presidential system; each side assumed it would win the elections, set for
September 1992. Their grim, zero-sum perceptions of one another persisted, leading to a breakdown in relations as the election outcome became
known. With dos Santos receiving 49.57 percent of the presidential vote
(and Savimbi 40.6 percent), a runoff election between the two main contenders became necessary. Savimbi, declaring that his opponent was determined "to cling to power illegally," charged electoral fraud and ordered
his army (still largely autonomous) into action.[38] In late November the
situation remained tense and the next step in the election process was
unclear. However, with MPLA leaders showing some willingness to include UNITA representatives in a national coalition and Savimbi urging
that the United Nations "completely take over the negotiating process,"
there was reason to hope that some kind of an agreement growing out of the
Bicesse Accords could still be salvaged.[39]

Following the 1992 elections, the military fortunes of the two adversaries swung like a pendulum, with each side determined to take advantage of
a shift in the balance of power to achieve military victory. In 1993 UNITA
held some 70 percent of the country, but neither the capital nor the oil-
producing enclave of Cabinda; in 1993–94 the government, greatly
strengthened by the purchase of some $3.5 billion in arms and ammunition
from abroad,[40] and by the retraining of its forces by a Pretoria-based
security firm, launched a sustained offensive that overran UNITA-held
diamond mines and penetrated UNITA strongholds in its heartland area.[41]
With UNITA's supply of military spare parts and fuel running down and
with the United Nations increasingly critical of its decision to resume the
war, UNITA found itself becoming more vulnerable and isolated.[42] The
increasing dominance of the government forces combined with growing
international and regional pressure, then, became the primary factors that
induced Savimbi to shift from a bid for total military victory toward
negotiation for what amounts to continuance of the Bicesse Accords.

Against this backdrop of sharp military encounters, heavy casualties, and
destroyed cities, a little more than a year of UN-mediated peace negotia-

tions ensued in Lusaka, Zambia, between Angolan government and UNITA representatives. In these long and often frustrating negotiations, the United Nations Special Representative to Angola, Alioune Blondin Beye, assisted prominently by U.S. special envoy Paul Hare and various Portuguese and South African diplomats, carefully worked out the Lusaka Protocol of November 22, 1994. The protocol was signed by Angolan foreign minister Venancio de Moura and UNITA's secretary general Eugenio Ngolo at a ceremony attended by the representatives of some thirty countries. In reaffirming the 1991 Bicesse Accords, the protocol set out details for a cease-fire, a second round of presidential elections, demilitarization, disarmament, the formation of a unified army and a national police force, and national reconciliation. Emphasizing the importance of reestablishing central control over the country's security forces, the general principles of the Lusaka Protocol affirmed that ''[t]he process of completion of the formation of FAA [the Angolan Armed Forces] under the verification and monitoring of the United Nations, will guarantee the existence of one single, national and non-partisan armed forces obeying the sovereign organs of the Republic of Angola.''[43]

Certainly there are differences between the political contexts surrounding the Biscesse and Lusaka agreements that raise hopes that Angola's fratricide will now come to an end. The change of regime in South Africa, the determination of United Nations authorities to deploy 7,000 observers to oversee the implementation process, and the provisions in the Lusaka Protocol for applying the principle of proportionality in recruitment all represent hopeful signs. Nevertheless, deep distrust prevailed on both sides, as fighting continued (in the area around Uige, for example) after the protocol took effect and as UNITA leader Savimbi failed to turn up for the signing of the protocol, and later made ominous allusions to the possibility of reverting to guerrilla warfare.[44] Unless the international community provides the United Nations with sufficient funding to oversee the transition to peace, the perseverance displayed by Alioune Blondin Beye and others was still in doubt. It was only on May 6, 1995, that the two rivals finally met and Savimbi acknowledged that his struggle was over.

Conclusions

Three important concepts have been explored in this chapter: changing incentives for state intervention over time, the roles of mediators in facilitating the peace process, and the ability of mediators to exert pressures and manipulate incentives effectively. In the interstate negotiations, movement by the major external actors—the United States, the Soviet Union, Cuba, and South Africa—from intervention in 1975 to disengagement in 1988 has been explained primarily by shifts in each actor's perceptions of the gains to be had from conflict as opposed to those to be had from nonconflictive behavior. In the late 1980s a new cooperative relationship developed between the two superpowers. As the Soviets stepped back from their political, military, and ideological competition with the United States and increasingly emphasized their own domestic objectives, possibilities for great-power collaboration were enhanced. The practical consequence in the Angolan case was important behind-the-scenes cooperation in the mediation process, with the Soviets exerting pressure on the Angolan government and the Cubans at key points, and U.S. mediators seeking to influence South African preferences regarding Angola and Namibia.

The internal negotiations at Gbadolite, Bicesse, and Lusaka, however, brought little fundamental change in the perceptions that the two adversaries had of one another. Because the great powers and the United Nations displayed a greater involvement and sense of urgency during the Bicesse and Lusaka mediation processes than was the case with the Mobutu-led initiative, they were able to facilitate an agreement despite the evident distrust that continued to divide the adversaries. Nevertheless, the continuing distrust between the MPLA and UNITA resurfaced in full force following the 1992 elections and in the aftermath of the Lusaka Protocol, and continues to represent a grave threat to the survival of the Bicesse and Lusaka agreements.

With respect to the roles of the mediators in promoting constructive outcomes, the situations in which the third-party intermediaries found themselves differed in important ways. U.S. assistant secretary Crocker showed great resolve in his search for an internationally acceptable solution to the Namibian independence issue, which, as shown throughout, was interconnected with events in Angola—although Crocker's initial attempt to link that issue with resolution of the Angolan conflict may have complicated that task for some years and made a peace settlement more difficult. Once the military stalemate on the ground was recognized, however, linkage became a means for face-saving and for addressing the differences among Angolans.[45] Crocker's pursuit of possible openings and his position as a representative of a global power, coupled with the change in the balance of military forces and the shift in superpower perceptions, created new opportunities for decisive moves toward an Angolan settlement.

At the internal level, however, no comparable convergence of opportunities took place at Gbadolite. The United States during the Bush administration backed Mobutu's initiative but expressed reservations about becoming a mediator in any formal sense. Lacking the diplomatic skills and determination displayed by Crocker in the earlier negotiations and unable to bring the resources of a great power to bear on promoting an internationally acceptable settlement, Mobutu was not in a position to alter the perceptions of or offer significant incentives to the MPLA and UNITA. Subsequently Portuguese mediators made concerted efforts to involve the superpowers in the negotiating process, with evident success. As a consequence the medium-power mediator was backed during the final, critical weeks of negotiations by the influence that the Soviet Union and the United States could bring to bear on their allies. The importance of the great-power role in the Bicesse mediation process was not lost on the rival Angolan leaders. Thus Savimbi noted, when expressing his appreciation for the Portuguese effort, that "without the Americans and Soviets on their side, Durao Barroso [the Portuguese mediator] would not have gotten anywhere."[46] In the subsequent United Nations–led mediation effort of 1993–94 at Lusaka, the international organization had important backing from the United States and the Portuguese, as well as from such regional powers as South Africa and Zimbabwe. With the changing balance of forces in Angola, the result was to leave Savimbi with little room to maneuver.

Finally, the mediators' credibility and capacity to mobilize resources had a direct bearing upon their ability to exert pressures and manipulate incentives. In the international negotiations on an Angola-Namibia agreement and in the internal mediation effort leading to the Bicesse Accords, the successful outcomes depended substantially upon parallel United States and Soviet pressures on their respective clients. At various points Crocker pressed the South Africans to cease their military assistance to UNITA and to agree to an international settlement; in the internal negotiations in 1991 American officials reassured MPLA leaders as to their good intentions while at the same time pressing UNITA, which relied heavily upon the United States for sophisticated military equipment, to make concessions on such key issues as the timetables for elections. Similarly, the Soviets, who had provided Angolan government forces with ideological support and extensive war matériel over the years, were in a favorable position to influence their MPLA allies. During the international negotiations Soviet diplomats were well placed to clarify critical points of contention and to encourage Luanda's leaders to bargain in earnest and adopt conciliatory positions on such questions as the redeployment and withdrawal of Cuban forces. At Bicesse the Soviets played an active part in facilitating an agreement, meeting with Savimbi at the Soviet embassy in Washington, helping to shape the Washington Concepts Paper, and pressing MPLA leaders to make concessions on important points of difference.

In contrast, Mobutu could bring no comparable pressures and incentives to bear on the disputing parties during the Gbadolite process. Through a combination of persuasion and pressure he did manage to get the rivals to the summit at Gbadolite and to extract an agreement on certain broad principles from a reluctant dos Santos and Savimbi. But once the Gbadolite conferees dispersed, Mobutu could exert little influence to overcome the stalemate. To be sure, the United States sought to pressure Savimbi to attend the Kinshasa summit, and some African leaders gave general support to Mobutu's mediatory effort, but these initiatives were intermittent and lacking in firmness and conviction.

The negotiations over the Lusaka Protocol involved active United Nations leadership in all its phases, although the United States (and Russia in a limited way) did play minimal roles under UN auspices. Because the principles hammered out at Bicesse were never repudiated following the resumption of hostilities in 1992, the mediators at Lusaka did not have to start from scratch but could use the Bicesse Accords as a guideline in their deliberations. In working out the Lusaka Protocol, the main incentives bringing the negotiating parties to an agreement were the Angolan government's desire to restore legitimate central authority in the country and UNITA's need to halt the military offensive against its weakening positions. Other factors at work included the guarantees in the protocol of full representation of UNITA's interests in national and local politics and international and regional pressures on Savimbi to agree to the settlement. With the costs of continued military engagement rising, Savimbi had little to gain from continuing the fight and agreed to what amounted to a fragile military truce. Taken together, these factors show that the structures of the four mediation processes were quite distinct, and thus account in part for the varying results from each peacemaking attempt.

Notes

1. Arthur Jay Klinghoffer, *The Angolan War: A Study in Soviet Policy in the Third World* (Boulder, Colo.: Westview, 1980), p. 13.

2. On these negotiations, see Michael Wolfers and Jane Bergerol, *Angola in the Front Line* (London: Zed, 1983), p. 6; John Marcum, *The Angolan Revolution*, vol. 2: *Exile Politics and Guerrilla Warfare (1962–1976)* (Cambridge, Mass.: MIT Press, 1983); Thomas Ohlson and Stephen John Stedman with Robert Davies, *The New Is Not Yet Born: Conflict Resolution in Southern Africa* (Brookings, 1994), pp. 79–82; and Larry C. Napper, "The African Terrain and the U.S.-Soviet Conflict in Angola and Rhodesia: Some Implications for Crisis Prevention," in Alexander V. George, ed., *Managing U.S.-Soviet Rivalry: Problems of Crisis Prevention* (Boulder, Colo.: Westview Press, 1983), pp. 157–63.

3. Cuban assistance to the MPLA, initiated in 1966, remained relatively constant until 1975. This assistance, consisting of arms and training programs in Cuba and in Congo-Brazzaville, was motivated by Cuba's ideological preference for the MPLA over its rivals. Following South African troop movements into Angola and South Africa's opening of training bases for the FNLA and UNITA in southern Angola in 1975, the MPLA appealed to Cuba for troop support. Cuba responded by sending several hundred troops. See William LeoGrande, "Cuban-Soviet Relations and Cuban Policy in Africa," *Cuban Studies/Estudios Cubanos*, vol. 10 (January 1980), pp. 7–11.

4. BBC (British Broadcasting Corporation) Monitoring Service, Publication ME/0557, September 9, 1989, p. B/5.

5. Jiri Valenta, "The Soviet-Cuban Intervention in Angola, 1975," *Studies in Comparative Communism*, vol. 11 (Spring/Summer 1978), p. 21.

6. Raymond L. Garthoff, *Detente and Confrontation: American-Soviet Relations from Nixon to Reagan* (Brookings, 1985), p. 529.

7. "President Ford Reiterates U.S. Objective in Angola," text of a letter from President Ford to Speaker of the House Carl Albert, January 27, in *Department of State Bulletin*, vol. 74 (February 16, 1976), p. 183.

8. *Statement of Henry Kissinger, Secretary of State, January 29, 1976, on U.S. Involvement in the Civil War in Angola*, Hearings before the Subcommittee on African Affairs of the Senate Committee on Foreign Relations, 94 Cong. 2 sess. (Government Printing Office, 1976), p. 7.

9. Congressional Research Service, "The Soviet Union and the Third World: A Watershed in Great Power Policy?" Report to the Committee on International Relations, House of Representatives (Government Printing Office, 1977), p. 7.

10. Robin Hallett, "The South African Intervention in Angola, 1975–76," *African Affairs*, vol. 77 (July 1978), p. 363.

11. Deon Geldenhuys, *The Diplomacy of Isolation: South African Foreign Policy Making* (Johannesburg: Macmillan South Africa, 1984), pp. 79–80.

12. Gillian Gunn, "A Guide to the Intricacies of the Angola-Namibia Negotiations," *CSIS Africa Notes*, no. 90 (Washington: Center for Strategic and International Studies, September 8, 1988), p. 12. See also Howard Wolpe, "Seizing Southern African Opportunities," *Foreign Policy*, no. 73 (Winter 1988–89), p. 61; I. William Zartman, *Ripe for Resolution: Conflict and Intervention in Africa*, 2d ed. (Oxford University Press, 1989), chap. 5.

13. Quoted in *New York Times*, November 16, 1988, p. 1.

14. For a discussion of the Soviet role, see Chester A. Crocker, *High Noon in Southern Africa: Making Peace in a Rough Neighborhood* (Norton, 1992), pp. 422–24;

and Donald Rothchild, "Regional Peacemaking in Africa: The Role of the Great Powers as Facilitators," in John W. Harbeson and Donald Rothchild, eds., *Africa in World Politics* (Boulder, Colo.: Westview, 1991), pp. 284–306.

15. Crocker, *High Noon*, pp. 456–58.

16. Interview with Fidel Castro, *Granma Weekly Review*, March 13, 1988, p. 7.

17. Charles W. Freeman, Jr., "The Angola/Namibia Accords," *Foreign Affairs*, vol. 68 (Summer 1989), p. 133.

18. Chester A. Crocker, "The U.S. and Angola," Statement before the Senate Committee on Foreign Relations, February 18, 1986, in *Current Policy*, no. 796 (U.S. Department of State, Bureau of Public Affairs, 1986), p. 1.

19. Jiri Valenta, "Comment: The Soviet-Cuban Alliance in Africa and Future Prospects in the Third World," *Cuban Studies*, vol. 10 (July 1980), p. 39.

20. Pauline H. Baker, "The American Challenge in Southern Africa," *Current History*, vol. 88 (May 1989), p. 245.

21. BBC Monitoring Service, Publication ME/0532, August 11, 1989, p. B/6.

22. BBC Monitoring Service, Publication ME/0491, June 24, 1989, p. B/1.

23. On the pressures used on dos Santos to encourage him to attend the summit, see *Africa Confidential*, vol. 30 (July 7, 1989), pp. 3–4; BBC Monitoring Service, Publication ME/0491, June 24, 1989, p. B/1.

24. See the interview by Margaret A. Novicki with Herman J. Cohen, U.S. assistant secretary of state for African affairs, "Forging a Bipartisan Policy," in *Africa Report*, vol. 34 (September–October 1989), p. 16.

25. BBC Monitoring Service, Publication ME/0494, June 28, 1989, p. B/1.

26. BBC Monitoring Service, Publication ME/0544, August 25, 1989, p. B/1.

27. Novicki, interview with Herman J. Cohen, "Forging a Bipartisan Policy," p. 17.

28. Kenneth B. Noble, "Rebel Head Agrees to Angolan Truce," *New York Times*, December 4, 1989, p. A7.

29. BBC Monitoring Service, Publication ME/0543, August 24, 1989, p. B/3.

30. Warren Clark, Jr., "National Reconciliation Efforts for Angola," Statement before the Subcommittee on Africa of the House Foreign Affairs Committee, September 27, 1989, in *Current Policy*, no. 1217 (U.S. Department of State, Bureau of Public Affairs, 1989), p. 2; BBC Monitoring Service, Publication ME/0574, September 19, 1989, pp. B/2, B/3. Savimbi also stated that the peace talks were not achieving their desired results "because they were not prepared properly." *Times* (London), September 13, 1989.

31. UNITA Ceasefire Appeal," *Africa Research Bulletin* (Political Series), vol. 27 (April 15, 1990, p. 9628.

32. Christopher S. Wren, "South African Chief in Zaire to Discuss Angola," *New York Times*, August 26, 1989, p. A4.

33. Lisa Hopkins, "Is Peace Finally in Store for Angola?" *Guardian* (New York), July 5, 1989, pp. 1, 21; Kenneth B. Noble, "For Angola Rebel, New Respectability," *New York Times*, June 26, 1989, p. A3.

34. U.S. Congress, Senate Committee on Foreign Relations, *Hearings* [on the nomination of Herman J. Cohen to be assistant secretary of state for African affairs, May 3, 1989] (Washington: Alderson Reporting, 1989), p. 26.

35. Martin Lowenkopf, "If the Cold War Is Over in Africa, Will the United States Still Care?" *CSIS Africa Notes*, no. 98 (Washington: Center for Strategic and Interna-

tional Studies, May 30, 1989), p. 5; Robert Pear, "U.S. and Angola Discuss Forging Diplomatic Ties," *New York Times*, January 27, 1989, p. A3.

36. Herman J. Cohen, "Cease-fire and Political Settlement in Angola," *U.S. Department of State Dispatch*, vol. 2 (May 6, 1991), p. 328.

37. Luanda Domestic Service, "Unita, Government Peace Accords Detailed," in Foreign Broadcast Information Service (FBIS), *Sub-Saharan Africa*, May 3, 1991, p. 7; London BBC World Service, interview with Jonas Savimbi by Tim Cabral, in FBIS, *Sub-Saharan Africa* (May 1, 1991), p. 16.

38. Jonas Savimbi, "The UNITA President Dr. Jonas Savimbi's Message to the Angolan Nation," March 10, 1992, p. 1. Typescript. Meanwhile, Luanda Radio charged that "UNITA did not have the least interest in the elections. UNITA wanted and wants power at any cost." "Commentary Blames Savimbi's 'Excessive Ambition'," FBIS, *Sub-Saharan Africa* (October 15, 1992), p. 21.

39. Lisbon Radio Renascenca, "Savimbi Seeks Support for UN," in FBIS, *Sub-Saharan Africa* (November 12, 1991), p. 16.

40. Desmond Davies, "A New Look at . . . Conflict," *West Africa* (December 5–11, 1994), p. 2066.

41. UNITA and other observers charged the Angolan government with using the security firm Executive Outcome to funnel some 500 to 3,000 mercenaries into Angola, many of whom were directly involved in the battles with UNITA forces. BBC World Service, as reported in FBIS, *Sub-Saharan Africa* (December 8, 1994), p. 10.

42. "Angola: The militarists on Top," *Africa Confidential*, vol. 35 (February 18, 1994), pp. 6–7.

43. *Lusaka Protocol*, General Principles, 1, p. 16.

44. Interview with Jonas Savimbi by Stephen Smith, in *Liberation* (Paris), in FBIS, *Sub-Saharan Africa* (December 22, 1994), p. 22.

45. For one participant in the mediation process linkage was the "only available framework for a settlement" (Freeman, "Angola/Namibia Accords," p. 133). See also Colin Legum, "Southern Africa: Analysis of the Peace Process," *Third World Reports* (London: CSI Syndication Service, January 11, 1989), L.B/1, p. 6; G. R. Berridge, "Diplomacy and the Angola/Namibia Accords," *International Affairs* (London), vol. 65 (Summer 1989), p. 471.

46. Sergio Trefaut, "UNITA Embarks on Electoral Campaign," *Semanario* (Lisbon), in FBIS, *Sub-Saharan Africa*, May 2, 1991, p. 16.

CHAPTER NINE

Negotiating an End to Mozambique's Murderous Rebellion

Ibrahim Msabaha

THE TERMINATION of Portuguese colonial rule in Mozambique in 1975 was followed by years of intense military conflict between the governing Front for the Liberation of Mozambique (FRELIMO) and the Mozambican National Resistance (MNR or RENAMO)—a conflict resolved by agreement only in late 1994. The intensity of the confrontation was matched by government efforts to resolve the hostilities, first by coercive methods using armed action, and after 1984 by a mixture of force and diplomacy: pacifying methods of mediation and negotiation were combined with military intervention in support of the government.

The diplomacy of violence produced the Pretoria Declaration of 1984, the Nairobi and Rome rounds of talks in 1989–92, three major protocols, and the Rome Declaration of Agreement in 1992. This diplomatic activity occurred against a background of several factors: the Nkomati Accord of 1984, a conflict management effort between South Africa and Mozambique; the introduction of troops from Tanzania and Zimbabwe into Mozambique in 1986 to halt the collapse of the government; changes in the international system brought about by the end of the cold war, the disinte-

This is to acknowledge with gratitude the research assistance of Bernard Membe, Kate Almquist, and Darin Ohlandt in preparing this chapter.

gration of the Soviet Union, and political revolution in Eastern Europe; a change in the balance of forces in southern Africa in favor of the liberation process, as reflected in the independence of Namibia achieved in 1989, the release of Nelson Mandela from prison in South Africa in 1990, and the completion of negotiations in 1994 to eradicate South African apartheid; and a new wave of devastating drought in southern Africa.

Against this backdrop of national, regional, and global developments the primary question for the analyst of these (or any) negotiations is what best explains the efforts toward conflict resolution through negotiation. The question has academic and policymaking relevance. Most analysis of international negotiation focuses on negotiations in the industrialized countries and on those concerning East-West economics and security.[1] Only recently has attention shifted away from East-West relations to North-South economic negotiations.[2] The reason for this is an inherited intellectual malaise under which the study of negotiations is a growth industry in the developed nations but is virtually nonexistent in African states. Yet today negotiation rules supreme in every aspect of public policymaking.

This chapter examines the applicability of general negotiation theory and concepts to the Mozambican conflict in order to improve the analysis of negotiations for academicians and the practice of conflict resolution. It also seeks to contribute to policymakers' understanding of the Mozambican conflict and the methods used to terminate that conflict in order to promote peace, security, and development in Mozambique.

The Mozambican war has been characterized by conflicts of interest and substantial costs, and therefore the need for a settlement between the belligerents. These salient features imposed their logic on diplomatic and military behavior. The protagonists must be viewed as pursuing the resolution of the conflict rationally, at least at the talks. However, in Mozambique as in most other cases conflicting parties, on their own, were incapable of resolving their conflicts and thus effective third-party intervention was a precondition for conflict resolution.

The Mozambican negotiations were a result of efforts by both the government and the Mozambican National Resistance to manage the complex environment that brought about the conflict. Rapid changes taking place in the international system were reflected in the will of the parties to negotiate. These changes eventually explain the motives, strategies, and tactics of the protagonists.

The end of the cold war and the collapse of communist regimes in central and eastern Europe precipitated a new revolution. Although the international system has remained in a state of transition, it has promoted the settlement of regional disputes by peaceful means. As is typical in a period of transition in the international system, negotiation as a peacemaking and policymaking instrument has regained importance in resolving old and new issues. Whereas East-West competition traditionally induced the superpowers to ignore the character of regimes they supported, the end of the cold war has been unfavorable to autocratic regimes and those that do not favor negotiated settlement of their conflicts. In short, this period of transition in the international system has produced a political climate conducive to negotiated settlements, both directly between conflicting parties and through mediation.

Background and Context

In his analysis of conflict and its resolution in Africa, I. William Zartman identifies four general causes of conflict: power struggles resulting from decolonization, consolidation following independence, leftover liberation movements, and ill-defined territories.[3] Decolonization power struggles originate in the fierce political competition and maneuvering among domestic groups and parties for political participation and control of political position. Consolidation confrontations follow the defeat of the common colonial enemy. Leftover liberation movements, on the other hand, relate to the legacy of the anticolonial struggle. As his study puts it, "the struggle for national liberation has legitimized anti-state politics and guerrilla movements; the successor states now have to live with their own legacy."[4] This classification is incomplete in that it neglects the socioeconomic asymmetries within nations and among states. But Zartman's identification of the causes of conflict is useful in the Mozambican case because in the Mozambican context his first three sources of conflict account for the hostilities between the FRELIMO government and the Mozambican National Resistance.

The achievement of independence by Mozambique in 1975 was a political and psychological threat to the white minority regimes in Rhodesia and South Africa. Strategically, an independent Mozambique, like an independent Angola, signaled a shift in favor of the decolonization movement in southern Africa. It afforded psychological and material support to Zimbabwean and South African liberation movements. The demonstrative effect of the changing balance of forces in southern Africa was vividly expressed in the Soweto uprising in South Africa in 1976 and in the intensification of the armed struggle in Rhodesia. Leaders of the Black Consciousness movement in South Africa were arrested for participating in an illegal rally to celebrate the independence of Mozambique, and in September 1976 one of them—Steve Biko—was murdered while in police custody. These events demonstrated South Africa's nervousness about the changing strategic balance in southern Africa. Mozambique thus became a prime target for Rhodesian and South African strategies to counter the tide of decolonization.[5]

Mozambique's historic dependence on South Africa and Portugal was its main structural weakness. Mozambique had been tied to South Africa since an agreement between Portugal and South Africa in 1901, under which the colonial state received 13 shillings for each Mozambican mine worker leased to South Africa, as well as 6 pence for each month's service beyond an initial one-year contract period. Consequently labor rent became Mozambique's main source of income and foreign exchange. For its part, South Africa agreed to use the port of Maputo for the imports and exports of the Transvaal region, thus exchanging transport for labor dependency.

Dependence on South Africa meant that any "domestic" conflict in Mozambique was inherently regional and that any bilateral encounter between the government and insurgents ultimately became multilateral, involving South Africa and other external powers. As a result there could be no purely internal solution. For instance, between 1975 and 1982 South Africa reduced the number of Mozambican mine workers from 120,000 to 45,000, thus denying Mozambique $3.2 billion in revenue.[6]

Formation and Roles of the MNR

A key element in the Rhodesian and South African strategy for countering decolonization was the creation of a Mozambican movement of national resistance by the Rhodesian regime's special branch in 1974, with the support of the Portuguese intelligence service, PIDE. From its inception the movement assumed many names as part of its evolution: Free Africa, Free Mozambique, Mozambique Resistance Movement (MRM), National Resistance Movement (MNR), and after 1980, the Mozambican National Resistance, or RENAMO. Ken Flowers, former head of the Rhodesian Central Intelligence Organization, in particular wanted to create a fifth column inside Mozambique whose members could be used as interpreters, guides, and scouts for Rhodesian army incursions into Mozambique in search of guerrillas of the Zimbabwe African Nationalist Union (ZANU), and for economic and political destabilization of areas in Mozambique used as bases by ZANU.[7] Mozambique's decision to implement sanctions against Rhodesia on March 3, 1976, gave the Rhodesian regime of Ian Smith an excuse for destabilization.

The Rhodesian regime capitalized on dissidence within Mozambique's ruling Front for the Liberation of Mozambique—the country's national liberation movement whose fifteen years of struggle had produced break-away factions even before independence in 1975. In the period 1965–69 a number of top FRELIMO leaders had been assassinated (including FRELIMO president Edward Mondlane), ethnic splinter groups were formed, and a special party congress in 1970 chose as Mondlane's successor Samora Machel, a Shangani from southern Mozambique, which was neither the most populous area nor the area where the anticolonial movement was most active. A number of leaders who were Ndaos from central Mozambique were assassinated, and others, including Machel's main rival, fearing for their lives, defected to Rhodesia or Portugal. One of the defectors was Orlando Cristina, four years later to become the MNR's first leader.[8] Dissatisfaction with the Marxist orientation of FRELIMO, its perceived Shangani leadership, and the shortfalls of independence produced further strains and a crisis in governance immediately upon independence. According to one study, "many FRELIMO guerrillas felt they deserved compensation for the many years of fighting in the bush, and that they had a right to take what they wanted. The FRELIMO leadership cracked down hard, and many ex-guerrillas were sent to re-education centers."[9] Dissension was coupled with peasant dissatisfaction with forced rural reorganization into regimented villages ("villagization") and with a lack of consumer goods.

All of these dissident elements formed the support for the Rhodesian-sponsored national resistance movement. They were joined by elements of the PIDE Fleches—commandos who had opposed FRELIMO all along—and by witch doctors and Portuguese-appointed officials deposed by FRELIMO at independence. The MNR was thus the only African guerrilla movement founded by "white spy masters" rather than indigenous groups.

When Rhodesia gained independence in 1980 the strategic situation changed for South Africa. South Africa took over the national resistance movement (now known as MNR), changing not only its patronage but also its strategy: MNR's main task would be to carry out destabilization through intelligence activities and by inflicting economic damage on Mozambique. As part of a so-called total strategy, the MNR was a useful instrument in

South Africa's regional policy of military intimidation and economic strangulation of the frontline states.[10] The objectives were to create a cordon sanitaire of states that would be perpetually dependent on South Africa and vulnerable to South African pressures, and to present Mozambique with security problems that would make it rethink FRELIMO support for the African National Congress (ANC) in South Africa (see chapter 7). The crisis in governance was to worsen the situation for the FRELIMO government.

Crisis in Governance

As in other African states at the time of independence, in Mozambique in 1975 there was an understandable and exclusive emphasis on national unity. In building a new Mozambican state, FRELIMO—a Marxist party— encouraged a focus on a single leader, Marxist ideology, and a single party. The emphasis on national economic reconstruction after years of guerrilla warfare put a high premium on collectivization, forced villagization, and nationalization of the major means of production and distribution. For instance, after the third FRELIMO party congress in 1977, at which the party changed from a broad mass party to a committed vanguard party, Mozambique moved to create huge state farms, incorporating 35,000 acres, to employ about 200,000 rural workers left idle by settlers who had fled the country in 1975. By 1982 government investment in state farms had reached $75 million for agricultural machinery such as tractors and combine harvesters.[11] Yet by the end of 1982 state farms accounted for only 20 percent of the national agricultural output. The villagization policy did not bear any better fruits. Although by 1982 about 1,400 villages had been established, with a total population of 1.8 million, fewer than 25 percent of the villages had agricultural cooperatives. Moreover, between 1979 and 1986 production on communal farms fell by 50 percent. Worse still, there was a general scarcity of consumer goods, and South Africa had decided to increase pressure on the FRELIMO government by reducing the number of Mozambican mine workers it employed.

Thus seven years after independence FRELIMO government policies and South African destabilization had combined to produce citizens' alienation from genuine political participation, underground opposition, political instability, and the clandestine support for antigovernment violence. The Mozambican state and society remained apart, and sustainable peace and security became impossible. By the late 1980s Mozambique was paralyzed: about 50 percent of the country was disrupted by RENAMO, nearly 1 million people had been killed and another 2 million displaced,[12] a collapsed administration made most of the country inaccessible from Maputo except by air, and the political and economic system faced pressures for change from the major Western powers. In short, the Mozambican state, unable to preserve peace and foster economic prosperity, lost the confidence of its citizens, especially those in the rural areas. It had lost not only the initiative, but also the ability to make the economic transformation essential to regaining the support of the rural population. Strikes after 1990 indicated that support also became difficult to sustain even in urban areas.[13] The security crisis brought about an urgent need for talks.

Paul Pillar contends that talks to end conflict arise out of three essential conditions: the parties to the conflict must realize that they could improve their lots if they struck a bargain with each other; mutual action must be undertaken to reach an agreement, preempting unilateral solutions; and several possible settlements must exist.[14] Parties to a conflict must appreciate that they need a solution and that to get one they must cooperate. Although warfare inflicts immense costs in terms of military and civilian lives, in Mozambique neither the government nor the insurgents could attain their objectives through military action—that is, neither could impose a solution. Thus a mutually hurting stalemate produced an impetus for negotiations at several points in the sixteen-year history of the conflict. The failure of those negotiations, as well as their occurrence, must be explained.

By 1983 destabilization had been identified as the main problem facing the young state, and the restoration of peace and security the main challenge. The fourth FRELIMO party congress, held that year, passed several resolutions aimed at combating the deteriorating security situation. In doing so the congress reversed the policy set by the third congress in 1977 that established state control over strategic sectors of the economy; criticized the heavy-handedness of the FRELIMO leaders; identified the family sector, rather than state farms, as the national priority in new policies; approved Mozambican economic cooperation with the Western world; and identified the regional organization, the Southern African Development Coordination Conference (SADCC), as an instrument to challenge South Africa's economic domination in southern Africa.[15]

It was against this background that the government negotiated the Nkomati Accord with South Africa in 1984, agreeing to withdraw its material support for the African National Congress in exchange for an end to South African support for RENAMO. However, the Nkomati Accord did not improve Mozambican security, and later in the same year in a follow-up agreement (Nkomati II), South Africa obtained Mozambican recognition of RENAMO as a player.[16] Continuing South African support for RENAMO precipitated Mozambican withdrawal, in October 1985, from the Joint Security Commission established under the terms of the first Nkomati Accord. Mozambican president Machel, going on a diplomatic offensive against South Africa, undertook a highly publicized tour of Western Europe to prompt the West, and especially the United States, to press South Africa into respecting the Nkomati Accord. Mozambique also signed a security agreement with Malawi, in 1986, under which RENAMO bases in Malawi would be dismantled, Mozambique would be allowed the right of hot pursuit across the border, and Malawian troops would help guard the strategic Nacala-Malawi railway line.

These approaches were undertaken by the government as diplomatic contacts with the insurgent movement continued. With the encouragement of South Africa, early contacts took place in Frankfurt am Main on May 29, 1984, between RENAMO's spokesperson in Europe—Evo Fernandes— and a Mozambican official.[17] RENAMO wanted a multiparty system and a government of national reconciliation in which its members would have a share of cabinet posts. The government, however, rejected the concept of power-sharing with RENAMO and offered only amnesty for RENAMO fighters. That first exchange constituted an exploratory stage in contacts to determine whether the two parties could meet at all.

Direct South African involvement in the next round of talks, held at the beginning of October 1984, produced the first attempt at serious negotiations. After a three-day meeting in Pretoria, South African foreign minister Pik Botha announced the Pretoria Declaration—agreement on a cease-fire and on the beginning of substantive negotiations on the basis of four principles: recognition of President Machel as Mozambique's head of state; cessation of all armed activities; South African involvement in implementing a settlement; and establishment of a joint commission to work for application of a settlement.[18]

The Pretoria Declaration did not lead to a cease-fire, and its failure precipitated a second meeting, on October 8–11, under South Africa's mediation. FRELIMO and RENAMO came with different agendas. The Mozambican government's priority was the cessation of armed hostilities at a fixed date; the insurgents wanted to reopen negotiations on RENAMO's political future in Mozambique. Just when it appeared that agreement was being reached, the insurgents broke off the talks under pressure from Portugal, which so far had not been involved in the negotiations.

Six years later, in 1990, an alleged lack of Portuguese involvement also became a factor in the failure of negotiations at Blantyre, Malawi. As a former colonial power, Portugal had a major stake in the outcome of negotiations between the Mozambican government and RENAMO. Mozambique had nationalized substantial assets of Portuguese investors, who thus had a stake in any denationalization that might result from a cessation of hostilities between the government and the insurgents. Potential peace dividends and its prestige as a former colonial power kept Portugal interested in Mozambican politics.

Following the collapse of talks in October 1984, it was to be five years before negotiations were reopened; talks resumed in Nairobi, Kenya, in 1989. The Mozambican domestic scene and the international environment had grown much more complex in the interim.

Analysis of Negotiations

Any negotiation must take certain preliminaries into account, among them a diagnosis of the motives and backgrounds of the parties and the implications of these for the prospective negotiations. The basic question is whether the conflict is negotiable at all—a question that arises from the asymmetrical nature of the government-insurgency relationship, as I. William Zartman points out in chapter 1.

The weakness of an insurgency rests on its uphill struggle to cover itself with the mantle of legitimacy, which is taken away from the government's monopoly. Even when it admits the standing of an insurgency as a negotiating party, the government remains a prisoner of its own notions of asymmetry; if it adopts reform as its platform, as FRELIMO was to do in 1989, it removes from the conflict what should be negotiated. The FRELIMO-RENAMO negotiations were to be plagued with the problem of unilateral enactment of positive reforms, which corrected grievances but robbed the insurgency of the very credits it needed for legitimization.

Nevertheless, although the structural features of asymmetry impose constraints, the presumed strength of the government becomes the basis for negotiation. The insurgency does acquire command of material resources to inflict damage on government credibility. Guerrilla attacks can be launched with relatively simple material resources. Yet a government must mobilize greater resources to protect vital installations and the population. Thus the greater the capability of the insurgency to impose insecurity, the greater the probability that the government will hold talks to enhance its security. That factor, as well as others that bring parties to talks—historical conjecture, stalemate, escalation, changes in the balance of forces, and third-party pressure—underlay government-insurgency negotiations in Mozambique.

The Pretoria Talks

The road to the Pretoria Declaration of 1984 was rocky. The basic issue of contention was one of legitimacy and recognition. Because of the insurgency's nature as an internal rebellion, the government defined the Mozambican National Resistance as an illegal organization devoid of legitimacy. The insurgents were considered to be a bandit group whose main objectives were senseless killings and the destruction of civilians, economic projects, and infrastructure. That definition, accurate as it was in principle, ruled out genuine negotiations. However, it was precisely RENAMO's tactics, brutal and inhuman as they were, that brought about the virtual collapse of civilian administration and the government's interest in negotiation to try to curb its own collapse.

The partial achievement of South Africa's strategic objectives in Mozambique, as reflected in the Nkomati Accords of 1984, was a complicating factor in the government-RENAMO relationship. South Africa found itself in the paradoxical position of transforming the nature of the negotiation from a bilateral to a trilateral structure. As a sanctuary for the insurgents South Africa was a party to the conflict, and as a host to the Pretoria talks it played a mediatory role. Thus South Africa did not legitimize RENAMO as an effective negotiator; it merely acted as RENAMO's agent.

The theory of negotiations contends that there are at least four negotiating dimensions in any bilateral talks: the horizontal, internal, and vertical, and shadow bargaining.[19] Horizontal negotiations are those that occur across the table; they are formal and structured. That setting gives the false impression that most substance is discussed at the table; the reality is quite different. Although the formality of horizontal negotiations is useful in that it sets the tone for future negotiations, provides an opportunity for information gathering and sharing, and allows posturing, most real negotiation takes place internally, vertically (that is, within each side), and in shadow bargaining away from the negotiating table. These characteristics of bilateral negotiations increase geometrically rather than arithmetically in trilateral or quadrilateral talks, such as those held during the Mozambican conflict.

On the face of it, it should have been in the interest of the Mozambican government and the Mozambican National Resistance to keep negotiations bilateral. However, "pure" bilateralism would have placed the insurgents at a disadvantage. It was in RENAMO's interest to bring South Africa and Portugal into the negotiations as a source of power, through the threat of continued external support and violence. South Africa and the Mozambican government also had an interest in a trilateral relationship. South Africa faced a choice between good neighborliness as a mediator and continued support for RENAMO as a bargaining chip with the government.[20] To be successful as a mediator, South Africa would be expected to deliver RENAMO's approval of an agreement—not an easy task. By 1984 South Africa had chosen a double-track policy of good neighborliness (by signing the Nkomati Accord) and continuing clandestine support for RENAMO.

FRELIMO had a choice among winning RENAMO away from South Africa, using South Africa to influence the insurgents, and seeking an accommodation with South Africa. FRELIMO opted for accommodation with South Africa, through the Nkomati Accord, hoping to use the Pretoria regime as a mediator to terminate the insurgents' destabilizing campaign.

Although the Pretoria talks of 1984 were the direct result of the Nkomati Accord, the question arises as to whether South Africa was at that time serious about good neighborliness. The evidence of continued clandestine support for RENAMO indicates that the Pretoria regime negotiated the Nkomati Accord only to curb Mozambican support for the African National Congress and to improve South Africa's international standing as a peacemaker.[21] As a rear base for the insurgents and thus an intervenor, South Africa could have coerced the insurgents into accommodation with the government if agreement had been its real objective.

The Pretoria talks also collapsed because of disagreement within RENAMO ranks and between the insurgents and their Portuguese backers. Internal negotiation within a party brings about complications because the negotiators represent and defend the positions of their constituencies rather than their own personal positions. Portuguese supporters of the Mozambican National Resistance felt that the Machel government was not ready to implement the major economic and political reforms that would justify a peaceful settlement. In short, for RENAMO and its backers the time was not ripe for resolution.

The Nairobi Talks

The principal impetus for the Nairobi talks of August 10–12, 1989, came from the emergence of Joachim Chissano as president of Mozambique and the changes in the international system. The government of President Machel was identified with the hard-line revolutionary policies of FRELIMO as a vanguard Marxist party. The party and the governmental structure over which Machel presided looked at negotiation with the Mozambican National Resistance as a compromise and a defeat for the Mozambican revolution. Under normal circumstances a party's security point is an important point of reference in negotiations, and especially in the initial decision on whether or not to negotiate. In Mozambique the deterioration in security between 1984 and 1986 and the consequent loss of the government's dominant position might have convinced FRELIMO that the time was ripe for negotiation. Instead, worsening security acted as a psychological barrier for the Machel government, producing a negative image that equated talks with defeat. To improve his position Machel opted to invite the intervention of friendly troops from Tanzania and Zimbabwe and to revive relations with the Catholic Church in Mozambique, meeting the pope in Rome in 1985. The Chissano government, coming to power in 1986, inherited both improved national security (especially from mid-1987 on as Mozambique no longer faced the threat of partition in Zambesia province) and improving relations with a potential mediator, notably through Jaime Gonçalves, the Bishop of Beira (Mozambique). The change of leadership produced the impetus to seize on the change.

A related impetus was the relaxation of tensions in East-West relations and political revolution in Eastern Europe, in which communist governments lost power. Diplomatic historians contend that history is marked by periods of transition from one international system to another and from one epoch to another, during which diplomacy is called into exceptional activity.[22] The withering away of the post–World War II international system produced a climate for negotiated settlements in regional and national conflicts,[23] and yet among African states offered greater possibilities for physical and psychological intimidation.

Since 1945 a socialist Eastern Europe, under the Warsaw Pact had acted as a mentor to a number of third-world regimes and a counterforce to the capitalist Western world and to NATO. But in 1986 the Soviet Union was wholly preoccupied with internal convulsions and politics, and its open declaration that the policy of perestroika implied noninterference in the

internal affairs of other countries was interpreted as an emerging isolation-
ism in Soviet foreign policy. Marxist revolutionary governments such as
FRELIMO could no longer bank on the Soviet political and military umbrella in regional conflicts.

With his succession to the Mozambican presidency in 1986, Chissano
prepared to defeat the rebellion by negotiation rather than purely military
means. The turning point came in July 1989 when the new leader of South
Africa's National Party (and president-to-be) F. W. de Klerk came to
Maputo and agreed to end aid to RENAMO. Chissano announced that
FRELIMO was ready for dialogue with RENAMO if the insurgent movement would renounce violence and agree to function under Mozambique's
constitution.[24]

Changes within Frelimo and Renamo

During the fifth FRELIMO party congress of July 1989 important decisions were taken in the direction of reform, breaking the deadlock on
negotiation. First, FRELIMO underwent a reverse transformation from a
vanguard party to a mass party. By its own admission in 1989, its decision
in 1977 to become a vanguard party had destroyed FRELIMO's representative character and had alienated grass-roots citizens, especially the peasants. At the same congress, Chissano also expanded multiethnic representation in top party circles to include Ndaos and other groups that were strong
in the Mozambican National Resistance. Second, the congress resolved to
expand democracy and to end single-party rule in Mozambique. Between
September 1989 and January 1990 a draft constitution was prepared and
debate on democracy and a multiparty system was launched. The draft
recognized universal suffrage, human rights of individuals, and the right to
strike, and prepared the way for a multiparty system. In August 1990
FRELIMO's Central Committee endorsed a multiparty system for Mozambique.

The third significant decision taken at the fifth party congress was the
renunciation of Marxism and the acceptance of economic reforms in which the
private rather than state sector would play a pivotal role. Mozambique accepted
an International Monetary Fund (IMF) economic recovery package that guaranteed private investment. In a fourth decision, the congress opened the way
for direct and open negotiations with RENAMO, which for the first time was
called by its name instead of being referred to as armed bandits. The congress
approved Chissano's authorization, given earlier in July, of contacts with

delegates of the Catholic Church and RENAMO, on the condition that RENAMO renounce violence and support constitutional rule.[25]

Changes taking place within RENAMO paralleled the internal changes in FRELIMO. Afonso Dhlakama, a former FRELIMO soldier, had taken over RENAMO leadership in 1979–80 as external sponsorship passed from Rhodesia to South Africa. He consolidated his own power and pounded RENAMO into a coherent political organization and centrally controlled military force.[26] Although RENAMO's military unity was to prove elusive, its political platform gradually began to appear after 1979. It took ten years for Dhlakama to consolidate RENAMO to the point where the movement could plan its first congress; it was held on June 5–9, 1989, six weeks before FRELIMO's fifth party congress. At its own congress RENAMO dropped most of its preconditions to negotiation and agreed to begin talks; many preconditions—elections, coalition government, an end to socialism, a market economy, respect for the church—were reduced to opening demands.[27]

Mediators and Proposals

The distinguishing features of the Nairobi talks of August 1989 were their indirect nature and the variety of mediators. Communications were largely carried out indirectly between the Catholic Church and the Mozambican National Resistance, with Presidents Daniel Arap Moi of Kenya and Robert Mugabe of Zimbabwe as mediators. In the Mozambican case both the advantages and the disadvantages of using third-party agents in conflict resolution were evident. The advantages are expertise, detachment, and tactical flexibility; the disadvantages are increased complexity in the negotiation process, possibilities for artifice and duplicity, and increased chances for unwanted side effects.[28]

As early as 1987 the Mozambican Catholic Church had issued a pastoral letter, "The Peace that the People Want," calling for direct negotiations. In 1989 the church asked the FRELIMO government for permission to contact RENAMO leaders to "ascertain their views on the conflict" and to determine whether or not any negotiations were possible.[29] At the same time, in February, having just concluded an agreement with Angola (see chapter 8), South African foreign minister Botha called for United States and Soviet intervention to settle the Mozambican conflict. RENAMO had rejected mediation by South Africa. RENAMO saw that its heavy dependence on the apartheid regime could be used to steamroll the movement into accepting conditions that it would rather evade. Just as FRELIMO was losing its external support from a withdrawing Soviet Union, RENAMO was losing its backing from a changing South Africa that had growing interest in conflict resolution; similarly, sympathy in the United States was heavily eroded by the publication of the Gersony Report officially detailing the terrorist nature of RENAMO's activities.[30]

The refusal of South African mediation was followed on July 21, 1989, by a formal request from the Mozambican government to Presidents Mugabe and Moi to become official mediators. The U.S. government was invited to intervene by pressuring the two main parties to reduce their aspirations and to become more accommodating to a wider peaceful settlement. That strategy relied on the perception that there would be further intervention by the major powers unless the belligerents settled the conflict between themselves, and that such intervention might carry the prospects of an imposed solution (as had happened in the superpower-sponsored agreements in Namibia and elsewhere). The Kenyan and Zimbabwean presidents were to integrate the two parties' lists of demands and compensate the parties for any losses, in an effort to find creative solutions that FRELIMO and RENAMO had been unable to discover.

Well before the Nairobi talks, the Mozambican government preempted the agenda by circulating to foreign embassies in Maputo a twelve-point plan to end the conflict with the Mozambican National Resistance. That plan included the following points, among others: the conflict was a destabilization operation and not a war between parties; before talks the MNR must therefore stop all acts of terrorism and banditry; dialogue would be open to all individuals, including those involved in violent destabilization; the constitution would be revised through popular debate, to enhance democratization of state functions; presidential elections would be by secret ballot; amnesty would apply to MNR bandits who voluntarily surrendered; the MNR must be reintegrated into society; and the MNR must end violence and respect individual and collective liberties, human rights, and democratic rights.[31] The emphasis in the government's plan was understandably on its own survival, and thus it called for a cease-fire, amnesty, and the introduction of government-instigated political and economic reforms.

In response, the Mozambican National Resistance circulated a sixteen-point program with emphasis on the withdrawal of all foreign forces from Mozambique, the creation of a multiparty system in which RENAMO could exist as an active political force, and commitment to a negotiated settlement.[32] The two plans were designed to address first the characteristic asymmetry of the situation by assuring the legitimacy of each party.

On August 7, 1989, Presidents Moi and Mugabe endorsed indirect exploratory negotiations and called upon all interested parties to support the initiative. The meeting in Nairobi a week later marked a first contact and laid the basis of both sides' legitimization. In January 1990 Moi and Mugabe produced a seven-point peace plan for direct talks, based on a document drafted by the United States embassy in December 1989, in which the two presidents suggested that a solution to the conflict must be found and that all attacks on civilians must stop; democracy in Mozambique must be based on freedom of expression and association and on economic liberation; all Mozambican citizens should be able to participate freely in the country's political, economic, social, and cultural life and to determine the country's national policies themselves; the people are sovereign and should be able to control the actions of their government through the right to vote; reconciliation and national unity must be the fundamental principles in the application of a peace plan; all parties must recognize the legitimacy of the Republic of Mozambique and its constitution, institutions, and laws; and any fundamental change in the Mozambican state should be carried out peaceably and democratically.[33]

As if to echo the new economic environment emerging in Mozambique and the government's new receptive thinking, the International Development Agency (IDA) approved a $50 million loan to enable the government to put into action a three-year industrial and agro-industrial restructuring project. The project had been conceived by the development consulting firm Arthur D. Little, was to be co-financed by Italy, France, and the United Kingdom, and would involve fifteen companies.[34]

The basis for negotiations had been laid down in the Nairobi process, but the parties were scarcely ready to come to a peace agreement. Both sides had recognized each other informally, but neither had granted formal recognition. Point six of the seven principles granted FRELIMO superior standing as the government. Moreover, at a summit meeting of nonaligned nations in Belgrade in September 1989, President Chissano declared that talks with RENAMO were not aimed at establishing a power sharing arrangement or altering the constitution of the Mozambican political order. On RENAMO's side, political consolidation was still incomplete and goals were uncertain, making RENAMO sensitive to matters of status. Even three years later RENAMO was to complain that mediators were "regarding the talks as being between a group of guerrillas and a government rather than between two political parties who have been at war for 15 years."[35] In that war RENAMO was now on the offensive; the government's last major counteroffensive had been in 1986–87.[36] Much more conflict between the parties and consolidation within each of them were needed before they could bring the process begun at Nairobi to fruition. For this they needed help from the outside, in the form of better mediators.

The Abortive Blantyre Round

Following the Nairobi round of exploratory talks and FRELIMO's new policy of openness, the Mozambican government and the Mozambican National Resistance prepared for their first direct talks, to be held in Blantyre, Malawi, in June 1990. There were to be four parties to the talks—the government, RENAMO, Zimbabwe, and Kenya, the latter two as official mediators, each with a ministerial delegation.

Before the talks could start, however, RENAMO objected to the venue on security grounds and issued three preconditions for the resumption of negotiations: withdrawal of Zimbabwean troops guarding the Beira Corridor, Zimbabwe's closest access to the sea across central Mozambique; suspension of a government military offensive against RENAMO bases then under way in Manica and Sofala provinces; and expulsion from Malawi of all Mozambican security officers in order not to compromise the security of the RENAMO team during the talks.[37]

The Mozambican government apparently wanted Blantyre as a venue for the talks in order to hold Malawi responsible for their outcome, and especially for adherence to any accord that might be reached. Such an arrangement was intended as a follow-up of a 1986 agreement under which Malawi would withdraw support for the Mozambican National Resistance. (Malawi had been used as a rear base by RENAMO, and in 1986 was the RENAMO base for an invasion of the Zambezi Valley.) The other reason appeared to be the dissatisfaction of the Mozambican government with Kenya as a mediator. Kenya was alleged to be siding with RENAMO and thus compromising its impartiality; yet Kenya would not deliver its ally's agreement to any accord. Moreover, Kenyan permanent secretary for foreign affairs Bethwell Kiplagat traveled to Blantyre on June 11 and left the next day in the same plane with Dhlakama, leader of RENAMO; Mozambicans regarded this as another symbol of Kenyan partiality.

In retrospect, it could be said that RENAMO, aware of the implications of the venue for the outcome of negotiations, was simply not prepared to negotiate seriously at Blantyre, and that RENAMO rejected Kenya as the mediator that might force its agreement.[38] RENAMO's dilemma was compounded by the government reform program, that emanated from FRELIMO's fifth party congress, because the insurgents needed time to respond and adjust to the reforms if they were to avoid being stampeded into an agreement. Thus the Blantyre round of negotiations was over before it started.

The Rome Negotiations

Following the collapse of the Blantyre round it became evident that a new venue and a new mediator were required. The Catholic Church was a willing candidate for the mediator's role. It was close to the more recalcitrant party, RENAMO, and therefore better placed to deliver that party's adherence to an agreement. Archbishop Jaime Gonçalves of Beira was particularly active in promoting mediation, and the Sant'Egidio lay community in Rome provided a location for negotiations. The Sant'Egidio community had been in contact with the Mozambican Catholic Church since 1976, arranging meetings between Gonçalves and Dhlakama and Gonçalves and Italian foreign minister Giulio Andreotti in 1988, as well as arranging Dhlakama's first trip to Rome in February 1990.[39] Then in March 1990, after a meeting with U.S. president George Bush, Chissano declared Frelimo's willingness to engage in a dialogue with RENAMO. The following month, as the Mozambican Catholic Church issued another pastoral letter, "Toward a Dialog for Peace," the Mozambican government asked the Sant'Egidio community to arrange a meeting with RENAMO.

A ministerial delegation from Mozambique met department heads of RENAMO in Rome under Sant'Egidio's auspices in a series of more than twenty rounds, beginning on July 8–10, 1990, and continuing to October 4, 1992. The first direct meetings were confidence-building occasions that accorded each party legitimacy. At the first meeting the government and the Mozambican National Resistance agreed "to set aside what divided them . . . and concentrate their attention on what unites them so as to create a common working basis . . . and to engage fully and in a spirit of mutual respect and understanding [to find] a working platform to put an end to war and create political, economic and social conditions conducive to a lasting peace and the normalization of life for all Mozambican citizens."[40]

At a second round, in August 1990, procedural issues blocked all others. FRELIMO insisted on a bilateral dialogue that would concentrate on military issues and would begin with a cease-fire, and on no United Nations

involvement. RENAMO insisted on inclusion of a mediator (again preferring Kenya) and on reaching an agreement on political reforms before
turning to military issues and elections; it wanted extensive UN involvement. The issues had been staked out.[41] The next round was boycotted by
RENAMO because of an offensive by Zimbabwean troops; talks were not
resumed until November 6, following intensive mediation by the Kenyan
and Zimbabwean presidents, to focus on the role and presence of
Zimbabwean troops as a new agenda item.

The talks then led rather rapidly to an early tangible outcome at the third
round on December 1, 1990, when a limited cease-fire, for a renewable
six-month period, was signed concerning the two main communications
corridors from Zimbabwe to Maputo and Beira. At the next round, in
mid-December, the Joint Verification Commission (CoMiVe) was created,
to be staffed by four African states (Zimbabwe, Kenya, Congo, and Zambia), four European countries (Portugal, Britain, France, and Italy), and the
two superpowers; Italy was designated chair of the commission and chief
mediator. However the cease-fire soon collapsed, CoMiVe's neutrality was
challenged by RENAMO, and much of 1991 was spent in fruitless negotiations and growing distrust.

The main obstacles to the peace process were the prevelant suspicion
(particularly on the part of RENAMO) arising from the two main parties'
asymmetry in status, both parties' unreal expectations of each other's
imminent collapse, and RENAMO's inability to develop clear goals and to
feel the pressure of the stalemate. The Mozambican National Resistance
was a fractionated organization with little central control over its various
guerrilla units in the field. It was animated by strong feelings of rebellion
against the FRELIMO government and its inadequacies, and had been more
interested in carrying out destruction than in seizing power. As long as its
units could roam the countryside and destroy government installations (and
local populations with them) it had little incentive to come to an agreement—much to the frustration of the Mozambican government, which was
beginning to feel the pressure of the hurting stalemate.[42] Only when the
rebels' external supporters started threatening to withhold their backing,
and when in late 1991 and 1992 a drought made conditions in the countryside unbearable, did RENAMO begin to feel the hurting stalemate and turn
its focus toward an agreement.

Also unhelpful to the negotiations were political reforms put into practice by the government as evidence of the characteristic asymmetry, and
thus particularly offensive to RENAMO. While the first rounds of talks

were going on, through the end of 1990, FRELIMO enacted multiparty reforms and constitutional amendments that covered the very issues under discussion in the negotiations. In so doing the government both undercut the negotiations and delegitimized the reform measures it had adopted. Nearly the first half of 1991 was spent restoring such issues to the negotiating agenda. The agenda was finally established in May 1991. It then took personal meetings with Dhlakama by Italian prime minister Andreotti, U.S. assistant secretary of state Herman Cohen, U.S. deputy assistant secretary Jeffrey Davidow, and Soviet ambassador Antoly Adamishin to secure RENAMO's agreement to the subjects and order of the agenda.[43]

Not until late 1991 was new progress made in the Rome talks. Ten rounds of negotiation produced an agenda of seven items: a law on political parties, a law on elections, provisions for military demobilization and the integration of forces, a cease-fire, political guarantees, a conference of aid donors, and a formal peace accord. A protocol signed on October 19 settled an important aspect of the asymmetry issue by registering a government pledge not to preempt unilaterally any potential subjects of bilateral agreement. During the next round, on November 13, 1991, a second protocol established criteria and modalities for the recognition of political parties, and on March 12, 1992, a third protocol established the principles of electoral rule. Minutes agreed to on July 2, 1992, prepared for a general cease-fire by improving the functions of CoMiVe. A Declaration of Orientation Principles for Human Assistance followed on July 16.[44]

The Rome Declaration

On August 4, 1992, after a year of preparation involving the presidents of Zimbabwe, Zambia, and Botswana, as well as the British investment firm Lonrho, Chissano and Dhlakama met personally in the presence of Mugabe, Roland Rowland of Lonrho, and the Sant'Egidio mediators to shake hands and sign a joint declaration guaranteeing complete political freedom and personal security for all Mozambican citizens and parties, and to accept international—especially United Nations—supervision of a cease-fire and elections. Negotiations in informal sessions and through Sant'Egidio shuttle diplomacy bogged down again as the target date of October 1 neared, requiring a second summit meeting of the two leaders in Gabarone, Botswana, on September 18. A formal peace accord, to be signed at a third summit in Rome on October 1, was delayed by last-minute disputes over the administration of RENAMO-controlled zones and the organization of a national army and security forces.

The Rome Accord was signed on October 4, 1992. It provided for an immediate cease-fire, military regrouping, demilitarization of combat zones, liberation of prisoners, formation of a new army to be composed of 15,000 members from each side, scheduling of parliamentary and presidential elections within a year, and convening of a donors' conference within a month. Important details such as peacekeeping measures by United Nations Operations in Mozambique (UNOMOZ) and funding remained to be specified, and the army was rebellious, but a peace accord had been signed.

The Rome Declaration was a result of successful mediation by Zimbabwe, Botswana, South Africa, Italy, and the Catholic Church, each contributing its bit at crucial moments as communicator, formulator, or manipulator. The Sant'Egidio community provided the essential element of goodwill, "the spirit of Rome," and an informal setting for generating formulas for agreement. Zimbabwe played a major mediating role, induced by the need to eliminate the cost of stationing 7,000 troops in Mozambique to combat RENAMO—a "reverse host" effect. Other state actors, notably the United States and Italy, backed informal and African efforts with pressure and technical expertise. The combination of nonthreatening goodwill without muscle and tough, leveraged backup gradually produced its result.

The war that had taken nearly a million civilian lives, half of them under the age of five, came to a gradual end with the cease-fire. Both exhausted parties saw a more rewarding future in politics than in violence. In 1993 alone Mozambique received more than $1 billion in international aid, including some $300 million from UNOMOZ, $400 million from other United Nations agencies, financial assistance from a dozen bilateral programs and the activities of 175 nongovernmental organizations (NGOs), and a $15 million UN political trust fund to pay the parties to convert to politics.[45]

Transition and Elections

The transition period took more than twice as long as had been planned, but that lengthy time assured the careful accomplishment of the transition and served as a double warning.[46] To the warning already provided by the failed parallel process in Angola, discussed in chapter 8, was added a reminder that the funds available from UN members for UNOMOZ were not unlimited—a reminder emphasized by a visit by UN secretary-general

Boutros Boutros-Ghali to Mozambique in October 1993. UNOMOZ was composed of 6,200 troops from twenty-two countries, 300 military observers, and 600 civilians, who set up forty-nine demobilization sites, supervised the conversion of the two opposing forces into political parties and a joint army, conducted a program for the return of 2 million refugees and from 2 million to 3 million internally displaced persons, and generally acted as a de facto government.[47] By the end of the first year after the cease-fire a third of the refugees and many of the displaced persons had returned, but demobilization activities—involving the collection of weapons, disbursement of back pay, and the preparation of armed forces personnel for civilian employment or enrollment in the new army—did not occur until the second year. As a result, the first multiparty elections in Mozambican history could not take place until October 1994, a year after the scheduled date.

Delay was the price of success in carrying out the provisions of the negotiations to end the internal conflict—a small cost for a successful operation. Elections were interrupted on their second day by Dhlakama's petulant withdrawal and return (mediated again by Mugabe and by South African deputy president Thabo Mbeki). The voting, judged free and fair in the end, took place from October 27 to 29. A 90 percent turnout reelected Chissano and Frelimo, and gave a large minority to RENAMO.[48] Negotiated success in Mozambique was the result of a gradually growing and mutually painful stalemate, which was gradually transformed from a ripe moment to a comprehensive set of agreements by a complex array of mediators. RENAMO was folded into a new political system so well that Dhlakama's final pout was not even heard, let alone obeyed by his followers.

Conclusions

The necessity to cope with the gradual transformation of both FRELIMO and RENAMO, a complex security equation, and a changed international environment brought about a settlement of the conflict in Mozambique. The Mozambican security environment became more complicated by the day and thus was the chief impetus for a negotiated settlement. Successful implementation of the various steps in the process depended on a variety of factors: the military situation on the ground—the worse it became, the greater the incentive for either of the parties to make concessions; changes inside South Africa—the faster the pace of change, the better the prospects for change in Mozambique; and the intervention of external powers (the

United States, Italy, Russia, Zimbabwe, Botswana, and South Africa)—the greater the pressure, the faster the progress toward settlement.

Social, economic, and political stagnation had threatened the survival of the Mozambican state. Although at independence in 1975 there was understandable and exclusive emphasis on national unity to promote national security, this objective was to become a political liability and a threat to state security. Exclusive emphasis on a single party—FRELIMO, a single Marxist ideology, and a single supreme leader produced the disenfranchisement of the citizenry from genuine political participation. The only strategic advantage for the government was that despite signs that it had lost the confidence of its citizens, RENAMO equally alienated itself through its brutal tactics. RENAMO has not so far been a political alternative to government. Since a military solution was neither desirable nor possible, there was no alternative to a negotiated settlement.

Parties to a dispute often need a mediator, as a communicator, formulator, or (with greater involvement) manipulator, as chapter 1 spells out. An internal conflict imposes special problems for mediators, however, and the Mozambican case was not an exception. South Africa, Kenya, and Zimbabwe were all accused of interfering in Mozambican internal affairs, by the government or by the Mozambican National Resistance. Thus RENAMO's toleration of President Mugabe as a mediator was based on the assessment that Mugabe could deliver the Mozambican government's agreement to an accord. This assessment was mirrored by the FRELIMO government's acceptance of mediation by the Sant'Egidio community and President Moi.

Mediation requires coordination—the pooling of strengths to fill in the weaknesses of the mediators. In the 1980s the United States, the Soviet Union, and South Africa mediated behind the scenes and Kenya and Zimbabwe served as formal intermediaries. Such proliferation offers the possibility of competing solutions unless the mediators consult and coordinate (see chapter 1). Mediators must also be sincerely concerned with producing a joint agreement of the parties, not merely with asserting their own primacy or favoring their allies. In Mozambique this problem was overcome when Italy, Zimbabwe, the United States, and Botswana took much more assertive roles in mediation following the disintegration of the Soviet Union.

The Sant'Egidio community's role was a glowing example of dedicated peacemaking by a nongovernmental organization, capitalizing on its strengths and assisted in overcoming its inherent weaknesses. The community's evenhanded goodwill, its concern for the affective and technical dimensions of asymmetry, its long-standing efforts to build relationships, and its honest search for solutions made it invaluable to the negotiation process. The community was present before it was needed, and possessed a patience that outlasted the parties' proclivity for delays. That meant that the community needed muscular backing, hard talking, and persuasive officials to confer status on the parties and urgency to the proceedings.

At first successful settlement was hindered by the parties' preoccupation with commitment and identity. The government and RENAMO were not even on speaking terms because the ontological issues of security, self-determination, dignity, and esteem were at stake. The Rome Declaration only began to resolve these issues, and they dogged the negotiation process to the end. The question of identity had strategic implications for the material needs of both parties and for their nontangible requirements, such as legitimacy. Direct meetings between Chissano and Dhlakama were difficult and necessary for both symbolic and decisional reasons.

Each party to the Mozambican conflict has had internal constituencies that called for peace. These internal divisions have become a central element in the dynamics of lasting solution. The evolution in the nature of RENAMO made it more capable of waging war and of making peace. Although they complicate the process, such internal divisions also offer possibilities for coalition building, as long as they do not threaten the parties' credibility. The essential task of the mediators in Mozambique therefore has been to identify this conjuncture and to encourage coalition building within each party and across conflict lines without threatening anyone's credibility—thus fostering the building blocks for durable peace in Mozambique.

Notes

1. See John C. Campbell, ed., *Successful Negotiations, Trieste: An Appraisal by the Five Participants 1954* (Princeton University Press, 1976); Daniel Druckman, ed., *Negotiations: Social-Psychological Perspectives* (Beverly Hills, Calif.: Sage, 1977); Fred C. Iklé, *How Nations Negotiate* (Millwood, N.Y.: Krause Reprint Co., 1976); Herbert C. Kelman, ed., *International Behavior: A Social-Psychological Analysis* (Holt, Rinehart and Winston, 1965); John Newhouse, *Cold Dawn: The Story of SALT* (Holt, Rinehart and Winston, 1973); and Thomas C. Schelling, *The Strategy of Conflict* (Harvard University Press, 1960).

2. See I. William Zartman, *The Politics of Trade Negotiations between Africa and the European Economic Community: The Weak Confront the Strong* (Princeton University Press, 1971); Robert L. Rothstein, *Global Bargaining: UNCTAD and the Quest for a New International Order* (Princeton University Press, 1979); and Gilbert R. Winham, *International Trade and the Tokyo Round Negotiation* (Princeton University Press, 1986).

3. I. William Zartman, *Ripe for Resolution: Conflict and Intervention in Africa* (Oxford University Press, 1985), pp. 3–17.

4. Zartman, *Ripe for Resolution*, p. 13.

5. Southern African Research and Documentation Centre (SARDC), *South Africa Imposes Sanctions Against Neighbors,* published for the Eighth Summit of the Non-Aligned Movement, held in Harare, Zimbabwe, September 1986. See also Robert S. Jaster, *South Africa in Namibia: The Botha Strategy* (Lanham, Md.: University Press of America, 1985); Colin Legum, *The Battlefronts of Southern Africa* (New York: Africana Publishing Co., 1988); Gilbert Khadiagala, *Allies in Adversity: The Frontline States in Southern African Security, 1975–1993* (Ohio University Press, 1994). On Biko, see Millard Arnold, ed., *Steve Biko: Black Consciousness in South Africa* (Vintage, 1979).

6. Joseph Hanlon, *Mozambique: The Revolution Under Fire,* 2d ed. (London: Zed Books, 1984).

7. See Carter Center of Emory University, "Beyond Autocracy in Africa: Working Papers from the Inaugural Seminar of the Governance in Africa Program" (Atlanta, Ga., February 17–18, 1989).

8. Allen F. Isaacman and Barbara Isaacman, *Mozambique: From Colonization to Revolution, 1900–1982* (Boulder, Colo.: Westview Press, 1983) pp. 96–99, 177.

9. Hanlon, *Mozambique,* p. 220.

10. Jaster, *South Africa in Namibia.*

11. Allen F. Isaacman, "The Escalating Conflict in Southern Africa: The Case of Mozambique," paper presented at the Conference on Regional Security in Southern Africa, co-sponsored by the Department of Political and Administrative Studies, University of Zimbabwe, and the International Institute for Strategic Studies, London; held in Harare, Zimbabwe, June 8–10, 1987.

12. Whitney Schneidman, "Conflict Resolution in Mozambique," *CSIS Africa Notes*, no. 121 (Washington: Center for Strategic and International Studies, February 28, 1991).

13. On January 22, 1990, strikes forced the closure of Maputo Hospital; on March 3, 1990, riot police broke up a demonstration by about two thousand teachers in Maputo who had initially demanded a 100 percent salary increment. See "Strike Forces Closure of Maputo Hospital," *Daily News* (Tanzania), January 23, 1990, p. 2; and "Maputo Teachers End Strike," *Daily News* (Tanzania), March 4, 1990, p. 2.

14. Paul R. Pillar, *Negotiating Peace: War Termination as a Bargaining Process* (Princeton University Press, 1983), p. 37.

15. Isaacman, "The Escalating Conflict."

16. Zartman, *Ripe for Resolution,* p. 221; Dan O'Meara, "Nkomati Accord," briefing paper (Ottawa: International Defence and Aid Fund for Southern Africa, November 1985).

17. Phylis Johnson and David Martin, eds., *Destructive Engagement: Southern Africa at War* (Harare, Zimbabwe: Zimbabwe Publishing House and Southern Africa Research and Documentation Centre, 1986), p. 32.

18. *Keesing's Contemporary Archives,* vol. 30 (November 1984), p. 33196.

19. See Thomas R. Colosi and Arthur Eliot Berkeley, *Collective Bargaining: How it Works and Why. A Manual of Theory and Practice* (New York: American Arbitration Association, 1986).

20. South Africa was never actually a host because RENAMO had no need for sanctuary.

21. Parties to negotiation pursue a variety of objectives. See Iklé, *How Nations Negotiate,* pp. 26–42.

22. See Gilbert R. Winham, "International Negotiation in an Age of Transition," *International Journal,* vol. 35 (Winter 1979–80), pp. 1–20; Henry A. Kissinger, *Nuclear Weapons and Foreign Policy* (Harper, 1957); Henry A. Kissinger, *The World Restored* (Houghton Mifflin, 1957); and Harold G. Nicolson, *The Congress of Vienna: A Study in Allied Unity, 1812–1822* (Harcourt Brace, 1946).

23. For a history of the postwar international system, see Daniel Yergin, *Shattered Peace: The Origins of the Cold War and the National Security State* (Houghton Mifflin, 1977).

24. Cameron Hume, *Ending Mozambique's War: The Role of Mediation and Good Offices* (Washington: U.S. Institute of Peace, 1994).

25. Leone Gianturco, "Mozambique: The Irrecusable Mediation," mimeographed, 1991; Jane Perlez, "Mozambican Government Ready to Start Meeting with Guerrillas, *New York Times,* July 18, 1989, p. A8; Christopher S. Wren, "Mozambique Party Backs Rebel Talks," *New York Times,* August 1, 1989 p. 3.

26. Alex Vines, *Renamo: Terrorism in Mozambique* (University of Indiana Press, 1991), pp. 77; Hilary Andersson, *Mozambique: A War against the People* (St. Martin's Press, 1992), pp. 53–55, 68–69. On comparable organizational problems see William Quandt, *Revolution and Political Leadership: Algeria 1954–1968* (MIT Press, 1969). See also Colin Legum, "The MNR," *CSIS Africa Notes,* no. 16 (Washington: Center for Strategic and International Studies, July 15, 1983).

27. "Mozambique: Renamo Congress Bids for Peace," *Africa Confidential,* vol 30 (July 7, 1989), p. 1.

28. See Jeffrey Z. Rubin and Frank E. A. Sander, "When Should We Use Agents: Direct v. Representative Negotiations," *Negotiation Journal,* vol. 4 (October 1988), pp. 395–440.

29. Gianturco, "Mozambique."

30. Robert Gersony, "Summary of Mozambican Refugee Accounts of Principally Conflict Related Experience in Mozambique," Department of State, Washington, 1988.

31. Hume, *Ending Mozambique's War;* see also Patrick Brogan, *The Fighting Never Stopped* (Vintage Books, 1989).

32. *Indian Ocean Newsletter,* no. 415 (January 27, 1990), p. 4.

33. *Indian Ocean Newsletter,* no. 415 (January 27, 1990), p. 4.

34. *Indian Ocean Newsletter,* no. 415 (January 27, 1990), p. 8.

35. Afonso Dhlakama, "Report from the Cabinet and President of Renamo Considering the Present Situation of Mozambique and Current Peace Talks in Rome," mimeographed, July 1992, p. 8.

36. "Mozambique: Time to Talk," *Africa Confidential,* vol. 30 (June 23, 1989), p. 2.

37. Based on a confidential document.

38. "Mozambique: Moving with the Times," *Africa Confidential,* vol. 31 (February 9, 1990), p. 1.

39. On the role of Sant'Egidio, see Gianturco, "Mozambique"; Kate Almquist, "The Role of Non-Governmental Organizations in International Mediation," School of Advanced International Studies (SAIS), Johns Hopkins University, 1994; Darin Ohlandt, "Elements of Change in Mozambique," SAIS, Johns Hopkins University, 1994; Douglas Johnston and Cynthia Sampson, eds., *Religion, the Missing Dimension of Statecraft* (Oxford University Press, 1994), pp. 327–29.

40. Joint Communique issued at Sant'Egidio (Rome, July 10, 1990).

41. Hume, *Ending Mozambique's War.*

42. On the collapse of the Mozambique state, see Barry Schutz, "The Heritage of Revolution and the Struggle for Government Legitimacy in Mozambique," in I. William Zartman, ed., *Collapsed States: The Disintegration and Restoration of Legitimate Authority* (Boulder, Colo.: Lynne Rienner, 1995), pp. 109–22; Andersson, *Mozambique.*

43. Hume, *Ending Mozambique's War.*

44. Ibid.

45. Paul Taylor, "In Mozambique," *Washington Post,* October 24, 1993, p. A35.

46. On the distinction between threats and warnings, see Schelling, *Strategy of Conflict;* and I. William Zartman and Maureen R. Berman, *The Practical Negotiator* (Yale University Press, 1982), pp. 75–78.

47. Paul Taylor, "Building a Nation in Mozambique," *New York Times,* October 11, 1993, p. A33.

48. Comissão Nacional de Eleições, Eleições Gevais 1994, "Apuramento Nacional," Maputo, November 19, 1994.

CHAPTER TEN

Internal Negotiations Among Many Actors: Afghanistan

Imtiaz H. Bokhari

THE AFGHAN conflict, which began in 1979, has involved a highly complex case of internal negotiations among a large number of actors with different agendas and different interests to protect. Conflict in Afghanistan was not a simple case of rebellion by a small group of insurgents or even by a minority of the people seeking regional autonomy or secession from a legally established government. It was a case of people rising against a regime that had come to power riding on the tanks of the neighboring superpower. In this respect the Afghan case differs from most cases of internal negotiations between government and insurgent groups. Yet when the popular uprising in Afghanistan reached success, the bonds of nationalism that held it together against its ideological enemy dissolved and the victors set vigorously upon each other in the name of old ethnic rivalries.

The nucleus of an Afghan resistance had been formed as early as 1973 in response to the overthrow of King Zahir Shah by Sardar Daud Khan and the proclamation of a republic in Afghanistan. The immediate precipitant of the Afghan conflict was the bloody coup in April 1978 that overthrew Sardar Daud Khan and brought to power Noor Mohammad Taraki, leader of the socialist People's Democratic Party of Afghanistan (PDPA), which had links to the Soviet Union.[1] There was serious and widespread opposition to the new "godless" regime, arising from the religious tradition of the Afghan nation and revulsion against alien ideas and foreign domination; the result was the near collapse of the socialist regime. To save the socialist regime the Soviet government, under the Brezhnev doctrine of protective intervention, moved military forces into Afghanistan at the end of December 1978 and installed Babrak Karmal, more pliable to Soviet interests, as head of the Afghan state. The number of resistance forces, or mujahideen, within the country increased rapidly following the Soviet invasion, as did the number of Afghan refugees fleeing to Pakistan and Iran. The mujahideen themselves were divided by geographic diversity, ideology, ethnic makeup, and personal rivalries.

The complexity of the negotiation process in Afghanistan can be judged from the number of actors involved, both directly and indirectly. The major ones were the two superpowers—the United States and the Soviet Union— which had become parties to the conflict; Pakistan, which received more than three million Afghan refugees, provided sanctuaries for mujahideen fighters, and acted as a conduit for all kinds of supplies for them; Iran, which was host to nearly two million refugees; China and Saudi Arabia, which were major providers of assistance and deeply interested in the outcome of the negotiations; a seven-party mujahideen alliance based in Pakistan (the Peshawar Seven); an eight-party mujahideen alliance with headquarters in Iran (the Tehran Eight); field commanders within Afghanistan (numbering about 500, of whom only 30 to 40 were militarily and politically significant); the Afghan regime in Kabul; and the United Nations. The negotiations, which were spread over a period of more than fifteen years (1980–95), can be divided into three phases: the search for unity (1980–87), the Geneva negotiations and Accords (1982–88), and the search for an alternative government (after 1988).

Politically and culturally Afghanistan had its own system and traditions, which directly affected the negotiation process and its outcome. In the monarchial period the king in Kabul functioned as an object of reverence and tribal allegiance rather than as a strong central authority. Sardar Daud's experiment with republicanism changed nothing. Political activity at the national level was expressed by calling a *loya jirga* (an assembly of tribal elders, important religious leaders, and other eminent persons) that had ceremonial rather than policymaking functions. There were no political parties. Afghanistan was a society of autonomous tribes in which loyalty was to the ethnic group and its chief, who ran affairs through a *jirga* (committee of elders). Another loyalty of the Afghans was to religious elders. Thus individualism and religious and tribal loyalties prevented the emergence of an effective political entity that could direct the political and military struggle of the mujahideen.

The Search for Unity

The 1978 coup divided the body politic of Afghanistan and coalesced it around two irreconcilable poles: the Marxists, who controlled the government in Kabul, and the Islamist opposition, which functioned both inside Afghanistan and outside. The ideological divide between the two ran deep and wide, leaving too large a gap for negotiations to bridge. Soviet military intervention strengthened the resolve of the opposition to rid Afghanistan of its Marxist regime. There was also great disparity between the two in their means to fight. The Kabul regime was strong, with a fully committed superpower as its partner; at the beginning at least, the mujahideen had only their antiquated personal weapons. The Kabul regime had the advantage of a valid spokesperson—the president—but the opposition, although widespread and intense, was divided into dozens of groups.[2] With such pronounced asymmetry in power and commitment, there was no ripe moment for negotiations between the government and the opposition; a ripening process was needed to create conditions for negotiations.

The mujahideen had to redress the asymmetry and strive for unity, which required having a valid spokesperson or spokesgroup. Yet they could achieve neither without resorting to negotiations among themselves. Thus when negotiations did occur, they took place in two distinct arenas: intra-mujahideen and inter-Afghan. The intra-mujahideen negotiations proceeded at various levels between various groups based in Peshawar, Pakistan; between Peshawar-based groups and groups based in Iran; and between mujahideen commanders inside Afghanistan and various mujahideen groups outside the country. The inter-Afghan negotiations took place between mujahideen groups (including their military commanders) on one side and the Kabul regime backed by the Soviets on the other.

For quite some time the inter-Afghan arena was empty. Although the Kabul regime was willing to negotiate, the mujahideen leaders were not, lest the regime gain a legitimacy that it had lost domestically as well as internationally. The intra-mujahideen parleys were not an unreserved success. Schisms among the groups were so deep that at times it seemed they were fighting more among themselves than against their common enemy, the Soviets. When the common enemy left, the ethnic schisms became predominant.

In Peshawar two of the largest resistance groups were Burhanuddin Rabbani's Jamaat-i-Islami and Gulbadin Hekmatyar's Hizb-i-Islami.[3] The first serious intra-mujahideen dialogue for unity was initiated by Rabbani, who established the National Liberation Front in June 1978, two months after the coup; that front claimed to represent eight right-wing groups. Within six weeks of its birth, however, the front collapsed. Another short-lived merger negotiated by Hekmatyar and Rabbani in September 1978 was reportedly induced by an Arab offer of U.S. $2 million. In December 1978 Sibghatullah al-Mojaddedi, a noted religious leader, established the Afghan National Liberation Front (ANLF), composed of the groups based in Peshawar; Hekmatyar's Hizb-i-Islami was the notable holdout. This front too did not achieve much.

Following the Soviet invasion of Afghanistan the six main resistance parties based in Peshawar agreed in principle to form a coalition. After only two negotiating sessions Hekmatyar's Hizb-i-Islami withdrew; the remaining five parties formed a loose coalition on January 27, 1980, which foundered five months later because of personal rivalries and ideological divisions. At the same time, however, a parallel and totally different effort at unification was made—an attempt to set up a democratic parliament with representatives from each district of Afghanistan. A loya jirga was planned for the eve of a meeting of foreign ministers of the Organization of the Islamic Conference (OIC) in May 1980, to proclaim a prospective Afghan government-in-exile. This initiative too proved stillborn, however, as it was considered a Trojan horse of the royalists.

Beginning in 1981 there was a clear bifurcation among mujahideen groups. Two alliances were established, the "moderates" and the "fundamentalists." In 1981 the Pakistan government decided to recognize only six Pakistan-based resistance groups; three parties in the Moderate coalition and three in the Fundamentalist (in 1983 Pakistan recognized five more parties). Only in 1985 did the Peshawar Seven form one alliance, the Islamic Union of Afghan Mujahideen (IUAM). The alliance was to be chaired by a spokesperson, and the position was to rotate among members every three months.

Although efforts for intra-mujahideen unity were making slow progress, contacts between a mujahideen military leader and the Soviets were reported in early 1983. Ahmed Shah Massoud, a leader of the military resistance and commander of resistance forces in the Panjshir Valley, refused to enter into negotiations with Babrak Karmal's government, but instead negotiated a truce agreement in February 1983 directly with the Soviets. The cease-fire in the Panjshir Valley remained intact for the stipulated period of one year, but negotiations for its extension did not succeed. In analyzing the negotiations it is worth noting the degree of autonomy exercised by major military leaders, their hesitancy to negotiate with the regime in Kabul, and the willingness of the Soviet Union to negotiate with mujahideen over the head of the Kabul regime.

During this period both the negotiation process and its outcome were hostage to the lack of unity among the resistance parties. For example, there was a total absence of inter-Afghan dialogue, even though the regime in Kabul made a number of offers to seek a political solution to the conflict. Pakistan and Iran would not enter into dialog with the Soviet Union or with the Kabul regime unless the mujahideen were a part of the delegation, and the mujahideen could not be a part of the delegation because they lacked a unified policy. Eventually Diego Cordovez, special envoy of the United Nations secretary-general, initiated an indirect negotiation process between the Kabul and Islamabad regimes, which was to lead to the Geneva Accords of 1988.

The Geneva Negotiations and Accords

Spread over six years (1982–88), nine shuttle missions, and eleven rounds of indirect talks, the Geneva negotiations represented a more successful track in the search for a solution to the Afghan conflict. Official parties to the proximity talks were Pakistan and Afghanistan, but the Soviets were always (except on one occasion) part of the Afghan delegation, and Pakistan closely coordinated its position with that of the United States, and consulted mujahideen leaders before and briefed them after each round of talks.

The Geneva negotiation process was initiated in pursuance of a resolution of the UN General Assembly of November 20, 1980, which authorized the secretary-general to seek a political solution to the Afghan problem.[4] The resolution listed four essential points that were to form the basis of a solution: the preservation of the sovereignty, territorial integrity, political independence, and nonaligned character of Afghanistan; the right of the Afghan people to determine their own form of government and to choose their economic, political, and social systems freely, without external intervention, subversion, coercion, or constraints of any kind; the immediate withdrawal of foreign troops from Afghanistan; and the creation of the necessary conditions for the voluntary return of Afghan refugees to their homes in safety and honor.

Afghanistan's was an international crisis needing an international approach to its resolution. Pakistan urged the UN secretary-general to pursue the resolution, and also suggested trilateral negotiations involving Pakistan, Iran, and the People's Democratic Party of Afghanistan in Kabul. The Soviet Union's stand on the question of negotiations was one of ambivalence. Although the Soviets supported a political settlement, they wanted only a minimal role for the United Nations in the negotiations, and pressed for recognition of the Kabul regime as a precondition to negotiations. Although willing to talk with the People's Democratic Party, Pakistan refused to recognize it as the Kabul regime, in accordance with a decision of the OIC foreign ministers. In December 1980 the Soviets told Pakistan that the Kabul regime was prepared to talk without raising the question of recognition.

The United Nations General Assembly resolution did not require the mujahideen to be a party to negotiations. Mujahideen leaders were not willing to talk to the Kabul regime in any capacity, even indirectly, lest such contacts confer legitimacy on the regime. Moreover, the mujahideen would have had to negotiate from a position of weakness. Assistance to the mujahideen by the United States was limited and covert, although from the start the Afghan conflict assumed the character of an East-West issue. (Pakistan too had declined to accept military and economic aid offered by the United States during the Carter administration.)

On August 24, 1981, eight months after the Soviets lent their support to talks and seven months after UN secretary-general Kurt Waldheim appointed Under Secretary-General Javier Perez de Cuellar as his personal representative, the government in Kabul indicated to Pakistan that it no longer insisted on bilateral talks, and the Afghan foreign minister, Shah Dost Mohammad, told Indian prime minister Rajiv Gandhi that the Kabul regime was "flexible" on procedural matters in negotiations.[5] As a result, Perez de Cuellar could report to the secretary-general that Pakistan and Afghanistan had agreed on a four-point agenda that was to form the basis of an eventual agreement: withdrawal of Soviet forces from Afghanistan, noninterference in each other's internal affairs on the part of both Pakistan and Afghanistan, international guarantees concerning noninterference, and the return of Afghan refugees.[6]

Following this breakthrough, the first indirect talks were held at United Nations headquarters in New York. Both parties hardened their positions. The Afghan foreign minister expressed readiness for bilateral or trilateral talks, but stressed that the talks should be direct, government to government, and that the timetable of a withdrawal of Soviet troops should be a bilateral matter between Afghanistan and the Soviet Union. Pakistan in turn refused to talk directly to the Kabul delegation, even if the delegation was participating as a representative of the People's Democratic Party.

Indirect Negotiations

After his election as UN secretary-general (succeeding Waldheim), Perez de Cuellar appointed Under Secretary Diego Cordovez as his personal representative for Afghanistan. The first round of talks between Pakistan and Afghanistan began in Geneva on June 16, 1982. The format was indirect, with Cordovez meeting with the two delegations in the same building but at different times; he then continued discussions through visits to Pakistan, Afghanistan, and Iran.

When Yuri Andropov, who had not supported the invasion of Afghanistan, succeeded Leonid Brezhnev as the Soviet chairman in December 1982, it was generally believed that he would have a more flexible position on the withdrawal of Soviet troops from Afghanistan. There was a heightened sense of optimism when, at Brezhnev's funeral, Andropov reportedly told President Zia ul-Haq of Pakistan that the Soviet Union wanted to get out of Afghanistan and would withdraw quickly if Pakistan ceased its support of the Afghan resistance. Even Cordovez saw a window for diplomacy. He carried a working draft of an agreement to Tehran, Kabul, and Islamabad in January 1983, and on March 25, with Secretary-General Perez de Cuellar, he met Andropov and Soviet foreign minister Andrei Gromyko in Moscow to secure their support for the Geneva talks. A second round of the talks, held on April 8–22, was adjourned to permit consultations with the respective governments. Cordovez reported that 95 percent of the draft text of a comprehensive settlement was ready, and that "only blanks in a withdrawal time-table had to be filled in."[7]

The optimism of Cordovez soon proved unfounded. During the Geneva meetings in June 1983 both sides hardened their positions again, although they did agree that Cordovez could initiate consultations with the Soviet Union and the United States to seek their agreement to act as guarantors. Soviet policy was also hardened by the succession of Nikolai Chernenko to Andropov. After a ten-month break in the negotiation process, Cordovez again visited Tehran, Kabul, and Islamabad, in April 1984. He was able to gain agreement on a new format for proximity talks, involving discussions alternately with the parties, which would be sitting simultaneously in adjacent rooms. He also reformulated the framework of the negotiations to include noninterference, international guarantees, the return of Afghan refugees, and interrelationships; "interrelationships" referred to the withdrawal of foreign forces, as the Soviet Union insisted that withdrawal was an issue between Kabul and Moscow only.[8]

Although the third round of Geneva talks, on August 24–30, 1984, did not achieve substantive results, both Pakistan and Afghanistan expressed their satisfaction with the proximity talks and agreed to continue them. For the first time the Afghan delegation was without a Soviet adviser; some observers saw this as a reason for the lack of significant movement in the Afghan position. In May 1985 Cordovez secured agreement that settlement should consist of the four instruments drafted in 1984 and spoke about the end of the deadlock that had prevailed since 1983.[9] According to a report by the UN secretary-general, all questions but that of interrelationships were resolved. Afghanistan insisted on concurrent action on noninterference and international guarantees, and Pakistan emphasized a time frame for the Soviet withdrawal.

At a fifth round of Geneva talks, on August 26–30, 1985, Afghanistan made a determined bid to force Pakistan to accept face-to-face negotiations. Pakistan refused, and after two days of deadlock Cordovez reverted to the format of shuttling between separate rooms. Nevertheless, the basic impasse remained. At the December 1985 meeting the deadlock over format continued, although Afghanistan reportedly gave Cordovez a withdrawal schedule; Pakistan refused this on the ground that it represented recognition of the Soviet-installed regime. In a letter to Cordovez on December 10, the United States expressed its willingness to be a guarantor in the context of a comprehensive and balanced agreement, in which the central issue of Soviet troop withdrawal was resolved. After further shuttle diplomacy in March 1986 Cordovez got from the Kabul regime a timetable for Soviet withdrawal and an agreement to continue indirect talks.

Upon his accession to power in early 1985, Mikhail Gorbachev intensified Soviet military operations against both the Afghan resistance and Afghanistan's civil population. He also increased pressure on Pakistan through border violations and terrorist acts. On May 4, 1986, Karmal was abruptly replaced as head of the Kabul regime by Najibullah, the chief of Afghan secret police, on the eve of another round of the Geneva talks. Some observers interpreted this move as a concession; others thought it was designed for a more effective prosecution of the war. Talks in Geneva were held on May 19–23 against a background of intensified Soviet military pressure. Two important developments took place: the Kabul regime withdrew its demand for direct negotiations, and for the first time the talks included consideration of the "interrelationship." Afghanistan sought three to four years to complete the withdrawal of Soviet troops, and Pakistan sought six months or less. The two sides did reach an agreement that the final document would be legally binding, signed by their foreign ministers, and enforced by an international monitoring team composed of representatives of mutually acceptable countries.

On July 26, 1986, Gorbachev called for the formation of an Afghan government "with the participation in it of those political forces which found themselves outside the country"—a reference to exiled resistance leaders, refugees, and the former king.[10] The week-long talks that began four days later failed to narrow the gap on the withdrawal time frame and on measures for monitoring and verifying compliance with an agreement. Cordovez could say only that "the process is very much alive and will continue." Five months later Najibullah announced the details of a plan for national reconciliation, which the mujahideen rejected. On December 9, however, after a November trip to the region, Cordovez declared that for "the first time the only issue remaining is the time frame."[11]

In the Geneva talks in February and March 1987 Pakistan and the United States stated that a solution to the Afghan crisis, to be acceptable, would have to involve political arrangements agreeable to the Afghan mujahideen, and that it would have to induce the refugees to return home. Positions on the timing of troop withdrawal narrowed down to eighteen months (the Kabul regime's proposal) versus seven months (Pakistan's proposal). The only achievement of a round of talks in September 1987, held at Soviet and Afghan request, was a further but slight narrowing of the withdrawal time frame—sixteen months versus eight months.

The Final Round

On the military front, the Soviets gave the Kabul regime a year to build a stable base of power with the help of Soviet troops. As Gorbachev reportedly told Najibullah during the latter's visit to Moscow in July 1987, "I hope you are ready in twelve months because we will be leaving whether you are or not."[12] In November, after the stalemate at Geneva, Cordovez received signals that the Soviets had decided to propose a shorter timetable for withdrawal, without linking it to the formation of a national government. After the summit meeting between U.S. president Ronald Reagan and

Gorbachev in 1987, U.S. under secretary of state Michael Armacost observed that "the Soviets do not link the withdrawal of their troops to prior resolution of issues of an interim government or transitional arrangements among Afghans."[13]

Following a twenty-day visit to the region by Cordovez, during which he laid the groundwork for an agreement, the final round of negotiations opened in Geneva on March 2, 1988. Within two days agreement was reached between Pakistan and the Kabul regime on a phased withdrawal of the Soviet forces, to commence on May 15—the date on which the agreement was to come into force. The withdrawal was to be "front-end loaded," implying that half of the troops were to be withdrawn by August 15, 1988, and that the withdrawal would be completed within nine months (half the difference between the previous positions).

The four instruments of the political settlement for Afghanistan were:

—a bilateral agreement between Pakistan and Afghanistan on the principle of mutual relations, in particular on noninterference and nonintervention;

—international guarantees of the settlement by the Soviet Union and the United States;

—a bilateral agreement between Pakistan and Afghanistan on the voluntary return of Afghan refugees; and

—an agreement on "interrelationships for the settlement of the situation relating to Afghanistan," signed by Pakistan and Afghanistan, and by the Soviet Union and the United States as guarantor states. This instrument provided for a phased withdrawal of foreign troops from Afghanistan, starting on May 15, 1988, and in fact completed on schedule on February 15, 1989.[14]

The final negotiations, however, soon stalled over new thinking on two issues: Pakistan insisted that Najibullah's government be replaced by an interim Afghan coalition government before the Soviets left Afghanistan, which was a reversal of Pakistan's previously stated position; and the United States demanded, under strong congressional pressure, that the Soviets stop supplying the Kabul regime simultaneously with a cut-off of U.S. arms deliveries to the mujahideen. Pakistan's demand was not accepted by Cordovez on the grounds that a transitional government was not called for in the four instruments that formed the basis of Geneva negotiations. Even Pakistan's scaled-down demand to "finalize the modalities and procedures" for the formation of a transitional regime was not acceptable to the Kabul regime.[15]

The two superpowers resolved the issue of a transitional government by agreeing that Cordovez should provide his good offices, in his personal capacity, to facilitate an agreement among various Afghan parties on a broad-based Afghan government. This provided a way out for Pakistan. On the question of symmetry, the two superpowers reached a side agreement that allowed the United States to continue giving military supplies to the mujahideen if the Soviet Union did not cut off its aid to the Kabul regime. The Geneva Accords were finally signed on April 14, 1988.[16]

The Search for an Alternative Government

With the signing of the Geneva Accords the intra-mujahideen and inter-Afghan negotiations gained considerable momentum. The different mujahideen groups (and the observing world) expected that the Najibullah government would crumble like a house of mud once the Soviet troops left Afghanistan, and thus each group was concerned more with the spoils of victory than with victory itself. Quarrels among mujahideen concerned division of the pie as each group attempted to secure maximum gains for itself, even at the expense of mujahideen allies. In inter-Afghan negotiations the Najibullah regime's concern was to secure membership in a future Afghan government to protect its interests. Mujahideen leaders negotiated separately with the Kabul regime in order to add to their bargaining power with other groups. These conflicting aims gave rise to a complex negotiation process that proceeded simultaneously on a number of tracks and levels.[17]

Intra-Mujahideen Negotiations

The need for a unified politico-military strategy by the mujahideen was never so great and urgent as after Geneva, so attempts to bring together mujahideen groups in both Iran and Pakistan were increased. These efforts first bore fruit in March 1988, when eight parties based in Iran agreed to form the United Council of Afghan Mujahideen.[18] As the end of 1988 approached and the deadline for the withdrawal of Soviet troops neared, the mujahideen leaders came under increasing pressure to set up a mechanism acceptable to the majority of Afghans for replacing Najibullah government. In the first week of December, a delegation of the Peshawar Seven under Burhanuddin Rabbani, leader of the Islamic Union of Afghan Mujahideen, made the first high-level direct contacts with a Soviet delegation (led by Yuli Vorontsov, Soviet ambassador in Kabul and first deputy foreign minister) in Taif, Saudi Arabia; they were to discuss a future Afghan government and other issues. During the same month Rabbani also led a delegation to Tehran to discuss with Karim Khalili, leader of the Tehran Eight, the convening of a *shura* (a consultation session) to elect an interim government once the Soviets had withdrawn. Earlier, both the Peshawar Seven and the Tehran Eight had rejected a plan proposed by Cordovez for the establishment of a national government in Kabul.[19] The new chairman of the IUAM, al-Mojaddedi, visited Iran in early February 1989 and reached an agreement with Khalili on the composition of a shura and a mujahideen council. Tehran-based mujahideen groups were to be allocated one hundred shura seats, seven ministries in an interim government, and six seats in an expanded Supreme Council (the mujahideen policymaking body, which until then was made up only of leaders of the Peshawar Seven).

Preliminary moves leading to the formation of an Afghan interim government fully exposed the limits and difficulties of intra-mujahideen negotiations. A shura of about five hundred representatives of the mujahideen was to meet on February 1, 1989, to elect an interim government. But mujahideen groups remained divided on the composition of a shura. The basic division was between Peshawar-based moderate and fundamentalist groups, which was further complicated by a division between Tehran-based Shi'as and Peshawar-based Sunnis. The accord reached earlier in February between al-Mojaddedi and Khalili was not acceptable to Peshawar-based fundamentalist leaders, notably Hekmatyar and his Hizb-i-Islami. The Tehran Eight decided to boycott a shura rather than accept reduced representation. Mujahideen leaders had also failed to build bridges with the field commanders in Afghanistan who had done most of the fighting and who were uncertain of their future in an interim government. In early February, Hekmatyar announced that a shura to be composed of 519 members, with 60 seats reserved for each component group of the IUAM, 80 seats for the Tehran Eight, and 19 seats for "good" Muslims from inside Afghanistan. The Shura that finally convened on February 10 in Rawalpindi was attended by neither the majority of the mujahideen field commanders, nor the Tehran-based mujahideen, nor the "good" Muslims from Kabul, and broke up within hours of opening.

The Shura was reconvened on February 14 and again the three groups that had boycotted the first meeting were conspicuous by their absence. Within a week a government headed by Ahmed Shah, a fundamentalist with support from the Saudis and the Pakistani Inter Services Intelligence Directorate (ISI), was proposed to the Shura for approval, but it failed to win the support of the moderates. The situation remained deadlocked for a week, until a voting formula was devised for electing a government. The 450 delegates in attendance selected a government from among the seven Peshawar-based leaders; a number of portfolios were given to each leader for his group.

Al-Mojaddedi received the highest number of votes and was appointed president, followed by Rasul Sayyaf, who was named prime minister. The others selected to form an interim government, in descending order, were Nabi Mohammedi, Hekmatyar, Maulvi Yunis Khalis, Rabbani, and Syed Ahmad Gailani. That interim government lacked credibility because it was composed only of members of the Peshawar Seven and was tainted as having been engineered by the Pakistani ISI. After the mujahideen launched an offensive against Najibullah's forces in the vital stronghold of Jalalabad and were repulsed without intervention of the Soviets, the interim government was marginalized and ceased to play any meaningful role in a political solution to the Afghan conflict.

Inter-Afghan Negotiations

While mujahideen leaders were trying to form an Afghan interim government, Najibullah was promoting his own initiatives. In October 1988, with Soviet support, he streamlined the People's Democratic Party of Afghanistan by providing greater visibility for its moderate elements in the hope that they could be part of any future power-sharing arrangements with the mujahideen. The Soviets also suggested that Afghan prime minister Hassan Sharq, who was not a member of the PDPA, should be named as Najibullah's successor—a suggestion rejected by both the Islamic Union of Afghan Mujahideen and the United States, which continued its interest as long as the Soviets remained in Afghanistan. Najibullah then appointed a commission to bring about fundamental changes in the manifesto of the People's Democratic Party. References to communism were eliminated. Radical elements were expelled from the party, its name was changed to Hizb-i-Watan (Homeland Party), and the name of the party newspaper was changed from *Haqiqat-i-Inqilab-Saur* (Reality of the Saur Revolution) to *Payam* (Message). Even the name of the country was changed from a revolutionary Democratic Republic of Afghanistan to Republic of Afghanistan. Perhaps Najibullah thought that by distancing himself from communism and reappearing as a nationalist, and by being flexible on Islam, he could increase his chances of securing a partnership with at least some mujahideen groups to form a national government.

As a goodwill gesture Najibullah announced, with Soviet agreement, a four-day cease-fire covering both Afghan and Soviet troops, to start on New Year's day 1989; but the cease-fire was rejected by the mujahideen. In an opening speech to a loya jirga convened on May 21, 1989, Najibullah appealed for active political involvement by opposition leaders. But his appeal was directed more toward mujahideen commanders inside Afghanistan, to whom he promised posts within the Afghan army and commands of men and weapons, and even possible autonomy for certain parts of Afghanistan. His attempt to divide the mujahideen was well timed, coming soon after the failure of the mujahideen's Jalalabad offensive and after a serious intra-mujahideen clash in which a unit of Massoud's Jamaat-i-Islami was ambushed and killed by Hekmatyar's Hizb-i-Islami.

During the same period an improvement in relations between Iran and the Soviet Union increased Najibullah's chances of effecting a power-sharing agreement with Iran-based mujahideen groups. Also, Soviet ambassador Vorontsov met with former Afghan king Zahir Shah in December 1988 to explore the possibility of broadening the base of the government in Kabul. In November 1989 a meeting of the Soviet foreign minister with the shah in Rome was followed by overtures by Najibullah to the former king to boost the foundering peace initiatives.

In early 1990 Najibullah issued another set of proposals for resolution of the Afghan conflict. The main points were a cease-fire between government and mujahideen forces; removal of the arms and ammunition depots of both sides, under UN supervision; cessation of arms supplies to both sides from the United States and the Soviet Union; and a UN Security Council guarantee of noninterference by outside actors. Prime Minister Rasul Sayyaf of the Afghan interim government rejected the proposal, as he had all others, on the grounds that the interim government did not recognize the Kabul regime as a party to the conflict.

The mujahideen's inter-Afghan negotiations were a two-track process. In one, the mujahideen openly negotiated with the Soviet Union, having consistently refused to talk with Najibullah; in the other, some mujahideen negotiated covertly with Najibullah. As the pressure provided by the Soviet withdrawal deadline was mounting, so was Soviet pressure on Pakistan to arrange talks with the mujahideen. In his first meeting with Vorontsov in Taif in December 1988, Rabbani had listed nine conditions for an agreement with the Soviets, adding that the Soviet Union must accept the IUAM as the sole representative of Afghanistan. Vorontsov then visited Iran and Pakistan in the first week of January 1989 for talks with the two mujahideen coalitions. In preparation for the visit, al-Mojaddedi, the new president of the IUAM, announced a three-point agenda: the withdrawal of Soviet troops, the removal of the regime in Kabul, and the right of self-determination of the Afghan people. The mujahideen, who also included representatives of the Tehran Eight, met with Vorontsov on January 6 at the Pakistani foreign office, but with no Pakistani official present. During the two rounds of talks the Soviets concentrated on a cease-fire and the future government in Afghanistan, acknowledging that they were not opposed to the Shura formula if it included representatives of the People's Democratic Party. They also invited the mujahideen to Moscow. Al-Mojaddedi later said that further talks would be held only when the Soviet Union withdrew unconditionally and refrained from imposing the PDPA on an Afghan government. Vorontsov too said that the "Kabul regime won't collapse after [Soviet] withdrawal."[20]

A visit by Soviet foreign minister Eduard Shevardnadze to Pakistan on February 4, 1989—the first visit by a Soviet foreign minister in two decades—was widely seen as a last and unsuccessful attempt by the Soviet Union to secure a place for members of the Kabul regime in any future mujahideen-dominated Afghan government. Shevardnadze was reported to have offered U.S.$1 billion in economic aid to Pakistan if the mujahideen would enter into negotiations with Najibullah.[21] The mujahideen rejected another opportunity to negotiate with the Russians when Soviet vice president Alexander Rutskoi, an Afghan veteran, visited Pakistan at the end of 1991 to seek the release of Russian prisoners held by the mujahideen. By not delivering the prisoners, the mujahideen not only failed to open channels of communication with the new Russian government of Boris Yeltsin but also embarrassed Pakistan.

Covert inter-Afghan negotiations had reportedly been arranged by Yasir Arafat of the Palestine Liberation Organization (PLO) during 1989. According to Arafat, meetings were held between a four-member PDPA delegation, which included General Sahabzada Yaqub Khan and Sulaiman Laig, and three members of Hekmatyar's Hizb-i-Islami in four different Arab capitals (including Sana', Baghdad, and Tunis) to avoid media attention. No details of the agenda or the substance of discussions of these meetings is known. Hekmatyar was also reported to have established contact with the Kabul government. It has also been reported that Najibullah met the leader of the National Islamic Front, Syed Ahmad Gailani, and representatives of former king Zahir Shah in Geneva on December 1, 1990, and that Najibullah met with two mujahideen leaders, possibly including al-Mojaddedi at Meshed in Iran. None of these reported covert contacts led to formal and open negotiations between the mujahideen and the Kabul regime.[22] If the reports are true, the meetings would have constituted important moves in the internal negotiation process.

United Nations mediation had also worked the inter-Afghan front. In July 1987 Cordovez changed his negotiating strategy and made his first attempt to bring all parties together and move them toward national reconciliation. Under the Geneva Accords he was required to use his good offices to seek the formation of an interim Afghan government. He increased his efforts for a UN-sponsored loya jirga that would include the Peshawar Seven, mujahideen commanders, tribal leaders, former king Zahir Shah and his loyalist groups, the Tehran Eight, and the People's Democratic Party of Afghanistan. This national jirga was to choose an interim government. Cordovez set September 1, 1988, as the goal for a cease-fire and creation of a "temporary" new government of Afghan technocrats of "recognized independence and impartiality," who were not to serve in any future Afghan government.[23] The temporary government would plan for the loya jirga that would set up a permanent government acceptable to all sides. In view of strong mujahideen objections, Cordovez suggested that such a loya jirga session should be held not later than March 1, 1989—two weeks after the Soviets completed their withdrawal. Mujahideen leaders viewed the whole exercise as an attempt to infiltrate Najibullah's men into the new government, and refused to meet with Cordovez. With this failure of the UN plan, the secretary-general relieved Cordovez as his personal envoy and assumed charge of the Afghan talks himself. The United Nations played a low-key role for almost two years.

The UN General Assembly resolution of November 1990 worked out by Pakistan and the Soviet Union impelled yet another attempt by the secretary-general at a political solution. A five-point plan outlined by Perez de Cuellar in May 1991 included preservation of the sovereignty, territorial integrity, political independence, and nonaligned and Islamic character of Afghanistan; the right of the Afghan people to determine their own future; creation of a credible and impartial mechanism for transition to a broad-based government, and an end to hostilities, to be worked out through inter-Afghan dialogue; termination of the supply of arms to all sides from all sources; and reconstruction of the war-ravaged country and the rehabilitation of Afghan refugees.[24] Pakistan and Iran tried to overcome initial mujahideen opposition to the plan. In July, after much hesitation and skepticism, a majority of the mujahideen groups decided to support the plan, but the three conservative leaders—Hekmatyar, Yunis Khalis, and Sayyaf—held out.

Two important breaks came in January 1992. On January 27 the Pakistani government declared that it had ''decided to implement the UN peace plan'' and hoped ''to persuade the Afghans to endorse it,'' and promised to stop supplies of arms to the mujahideen.[25] This was a major turning point in Pakistan's Afghan policy. At the end of the month Najibullah gave assurances that he would quit as soon as a transitional government was formed. That removed the greatest obstacle to resolution of the Afghan conflict. But the three conservative leaders continued to insist that the Najibullah government leave immediately in favor of a mujahideen government, even though the mujahideen leaders were unable to agree to form one.

In an urgent effort to bring peace to Afghanistan and to hold off the pressures of time, Benon Sevan, newly appointed envoy of the UN secretary-general, engaged in protracted shuttle diplomacy from late February to early April 1992, which took him six times to Islamabad, five to Kabul, thrice to Tehran, and once to Saudi Arabia. He sought to implement the five-point plan by convening a meeting of up to two hundred Afghans representing all shades of political spectrum—the mujahideen groups, mujahideen commanders, members of the Watan Party, and neutral Afghan notables—in Vienna in mid-1992 to nominate a thirty-member Afghan consulting body. That body, together with other Afghans, would nominate delegates to the first session of a loya jirga, which in turn would elect an interim government, write a new constitution, and hold elections. However, the three conservative mujahideen leaders refused to provide a list of their representatives to a loya jirga, now scheduled to meet in the last week of April. Pakistani prime minister Nawaz Sharif failed to get the three hardline parties to agree to a transitional government, but nevertheless urged the UN envoy to convince Najibullah to quit even before an assembly could be convened.

By now events inside Afghanistan had picked up a momentum of their own that overtook Sevan's diplomacy. Sensing Najibullah's fast-deteriorating position, Sevan in April proposed a pretransition council of fifteen prominent but politically neutral Afghans to form a government in Kabul quickly; implementation of other proposals would follow.[26] Before the initiative could take effect, Najibullah was ousted in a low-key coup on April 15 and sought refuge in the United Nations headquarters in Kabul, where he remained for years. Events initiated by the United Nations had overtaken its own plan.

The Peshawar and Islamabad Accords

After the cold war the two superpowers acted more like allies than adversaries in handling international crises. They agreed to cut off supplies of arms to both sides in Afghanistan as of January 1, 1992, and urged Afghan leaders to seek a political solution. Then just when conditions in the Afghan conflict seemed ripe for resolution—that is, when all major actors (the United States, Russia, Iran, Saudi Arabia, and Pakistan) lent their full support to the UN peace proposals and when Najibullah was finally willing to step down—the situation burst. When Najibullah announced that he was willing to hand over power to an interim government under the UN peace plan, his statement caused panic among Watan party leaders and the regime's military commanders. Sensing the trend of events, they began negotiations with various groups of mujahideen.

The chain of events that set in motion Najibullah's fall started in January 1992 when General Abdul Momin, commander of the government's Herat garrison in the north, rebelled when he was to be replaced by an officer who was a Pushtun from the south. In March General Abdul Rashid Dostam, a powerful government commander in the north with headquarters on the Uzbekistan border at Mazar-i-Sharif, and General Syed Jafer Naderi, an Ismaili leader, switched sides rather than accepting replacement by Pushtun officers; they formed an alliance with Ahmed Shah Massoud, a Tajik commander of Rabbani's moderate Jamaat-i-Islami, who controlled the mostly Uzbek and Tajik north. Najibullah was removed from power on April 15 through a coup by Kabul garrison commander General Nabi Azimi, a Tajik, who was supported by other leaders of the Watan party, including Foreign Minister Abdul Wakil. In the brutal political culture of Afghanistan, Najibullah was defeated not by his enemies but by his own men.

Najibullah's ouster caused most local militia to sever all links with the old regime and either surrender to or enter into power-sharing arrangements with local mujahideen commanders. In this way all the major towns fell into mujahideen hands peacefully. But the new alignments sharpened the south-north or Pushtun-Tajik–non-Pushtun divide and the fight for Kabul became its symbol. While Massoud and Hekmatyar were making military moves to secure strategic advantage, leaders of the Kabul garrison were engaged in inter-Afghan negotiations not only to secure the best terms for surrender but also to ascertain which of the two mujahideen leaders could be most trusted.

With General Azimi and Abdul Wakil negotiating with Massoud and Hekmatyar inside Afghanistan, Pakistani prime minister Sharif personally took charge of negotiations with mujahideen leaders in Islamabad. In Pakistan the venue of talks shifted to Peshawar, where the mujahideen leaders had their headquarters. By April 18 Pakistan had convinced most of the leaders to accept a formula for the transfer of power. Hekmatyar's Hizb-i-Islami and the Iran-based Hizb-i-Wahdat opposed the formula. Thus on April 24, instead of achieving consensus, a majority decision was taken by mujahideen leaders in favor of a three-stage plan—the Peshawar Accord.[27] The plan called for a fifty-one-member Islamic Jihad Council (IJC) to run the administration in Kabul for a period of two months. The council was to be composed of thirty field commanders, ten 'ulema (religious leaders), and ten nominees of the mujahideen parties. Al-Mojaddedi was elected interim president and leader of the council. His main function was to oversee the transfer of power to an interim mujahideen government, which was to come in the second stage of the plan. In the interim government the president was to be from Rabbani's Jamaat-i-Islami, the prime minister from Hekmatyar's Hizb-i-Islami, and the defense minister was to be Massoud. Other parties were to get the remaining portfolios. The interim government was to be in effect for a period of four months; its main task was to make arrangements for holding free and fair elections, and then to hand over power to the elected representatives of the people.

The Peshawar Accord was immediately accepted by Massoud. The interim government that seized power from Najibullah also agreed to hand over power to a joint mujahideen council. But Hekmatyar rejected the accord and moved to take Kabul by force. Only after he was badly bruised militarily and deprived of most of his gains in Kabul by his much stronger and better-organized foe, Massoud, did Hekmatyar agree to a cease-fire engineered by Prime Minister Sharif and Saudi Arabian intelligence chief Prince Turki al-Faisal.[28] By the end of April 1992 Massoud held the capital and a sixty-day interim coalition government had been installed, without benefit of a cease-fire, the UN plan, or a mujahideen assembly. Only after the cease-fire was al-Mojaddedi able to reach Kabul, under Massoud's protection, and assume charge as interim president.

Negotiations then shifted to peacemaking efforts between Jamaat-i-Islami and Hizb-i-Islami, the two main factions. A thirty-one-member mediation commission of mujahideen leaders worked over the following month to bring the factions' leaders, on May 25, to subscribe to a cease-fire and to division of the country into northern and southern zones, with a neutral zone between the two around the capital, to be patrolled by a neutral military force. The factions then agreed to a ten-member Islamic Jihad Council and, at the end of the designated interval, the installation of Rabbani as a new president for the designated 120-day period. No clear procedure was established for thereafter. Rabbani's charge was to prepare elections; instead, in December 1992 he called a new session of the Loya Jirga. Although boycotted by five of the nine factions, the Loya Jirga chose Rabbani to succeed himself. The factions remained strong, interfactional violence continued, and institutional structures were not decided upon.

Pakistan again intervened the following spring to broker a new agreement that would reflect the shifts in power. Through constant artillery pounding of Kabul, Hekmatyar's forces were able to impose a new attempt to organize a government, even though they were unable to capture the capital. Under the Islamabad Agreement of March 1993, Hekmatyar became prime minister, Rabbani remained president, and Massoud was forced out of the government, although he continued to serve as an informal defense minister to the president. While Rabbani remained in Kabul, Hekmatyar exercised his functions from his base in Sarobi, fifty kilometers to the east in the Pushtun region, near the Pakistani border. At the holy city of Mecca, with Saudi king Fahd as witness, all parties vowed to honor the Islamabad Accords.[29]

After 1992 the rising force in the north of Afghanistan came to be General Dostam, the commander of Najibullah's army whose shift in loyalties ended the communist regime. Uzbek Dostam and Tajik Massoud headed the armed support behind Rabbani's government. In the fall of 1993 there were reports that the northern forces were preparing to launch an offensive to destroy the forces of Hekmatyar.[30] But Hekmatyar played on his own rising power and on the ambitions of Dostam, who called himself "president," and when Rabbani refused to resign on Dostam's demand, Dostam shifted alliances and on New Year's Day 1994 joined Hekmatyar in attempting to overthrow Rabbani and Massoud in Kabul.[31] Again Pakistan and the United Nations produced a series of cease-fires, but none brought an end to hostilities or a political structure agreed to by all factions. The Hekmatyar-Dostam alliance is even less stable in the long run than the preceding Massoud-Rabbani-Dostam alliance because Dostam remains opposed to Hekmatyar's Islamic fundamentalism. Whether in success or in failure against their rivals, the Pushtun-Uzbek alliance centered around Hekmatyar and Dostam contains seeds of its own collapse, but then so did the Tajik-Uzbek alliance of Massoud and Dostam that preceded it.

A year later, it was a new force drawing on Pushtun groups from the southern part of Afghanistan around Kandahar that was suddenly mobilized, with Pakistani support, in an attempt to break the deadlock of war and fatigue. The Taleban (Islamic students) force drained Hekmatyar's support and pushed back his forces, without eliminating them. The rapid drive of the Taleban force, in January and February 1995, had its immediate effect in destroying yet another attempt at UN mediation, under the Tunisian Mahmond Mestiri, in that its members refused to join the proposed executive commission of twenty-five mujahideen and independents that would replace Rabbani. Another faction was thus added to the list of parties seeking power.

While this cycle of instability is being played out, the Shi'i forces of the Hazara ethnic group in the west, related to the Tehran Eight, and the Taleban forces of the Mohammadzai Pushtuns of the south, related to the former king, also need to work out their relation to national politics. As long as the possibility of improving fortunes by shifting alliances remains, there is little chance for stalemate in Afghanistan, and as long as personal, ethnic, and religious passions animate the factions, there is a continual impetus to bolt and beat in a coalition game.[32] Only fatigue, a change in leadership, a uniting ideology, or enforced collaboration from a coalition of surrounding host-country patrons (four conceptual possibilities in declining order of likelihood in the 1990s) would produce the conditions for a power-sharing coalition among tolerant partners in Afghanistan. In real terms, this would mean either a coalition of ethnic factions based on regional control, who would negotiate a new Peshawar or Islamabad accord on central cooperation; or, alternatively, a fundamentalist victory that would submerge ethnic differences under a politico-religious ideology.

Analysis of the Internal Negotiation Process

The internal negotiation process in the Afghan conflict does not represent a case of resounding success. But its failures are as useful in providing theoretical insights into an internal negotiation process as are its successes. Spread over a fifteen-year period, the intra-mujahideen, inter-Afghan, and Geneva negotiation processes taken together highlight the variety of variables affecting the negotiation process—for example, the role of culture, the importance of the moment, and the weight of outside actors' interests. Here the Afghan negotiations are analyzed according to their structure, the negotiation process, and the ripening process leading to a ripe moment.

The Structure

Structurally, negotiations in the Afghan conflict followed two different tracks, with two very distinct and divergent destinations. On one track, or set of contests, the mujahideen sought to replace the Kabul regime and the government in Kabul tried to liquidate the insurgents. The two parties—and then the two shifting coalitions when one party had won—were locked in total confrontation and their objectives were mutually exclusive, leaving little room for negotiation. This track represented a classic zero-sum case, which was not easy to turn into a positive-sum situation.

On the other track were the Geneva negotiations and Accords, under the aegis of the United Nations. The Soviet Union was an active participant in the Afghan conflict and had hoped to accomplish quickly its mission of finishing off the insurgency with a well-equipped 115,000-man force. Only when the United States too became a party to the conflict, even though indirectly, and the insurgency grew stronger instead of weakening, did the Soviet leadership agree to let the United Nations initiate a negotiated solution to the crisis. Initially the Soviet Union thought to win on the table what it failed to win on the ground. The United Nations sought to de-escalate the conflict from its East-West and regional levels to an inter-Afghan level. Ultimately the Soviet army turned to extracting itself from the conflict in exchange for maintenance of the Kabul regime, and negotiations on those terms became possible.

Symmetry is an important structural component of successful negotiations. But insurgencies are normally asymmetrical, as it is de jure government that has access to the instruments of power and the legitimacy to use them, thus making it stronger than the insurgents. Insurgents have to fight for attention, for legitimacy, and for access to the means to continue their struggle. In regard to asymmetry, the Afghan situation differed from other conflicts in that the degree of asymmetry was not so marked; all male Afghans carry arms (albeit primitive ones) as a tradition, and the asymmetry that did exist was rapidly redressed by large-scale defections from the Afghan army to the insurgents, by which the insurgents also gained better weapons. Even then asymmetry was more pronounced during the pre-

Geneva phase of the conflict than later, as the insurgency, although widespread, was then in its infancy and lacked organization.

By not losing to a superpower for so long, the mujahideen were in fact winning, and that helped the United States to make the decision to come out openly and boldly in their support. Thus by the mid-1980s the mujahideen were assured of substantial supplies of modern weapons, including the latest shoulder-fired antiaircraft missiles—Stingers—which had a telling effect particularly on the Soviet Mi-24 Hind helicopter gunships that were highly feared by the mujahideen. The progressive improvement in the political, financial, and military strength of the mujahideen directly affected the pace of the negotiations. Following the Geneva negotiations it was generally expected that Najibullah would fall soon after the last Soviet soldier left Afghanistan. But he did not. The mujahideen's strength became their weakness as their divisions became more intense.

Commitment to Islamic ideology more than compensated for the mujahideen's asymmetry in the means to fight. From the mujahideen point of view a communist government in Afghanistan, installed and supported by the leader of the communist bloc, was perceived as anti-Islamic and thus had to be removed irrespective of the cost. In this struggle the mujahideen had the support of the entire Muslim world, which in a way redressed the asymmetry. The Afghan conflict was not a simple rebellion against an established authority; nor was it merely a protest against a denial of political or economic opportunities, or against the tyranny of a majority. In Afghanistan it was the majority itself that wanted to replace an ideologically unacceptable regime without regard to the cost; in this way the Afghan situation resembled that in South Africa. In the Afghan case it was the Kabul government whose legitimacy became suspect.

To find a valid spokesperson is usually not a problem for a government in power, even an illegitimate government; but for insurgents it is a major and multidimensional challenge. The Afghan internal negotiations ran into the problem of finding a valid representative for the mujahideen, a collectivity that had no de jure standing or organizational unity. The problem was accentuated by the sheer size of the insurgency. More than five and a half million people—more than a third of the entire population of Afghanistan—were outside the country as refugees in Pakistan and Iran. The number of refugees within Afghanistan was also substantial. Moreover, an active and effective insurgency was divided by mountains and valleys.

Apart from the problems of size and dispersion over wide geographic areas, mujahideen leaders (who had emerged by the dozens) were deeply divided by personal, ethnic, tribal, religious, and sectarian factors. The fissures were so deep that organizations within Pakistan had to be very careful in arranging meetings of and with Afghan leaders. Initially only individual and like-minded leaders were called together at any one time. It was only over a period of time that leaders of different groups reached a stage of talking with one another. Even then two senior leaders reportedly drew their pistols in one meeting. In due course Pakistan recognized only eleven of the mujahideen groups based in Peshawar. Eight groups were based in Iran, and a large number of mujahideen field commanders acted almost as independent entities. With such diversity among the mujahideen, both the prosecution of war and negotiation for peace suffered considerably.

During the post-Geneva period, when the mujahideen were burdened with the task of forming an alternative Afghan government and the need for unity was much greater, their infighting and inflexibility increased. The deaths of Pakistani president Zia ul-Haq and General Akhtar Abdur Rehman in August 1988 in an air crash were a factor in the worsening of the situation as these two leaders had the confidence of the mujahideen and could influence even the most inflexible of the Afghan leaders. Even when the mujahideen had managed to put some structure and organizations like the IUAM in place, their spokespersons suffered from undefined authority. For example, al-Mojaddedi's agreement with Karim Khalili, leader of the Tehran Eight, was rejected by the mujahideen hard-liners in Peshawar, thus scuttling a promising chance to form a widely representative and viable Afghan interim government, which in turn might well have brought the Afghan conflict to a resolution. Although infighting among insurgent groups when victory comes within grasp is not peculiar to the mujahideen, as chapter 1 indicates, Afghanistan provides one of its extreme examples.

The Process

The structural complexity of the Afghanistan negotiations directly affected the negotiating process and its outcome. National interests of so many countries had been affected by the developments in Afghanistan that it would be natural to expect their direct or indirect involvement to safeguard those interests. It is not unusual for an insurgency to spill over into neighboring states, involving them in a situation that is essentially an internal affair. Such a spillover regionalizes and then internationalizes a conflict, in turn providing legitimacy for external attempts at mediation. In the case of Afghanistan, the UN-mediated proximity talks were officially between Pakistan and the Kabul regime, but the negotiation process was pentangular, with the Kabul regime, the mujahideen, Pakistan, the Soviet Union, and the United States as active participants (Iran had opted out, but was kept informed and frequently consulted). As host to more than three million Afghan refugees and sanctuary and conduit for the mujahideen, Pakistan particularly was under direct military threat from the Afghan and Soviet forces. Pakistan was in a hurting stalemate (similar to the military situation in Angola in 1987–88), with its costs not only heavy but rising, thus creating conditions in which Pakistan had to take into consideration its own national interests in either facilitating or avoiding a negotiated approach to the conflict.

The withdrawal of the Soviet forces addressed the security concerns of most major actors involved, and was seen as a major accomplishment of the United Nations. Could the Geneva Accords have been accomplished by any other actor? It appears unlikely, because the Afghan conflict was not a simple case of insurgency. It became an international conflict when a Soviet military force invaded Afghanistan to uphold the Brezhnev doctrine, a large number of refugees fled to Pakistan (where the mujahideen established their bases), the Muslim members of the nonaligned movement in the Organization of the Islamic Conference condemned the Soviet invasion, and the United States supplied weapons to the mujahideen to counter a perceived Soviet threat to critical interests of the industrialized West and Japan. By debating the Afghan conflict every year the UN General Assembly kept the issue before the world's attention, and by placing its authority behind the UN secretary-general's efforts for a political settlement, the General Assembly created the conditions for the Soviet withdrawal. In a conflict involving the superpowers, only the United Nations has the moral standing to attempt mediation. Perez de Cuellar and Cordovez mediated many a deadlock between Islamabad and Kabul to keep the talks alive.

The mediation succeeded because of the mediators' tenaciousness and innovative intervention at crucial moments. It took thirty months and three diplomatic shuttles by Perez de Cuellar and Cordovez to get Pakistan and Afghanistan, with diametrically opposed views of the negotiations, to hold their first indirect round of talks in Geneva. The regime in Kabul insisted on direct talks so that it could gain recognition and international legitimacy. Pakistan, for the opposite reasons, was equally insistent in opposing direct negotiations with the Kabul regime. Cordovez, diagnosing the situation, worked out a format for indirect talks through a ''shuttle'' within the same building. As a result, a four-point agenda that included reference to the withdrawal of Soviet troops was the basis of the first round of proximity talks in Geneva in June 1982. A second opportunity for creative redefinition arose when the Soviet Union objected to inclusion of the withdrawal of troops on the agenda, although initially the Soviets had cleared the reference. Cordovez resolved the impasse by replacing that issue on the agenda with an instrument of ''interrelationships,'' under which a separate agreement between the Kabul regime and the Soviets would cover the question of withdrawal of Soviet troops.

Later, agreement again became stuck over whether the formation of an interim Afghan government should precede the Soviet withdrawal, as the Soviets demanded, or follow it, as the Pakistanis wished. The Soviets wanted to make sure that there would be a place for Najibullah's people in the interim government, whereas Pakistan and the mujahideen expected the Kabul regime to disintegrate once the Soviets left. When the Soviets unlinked the two issues an agreement seemed ready to sign, but at the start of the final round of Geneva talks, on March 2, 1988, Pakistan reversed its position and refused to sign before an agreement was reached on an interim government to replace the Najibullah regime. Another source of last-minute disagreement was a U.S. demand for symmetry, under which the Soviet Union and the United States would simultaneously halt aid to their respective clients. The Soviet Union blamed the United States for advancing ''new terms'' to thwart the Geneva Accords; the Soviet news agency Tass justified Soviet assistance to the Kabul regime on the basis of bilateral agreements and the Soviets' 1921 treaty with Afghanistan; Afghan foreign minister Wakil said that ''aid to terrorist groups'' was ''totally different from assistance given by one state to another.''[33]

It was a new situation demanding a new approach by the United Nations mediator. Cordovez rejected Pakistan's demand as not falling within the agreed four-point agenda, but got support from the two superpowers and then from Pakistan and Afghanistan for personal use of his good offices to bring about an agreement among the Afghan parties on the formation of a broad-based Afghan government. The formula provided Pakistan with a way out from an isolated position. The Soviet Union rejected the U.S. demand for a moratorium on military aid by both sides (positive symmetry) during the period of Soviet withdrawal. U.S. secretary of state George Shultz offered a compromise under which the United States would reserve the right to supply military equipment to the mujahideen as long as the Soviet Union supplied the Najibullah regime (negative symmetry). The

Soviet Union finally agreed, thus opening the Geneva Accords for signature. The protracted Afghan negotiations show the importance of the mediator in diagnosing new situations and devising their resolution.

During the post-Geneva period, in addition to making arrangements for the return of Afghan refugees, mine-clearing operations, and the reconstruction of destroyed infrastructure, the United Nations was actively involved in seeking a political inter-Afghan settlement. That progress remained stunted was not due to any lack of effort on the part of Cordovez and Sevan, but rather to the intransigence of the Afghans themselves and to the lack of a firm Pakistani policy on Afghanistan after Zia's demise. In the end, Pakistan and Sevan did work together to hammer out a political accord, following Najibullah's exit.

The Geneva process was a case of both internal and international negotiations. In the pre-Geneva phase, the mujahideen were spectators, cheering on the players; during the Geneva Accord negotiations, the mujahideen were coaches, deeply involved in the outcome but able to instruct the players only before and after the rounds of talks; and in the post-Geneva phase, the mujahideen themselves were the players. Input by the mujahideen was informal in the Geneva process, but they were consulted and informed at every stage. Pakistani president Zia routinely invited leaders of the Peshawar Seven to consultations before the start of a round of negotiations and to briefings at the conclusion of talks. Even though the mujahideen rejected the Geneva Accords, Maulvi Yunis Khalis, then chairman of the IUAM, met Cordovez in Peshawar on February 6, 1988, at the request of President Zia, after the mujahideen leaders had refused to meet with Cordovez on three previous occasions. The United States also kept in close contact with mujahideen leaders and consulted with and briefed them on major developments. After the summit meeting in Washington, D.C., between Gorbachev and U.S. president Ronald Reagan in December 1987, U.S. under secretary of state Armacost met with five of the seven main mujahideen alliance leaders on January 5, 1988, in Peshawar.[34] The United States had also appointed an ambassador to the mujahideen, who acted as an important contact between the U.S. government and the mujahideen.

In the post-Geneva period, when the Soviet forces had withdrawn, it was the Afghan game—the Buzkashi—that dominated inter-Afghan and intra-mujahideen politics.[35] Hekmatyar's Hizb-i-Islami reportedly kept its communications open with the People's Democratic Party and the Soviet Union, and was involved in a failed coup by General Shah Nawaz Tanai against Najibullah. Massoud too was consolidating his position in the northern part of Afghanistan. Some other leaders of the Peshawar Seven reportedly held secret meetings with either Najibullah or his representatives. It is hard to understand and explain how, in their individual capacity, the mujahideen leaders met and made alliances with PDPA leaders but rarely owned up to them, while at the collective level the mujahideen rejected all offers of reconciliation from Najibullah and were firmly against any dealings with the People's Democratic Party. When Najibullah fell in mid-April 1992, both Massoud and Hekmatyar scrambled to make alliances with different leaders of Najibullah's regime in order to secure positions of advantage.

The Ripening Process and the Ripe Moment

Apart from the structure and the process of negotiations, it is the presence or absence of the ripe moment that determines their success or failure. The concepts of the ripening process and the ripe moment are essential tools in analyzing as well as explaining the success of the Geneva Accords negotiations, but other elements are required to provide an adequate theoretical explanation of the events of the post-Geneva phase.

After the Soviet military intervention in December 1979, it was not until mid-1981 that the Soviet Union and the Kabul regime agreed to negotiate with Pakistan and the mujahideen without insisting on prior recognition of the Kabul regime and on direct talks only. It took yet another year for the two sides to actually start indirect negotiations. That delay of two and a half years allowed the ripening process that built a hurting stalemate for both sides, but one that differed in nature for each. For the Afghans and the Soviets the stalemate did not hurt as much in military as in political terms. There was no letup in the international condemnation of the Soviet military action in Afghanistan. It was even turning more hostile, and some allies and friends of the Soviet Union were themselves very vocal in demanding withdrawal of Soviet troops. Despite the long stalemate, Pakistan was not willing either to recognize the Kabul regime as a price for negotiations or even to enter into direct talks with it. The Afghan government had lost its legitimacy. The point had come when continued refusal to enter into a political dialog was futile for the Afghan regime. Its agreement to UN-sponsored proximity talks was considered an important means of defusing hostile international reaction.

Soviet military intervention in Afghanistan created a severe security problem for Pakistan. The mujahideen were not militarily in a position to drive the Soviet forces out of Afghanistan; it was only through a political settlement that the Soviets could be persuaded to withdraw. In addition, the more than three million Afghan refugees were a severe economic and social strain on Pakistan. The refugees could return home only through a settlement of the Afghan problem. Therefore the start of the negotiation process on June 16, 1982, was the first ripe moment of that process in the sense that it was the only way out of a hurting stalemate for both sides.

From the June 1982 session until April 1983, there was a serious attempt by all parties to arrive at some negotiated settlement of the Afghan problem. Apparently the Soviet Union then concluded that the Kabul regime was not yet strong enough to sustain itself without continued support of Soviet troops. There were also signs of military weakness on the part of the mujahideen, and even divisions among the mujahideen, as Massoud had concluded a cease-fire agreement with the Soviet Union independently of other leaders. For the Soviet Union this was not the ripe moment to conclude an agreement, so the June 1983 round of Geneva talks saw the beginning of another ripening process. The Soviet aims at the time were, on the one hand, to strengthen the Kabul regime so that it could withstand mujahideen military pressure without direct Soviet involvement, and, on the other hand, to weaken the mujahideen militarily. The Soviets stalled the negotiating process by raising the terms of their offer and introducing new elements. The United States and Pakistan were not oblivious to the Soviet intention. The result was provision of greater supplies of military equipment to both sides. This ripening process continued for nearly three years, and it was not until May 1986, in the seventh round of Geneva talks, that the interrelationships instrument was discussed for the first time.

When Gorbachev came to power in 1985, the ripening process employed by the Soviet Union became much more sophisticated and multidimensional. The Soviets intensified military operations against the mujahideen, increased border violations and operations against Pakistan, mounted subversive and terrorist acts within Pakistan, augmented the supply of military equipment to the Kabul regime, removed Karmal as Afghanistan's fig-leaf leader, and supported the Geneva talks. In his two-pronged strategy Gorbachev shrewdly increased the cost of Pakistan's support for the mujahideen and brought the lesson home to the people of Pakistan through terrorist acts; but the Soviets also provided Pakistan with a way out through the Geneva talks. At the same time, by providing increased military supplies to the mujahideen, Pakistan and the United States raised the cost of continuing the conflict for the Soviet Union and Afghanistan. The intensi-

fication and escalation of the conflict by both sides was viewed as dangerous, and resulted in greater efforts for a political settlement.

By late 1987 and early 1988 the pace of events and of the negotiations
dictated that the process either succeed or fail; results could not be post-
poned indefinitely. The stalemate was hurting all parties. At this crucial
phase of the negotiation process there were divisions among the
decisionmakers in both Pakistan and the United States. In Pakistan, Prime
Minister Muhammed Khan Junejo and the Foreign Office wanted to meet
the Soviet deadline of March 15 for signing the accords so that the withdrawal could start on May 15, whereas President Zia and the military did
not favor signing until the Soviet Union had agreed on the formation of an
interim Afghan government. In the United States, the Department of State
wanted to sign the agreement, whereas Congress was more hawkish. Finally it was Junejo in Pakistan and the Department of State in the United
States that prevailed, and the agreement was signed on April 14, 1988.

The withdrawal of Soviet forces in February 1989 should have brought
the different Afghan groups together to seek a political resolution of the
conflict. In fact, the reverse happened. The presence of Soviet troops had
acted as a kind of glue that kept the divergent mujahideen groups together.
Once the presence of Soviet troops was no longer an issue, infighting and
hardening views became more prevalent among the mujahideen. Their
inability to form a more representative interim government, and their military fiasco at Jalalabad, contributed to the reversal of their expectations of
Najibullah's early fall. The mujahideen were left groping in the dark. They
continued to refuse to talk about any formula for an interim government that
would incorporate members of the PDPA, but they were unable to do much
militarily. A Watan party leader commented that "the psychology of reconciliation has not yet ripened on both sides."[36] The same unripeness was
registered by the two major remaining supporters of the mujahideen, Pakistan and Saudi Arabia. Thus a fairly long stalemate resulted, and even
mediatory efforts by the United Nations moved into a low gear.

During that stalemate two mujahideen leaders, Massoud and Hekmatyar,
were busy in expanding their power bases—at times at each other's expense. The next breakthrough in the Afghan stalemate came when the
Soviet Union became deeply involved in its own internal crises, which led
to its breakup in mid-1991. During the same period the superpowers
reached an agreement on positive symmetry, effectively cutting off all
military supplies to both sides in the Afghan conflict as of January 1, 1992.
Deprived of military and even political support, Najibullah's power base

crumbled quickly—too quickly for UN negotiator Sevan to seize the ripe moment and achieve an agreement. Thrice the situation was salvaged by the intervention of the Pakistani prime minister, through the Peshawar and Islamabad agreements of April 1992 and March 1993, respectively, and the cease-fires of January 1994; twice a mujahideen government of all factions was formed; and thrice bloody civil war broke out over the capital of divided Afghanistan, among shifting coalitions seeking power. The element that made the difference between the rounds was the shift of General Dostam from one coalition to another. But the possibilities for new coalitions among the players remain many, and none of them are likely to produce a stable solution to the Afghan conflict.

Conclusions

The Afghan conflict has been one of the most intensely mediated of conflicts. The mediators' strategy, written as it were by the evolution of the bipolar confrontation, was to remove the external elements to the conflict and then help the internal parties to work out their own settlement. Before and during the Geneva Accord negotiations, the governing rationale for the intra-mujahideen negotiations was to forge a unified political stand to present to the world, in order to seek political, economic, and military assistance to redress the asymmetry of the mujahideen struggle. The Geneva Accords were an important success story in large part because of the way the negotiation process was conceived: aims were kept limited, the art of the possible was stressed, and the mujahideen were excluded from the process.

From Pakistan's point of view, the Geneva talks provided an opportunity to secure a political settlement to a problem that would have defied a military solution—and a military solution possibly would have been against the interests of Pakistan. Pakistan succeeded in securing an agreement for the withdrawal of Soviet troops from Afghanistan, but it did not succeed in bringing about an environment conducive enough for the Afghan refugees to return home. Thus Pakistan could manage only half a loaf. In negotiations for the Geneva Accords the interests of the host state—Pakistan—became entangled with the interests of the resistance forces, which sought and operated from sanctuaries provided by the host state.

In the post-Geneva period, the mujahideen were back at center stage and faced with the difficult challenge of putting into place a viable, broad-based government as an alternative to the regime in Kabul. This was also a period of several missed opportunities for negotiating an end to the conflict. The Soviet Union desired to negotiate a formula with the mujahideen that would allow some role for the People's Democratic Party in any future Afghan government. But the mujahideen were not about to oblige. By failing to accommodate the Tehran Eight in an interim Afghan government, and failing in their military attack on Jalalabad, the mujahideen further delayed resolution of the conflict. At the same time, the collapse of the central government's authority throughout the country, and the independence movements in the former Soviet republics of central Asia, such as neighboring Tajikestan and Uzbekistan, gave impetus to the reemergence of violent ethnic divisions within mujahideen ranks. Such divisions are seen in the fundamentalist Pushtun control of the east under Hekmatyar, the Tajik revolt in the north under Massoud, the revolt in the central autonomous region under Uzbek leader General Dostam, Shi'i control of the west, and the sudden emergence of the Pakistani-backed Pushtun Taleban force in early 1995. Pakistan was able to hammer out a series of negotiated power-sharing settlements for the establishment of an interim Afghan government, but these proved to be only momentary pauses in a cycle of unstable coalition dynamics. The commitment of the Afghan rebellion splintered along with its factions once the insurgents had overcome the power of the Soviet-backed regime, thus blocking the possibilities for a negotiated power-sharing agreement.

Notes

1. On the background of the Afghan conflict, see Carol Rose, "Afghanistan and Empire," report CVR 1 (Hanover, N.H.: Institute for Current World Affairs, November 1, 1990); and Carol Rose, "Afghanistan at the Crossroads," report CVR 2 (Hanover, N.H.: Institute for Current World Affairs, December 1, 1990). On women and the revolution, see Carol Rose, "Night Letters," report CVR 20 (Hanover, N.H.: Institute for Current World Affairs, January 15, 1992).

2. For details on the evolution of the resistance groups, see J. Bruce Amstutz, *Afghanistan: The First Five Years of Soviet Occupation* (Washington: National Defense University Press, 1986), especially pp. 97–110; André Briot and Olivier Roy, *The War in Afghanistan: An Account and Analysis of the Country, Its People, Soviet Intervention and Resistance* (Brighton, England: Harvester-Wheatsheaf, 1988), especially pp. 106–07; and Imtiaz Bokhari, "The Afghan War, A Study in Insurgency and Counterinsurgency," *Strategic Studies* (Islamabad), no. 573 (Spring 1992).

3. For a revealing interview with Hekmatyar, see Carol Rose, "Gulbuddin Hekmatyar in Person," report CVR 22 (Hanover, N.H.: Institute for Current World Affairs, March 21, 1992).

4. For a chronology of the negotiations, see Richard Cronin, "Afghanistan Peace Talks" (Washington: Congressional Research Service, Library of Congress, 1988); and Rosanne Klass, "Afghanistan: The Accords," *Foreign Affairs*, vol. 66 (Summer 1988), pp. 922–45.

5. Michael T. Kaufman, "Afghan Official, in India, Espouses New Flexibility," *New York Times*, September 8, 1981, p. A13.

6. Ted Morello, "Sweet and Sour Diplomacy," *Far Eastern Economic Review*, vol. 113 (August 28, 1981), p. 31.

7. Agha Shahi, "The Geneva Accords," *Pakistan Horizon*, vol. 41 (July 1988), p. 34.

8. Romey Fullerton, "Cordovez Starts Over," *Far Eastern Economic Review*, vol. 124 (April 12, 1984), pp. 26–27.

9. Lawrence Lifschultz, "Afghanistan: The Choice Ahead," *The Muslim* (Islamabad), August 5, 1985, pp. 1, 8.

10. Barnett Rubin, "Afghanistan: The Next Round," *Orbis*, vol. 33 (Winter 1989), p. 61.

11. "Gains Reported in Afghan Talks," *New York Times*, December 10, 1986, p. A10.

12. Rubin, "Afghanistan," p. 61.

13. Nayan Chanda, "Time to Go Home," *Far Eastern Economic Review*, vol. 138 (December 24, 1987), p. 30.

14. For a summary of the Geneva Accords, see Shahi, "Geneva Accords," pp. 23–24; and *Afghanistan Report*, no. 49 (Institute of Strategic Studies, Islamabad, May 1988), pp. 44–55.

15. Agha Shahi, "The Geneva Accords," *Pakistan Horizon*, vol. 41 (July 1988), p. 26.

16. For the text of the Geneva Accords, see William Maley and Fazel Haq Saikal, "Political Order in Post-Communist Afghanistan," International Peace Academy Occasional Paper Series (Boulder, Colo.: Lynne Rienner, 1992), pp. 59–68.

17. An excellent analysis of the issues in the internal negotiations for an Afghan government is found in Maley and Saikal, "Political Order in Post-Communist Afghanistan." On the evolving sociopolitical context, see Myron Weiner and Ali Banuazizi, eds., *The Politics of Social Transformation in Afghanistan, Iran and Pakistan* (Syracuse University Press, 1994).

18. *Afghanistan Report*, no. 48 (Institute of Strategic Studies, Islamabad, April 1988), p. 49.

19. "Riyadh Backs Early Formation of Broad-Based Afghan Government," *The Muslim* (Islamabad), July 13, 1988, pp. 1, 6; and "Gailini Willing to Consider Cordevez Proposal," *The Muslim* (Islamabad), July 15, 1988, pp. 1, 6.

20. *Dawn* (Karachi), January 24, 1989, p. 1; on al-Mujaddedi's statement, see *Pakistan Times*, January 10, 1989, p. 1.

21. *Keesing's News Digest*, February 1989, p. 36448.

22. *Frontier Post* (Peshawar), December 29, 1990; November 20, 1990.

23. Ali T. Sheikh, "The Afghan Conflict," in Ami Ayalon and Haim Shaked, eds., *Middle East Contemporary Survey*, vol. 12, 1988 (Boulder, Colo.: Westview Press, 1989), p. 74.

24. Raisul B. Rais, "Afghanistan and Regional Security after the Cold War," *Problems of Communism* (May–June 1992).

25. *Newsline* (Islamabad), February 1992.

26. *The Economist*, April 11, 1992.

27. *Herald* (Islamabad), May 1992.

28. *The News* (Peshawar), April 28, 1992, p. 1.

29. On the negotiations, see *Arab News* and *Saudi Gazette*, March 3–6, 1993.

30. "Strange Calm in Kabul," *Economist*, September 18, 1993, p. 42.

31. Jan Afar Abbes, "The Battle for Kabul," *Herald*, February 1994, pp. 41–45.

32. On the dynamics of such a situation, see Anatol Rapoport, *N-Person Game Theory: Concepts and Applications* (University of Michigan Press, 1970).

33. *Keesing's News Digest*, March 1988, p. 35785.

34. Ibid.

35. A ruthless Afghan polo-like game that involves picking up a dead goat from the ground. On the subsequent events in Afghanistan, see *Keesing's News Digest*, March 1990, p. 37315.

36. Steve Coll, "Afghan President Takes Zig-Zag Path to Survival," *Washington Post*, September 20, 1991, p. A18.

CHAPTER ELEVEN

Colombia: Negotiations in a Shifting Pattern of Insurgency

Todd Eisenstadt and Daniel Garcia

IN THE WEAK Colombian state experiencing constant challenges to its authority, leftist insurgents are but one threat to internal security. Guerrilla warfare has been the state's most consistent internal threat since the 1960s. But the governing regime has also been increasingly challenged since the mid-1980s by drug lords and their military and economic apparatus, and by the paramilitary right, which has tried to take matters into its own hands whenever it perceived its interests threatened by the government's handling of affairs. The resulting multifaceted contestation of the regime in some respects bears more similarity to an environment of generalized violence than to a simple internal conflict between the state and a single insurgency.

Historically, Colombia has experienced a continuous streak of civil violence since its early national consolidation in the 1820s, and the state has never been fully brought under the kind of strong centralist rule experienced in many Latin American countries in the late nineteenth and early twentieth centuries. Instead, in Colombia political order was established through the creation of strong political parties in the 1850s—parties formed to channel citizen participation away from violent expression, but which provoked a return to violence in the 1950s, 1970s, and 1980s as the politically disenfranchised desperately sought an outlet for expression. To this day entire regions of the country lie outside the state's control, serving as battlegrounds for guerrillas and narcoterrorists (and for paramilitary vigilantes intervening against the rebels) trying to consolidate control over peasant leagues and their local economies, over resources such as oil pipelines and emerald mines, and over geographical spaces from which to launch larger attacks. Structural obstacles impede the resolution of the soft stalemate between the government and the insurgencies, although the long peace process that commenced in 1982 has not been entirely fruitless. In the Colombian conflict fatigue has been the real conditioning factor behind negotiations; the deaths of guerrilla leaders and the endpoints of violent episodes have provided the ripe moments for settlement.

The negotiation of internal conflict has had at least a limited success in Colombia. The treaty signed in March 1990 between the leftist rebels known as M-19 and the government, which brought that group of some 1,000 insurgents into the democratic fold, should be viewed as a limited victory for mediation of internal conflict.[1] Similar treaties have since been signed by the government and the 2,000-member Popular Liberation Army (EPL) (in March 1991) and two smaller groups, the People's Revolutionary Party (PRT) and the Quintin Lame Indigenous Movement (in April and May 1991, respectively). Most recently, a dissident group of some 850 guerrillas from the Army of National Liberation (ELN) agreed to disarm in April 1994, although the majority of that group have not laid down their arms. Despite these achievements, some 10,000 guerrillas are reportedly still active, mainly in ELN and the Revolutionary Armed Forces of Colombia (FARC), Colombia's oldest insurgency.

The incorporation of the insurgents into electoral participation has also met with mixed success. In elections in October 1991 M-19's political arm, the Democratic Alliance of M-19 (AD/M-19), garnered about 10 percent of the vote, substantially less that its 27 percent showing in a December 1990 vote for a constituent assembly, but still significant for a group previously consigned to military displays of authority. However, by 1994 the Democratic Alliance vote was substantially lower. Winning only 4 percent in the first round of presidential balloting, AD/M-19 candidate Navarro Wolf urged supporters to cast blank ballots in the next round; 1 percent of the voters did so in the June 1994 runoff. And even inclusion of the guerrillas in the electoral system has not caused a letup in the violence. The end of the twenty-year armed insurrection by M-19 and EPL against the state represents an advance on but one of the fragmented Colombian state's insurgent fronts.

But in several other internal struggles government initiatives have been rebuked, stalemated, or ignored. Negotiations drag on between the government and several other guerrilla groups, united under the banner of the

Simón Bolívar Guerrilla Front (CGSB), which is composed mainly of FARC, ELN, and several smaller groups.

Other insurgencies refuse to be silenced. The narcoterrorism wrought by the Medellín and Cali cocaine dealers continues to provide a constant and violent distraction from the peace efforts of both the leftist guerrillas and the government. Colombian president César Gaviria Trujillo, upon taking office in 1990, reversed the hard-line antinarco policies of his predecessor Virgilio Barco Vargas. In August 1989 Barco had launched a major offensive against the Medellín cartel, which had precipitated a "total war" by the drug cartel against the state. That conflict had resulted in the killing of hundreds of police, scores of reporters and judges, and three presidential candidates. Gaviria's approach was more diplomatic, promising drug cartel leaders such as Pablo Escobar reduced sentences in exchange for their surrender. Drug terrorism dropped after Gaviria made these offers, but the drug trade has continued to thrive. External pressures to halt drug trafficking continue to be applied against Gaviria's successor, Ernesto Samper Pizano, particularly by the United States. Financial assistance designated for stemming the drug flow to the United States has reportedly been spent by the Colombian military in battling the leftist insurgents.[2]

There is an apparent overlap, to be sure, between the leftist insurgents and the drug lords, although it is unlikely that much of the guerrillas' funding is generated by the drug trade, as the insurgents and the drug cartels share few permanent interests. At certain moments the drug lords' Hobbesian social order supplants the leftist insurgents' idealistic quests as the state's greatest threat. In so doing the drug lords sabotage the agendas of both the government and the insurgents, neutralizing what would otherwise be the state's advantage in manipulating power asymmetries toward a negotiated settlement. Inevitably, reprisals by the state against the drug dealers result in a backlash against the guerrillas, particularly by the military, which often acts autonomously without regard for the rest of the government.

For the purposes of this chapter, the lessons to be drawn about internal conflict resolution from the Colombian case must focus necessarily on negotiations between the state and the leftist insurgents. The narcoterrorist insurgency, which is much more dependent on exogenous factors (such as the retail price of cocaine on the U.S. market), is not explicitly addressed. That the Colombian state, the guerrillas, the narcoterrorists, and the quasi-civilian militias of the paramilitary right are already mired in violence differentiates the Colombian case from other insurgencies, in which violence is used to increase the stakes and challenge one of the fundamental rights of the state—its monopoly on the legitimate use of force. In Colombia a penchant for violence is almost the ante for entering the game of power contestation, not just a mark of escalating frustration. It is ironic that some Colombian guerrilla groups have been able to take advantage of ripe moments for conflict resolution by resorting to peace as a novel attempt to redress their asymmetry with government forces. A key to the Colombian case, then, is the civil fatigue of the populace with the ever-escalating violence of guerrilla groups and other forces external to the state as they compete for the government's attention.

A second key to understanding the Colombian case lies in the ambiguity of the actors. It is often necessary to distinguish between the military and the executive, as the military's interests sometimes actively oppose those of the regime's executive (here referred to as the government, whereas the state is considered more broadly to be the entire array of social and economic forces that the guerrillas oppose). During the three presidential administrations in power at the time of the peace process considered in this chapter (1982–95), there were several open strategic debates between secretaries of defense and the president or ministries representative of the president's civil authority. Furthermore, some right-wing sectors of the military have overcome frequent bureaucratic deadlocks by supporting or even participating in paramilitary vigilante groups, whose objective is usually to obliterate the guerrillas and all other ideological opposition to the state.

Among the guerrillas, too, ideological and tactical divisions have led to profound fragmentation. It can be difficult to ascertain exactly who the guerrillas represent. Does their increasingly outdated world view espouse the views of the peasants they claim as their rural support base? Or, more probably, do they represent the only successful medium for drawing attention to the plight of the disenfranchised rural masses who, left to themselves, would petition the state with more practical grievances, unfettered by ideology? Expressed in other cases in this book as the search for a valid spokesperson, the overlap between interest groups can be so acute in the Colombian case that in addition to seeking a valid interlocutor in negotiations between the government and the guerrillas—an interlocutor acceptable to both sides—each side frequently has questioned whether any spokesperson can accurately represent the constellation of interests present.

A third key to the Colombian case lies in the intensity of the objectives of both sides. Do the guerrilla insurgencies express deep-seated ethnic conflicts, or just instrumental tensions? Whatever that answer, the more practical issue is how well different factions have overcome differentiating cleavages in the pursuit of common ends. When the government and the armed opposition have presented concrete objectives for peace talks and specific steps for attaining such goals, satisfactory results have been obtained. At all other times there has been no agreement. The degree of ideological cohesion of the various actors, and the obstacle such cohesion poses to finding compatible long-term goals, is at the bottom of this polemic. The tenacious Marxism of FARC (even after the cold war) calls for replacement of the incumbent regime with a new central government, whereas M-19 has espoused moderate and reformist rather than doctrinaire and revolutionary views.

The government has been alternately tolerant of and resistant to challenges to its legitimacy. After particularly strong waves of violence (often perpetrated by external actors—the drug cartels and the paramilitary right) exasperation sets in, facilitating ripe moments for governmental policy shifts. Moreover, high tolerance of challenges to the regime has been evident during presidential transitions, when each incoming president has differentiated his policies from the failures of his predecessor. However, even given such ruptures at the policy level, there has been a philosophical continuity among the last three presidential administrations: in contrast to their predecessors, all have believed that the guerrillas have had legitimate grievances worthy of state attention. Thus despite differences in personality and in the circumstance in which each executive has found himself, the peace process has evolved incrementally during each administration.

The analysis of Colombia's internal peace process in this chapter gives special consideration to three factors: the struggle of civil society to assert its own space, the difficulties posed by the extreme fragmentation and division of interests even among groups represented by a common interlocutor, and the often insurmountable obstacles posed by ideological rigidity.

Endemic Violence?

Analysts of culture and history, both from Colombia and abroad, often base their studies of the country on the assumption that its violence is permanent, chronic, and endemic. According to this reductionist thesis, contemporary car bomb explosions, machine gun massacres, and guerrilla ambushes are merely the modern expression of a recurring theme of violence. In this interpretation the primordial recurrence to violent expression was inherited from the bellicose nature of the country's pre-Colombian indigenous cultures, then fortified by the cruelty of the Spanish conquistadors, renewed during the country's movement for independence from Spain, embedded during the notorious nineteenth century civil wars, and reinforced yet again during the bloody mid-twentieth century confrontations between Liberals and Conservatives, which culminated during the 1950s in the period termed La Violencia. However, as noted by Daniel Pecaut, although violent convulsions have continued to sweep Colombia, at the institutional level the country has been one of the most stable civilian-ruled democracies in Latin America, and has had only one interlude of military rule—from 1953 to 1958—in recent history.[3] Yet even though the government has been formally democratic, access to political participation was for long limited to the ruling elite's two main political parties. The administration of Belisario Betancur (1982–86) was the first to acknowledge that there existed objective causes of the social crisis that led many of the country's youth to join guerrilla movements during and after the 1960s.

A National Front agreement implemented in 1958 ended a decade of La Violencia, after the loss of some 200,000 citizens' lives. That conciliation initiated a power-sharing arrangement under which the two oligarchical elites—the Liberals and Conservatives—rotated in power from 1958 until 1974. Although the National Front coalition had been opened slightly in 1972 by provisions for third-party electoral victories and by the formal end to the presidential rotation between Liberals and Conservatives in 1974, the coalition's constant state-of-siege measures, its legal obstacles to the formation of an opposition, and its wide tolerance of the military (particularly after 1975) were conducive to rebellion by the disenfranchised masses. The bipartisan governing coalition blocked participation by popular sector, thereby prompting the deinstitutionalization of social and union-based struggles, which overflowed legal bounds into illegal strikes and armed insurrections.[4]

In 1964 the military attempted to curtail the rise of autonomous "independent republics" in some of Colombia's most remote areas, but instead provoked the unification of rebels who had fought with the Liberals during La Violencia, under the banner of the Revolutionary Armed Forces of Colombia (FARC). That pro-Soviet group, which had close ties to the legally constituted Colombian Communist Party, was built on rural support acquired through peasant networks in several regions over dozens of years before the movement was formalized. Upon its creation in 1964 the Army of National Liberation (ELN), a Cuban-styled insurgency, became the country's second largest guerrilla militia; it was built upon an urban constituency of university students and other followers of Ernesto "Che" Guevara, and had strength in the Santander and Arauca regions. In 1965 another rural communist insurgency was formed, the Popular Liberation Army (EPL); it was a Maoist alternative to FARC, with strength mainly in the Uraba and Cordoba regions.

Political protest, rather than fundamental disagreement with the socioeconomic structure of the society, led to the creation of the last of Colombia's major insurgencies in 1972. The urban-based, ideologically heterogeneous M-19 was composed of a mixture of disillusioned FARC members tired of that group's rigid discipline and dogmatism, as well as dissidents from the left wing of the National Popular Alliance (ANAPO). That alliance was a populist political expression of loyal opposition, which had suffered a narrow electoral defeat (according to official results) in controversial presidential elections on April 19, 1970. The elections were widely viewed as marred by fraud. Formed to protest that particular political outcome rather than to promote an ideological restructuring of society, the non-Marxist M-19—whose full name was the April 19 Movement— was launched two years after the election with an ambiguous political agenda that drew on nationalism, populism, and democratic reform. Probably the smallest of the guerrilla groups, M-19, with its constituency of middle-class professionals and intellectuals, has nevertheless been the most popular among urban Colombians as well as those in the rural areas of the Cauca, Cauca Valley, and Caquetá. M-19 has usually opted for political activism and public displays of bravado rather than military maneuvers, preferring to capture attention through bold and nationalistic acts (such as the theft of Simón Bolívar's sword) rather than through brute strength. However, occasionally M-19 has chosen violence over cunning, and it has undergone the most drastic leadership changes (as a result of assassinations) of the major insurgent groups. Such periodic crises have also caused abrupt directional changes in M-19's tactics and prompted revised estimates of the insurgency's ripeness for resolution.

The showdown leading to a peace process between M-19 and the government, which at various times has also involved other guerrilla groups, began in the late 1970s. Half-hearted attempts by the administration of Alfonso López Michelsen (1974–78) to initiate a dialogue with the armed rebels had been blocked by the military. Liberal president Julio Cesar Turbay Ayala (1978–82) then declared a state-of-siege statute to broaden the military's powers. In response to the offensive by the government and the military, flamboyant M-19 leaders managed to steal some 5,000 arms from the Canton Norte military base in Bogotá. In retaliation, the government ordered the arrest of thousands of citizens, the "disappearance" of hundreds more, and widespread resort to torture and other forms of repression. The government's harsh measures only served to deepen popular resistance and broaden support for all the guerrilla groups. Early in 1980 an M-19 commando unit raided the embassy of the Dominion Republic, taking hostage twenty-three ambassadors, including those of the Vatican and the United States.[5] This daring act allowed M-19 to break the asymmetry between state and opposition, claim the public spotlight nationwide, and emerge as the legitimate representative of the "underdog" opposition in many Colombians' views.

Aside from negotiating with M-19 for the release of the captive diplomats, Turbay maintained a hard line until critics, including many in his own party, began calling for amnesty and a negotiated settlement. Turbay then indicated willingness to consider a limited amnesty agreement, although he rejected all concrete propositions. For example, he agreed to negotiate with an independent peace commission composed of third-party intermediaries, but summarily rejected the commission's recommendation that the government deal directly with the guerrillas. The peace commission collapsed in 1982. Rebel movements thrived even as the Colombian military vowed to eliminate all of them and was joined in its resolve by newly created right-wing paramilitary groups. Several weeks before leaving office Turbay did lift the state of siege, making way for the decade-long peace process commenced by Belisario Betancur.

Betancur's Short-Lived Initiatives

Immediately upon taking office Betancur declared that signing a peace agreement with the rebels would be his administration's top priority. With Colombia still largely free from the wholesale narcoterrorism that would soon divert attention from the peace process, Betancur departed from the policies of Turbay. He acknowledged that there were objective causes of social violence, whose solution would require state resources, that Colombian democracy should be extended to groups shunned by the National Front (he did not specify how he might accomplish this), and that negotiations with the rebels would be necessary until they disarmed and reentered political life. Under his Plan of National Rehabilitation (PNR) the new president established social relief and development programs for destitute areas, which were designed to turn the populace away from the guerrillas and toward the state. To mediate negotiations Betancur formed a peace commission consisting of forty citizens representing political party members, the clergy, journalists, business representatives, and academics. He also declared an immediate and unconditional amnesty for all guerrillas, and economic subsidies to assist their reentry to civilian life.

The Colombian armed forces, initially opposed to amnesty for the guerrillas, eventually acceded, but only after the president raised the penalty for possessing arms, increased the budget for new weapons and facilities, and expanded the military's component of the budget for the Plan of National Rehabilitation. In early 1983 Defense Minister Fernando Landazábal made his dissatisfaction public after Attorney General Carlos Jiménez published a report on the origins of a certain paramilitary group—a report that officially acknowledged the existence of vigilante death squads involving active military personnel. Landazábal's dismissal shortly thereafter signaled the credibility of Betancur's commitment to the peace process.

Public approval was a prime consideration in Betancur's decision to seek a settlement with the Revolutionary Armed Forces of Colombia rather than with M-19 or the Popular Liberation Army (the Army of National Liberation rejected proposals by the peace commission). Because FARC was the oldest and largest rebel group, negotiations with them was seen as the best way to bring prestige to Betancur's peace process.[6] The Revolutionary Armed Forces also perceived great benefits from an agreement, and in fact decided to lay down their arms (albeit temporarily) in March 1984. FARC leaders and members of the peace commission signed an accord—the Uribe Accord—which laid out a vague cease-fire process promoting political and social reforms, thus allowing the commission to attest to the government's future intentions without formally committing it to any specific programs. Thousands of rebels laid down their arms, as FARC leaders acquired instant political legitimacy with the battle-weary Colombian public.

This breakthrough, prompted by a ripe moment during which a new president was able to communicate with a guerrilla vanguard that was willing to try a new tack, gave justification to two years' frustrating negotiations. Asymmetry between the authority of the rebels and that of the government was broken, as the FARC leaders acquired national political stature as well as a military profile. Finding national resonance in a new political space, the leadership of the Revolutionary Armed Forces set about organizing a political party—the Patriotic Union (UP)—and discerning a way to verify the cease-fire.

Aggressions by M-19, anxious to draw attention to themselves and launch their own peace negotiations with the government and thereby break asymmetry, were forgiven when Betancur opened a second negotiating front with them.[7] The president clearly wanted a negotiated settlement, and his view prevailed during the first two years of the administration, when threats to national security were minimal and Betancur could keep the military reigned in. The disciplined and hierarchical nature of the Revolutionary Armed Forces had made it an ideal group for the first attempt at negotiations. Many M-19 leaders were released from prison under Betancur's amnesty, but the death of Jaime Bateman, the group's founding leader, served to fragment that guerrilla movement. Furthermore, M-19's insistence that negotiations be broadened to a national dialogue with all sectors of society over the future of Colombian democracy may have added too many variables to the talks for a government–M-19 agreement to be reached.

The Revolutionary Armed Forces, more specific in their demands than M-19, had given official negotiators a better indication of exactly what would be required of negotiations. However, after the Uribe Accord was struck, M-19 (along with the Popular Liberation Army) criticized the agreement as imprecise about the nature of future reforms and pressed the government's negotiators to link political reforms directly to a cease-fire. Although M-19 was critical of the government's deal with FARC, M-19 leaders did agree to meet with Betancur, and leaders of both M-19 and the Popular Liberation Army agreed to meetings with the peace commission, thus increasing the prestige of M-19 as a legitimate social force. By playing M-19 and the Revolutionary Armed Forces off against each other, the government kept them divided. Meanwhile, the Popular Liberation Army began a deep internal discussion, which eventually led it to take a position in favor of negotiations.

The development of any ripe moment for further guerrilla-government agreements was cut short in April 1984 by the abrupt slaying of Justice Minister Rodrigo Lara, apparently by hired guns of the drug lords. A shocked Betancur declared a state of siege, suspended peace talks, and announced a hard line against the drug traffickers. Thus events external to the peace process reclaimed the agenda precisely at a moment when government talks had been advancing. Several drug lords sought refuge in Panama, where they offered to surrender to authorities, cease their involvement in the drug trade, withdraw from political life, and repatriate more than $2 billion in drug profits in exchange for amnesty. Betancur negotiated with the drug dealers initially, thus making himself vulnerable to further attacks from the right, which was already assailing him for negotiating with the leftist rebels.

Despite these setbacks, in August 1984 the government's peace commission signed agreements in Corinto with M-19 and in El Hobo and Medellín with the Popular Liberation Army. Like the Uribe Accord, these agreements included a cease-fire and calls for further dialogue. The Betancur administration's efforts to talk with the rebels did lift some of the hatred of both parties for their common enemy, the drug lords, but nevertheless focused increasing external contempt on the government (and the guerrillas) from the paramilitary right. By 1985 the right was gaining strength in guerrilla strongholds such as the Middle Magdalena Valley and the Córdoba and Uraba regions.

Growing paramilitary pressure (often supported by the feuding Medellín and Cali drug cartels, who were vying for control) increased violence in several local areas, and assassination attempts were made on the lives of leftist leaders. Disillusioned, M-19 broke its cease-fire and immediately was confronted by all-out government retaliation: a military offensive to expel the insurgents from strategic areas, in the course of which, in August 1985, several luxurious homes in a Cali neighborhood were razed in pursuit of one M-19 leader. The guerrillas retaliated by attempting to assassinate the new defense minister—the attempt was unsuccessful—and then, in November, by taking over the Colombian Supreme Court building. They captured hundreds of hostages, including eleven justices.

During the army's attempts to retake the building nearly one hundred people were killed (including the justices and the entire guerrilla commando unit) and the nation's federal legal archives were destroyed. M-19 apparently thought that negotiating space could be pried open by force, and that Betancur would bow to direct negotiations after his administration had been punished for failing to control the army and to enact widespread reforms. Instead, the unbridled military, which years later would be chastised for acting without specific presidential authority, dispatched armored tanks through downtown Bogotá to reclaim the building.

In sum, the results of the Betancur peace process were quite mixed. The Revolutionary Armed Forces continued to seek civil space as a political party (the Patriotic Union) and to perpetuate its guerrilla organization. M-19 and the People's Liberation Army (whose two top negotiators were killed by paramilitary death squads) and the hard-line Army of National Liberation hardened their resistance by forming the National Guerrilla Coordination Front (CNG). The front lacked internal cohesion, but its mere creation was a step toward overcoming problems of collective action and recognizing common goals. Betancur's initial accomplishment of framing the internal struggle as a legitimate result of Colombia's socioeconomic and political inequities was soon lost. The administration's inability to control the military, its lack of resources to follow up on the promises made by the Plan of National Rehabilitation, its vagueness in the Uribe Accord, and its indecisiveness in the aftermath of the Supreme Court debacle led the populace and the guerrillas to question the president's effectiveness and good faith.

Barco Reclaims the Negotiation Agenda

Running against Betancur's weak handling of the insurgent left, Virgilio Barco, a Liberal, won a resounding election victory in May 1986. A third-party challenge did come from the Patriotic Union, and although its candidate, Jaime Pardo, got more votes than any other left-leaning candidate in Colombian history, the UP vote was still a footnote to the returns. Unlike Betancur, Barco immediately sought to remove the guerrillas' platform by deemphasizing the importance of the peace process and subverting it to a broader agenda of social and political reform. The new president built on Betancur's realization that Colombia's political violence indeed had structural roots, calling for broader development programs and treatment of poverty and social inequality at the local and regional levels. The Barco government sought to delegitimize the guerrillas as the sole interlocutors between the government and the impoverished classes by negotiating directly with local and regional leaders of civil society.

Simultaneously, Barco attempted to legitimize the Patriotic Union and institutionalize its role as a third-party opposition. He sought to replace the National Front coalition with a government-opposition model under which the winning party in an election would govern without the complete incorporation of the losers into the administration. The losers would instead serve in the Congress, along with the Patriotic Front, in the institutionalized role of loyal opposition. The idea was to bolster the state at the expense of the two principal parties; those parties had evolved into elite bastions rather than vehicles for mass political participation, and had become outlets for personalities rather than platforms.

Barco's stated policy of "rehabilitation, normalization, and reconciliation" also set different and more stringent prerequisites for direct talks with the guerrillas. These included establishing a timetable for disarmament, to prevent open-ended deliberations; limiting negotiations to the narrow issues of the guerrillas' demobilization, disarmament, and reincorporation into civilian life; and transferring the burden of demonstrating a will to peace from the government to the guerrillas (thus remedying Betancur's failure to articulate a way out). He also threatened military reprisal against those who did not cooperate. During Barco's watch the violence in Colombia extended beyond random acts by drug lords and occasional skirmishes between the guerrillas and the army to all-out civil war.

By mid-1987 the Revolutionary Armed Forces were disillusioned with the new president's rigid stance, and a gap developed between the group's legal expression as the Patriotic Union and its military initiatives. The paramilitary right's extermination campaign began to extract a heavy toll. In July 1987 the Revolutionary Armed Forces ambushed an army squadron in Caquetá, killing all seventeen of its members in what the government viewed as a decisive act of provocation to break the truce. The government then announced offensive maneuvers against FARC, nullifying all the gains of the Betancur peace process. The violence escalated as Barco simultaneously stepped up the war against the drug traffickers, who had assassinated the editor of Colombia's second-largest newspaper. The assassination unleashed a tempestuous series of arrests and raids by the military, which in turn provoked reaction from the drug lords, including the assassination of a Supreme Court justice. The paramilitary death squads were also active at this time against the guerrillas and their sympathizers. Barco remained silent while his ministers of defense and justice publicly defended the right of the military to arm rural vigilante death squads—the so-called autodefensas.

As if to erase any doubt about the will of the Revolutionary Armed Forces, in September 1987 FARC joined the other rebel groups of the National Guerrilla Coordination Front to create the Simón Bolívar Guerrilla Front (CGSB), which unified, for the first time, the four major guerrilla groups and two smaller ones under one umbrella. The assassination of former presidential candidate Jaime Pardo of the Patriotic Union in October further signaled the end of any ripe moment between FARC and the government. All the groups within CGSB, however uncoordinated their efforts sometimes were, unified in support of military rather than political pressure as the means to break asymmetry.

Again the support of the battle-fatigued public became critical, as the political struggle between the guerrillas and the state was increasingly perceived as a contest between two legitimate forces, with the drug kings occupying the role of the destabilizing common enemy. Although rising violence doomed Barco's efforts to address the socioeconomic roots of the Colombian internal crisis, he did further dismantle the National Front governing arrangement, bypassing Congress and gaining public approval in March 1988 to hold a national plebiscite.

M-19 sought to harness powerful public sentiment against the violence and thus overcome the infamous reputation it acquired after attacking the Supreme Court. After another leadership purge, the group's new chief, Carlos Pizarro, approached the government about entering into a dialogue in May 1988. Barco's predictably cold response was met by M-19 with the kidnapping of functionaries associated with the Conservative politician Alvaro Gómez—an apparent reversion to tactics of extortion. However, M-19 soon turned back to reconciliation, freed Gómez unharmed, and gained public sympathy.

Signaling its permanent switch from a strategy of control to a strategy based on popular support, M-19 convoked the leaders of societal sectors such as the Catholic Church, political parties, labor, industry, and Congress (with congressional leaders in their capacity as private citizens) to consider negotiation strategies, starting in July 1988. Soon M-19 agreed to abide by Barco's rules if the government would consider political reforms as a condition for disarmament. Barco agreed in September 1988, unveiling a peace initiative that M-19 embraced, although it did so without the endorsement of the other groups in the Simón Bolívar Guerrilla Front.[8]

As the government moved toward negotiations with the insurgency it began to distance itself from the right wing of the military. In September 1988 the Department of Security Administration (DAS) presented Barco with a confidential report that condemned paramilitary activities in the Middle Magdalena region.[9] The report was leaked to the press, and the government publicly endorsed its findings, promising to investigate further. That same month several military officials and the mayor of Boyacá were indicted on charges of complicity in the massacre of dozens of peasant supporters of FARC in the Uraba and Córdoba regions earlier in the year. The implication—for the first time during Barco's presidency—that there was collusion between the military and the death squads severely strained military-executive relations. Many in the Colombian army viewed Barco's new peace overtures as a repeat of Betancur's "soft collapse." In a replay of the Betancur-Landazábal clash, Defense Minister Rafael Samudio took public exception to Barco's policies and was promptly dismissed from office by the president. A further demonstration of changing sympathies was evident in May 1989 when the Supreme Court declared unconstitutional a 1968 law allowing the military to arm civilian vigilante groups. On the whole, Barco was much more successful in keeping the military under control than Betancur had been, despite occasional friction.

Unlike the Betancur administration, the Barco team had articulated a precise set of conditions and steps toward a negotiated solution with the insurgents, and it dominated the military right-wing fringes that offered the only real dissent to negotiations. Even so, the guerrillas could not concur. Pizarro of M-19, hoping to involve the entire Simón Bolívar Guerrilla Front in negotiations, appealed several times to the front, but found resistance from the Revolutionary Armed Forces and the Army of National Liberation. The hard-liners wanted negotiations at the ministerial level rather than through lower-level intermediaries; they perceived the peace initiative to be a defeatist solution for those willing to bargain away the guerrilla gains; they felt that accepting the government offer would boost Barco's sagging political fortunes without a commensurate benefit to themselves; and they still believed a military victory was attainable.

The Simón Bolívar Guerrilla Front did recognize that rejecting any peace talks outright would carry a high political cost, so it took a lesson from Barco, embracing the idea but attaching conditions it knew would be unacceptable to the other side. In October 1988 the CGSB leadership welcomed the spirit of the peace initiative but insisted that any negotiations be held directly with the ministers of defense and government. Barco categorically rejected this offer, and the government-CGSB dialogue reached a standstill.[10] Discussions did take place between Pizarro and Rafael Pardo, a young presidential adviser, but M-19, still debilitated both militarily and politically in the wake of the Supreme Court bloodletting, did not want to strain relations with the Guerrilla Front, and the government, uncertain of the guerrillas' real intentions, did not wish to suffer a letdown.

Public opinion seemed resigned to the failure of such low-level talks, until a new fault line developed in relations between the military and the state when in January 1989 twelve judicial investigators were murdered as they researched paramilitary activity in the Middle Magdalena region. As a rebuttal to that affront by the military (and perhaps as a gesture of concern for the guerrillas' safety), the government established a safe haven for the guerrillas in Santo Domingo, Cauca, where M-19 set up its political base in March, without a constant military presence.

The Revolutionary Armed Forces, noting that M-19 was getting the upper hand in articulating its political message, launched its own peace process, naming a "commission of notables" to mediate negotiations with the government. The Barco administration resented this political intrusion, but could not openly refuse the offer without offending the commission, which included former Colombian presidents López and Michael Pastrana Borrero and leaders of industry and the clergy. The effort of the Revolutionary Armed Forces achieved little more than splintering the Guerrilla Front, however, with the Popular Liberation Army and the Army of National Liberation splitting over whether to join the peace process. The Patriotic Union, which perhaps should have politically exploited FARC's reformist mood, could not capitalize on the situation because its most able leaders had been killed.

Negotiations Sabotaged

While the government-guerrilla dialogue floundered, the death squads and the narcoterrorists continued to raise the cost of ignoring their propensities for violence. A wave of assassinations in early 1989 claimed the life of a Patriotic Union congressman (and gravely injured Liberal senator Ernesto Samper Pizano, later to become Colombia's president). Also slain were outspoken reformers such as the antinarco governor of the state of Antioquia and the leader of a police anticorruption campaign in Medellín, as well as more than 1,000 Patriotic Union members. But the most dramatic assassination to date was the slaying in August 1989 of the popular Liberal senator and presidential candidate Luís Carlos Galán at a political rally near Bogotá, presumably by the drug lords. César Gaviria, a former minister of finance and government in the Barco administration, replaced Galán, calling for national reform through a constituent assembly and a new constitutional mandate to open up the country's political system.

Barco was incensed at the Galán slaying and closed ranks on all the state's internal security threats, although the focus of his anger was on the narcoterrorists. Galán's death ushered in the most violent period of the Barco regime, as the president declared a state of siege against the narcoterrorists, authorized government confiscation of the properties of accused drug lords, and expedited the efficiency of the courts in the judicial process.

With the government's attention on the narcoterrorist front, some maneuvering room may have been left for M-19 on the government's rebel front. Although most of his attention was elsewhere, Barco never did withdraw his peace initiative. In November 1989 representatives of M-19, the government, the Liberal Party (represented by former president Turbay), the Church, and Congress signed a political pact, under which working groups would address different facets of the insurgent problem; their conclusions would be presented to Congress for ratification and submitted to a nationwide referendum in January 1990. The agreement also allowed for a one-time ascension of M-19 to Congress to compete with more established political parties. The M-19 rebels, in turn, agreed to hand all weapons over to an independent international organization on the day of the referendum, regardless of whether it passed; they also agreed to integrate themselves into the legal civilian state before local, congressional, and presidential elections early in 1990.

Before these openings, or ripe moments, could be seized permanently for an M-19–government pact, they were all slammed shut by the drug lords. Despite being persecuted, the drug lords reiterated their 1984 offer to abandon the drug trade in exchange for pardons and for guarantees that those outside the country would not be extradited. Negotiating room was seemingly left for the drug lords in Barco's proclamation of the peace initiative, in which the president appeared to extend overtures to the drug traffickers as well as the guerrillas:

> The Peace Initiative is directed at solving the different forms and manifestations of violence, not only that which is generated by the guerrilla groups. . . . It can be said that in simple terms there is one form of violence that is realized by the insurgents and another which has nothing to do with subversion. This initiative is directed at both of these two major disruptions of the public peace.[11]

There was no success in negotiations between the drug lords and the state. The drug lords again escalated their violence, blowing up an Avianca commercial airliner in December 1989 as it left the Bogotá runway (killing all 107 passengers) and exploding a bus bomb that destroyed DAS headquarters in Bogatá and killed dozens of bystanders. Displaying a new array of political might, the drug lords also managed to sabotage efforts for the January 1990 plebiscite on a constitutional convention. Several members of the Liberal congressional delegation buckled under to narcoterrorist demands, pushing to allow the inclusion of an anti-extradition referendum as part of the plebiscite, to Barco's dismay. The frustrated president received no cooperation from his party, and decided to sacrifice constitutional reform and peace with M-19 to avoid the appearance of caving in to the narcoterrorists. The drug lords' pressures had thus sabotaged M-19's opportunity for dialogue with the government, ruined Barco's reform record, and drawn attention to the frequent incoherence of the ruling party's platform. Even in failing to get their referendum on the ballot the drug lords demonstrated that their knack for sabotage and subterfuge could be expressed in legislative chambers as well as on the streets.

The onslaught of violence prompted a reconfiguration of actors' strategies. The killing in December 1989 of one of the Medellín cartel's paramilitary leaders by a government police force further provoked narcoterrorist belligerence. The cartel began to kidnap relatives of distinguished Colombian elites, prompting a group of prominent political figures to insist on release of the hostages and an end to the drug trade. The drug lords, accepting a victory by the state for the first time, responded by announcing they would lay down their arms and suspend the drug trade.

The diminution of drug-related violence was countered by an increase in violence by the Simón Bolívar Guerrilla Front (now without M-19). With the failure of peace talks the front sought to overcome asymmetry through another means, and to take advantage of the government's distancing itself from the paramilitary right (thus exposing the autodefensa groups in the Middle Magdalena region). Meanwhile, M-19's pro-peace position held. A new generation of leaders realized that in laying down their arms in March 1990 they would be taking an irreversible step that would cost them any rapid deployment advantage they may have held. The M-19 leadership proceeded under the assumption that once commenced, the insurgents had little strategic choice but to complete the transition to civilian life, thereby ossifying the positions of the Revolutionary Armed Forces, the Army of National Liberation, and the hard-liners in the Popular Liberation Army (who viewed M-19 disarmament as a sellout).

As M-19 candidates, both Carlos Pizarro and Navarro Wolf ran strongly in the mayoral elections in March 1990, losing only by narrow margins. The slaying of a Patriotic Union presidential candidate, Bernardo Jaramillo, sent some UP supporters to Pizzaro, who planned to run in May elections as the candidate of the Democratic Alliance of M-19. However, Pizarro was also assassinated, thrusting Navarro forward as the unified left's only surviving candidate. Navarro reiterated Pizarro's pledge of peace. Although Gaviria won a plurality of the votes and the Conservative Gómez placed second, Navarro did finish third, ahead of the other Conservative candidate of the traditional or ultraconservative Pastrana wing of the party. Most significant for the peace process, a referendum on a constituent assembly to restructure the Colombian constitution was approved.

The new leadership of M-19 seemed to agree with the battle-fatigued sectors of civil society on the need for a negotiated solution to the insurgency. The ascent of M-19 moderate Navarro made this possible, even as the drug lords and the death squads sought to steal the insurgents' thunder.

Despite his tough stand against the guerrillas, Barco had by the end of his four years in office achieved the disarmament of M-19. An elite patrician rather than a populist reformer, Barco had taken a no-nonsense position against the military, the drug lords, and the socioeconomic elites, and had managed to clean house among the military, open the political system at least one notch, and pressure the drug mafia, even though those terrorists pushed the threshold of violence even further.

Gaviria Institutionalizes the Peace Process

Like Barco and Betancur before him, on taking office Gaviria immediately sought to distinguish himself from his predecessor by staking out distinct policy positions. However, unlike those former presidents, who owed part of their political fortunes to support by oligarchical elites, Gaviria designed policies that recognized the mass base of his political support—a base that stood apart from the traditional party apparatus. Gaviria appealed to a new inclusionary spirit, and in contrast with the Barco model of government-opposition relations, he sought to accommodate even parties that were out of power (such as the Conservative Gómez and Pastrana factions and the Democratic Alliance of M-19). Similarly, Navarro owed his sudden political rise to a chord that the M-19 disarmament had struck within Colombian society. As fellow heirs of reformist martyrs, Gaviria and Navarro shared an unusual affinity; thus it was not surprising that Navarro accepted Gaviria's offer to serve as minister of health. Gaviria promised to convoke a constituent assembly within months of his election, to continue negotiating with the guerrilla groups, to speak directly with members of the Simón Bolívar Guerrilla Front, and to curtail military autonomy.

A New Political Configuration

In consultation with all of the country's major political factions (including the AD/M-19), Gaviria set the rules for selecting members of a national constituent assembly, to be composed of seventy members, who would be chosen in a national election in December 1990. Gaviria wisely played up the importance of participation in writing the new constitution and offered a role in the constitutional convention as a reward for guerrillas who turned in their arms. Several fledgling guerrilla groups accepted Gaviria's offer upon witnessing that the new president was making good on his promises to M-19. Rebels from the Popular Liberation Army and two minor insurgencies disarmed in April 1991 in exchange for a total of four seats in a 72-member constituent assembly. Once again, public opinion played a key role in consolidating the positions of the government and the guerrillas. Student demonstrations and opinion polls helped guide the government response to calls for a constituent assembly, and elections became legitimate gauges of citizen satisfaction.

A strong slate of candidates ran from the left for the constituent assembly, including Navarro and the coach of the Colombian national soccer team. Internal splits among both the Liberals and Conservatives allowed the Democratic Alliance of M-19 to garner the most votes, double those of the second-place National Social Movement (the Gómez conservatives) and greatly outnumbering the various Liberal slates. Pastrana's Social Conservatives and the Patriotic Union fared poorly. Several new parties, including the Indigenous Peoples Party and the Protestant Evangelists Party, appeared for the first time, adding important new dimensions to traditionally bipartisan Colombian democracy.

The December 1990 election produced an entirely new political configuration, but voter turnout was low, demonstrating that most political battles were local rather than national in nature, and calling into question the ability of any government to keep order. Voter turnout was especially low in the election for the constituent assembly, as compared to the turnouts in the other elections in 1990. Although more than 8 million voters had cast ballots in local and state elections in 1990 and 6.2 million had participated in the May 1990 presidential election, only 3.5 million voted in the December selection of constitutional delegates. Only about 5 million of the country's 16 million eligible voters participated in the October 1991 congressional and gubernatorial election. In this first balloting after enactment of the new constitution in July, the Liberals won 57 out of 102 Senate seats, the traditional Conservatives won 15 seats, the New Democratic Force and National Salvation factions of Conservatives claimed 13 seats, the Democratic Alliance of M-19 claimed 9, and the Indigenous Peoples Party 3 seats (the rest of the seats went to even smaller parties). In the House of Representatives, the 162 seats were awarded as follows: Liberals, 87 seats; traditional Conservatives, 27 seats; M-19, 13 seats; other Conservatives, 11 seats. The rest went to minor parties.[12]

The 1991 election was seen as unlocking the stranglehold of National Front on Colombia's political structure. Despite the high abstention rate, Gaviria's approval rating remained consistently high. Participating third-party groups adjusted their tactics to their new status. The drug lords, lulled by Gaviria's guarantees in 1990 of their civil rights and further encouraged by an extradition ban to be included in the new constitution, eased up their violence. A fierce debate continued on the right, however, over the appropriateness of Gaviria's policies, as interpreted by the national security orientation of the military right. Criticism from the far right was sparked by the attorney general's dismissal of an army commander who had ordered the use of tanks and artillery to retake the Supreme Court building during M-19's 1985 takeover. Similarly, in June 1991 traditional political forces protested when Gaviria accepted the constituent assembly's suspension of the existing Congress for seven months, giving the president and the constituent assembly almost unrestricted powers until a convocation of a new Congress in December 1991. (The constituent assembly had met in February 1991.) Vested interests within the government, including the military, reacted vehemently to the government's structural opening, but Gaviria's coalition, backed by strong popular support, suppressed any impulses toward internal rebellion.

Progressive forces were favored by a Supreme Court ruling in October 1990 that Gaviria's "acuerdo politico," delineating the agenda for the upcoming constitutional convention, was illegal, and that the constitution's authors had to be free to alter any portion of the national charter. The new constitution, promulgated in July 1991, contained dramatic reforms of the electoral and judicial systems, granted the Congress greater authority as an executive branch counterweight, and provided for the direct election of state governors. Perhaps most significant in terms of governability, the new constitution institutionalized the ban on extradition of drug traffickers to the United States, thus clearing the way for the immediate surrender of more than a dozen top operatives of the Medellín cartel, including Pablo Escobar.

The Insurgent Front

The conventional Liberal and Conservative parties, under pressure from heavy electoral competition, divided into subgroups or factions, each possessing a narrow political agenda. Similarly, the departure of the Democratic Alliance of M-19 and the People's Liberation Army from the Simón Bolívar Guerrilla Front left only the Revolutionary Armed Forces and the hard-liners of the Army of National Liberation in the CGSB coalition. That coalition was now an ideologically more cohesive group; although it was directly at odds with the Colombian state, it at least represented a specific set of interests. Gaviria sought a dialogue with these ideologically regimented factions of FARC and ELN, acceding for the first time in history to FARC requests that negotiations be held outside Colombia.

Gaviria reiterated his position that the guerrillas could help draft the new constitution in exchange for their disarmament, thus retaining Barco's condition that the government would conduct negotiations only if the final objective was disarming the guerrillas. A further incentive to negotiation was the offer of adjustment compensation during the reentry of the guerrillas into civilian life.[13]

However, chances of negotiating the CGSB insurgents' entry into the constitutional process were ruined in December 1990, on the day of the constituent assembly elections, when the armed forces attacked the FARC commander's home. This unprecedented show of strength was apparently made without presidential authorization. Once again military interference had exposed internal splits in the executive, but this time the president was unwilling to enter into direct confrontation with the army. In response, the Guerrilla Front launched one of its most ferocious attacks—bombing energy plants, burning buses, and blowing up pipelines all over the country—on the day in February 1991 when the National Constituent Assembly convened its proceedings.

Prospects for a Broader Peace

Gaviria apparently considered the three keys to understanding the Colombian internal conflict—the use of civil fatigue to mobilize public support for peace negotiations, the isolation of cohesive core groups within ideologically ambiguous umbrella fronts, and the identification of the groups' true objectives—in order to cut through protocol to the essence of negotiations. With the breaks in drug-related and paramilitary violence, he also had the time and resources to focus on negotiations with the guerrillas. In regard to the first key, Gaviria heeded the dictates of public opinion, riding a wave of reformist sentiment to office, and then implementing constitutional changes swiftly and decisively. He recognized the public's potential for sympathizing with the guerrillas, and tried to harness that sympathy for the government by launching rehabilitation programs for former guerrillas. He also initiated a $6 billion "peaceful revolution" to pull 4 million of Colombia's 13 million poor above the subsistence level, extend education to 95 percent of the rural population, and vastly improve basic sanitation.

As to the second key, Gaviria attempted to bring the military into line by appointing the nation's first civilian defense minister—former peace commissioner Rafael Pardo—and by attempting to assert more control over a professionalized military with an expanded budget. However, right-wingers displeased with the Gaviria government advocated discontinuation of negotiations with the Guerrilla Front on the grounds that Marxist guerrillas could not negotiate in good faith.

Doctrinaire positions persisted among sectors with the most to lose through political change, among both the military and the guerrillas. Small wonder, then, that in the case of the third key—clarity of objectives—Gaviria also made progress, but reached a dead end. Peace was made with all cooptable groups who were fighting for a role in the newly opened political system. The remaining guerrillas of the Revolutionary Armed Forces maintained intransigent positions and were at loggerheads with the government, although they eventually abandoned the traditional Marxist goal of winning total power and moved closer to the reformist image of the new Colombian reality. Peace talks between the government and the Simón Bolívar Guerrilla Front were launched in Venezuela during the spring of 1991, away from the obstructions posed by the violence of the drug lords and the paramilitary right. Those negotiations reached an impasse because the Guerrilla Front called for a complete government retreat from the intermediate or "distention" zones in which the insurgents were to gather before laying down their arms. Suspended in November, resumed again in Mexico City early in March 1992, the peace talks were again suspended after less than one month when the Popular Liberation Army took credit for the death of a former government minister who had been taken hostage.

Before that suspension the government had acceded to broadening the negotiating agenda to cover the economic opening and its social effects. But the collapse of a possible breakthrough in the spring of 1992 left little prospect for a negotiated settlement. The world view of the guerrillas had been conditioned by nearly three decades of camping in the mountains, and their ideological ossification was not easily overcome, even by historical forces. Thus even the disintegration of the Soviet Union and the troubled isolation of the greatest guerrilla icon, Fidel Castro, were slow in forcing the CGSB to overcome ideological rigidity and to adopt more pragmatic, political demands. Peace talks finally did succeed in prompting another disarmament, but only by some 850 dissidents of the still-Marxist Army of National Liberation, who commenced their transition back to civil society in April 1994.

The success of government talks with that dissident group has been the exception to three years of negotiation gridlock. The military victories of the Guerrilla Front, and the ill fate of the Patriotic Union—and now probably of the Democratic Alliance of M-19—as electoral forces, seem to have convinced some elements of the CGSB that they are winning and should not give up. But even if the social welfare components of Gaviria's negotiating policy are extended by his successor, Ernesto Samper, and thus win the loyalty of the countless peasants who have used the guerrillas to voice their frustrations, peace will have to be offered to the holdout insurgents in broader terms than were given in the treaties signed with and by other insurgent groups. Specific solutions will have to be offered to redress the historic roots of political and social violence, particularly in the countryside.

Moreover, the now-institutional left has even come to question the choices it has made. Leaders such as Navarro, who have no doubt prospered since disarming, can continue to admit without shame that for the new Democratic Alliance of M-19 "our profile is very well defined, not by the gun but by our political ideas. Of course, changing the forms of struggle has its consequences. If you achieve military victory you can impose an entire program, but if you choose the party of elections and agreement, you must make concessions."[14]

The spoils of institutionalized political participation may turn out to be few and unevenly distributed, thus prompting fragmentation of the political-electoral left. Legislators of AD/M-19 have been critical of the party's leadership shortcomings, noting that the skills of warriors are not necessarily those needed by politicians. They have also been critical of the party's top-down structure and have noted the electoral disadvantages of not belonging to one or the other of the two parties that have run Colombia for decades. Those two parties developed elaborate patronage networks that delivered the spoils and other resources in ways that benefited themselves. Although other parties may formally challenge the Liberals and Conservatives, they can make few inroads against these patronage networks. The 1991 constitution formalized access to public resources by all political parties, but opposition leaders suggest that in practice the government has not lived up to the constitutional promises.[15] Furthermore, the ripe moment for participation by the Simón Bolívar Guerrilla Front in the landmark National Constituent Assembly was fleeting, leaving the remaining guerrillas with diminished expectations for potential gains from peace.

A Comparison of Negotiation Processes

The failure of government negotiations with the Revolutionary Armed Forces after such a positive start under Betancur, and the success of the government's dealings with the April 19 Movement under Barco and Gaviria after such dismal failure under Betancur, offer a stark contrast. Even in 1982 it was evident that the two insurgencies took distinctive tacks. The April 19 Movement, playing to its urban and educated constituency, insisted that the offer of unconditional amnesty could be only a first step toward a comprehensive peace, and should be followed by a cease-fire and a national dialogue. The Revolutionary Armed Forces, trying to broaden its rural political base and deemphasize its strong military foundation, wanted to take advantage of the contradictions in state policies and thus wavered between a will to genuinely negotiate and a desire to merely stall for time. M-19, with its public relations acumen, did not need the political legitimacy offered by an amnesty to break asymmetry. But M-19 did need a strengthened military hand, and early in 1983 it announced that amnesty did not mean peace and that the guerrilla war would continue. FARC, on the other hand, pursued a negotiated solution to bolster the public credibility it had gained through amnesty. It wanted a timetable for a cease-fire, a truce, and then a peace treaty—but it got only a general agreement. Early on, M-19 and FARC had discussed the prospect of a common front and arrived at a concurrent resolution, but that resolution said very little and stumbled over tactical questions. According to Alfonso Cano of the Revolutionary Armed Forces, "there were two different sets of criteria [regarding negotiations], and this led to a joint declaration that was only very general, where the most concrete thing that was stated was that we had common objectives."[16]

When the Revolutionary Armed Forces reached a separate peace with the government, undermining the stronger position of the April 19 Movement before the Colombian people, M-19 leaders such as Alvaro Fayad protested: "FARC fell for their [the government's] game. . . . It was stupidity because we had already secured a direct channel (with the president) and we wanted a collective agreement that would have demonstrated to the entire nation our combined strength, in all its dimensions. . . . They [FARC] had very little collective vision and they broke the agreement we had with them."[17] Whether or not the government intentionally exploited a chance to divide and conquer, such an opportunity presented itself in 1984 when FARC agreed to a cease-fire. That agreement allowed the government's armed forces to concentrate their fire on the militarily inferior M-19, which may have contributed to M-19's desperation as the group's leaders planned the Supreme Court takeover.

The apparent miscalculation by M-19 that led to the grandstanding effort at the Supreme Court, and a swift backlash by the army, provided the turning point for changes in attitude by the guerrilla groups, the military, and the civilian population. The April 19 Movement, which prided itself on craftiness rather than violence, had to regroup. The Revolutionary Armed Forces, seeing the force of the military reaction against M-19 and the Patriotic Union, realized that no insurgency, whether in a cease-fire or not, was immune to such attacks. The Patriotic Union, for all the fanfare surrounding its respectable showing in elections, had only a minor impact on the 1986 presidential election—a factor that no doubt led FARC to reconsider the viability of a legal course.

By the end of the Betancur administration, escalations in drug-related violence had blurred distinctions among the different internal security threats—distinctions that many factions in the military considered irrelevant. Barco, whatever his declarations for peace and negotiations, reasserted the position that guerrillas and drug lords were to be defeated by the same kinds of tactics. Barco's strict conditions for negotiations also provided a disincentive that led the guerrillas to their decision to break the Uriba treaty in 1987. As the Revolutionary Armed Forces became further alienated from the state, FARC turned back to violence as its primary means of breaking asymmetry. On the other hand, the revamped M-19, under the savvy leadership of Pizarro and Navarro, took up its cause with the Colombian government.

The escalation of bloodshed in 1989 provided a ripe moment for M-19 when two like-minded leaders—Navarro and Gaviria—were created by circumstances. Popular agitation for a constituent assembly gave the April 19 Movement a platform, and the Gaviria government recognized the need to accommodate M-19 in order to achieve a quick political victory, and perhaps to encourage other negotiated solutions. However, as M-19 opted increasingly for peace, FARC was pushed back into violence. The gains negotiated by Navarro—inclusion of M-19 in the constitutional convention, rehabilitation for reformed insurgents, and redress of grievances through a strong third-party political framework—were also opened to the Revolutionary Armed Forces, but M-19, by being the first to take advantage of these reforms, gained the most. FARC reverted to its earlier position of showing military strength, and the peace process was forced into a new gridlock.

Conclusions

Colombia's highly restrictive democracy, with its authoritarian trappings, precedents for sharing power only among oligarchical National Front elites, and lack of control over the military, has managed to transform itself, without drastic interruption in its institutional development, through legalistic methods. One point made in this chapter is that the violence of the leftist guerrillas was born of a legitimate quest for political space in which to express social concerns. The violence arose in the 1960s and has been institutionalized not as a cultural characteristic, but as an effective form of political contestation for the guerrillas and their constituents. Until the political openings of the 1990s, insurgency may have been the only real means of contestation available to many of these groups. The peasants who organized autodefensa groups were only fighting to protect their families from the paramilitary backlash to the guerrilla threat. Even the narcoterrorists, it may be argued, took up arms to defend their interests from arbitrary encroachments by the state—which benefited economically from drug-export labors, albeit indirectly. In a civil society desensitized by violence, discontented actors often faced the dilemma of having to up the ante to be noticed and to be heard.

Raising the stakes often involved escalating the violence. Some of the craftier actors—the Revolutionary Armed Forces in 1984, the April 19 Movement in 1990, the dissidents of the Army of National Liberation in 1994, and the government itself in its lucid moments (such as its convocation of the 1991 constituent assembly)—attracted attention by changing tactics in midcourse, leaving civil society wondering, but winning desired platforms, at least temporarily. Only the most rigid of political actors—the military right and the hard-line Marxist guerrillas—proved intractable in their positions. Ironically, the historical predisposition to violence on the part of some Colombian actors also gave power to the promise of peace. As the shock value of violence wore off and guerrilla leaders, narcoterrorists, paramilitary commanders, and army leaders escalated their excesses just to get attention, the social and political roots of the internal conflicts were bypassed.

The destruction of oil pipelines, buses, and energy facilities, and the wholesale execution of bystanders, certainly did not square with any of the guerrillas' stated objectives of social justice and equality. Futile and ruthless acts of violence such as the slaying of hostages during the takeover of the Supreme Court by M-19, paramilitary massacres of innocent civilians, and the bombing of a passenger airliner by narcoterrorists all undermined the coherence of the messages those acts were supposed to convey. At several junctures the efficacy of violence degenerated to the point that it only tarnished the image of its users. All political meaning was lost, as messages could not be heard above the gunfire of their deliverers. At these low moments actors with the courage to play peace politics found they could enhance their legitimacy by shaping public opinion favorably. Ultimately, however, it has been the escalation of violence itself that has in most cases led to successful negotiations when the costs of further escalation have grown too expensive. The Turbay military crackdown prompted the Betancur peace process, two years of intense warfare provided the space for Barco's peace initiative, and a wave of assassinations and violence by drug lords gave salience to Gaviria's inclusionary platform.

The drug lords have always made their peace amid the most aggressive government offensives against them, as in June 1984, July 1988, January 1990, and July 1992 when Pablo Escobar's escape prompted a crackdown that ended with his death eighteen months later. The idea that some of Colombia's leading narcoterrorists might turn themselves in was unthinkable at the height of their violent mobilization in the mid-1980s; similarly, the autodefensas and the paramilitary right commenced their demobilization processes after the state bore down on them.

The Problem of Blurred Distinctions

Another complicating factor in Colombia has been the difficulty of drawing distinctions among different political actors. For example, on several occasions there was found to be little separating the paramilitary right from the drug traffickers. Attention has been focused here on demonstrating the murky distinctions that sometimes existed between the government's executive and the military, and even within the executive and within the military branches. Perhaps even more difficult has been discernment of the true positions of rural peasants, whose support gave FARC and ELN their political authority. The vast majority of peasant guerrilla sympathizers have no doubt been apolitical, wanting merely a medium for petitioning the state rather than to raise any particular ideological banner.

Huge ideological gaps among the guerrillas precluded their representation by one voice such as the Simón Bolívar Guerrilla Front, although in the early part of the peace process some groups attempted common negotiations. Communications among the various quasi-governmental and quasi-private commissions have also been ambiguous at times, as channels to high-level government officials remained ad hoc, and often little agreement existed among the diverse memberships of these groups. All parties seemed to recognize these ambiguities and sometimes managed to employ them in their own favor. Even so, the blurred distinctions among interests in the negotiations complicated every step in the process of internal conflict resolution, and continue to do so.

In Colombia the search for valid spokespersons may be an interminable quest. Given their constant flux, as demonstrated in the wholesale slaying of the M-19 leadership in 1985 and 1990, the divisions in the Popular Liberation Army in 1984 and 1990, and the pro-peace faction's break from ELN in 1989, the guerrillas of those groups have faced difficulties in maintaining internal order, not to mention in cooperating with other guerrilla fronts. Maintaining the unity of groups within the Simón Bolívar Guerrilla Front has been quite difficult, but not nearly as complicated as unifying the government and the armed forces behind one voice. Discord between military and civilian officials, such as the Landazábal-Betancur disputes in 1984 and the apparently unordered military attack on FARC headquarters in 1990, have undermined the government's credibility as a negotiator. Squabbling between presidents and their defense ministers in each of the administrations discussed has undermined the president's position as head of a unified state. Furthermore, a president's inability to deliver (as Barco was unable to do in regard to his December 1989 bid for approval of a constituent convention) critically weakened his position as interlocutor for the state.

Further Reforms and Likely Outcomes

Consistent with the three keys for understanding Colombian attempts at internal conflict resolution, further reforms could be implemented to improve the expression of grievances by the public, to tighten control of the civilian government over the military, and to address the deadlock reached within the Simón Bolívar Guerrilla Front. In regard to the first of these reforms, any topic of concern to citizens must be brought within the scope of public dialogue—a principle Gaviria finally accepted (at least tacitly) with his acquiescence to the rebel demand that peace negotiations have no limit in scope. Whether or not significant political change may result under the current presidency of Ernesto Samper, educating citizens about their rights in a full democracy—particularly citizens in the marginalized countryside—would address the communications problems that gave rise to the guerrillas and prevent new groups from resorting to violence. In regard to the second, the president must continue the thorough clean-up of the armed forces and police, already begun, to rid those groups of influence from the paramilitary right, the autodefensas, and the drug cartels. As to the third reform, the government must recognize that unlike M-19 and other smaller and less extremist groups, the Revolutionary Armed Forces and the Army of National Liberation will require much more than permission to become legal parties before they agree to turn in their arms. Indeed, some ten thousand guerrillas from FARC and ELN (plus a few from newer and more transient organizations) are thought to exert a rebel presence in half of Colombia's 1,038 municipalities.

The Revolutionary Armed Forces in particular is backed by a huge network of peasant organizations, and has effectively exercised control, as the de facto state authority, over vast expanses of the country. Thus a broad land reform may be necessary in the areas that FARC controls, as may a power-sharing arrangement in which FARC maintains local control over certain areas in cooperation with the state government. There has already been discussion of converting the guerrillas into a local civic police force under control of the national government, but with autonomy comparable to their current status. Such a program would imply increasing social and economic assistance to guerrilla-occupied areas, thereby linking them to the rest of the country and demonstrating that the state is capable of attending to the basic needs of all its citizens.

As in most cases of internal conflict resolution, perhaps the central issue in Colombia is not how well the guerrillas and the government can compromise so that the state may reincorporate the disaffected rebels, but rather how extensive a role the state should play in the lives of all its citizens. Until 1991 Colombia had been governed under the same constitution since 1886. The state had been a weak, centralized, oligarchical structure that, unlike government in most democratic nations, had served the limited function of mediating between warring factions to minimize violence. Rather than molding society to its rules, the Colombian state had to be fluid enough to separate groups of hostile elites and referee between them. But the very system conceived to mitigate Colombia's long periods of civil violence (and only secondarily to govern) came to provoke violence by those excluded from the spoils. Great socioeconomic changes after the creation of the National Front in 1958—including urbanization, improvements in education, and changes in the composition of the work force—realigned the composition of the electorate. The public modernized more readily than the country's two-party system, which emerged as a singular oligarchical monolith of the traditional elites, whose interests were tended by each administration, whether Liberal or Conservative. As Jonathan Hartlyn has observed, ''the traditional parties increasingly lost ideological or programmatic content and came to be dominated by regional politicians with almost exclusively brokerage and clientelist motivations.''[18] Gaviria's attention to the socioeconomic roots of the guerrillas' grievances resulted in socioeconomic and political reforms intended to open up governance to a broader range of citizens, but that ambitious task has not been completed. Samper's challenge is to assure Colombia's underprivileged millions that they will have advocates in a desperately needed reconfiguration of whom the government truly represents.

The guerrillas, in spite of all the anguish they have wrought, did help to catalyze the state's limited political opening. As the state grew more pragmatic with the realization that both traditional political parties represented the same interests and that there was no use squabbling internally over platforms, the guerrillas dug in ideologically and prepared themselves mentally for an extended insurgency. The remaining insurgencies of the Simón Bolívar Guerrilla Front may appear to be completely unyielding, especially when contrasted with the state's more accommodating attitude, but the burden of proving good faith lies with the state, which claims to represent all societal interests. The rebels never have claimed to represent anything but their own specific social and political base. Yet the state cannot purport to effectively represent the needs and interests of society, including the guerrillas, if it does not control the national territory.

Thus the state finds itself in a dilemma, exacerbated by the internal autonomy of the narcoterrorists and the paramilitary right, as well as by the leftist insurgencies. The government would appear to be unable to negotiate if it cannot effectively and humanely administer the state. But if the government were in control of the national territory and represented civil society, it would have no need to engage in a dialogue with the rebels. Such soft stalemates have only been overcome after tumultuous violence that demonstrated to one side or to both sides how high the stakes really were, thus turning attention toward finding peace and away from political posturing.

Throughout the cycles in which wily actors have sought leverage alternately from the potency of violence and from the ideal of peace, there have also been continuities in the strategies of both the guerrillas and the government. Despite each successive president's declaration that he would differentiate himself from his predecessor's policies, Betancur, Barco, and Gaviria built on their predecessors' experiences. All three recognized (at least during their most effective moments of governance) that any peace plan had to be built on economic and social reform as well as on political opening— that is, that the objective causes of the guerrilla mobilizations were real. In addition, negotiations with the guerrillas were always going on at some level (except during a one-year period in 1987 and 1988), and some communication outlet was available to most of the guerrilla factions, however unofficial or indirect. For their part, the guerrillas continued to pay homage to their ideals of peace even as they grew comfortable with the life-style of warriors. For many members of the Simón Bolívar Guerrilla Front violence became a modus vivendi, in many ways isolated from the changing political realities of the nation.

The solution for the Colombian government, if there is one besides waiting years for the guerrillas to die out, lies in meeting peasant demands for agrarian reform and change at the local level, thereby undercutting the insurgents' base, and then negotiating compromises with the guerrillas over control of guerrilla-held regions. The Gaviria administration made strides toward clearing away the obstacles to such essential negotiations, overcoming external pressures from the United States to crack down on the drug cartels, and curtailing narcoterrorism, if not the drug trade, through negotiations. The paramilitary death squads, although they still exist, have also been reigned in, at least for the moment, through continuing efforts to clean up the armed forces. As the configuration of Colombia's internal conflict more closely approximates a single-front insurgency rather than a multi-front civil war, successful resolution or an enduring soft stalemate seems the more likely outcome. Peruvian journalist Gustavo Gorriti, studying the Peruvian Shining Path, has even gone so far as to suggest that there are conditions under which fragile democracies can consolidate themselves through suppression of internal conflicts.[19] Unfortunately for President Samper, backsliding may occur as Colombia's guerrillas become disillusioned with the meager benefits accorded to M-19 and other, lower-profile groups for surrendering their weapons and waging only political battles.

A lasting peace may remain elusive in Colombia, but in the twelve-year negotiations between the government and the distinct guerrilla groups, precedents have been set for partial success, at least. The lack of political access that provoked the guerrilla movement some thirty years ago does still exist, but the National Constituent Assembly has made strides toward reincorporating Colombia's disenfranchised peasants and urban slum dwellers, who have been the guerrilla movements' greatest base of support. After La Violencia, it can only be hoped that the convocation of the Constituent Assembly will turn out to have been a turning point—the end of the violence and the beginning of La Paz (the peace). Unfortunately, this is not likely in the short term. However, provided that the Colombian people and their leaders have learned from their painful decade of democratic opening, that civil society continues to prevail over the military, and that popular opinion is heeded, there is little danger that the soft stalemate will degenerate into a hurting one. The Revolutionary Armed Forces and the Army of National Liberation show no signs of conceding their struggles, but perhaps they can be persuaded to contain them within bounds. A not insignificant accomplishment, this would be a cautiously optimistic signal that a more definitive resolution is possible in the longer term.

Notes

1. On the identity of the M-19 rebels, see the section on Endemic Violence, below.

2. Peter R. Andreas and Kenneth E. Sharpe, "Cocaine Politics in the Andres," *Current History,* vol. 91 (February 1992), p. 79.

3. Daniel Pecaut, "Guerrillas and Violence," in Charles Bergquist, Ricardo Peñaranda, and Gonzalo Sánchez, eds., *Violence in Colombia: The Contemporary Crisis in Historical Perspective* (Wilmington, Del.: SR Books, 1992), pp. 218–21.

4. For a full discussion of deinstitutionalization, see Eduardo Pizarro, "Revolutionary Guerrilla Groups in Colombia" in Bergquist, Peñaranda, and Sánchez, *Violence in Colombia,* p. 174. On the early peace process, see Ricardo Santamaria and Gabriel Silva Lujan, *Proceso Político en Colombia* (Bogotá: Cerec, 1984).

5. Diego Asencio, *Our Man is Inside* (Boston: Little, Brown, 1983).

6. Interview with John Agudelo, former director of the Peace Commission on January 18, 1989.

7. Patricia Lara, *Siembra vientos y recogerás tempestades* (Bogotá: Planeta Editorial, 1986), p. 217.

8. See Ana Maria Bajarano, "Estratégias de páz y democrácia," in Francisco Leal and Leon Zamosc, eds., *Al filo del caos* (Bogotá Tercer Mundo Editores, 1990), pp. 93–96.

9. Jacobo Arenas, *Vicisitudes del proceso de paz* (Bogotá: Editorial La Abeja Negra, 1990), pp. 80–82. On the entire peace process, see Presidency of the Republic, *El Avance hacia la Reconciliación: Historia de un Proceso* (Bogotá: Presidency, 1990); and Jesús Antonio Bejarando, ed., *Construir la Paz* (Bogotá: Presidency, 1990).

10. Arenas, *Vicisitudes del proceso de paz,* pp. 80–82.

11. "La bomba del diálogo," *Revista Semana,* no. 388 (October 10, 1989), p. 26.

12. Juan Jaramillo and Bertriz Franco, "Colombia," in Dieter Nohlen, ed., *Enciclopedia Electoral de Latinoamerica y del Caribe* (Instituto Interamericano de Derechos Humanos, 1993), pp. 135–82.

13. Thousands of insurgents have since received a subsidy of $85 a month, low-cost loans, and assistance for education and starting up small businesses and farms.

14. "Has the M-19 Tiger Changed Its Spots?" in *Latin American Regional Reports: Andrean Group Report,* Latin American Newsletters, Ltd., April 18, 1991. pp. 8–9.

15. A critique of the 1991 constitution's terms may be found in Harvey F. Kline, "Conflict Resolution Through Constitution Writing: The Colombian Constituent Assembly of 1991," paper presented at the annual meeting of the Southern Political Science Association, 1992.

16. Quoted in Marc W. Chernick, "Negotiated Settlement to Armed Conflict: Lessons from the Colombian Peace Process," *Journal of Interamerican Studies and World Affairs,* vol. 30 (Winter 1988–89), p. 67.

17. Fayed, quoted in Chernick, "Negotiated Settlement," p. 68, citing A. Alape, *La Paz, la Violencia: testigós de excepción* (Bogotá: Planeta Editorial, 1985), p. 341.

18. Jonathan Hartlyn, "Columbia: The Politics of Violence and Accommodation," in Larry Diamond, Juan J. Linz, and Seymour Martin Lipset, eds., *Democracy in Developing Countries: Latin America,* vol. 4 (Boulder, Colo.: Lynne Rienner, 1989), p. 322.

19. Gustavo Gorriti, "Latin America's Internal Wars," *Journal of Democracy,* vol. 2 (Winter 1991), pp. 94–95.

CHAPTER TWELVE

Playing Two Games: Internal Negotiations in the Philippines

Daniel Druckman and Justin Green

NEGOTIATIONS in the Philippines between the National Democratic Front (NDF) insurgency and the government of Corazon Aquino are analyzed in this chapter in terms of the concepts of ripeness and formulas. Internal politics is viewed as a competitive game in which groups try to amass sufficient power to maintain or change the prevailing order or influence its policies. The balance of power is monitored by groups in terms of changes in effective power and legitimacy. The decision to negotiate, made by both the National Democratic Front and the government in August 1986, is explained in terms of an NDF calculation that its effective power was increasing while its legitimacy remained constant, and a government calculation that its power was decreasing while its legitimacy remained unchanged. That particular intersection is regarded as a definition of ripeness.

The decision to negotiate does not assure a successful negotiation process. The process is sustained to the extent that the parties continue to perceive the issues as negotiable. Negotiation is a cooperative game influenced by an interplay between values (or ideologies) and interests: changes in ideological polarization intensify or reduce perceived conflicts of interests, which in turn influence the extent of polarization. In the Philippines case the negotiations between the National Democratic Front and the government are construed in terms of such cycles, which are shown to be affected by intraparty divisions and mediation. Insurgent moderates served to depolarize the NDF positions early in the talks, but gave way to extremists who later polarized positions, which led to a breakdown in the talks. A framework for the talks, presented by Senator Jose W. Diokno, was accepted by both sides as a formula, only to be rejected as too vague to address the fundamental differences between the parties. These processes played a role in decisions to continue negotiating or to abandon the talks, and influenced the transition from one type of game—cooperative or competitive—to another. Progress also affected calculations of relative power and legitimacy, which in turn influenced decisions to continue negotiating.

Introduction

Insurgency, guerrilla warfare, and low-intensity conflict are similar forms of internal conflict. Each usually involves a reasonably well-organized group of citizens who arm themselves to engage the government's troops in an effort to weaken the regime's military strength and to gain additional weaponry, which, when combined with purchased or donated weapons, increases the strength of the insurgent group. "People power," on the other hand, can be considered as an insurgency without weapons. Masses of people in growing numbers are mobilized in the streets. The massed citizenry disables the government, and, if its numbers are large enough, such pressure drastically limits a regime's ability to use its armed forces against its citizens. After all, soldiers are citizens too.

Although the means of the armed and the unarmed are different, the goals of both are the same. Insurgency—such as the Philippines' New People's Army—and people power—in the Philippines spearheaded by Corazon Aquino's candidacy—are, in Clausewitz's words, "politics by other means." However, normal politics involves policy issues, whereas policy changes are not the primary purpose of either insurgencies or people-power revolutions, though both often result in policy changes as a secondary benefit. Rather, insurgencies and people-power revolutions seek to change regimes; their expectations are that the new regime will sweep out the misguided policies of the old and develop new programs that represent the ideals that fueled the revolutions. These were the goals of both the insurgent New People's Army and Corazon Aquino's challenge to the Marcos regime in 1986.

Seen as part of the political process, insurgencies and people-power revolts can be analyzed as unstable outliers on a normal spectrum ranging from political stability to political instability that applies to all nations. Thus a model that purports to explain the degree of stability or instability of any regime also explains the potential for that regime's demise, as well as the political events that lead to normalized relations between the armed rebellion and people power. The model is therefore useful in explaining the decision to negotiate and the possible outcome of negotiations between insurgencies and regimes.

Such a model is applied in this chapter in analyzing negotiations in 1986–87 between the Philippines' Aquino government and that country's major insurgency, the New People's Army of the National Democratic Front (NPA/NDF), as well as the interactions leading to the negotiations. The analysis is in two parts. The first examines the conditions leading to the decision to negotiate a cease-fire, which began on December 10, 1986, and the decision to negotiate over the political and substantive issues that divided the parties, which began on January 6, 1987. The conditions are defined in terms of a model of competitive group politics we have used to estimate the stability of the Ferdinand Marcos regime during the 1982–83 period.[1] Concepts from the model are used to define a ripe moment considered to be propitious for negotiation. The second part of the analysis focuses on the substantive talks held during January 1987; those talks ended in an impasse on January 22. In focusing on issues, the analysis superimposes a framework that takes the form of propositions that emphasize the interplay between ideologies and interests. Among the propositions tested by the events is the impact on progress of a formula proposed by a mediator. The concepts of ripeness and a formula are central in the analysis of the Philippines case. To help the reader follow the unfolding events, a chronology is provided in an appendix to the chapter, and additional context is provided in the next section—a history of the Philippines' insurgencies from the early postwar movements to the National Democratic Front activities in the first year of the Aquino regime.

A History of the National Democratic Front Insurgency

For approximately one hundred and fifty years the Philippines has been plagued by revolutions, insurgencies, and religious or quasi-religious millenarian movements. Except for the nationalist revolution, which took place around the turn of the twentieth century, none of the movements was a serious threat to the existing regime. This pattern changed, however, in 1945 at the conclusion of the Second World War.

During World War II the small Parti Komunista Pilipinas (PKP) gained control of an anti-Japanese guerrilla movement active in the central part of the main Philippine island of Luzon. Called the Hukbalahup (shortened to Huks), these guerrillas buried their rifles when the war ended in the hope that the emerging Philippine government would provide justice for central Luzon's small landowners, tenant farmers, and laborers. The Parti Komunista members who led the Huk movement also hoped to find a legal place in postwar Philippine politics. When neither of these goals materialized, the Huks resorted to armed struggle designed to overthrow the Philippine government. They had early success. However, the insurgency declined, in large part because of the combined effects of offers of land to the landless by the regime of the charismatic Ramón Magsaysay (1953–57), better tactics on the part of the Philippine military (devised by U.S. adviser Colonel Edward Lansdale),[2] and the failure of the Huk movement to grow beyond its geographical and linguistic area. By the mid-1960s the Huks were more bandits than insurgents and were no longer a serious threat to the regime. Never long on ideology, the tired and aging leadership of the PKP emerged from the jungle to serve an occasional short prison term, but in the main retired to a life in the sun.

A new generation of radical leadership emerged from student ranks at the University of the Philippines and other universities. This new leadership developed in the worldwide climate of student radicalism of the 1960s. It was nurtured on anti-Americanism and Philippine economic nationalism and, with youthful idealism, sought social justice in the Philippines. The new radicals opted out of the Philippine Communist Party and began their own revolution. In response to Mao Tse-tung's Cultural Revolution in China, with its emphasis on youth, self-help, and learning from the masses, a group of young radicals founded the Communist Party of the Philippines (CPP) in 1968. Its military wing, the New People's Army, was born when Commander Dante, a former Huk guerrilla leader, seceded with a few dozen troops from a faction of the old Huk army and affiliated himself with the CPP.[3] The National Democratic Front, the underground political front for the party, was conceived before the imposition of martial law by the Marcos regime in 1972. The NDF is an alliance of activist organizations whose aim is to bring nonparty groups and individuals into closer contact with the CPP and the NPA.

In 1972 President Ferdinand Marcos declared martial law ostensibly because of the threat of the New People's Army to Philippine national life, the growth of private armies, and widespread criminality. It may be suggested that the primary motive of Marcos was to perpetuate himself in office and to enjoy the perquisites that come with power. For almost seven years, despite some grumbling, Marcos gave most Filipinos what they wanted: an efficient, if not honest, government controlled by technocrats; a more effective land reform program than those of the past; an economic growth rate high by Philippine standards; and more law and order. There were disadvantages. A Muslim rebellion on Mindanao, perhaps inevitable, was certainly hastened by Marcos's attempt to collect all firearms. Political enemies went into exile and a few, such as Ninoy Aquino, were jailed. The press passed into friendly hands and was tightly controlled by the regime. Human rights of some citizens were violated; those suspected of being communists or other enemies of the state were tortured, disappeared, or suffered other forms of military and political brutality. Yet despite these negatives Marcos's martial law regime in its early years (1972–79) could be characterized as relatively benign authoritarian rule. Moreover, Marcos gained legitimacy during this period by holding a series of informal plebiscites, beginning a parliamentary system under a new constitution, and eventually holding elections for seats in that body.

Meanwhile, the New People's Army found it difficult to press its cause in the mainstream of Philippine life. Through the occasional ambush of government troops, it was able to provide enough new weapons to support its slow growth rate. However, the NPA did not receive help from communist parties or nations outside the Philippines. Nor were its early efforts to establish units in distant but relatively well-settled areas, such as Cagayan and Bicol, successful. To survive the New People's Army was forced to move all of its efforts to the backcountry of Samar. As progress was made in organizing remote villages, the NPA began to spread into the mountainous, jungle-covered regions of Negros, Panay, and the non-Muslim areas of Mindanao.

By 1979 the positive effects of martial law had begun to wane. The worldwide depression after 1979 hit the Philippines very hard: the cost of imported oil rose astronomically, employment fell along with the economic growth rates, demand for Filipino guest laborers abroad fell dramatically, and government funds were no longer available to support farmers who had obtained land. People of all classes were angered by the activities of a growing and less well disciplined military, whose new officers and poorly trained recruits brutalized barrio residents in the name of anti-insurgent activities. In the cities the growing middle class, hurting from the economic recession, began to weigh its losses against its gains by acquiescing to martial law. By 1982 several groups had made their opposition to the regime known. The more radical wing of the Catholic Church was no longer support- ing the Marcos regime. Moreover, the wealth and ostentation of the Marcos family, especially of the president's wife, Imelda Marcos, and the growing corruption of crony capitalism were increasingly evident. In scale both of those developments had crossed the boundary of acceptable behavior.

It was in this period, as the legitimacy of the Marcos regime fell, that the New People's Army grew both in military strength and in the effectiveness of its efforts to mobilize support among peasants living in relatively iso- lated rural barrios.[4] Between 1979 and 1985 the New People's Army insurgency grew rapidly from an armed base of about 2,000 to more than 12,000 soldiers.[5] The assassination of Ninoy Aquino in 1983, whether initiated by Marcos himself, by underlings who thought that his death was what Marcos wanted, or by old elite rivals who wanted to eliminate a potentially strong candidate for the Marcos succession, shook the founda- tions of the regime. The head of the Catholic Church, Jaime Cardinal Sin, began to move toward active opposition, and Manilanos of all socioeco- nomic levels used Aquino's murder as an excuse for blaming the regime for their unhappiness and ills.

An aging, ill, and increasingly withdrawn Marcos was no longer capable of finding the will and the strength to make the decisions and policy choices necessary to restore his own legitimacy. He thought he could ride out the increasing unrest, and must have believed that the majority of Filipinos, particularly the peasants, still supported him. Thus when pressed to act by his local opposition and by Ted Koppel on a *Nightline* telecast, Marcos agreed to hold a snap election in February 1986. He felt that he would either win in a fair election or that he could control the counting of votes to ensure his victory. Neither of these was possible, although he did attempt the latter.

The people took to the streets. One portion of a divided military defected and the pressure of foreign media limited the effectiveness of the remaining loyal armed forces. Marcos was forced to flee the country with help from the United States. Corazon Aquino, widow of Ninoy Aquino and the ostensible winner of the election, declared herself president. The new regime pledged a fair and honest democratic government with social justice for all, land reform, and healing of all the divisions in Philippine life, including the cleavages between the government and the National Demo- cratic Front and its New People's Army.

It was at this time that the insurgents, by their own admission, made a tactical mistake. They refused to participate in the snap election and urged its boycott. Although they were able to partially recover from this error by actively partaking in a people-power revolt just after the election, their contribution was lost because of the widespread participation of a broad spectrum of Filipinos. Thus at a crucial juncture in the insurgency's history, when participation in the snap election might have led to a direct role in the Aquino government, the National Democratic Front and its military arm made the wrong choice, thereby setting the stage for the negotiations that began in January 1987.

Modeling Regime Stability

The history of interactions between the New People's Army and the Marcos regime highlights a process of competitive group politics as a zero-sum situation; the outcome of a contest for power consists of winners and losers. This concept of internal group politics is captured in the structure of the model of political stability discussed above. Developed primarily for analysts, the model is a device for monitoring changes in the effective power and legitimacy of groups, and leads to estimates of a regime's vulnerability.[6] It can also be used for retrospective and prospective forecasts of collective-action decisions.

In the model estimates of a group's effective power are based on measures of group assets (such as coercive, economic, opinion-formation assets), group skills, and group characteristics related to mobilization potential. The model aggregates the various indicators to form an index that captures both resources and the way they are used by each group—both contenders and the governing regime. Legitimacy is based on indicators of a group's structure (its age and constitutional legality), whether its leadership is charismatic or not, endorsements from leaders of other countries, and the group's performance as evaluated in relation to the expectations or standards of other groups—in the case analyzed here, other groups in the Philippines. Stability estimates derive from the produce of differences between the regime and the contenders in effective power and from the ratio between these groups in legitimacy. Comparisons between the regime and various contending groups indicate the extent to which a regime is vulnerable to challenges at a particular point in time; an earlier analysis showed that the Marcos regime was more vulnerable to challenges after the Aquino assassination than before that event.[7] Changes in the indicators through time depict a fluid situation in which the relative advantages of insurgents and regimes may shift dramatically in favor of one or the other group.[8] The changes may also enter into a group's calculations concerning whether to fight or to negotiate for political influence.

The political stability model provides a context for strategic decisions. The context is the ongoing competitive struggle for power (in the Philippines, the NPA versus the regime) in which each group evaluates its position relative to other groups. The evaluation is made in terms of relative power and legitimacy, which are the conditions for deciding whether to negotiate, fight, or take another course of action. For example, a deteriorating situation, indicated by decreasing power and legitimacy, may lead to negotiation in desperation; an improving situation, when both variables are increasing, could encourage a decision to negotiate for gains as the groups approach equal strength. But an actual negotiation will only occur when both parties decide to negotiate; unilateral decisions are necessary but not sufficient conditions for getting to the table. It is the intersection of decisions made by both groups that determines whether or not the situation is indeed ripe for negotiation.

The analysis in this chapter is interpretive. The concepts, rather than the measures, of effective power and legitimacy are used as a framework for making judgments about the situation facing the regime and the NDF at different times. These judgments are the bases for inferences about whether one or the other (or both) parties are likely to go to the table—that is, whether the timing is ripe for negotiations.

Getting to the Table

The stability model suggests that the outcome of political interactions is based on the balance of strength between the actors as measured by the difference between them in effective power and legitimacy. When considering whether to change from a strategy of armed struggle to political competition, for example, each group judges the likelihood of achieving its goals by negotiation according to calculations of increased or decreased power and legitimacy. The model posits that political actors act "as if" these considerations influence their decisions. Just how the model's dimensions combine to result in decisions is represented by the matrices in table 12-1. The decision to negotiate or not is a result of an intersection of current levels of power and legitimacy depicted as decreasing, constant, or increasing.[9]

Table 12-1. Conditions under which Insurgents and Regimes would
Consider Entering into Negotiations

Insurgents: relative legitimacy	*Relative power (insurgents versus regime)*		
	Decreasing	Constant	Increasing
Decreasing	1A Negotiate	2A Do not negotiate	3A Do not negotiate
Constant	4A Do not negotiate	5A Do not negotiate	6A Negotiate
Increasing	7A Do not negotiate	8A Negotiate	9A Negotiate
Regime: relative legitimacy			
Increasing	1B Negotiate	2B Negotiate	3B Negotiate
Constant	4B Negotiate	5B Negotiate	6B Negotiate
Decreasing	7B Do not negotiate	8B Do not negotiate	9B Negotiate
	Increasing	Constant	Decreasing
	Relative power (regime versus insurgents)		

Source: Authors' calculations. See text.

The matrices illustrate the various combinations of legitimacy and power for the insurgents on the one hand and for the regime on the other. Each of two matrices consists of nine cells that describe the possible situations for each party. Because these dimensions (power and legitimacy) change relative to one another, the cells of the insurgent matrix are the mirror image of those of the regime matrix. For example, if the insurgent's power and legitimacy are both decreasing (cell 1A), it need not follow that the regime's power and legitimacy must be increasing (cell 1B). Both parties can be losing power and legitimacy. It must follow, however, that one party is losing at a faster rate than the other to ensure that each group's judgments relate to the other's. Thus when the cells represent decisions to negotiate or not to negotiate, the two matrices can be overlaid to reveal similar or dissimilar decisions indicating the conditions (of power and legitimacy) under which negotiations are likely to take place.[10] The following subsections examine the conditions of power and legitimacy under which the Philippine insurgents and regime are likely to consider negotiating.

The Insurgents

Application of the model to the Philippine case indicates that a regime with a loyal military will be more powerful than an insurgency, notwithstanding other reasons for changes in relative power.[11] Therefore insurgent power is unlikely to exceed regime power, although it may increase in relation to the regime's advantage. Because of this asymmetry the insurgents will negotiate only under the best possible conditions or when their survival is jeopardized. They will negotiate under three conditions: in desperation (cell 1A in table 12-1), in triumph (cell 9A), or when either their power or legitimacy is relatively constant and the other dimension is increasing. The latter conditions are represented either by cell 6A, where power is increasing and legitimacy is constant, or in cell 8A, where legitimacy is increasing and power is constant. In each of the other cells one dimension is constant while the other is decreasing (cells 2A and 4A), one dimension is increasing while the other is decreasing (cells 3A and 7A), or both dimensions are constant (cell 5A).

Negotiation is feasible for an insurgency that is progressing toward its goal of influence, as indicated by cells 6A and 8A. In an effort to halt such progress, the regime may attempt to recover its advantages by either continuing the armed struggle (cell 8B) or negotiating (cell 6B). Several reasons can be given for the insurgents' decision not to negotiate, as shown in cells 2A, 3A, 4A, 5A, and 7A: on the down side, the insurgents will not negotiate because they are losing ground on only one dimension and their survival is not yet an issue; on the up side, the insurgents have not attained a sufficient advantage relative to the government to feel confident about making gains at the bargaining table. In both instances, the insurgents are presented with the possibility of taking actions that serve to change dimensions on which they are at a disadvantage. For example, either appropriate moves by the New People's Army or the regime's misdeeds can change the direction of legitimacy in cells 2A and 3A.

The Regime

Assuming that the military remains loyal, the government will maintain a considerable advantage even if its power may be falling relative to the insurgents' power. Thus the regime is seen to be unwilling to negotiate when its legitimacy is falling, as in cells 7B and 8B in table 12-1. Put the other way, the regime will negotiate when its legitimacy is growing or constant, as in cells 1B to 6B. The government may conclude that in the situations represented by these cells it is likely to emerge from negotiations having made few concessions. When both power and legitimacy are falling precipitously, as in cell 9B, the government may either negotiate a surrender, or, fearing a total loss, may hope to emerge from negotiations with a role in a successor regime or a coalition government. A recent example of cell 9B negotiation was the behavior of communist regimes in Eastern Europe in 1989: with legitimacy long gone, and no longer supported by the threat of Soviet military power, those regimes in effect negotiated themselves out of power.

Symmetry

The three symmetrical cells in table 12-1 (those cells indicating that both sides are willing to negotiate) suggest alternative explanations for the negotiations. They may occur because of desperation on the part of the insurgents (cell 1A) or on the part of the regime (cell 9B). Or they may result because the power of the insurgency is increasing relative to that of the regime (cells 6A and 6B). The history of the Philippine insurgency suggests neither a trend toward a weakened movement nor a desperate regime. The power and legitimacy of the New People's Army increased slowly but steadily for about thirteen years, making an explanation in terms of cell 1A implausible. Although the Aquino regime may have lost some power, in part because of uncertainties regarding the military's loyalty, its legitimacy remained relatively strong throughout its first year in office. There was no need for the regime to negotiate its surrender, as is suggested by the conditions of cell 9B.

If this analysis is correct, measurements taken shortly after Aquino assumed office in 1986 should support the hypothesis that both the National Democratic Front and the government were at the intersection represented by cells 6A and 6B in the matrices. Those cells indicate that relative legitimacy was constant for both groups, and that the direction of relative power was changing in favor of the insurgents.

The Onset of Negotiations

The estimates of relative power and legitimacy for the Philippine regime and the NDF insurgents are summarized for selected years in table 12-2. The bases for these estimates vary by year (see the source note for table

Table 12-2.   Estimates of Power and Legitimacy for the Regime and Insurgents, Selected Years, 1972–92

Year	Regime		Insurgents		Results
	Power	Legitimacy	Power	Legitimacy	
1972					
Macros declares martial law	Increasing	Increasing	Decreasing	Decreasing	Negotiations if the NDF had not been new and the regime had lacked confidence
1979 (early)					
Sustained economic growth, 1972–79	Constant	Constant	Constant	Constant	No negotiations
1982					
Post-1979 world economic crisis	Increasing	Decreasing	Decreasing	Increasing	No negotiations
1983					
After Ninoy Aquino assassination	Constant	Decreasing	Constant	Increasing	No negotiations
1985					
Macros calls snap election	Decreasing	Decreasing	Increasing	Increasing	Negotiations if Marcos had stolen the election from Corazon Aquino and repressed People Power
1986					
Corazon Aquino comes to power; NPA boycotts election	Decreasing	Constant	Increasing	Constant	Cease-fire negotiated; political talks begin
1987					
Constitutional referendum	Constant	Increasing	Constant	Decreasing	Insurgents call off negotiations
1992					
Ramos elected; cold war has ended	Increasing	Constant	Decreasing slowly	Decreasing	Insurgent surrender likely, timing uncertain

Sources: Estimates for 1972 and 1979 are expert judgments derived from the literature of the periods and from discussions with other scholars of Philippine politics. Estimates for 1982 and 1983 come from measurements reported in Druckman and Green, *Political Stability* (cited in note 1). For 1985, 1986, and 1987, estimates for insurgents are based on extrapolations from the calculations for 1982–83 as reported in Druckman and Green, *Political Stability*, and estimates for the regime are based on new data collected for 1985–87 and processed by the formulas presented in Druckman and Green, *Political Stability*. Estimates for 1992 are based on information reported in the *Daily Express* (Manila) and other Philippine newspapers of that time.

12-2). Most estimates lend support to the hypotheses summarized in table 12-1. Exceptions are the estimates for 1972 and 1985 when expected negotiations failed to materialize. Some explanation for the unexpected results is in order. A small and inexperienced New People's Army in 1972 was not regarded by Marcos as a sufficient threat to his rule; nor was the NPA sufficiently self-conscious about its own predicament to concede on the regime's terms. By 1985, however, the Marcos government's legitimacy was falling in light of the Ninoy Aquino assassination, a deteriorating economy, and a military that had become riddled with disobedient factions. The New People's Army, on the other hand, was slowly gaining strength and rapidly gaining legitimacy. An eventual negotiation between the NPA and the regime (indicated in cells 9A and 9B in table 12-1) could well have occurred if there had been no snap election or if Marcos had stolen the snap election from Corazon Aquino; a continuing slide in Marcos's power and legitimacy, had he stayed in office, would have set the stage for talks with the New People's Army between 1986 and 1988.

Corazon Aquino's victory in 1986 restored legitimacy to the government. At that time the legitimacy of the New People's Army and the National Democratic Front eroded because of the tactical error of boycotting the election. (Note that this occurred after their participation in the people's revolt against Marcos, an act that may have served, temporarily, to increase their legitimacy.) That situation, represented by cells 6A and 6B in table 12-1, was propitious for the onset of negotiations, as indicated in table 12-2. Construed in this way, the particular intersection of relative power and legitimacy defined in cells 6A and 6B (as well as those defined in cells 1A, 1B, 9A, and 9B) is a definition of a ripe moment.[12] Extending the analysis further, and anticipating the discussion in the next section, a series of events during the 1986–87 negotiation period led to decreased insurgent legitimacy, thus moving the situation asymmetrically into cell 2A, where the insurgents break off negotiations despite willingness by the government to continue talking (cell 2B).

The Negotiation Process

Negotiation between insurgents and regimes takes place within the context of a competitive game of group politics, as noted earlier. Under the stability model, groups monitor their competitive status in terms of relative power and legitimacy; the decision to negotiate is made on the basis of these indicators, as shown in table 12-1. Although cognizant of changes in the balance of power during negotiations, the contending groups must confront substantive differences on the issues in order to gauge the prospects for agreements. In so doing, differences in ideology and interests become apparent.

Ideology is a key dimension of difference between insurgents and governments. Insurgents define themselves in terms of an ideological orientation, usually on the far left of the political spectrum; to get elected, and remain in power, a government must define itself closer to the center of the spectrum. Thus ideology is an issue in negotiations. It is addressed directly and is linked to the interests reflected in the parties' positions. To the extent that ideology is explicit and differences are polarized, negotiation is very difficult. To the extent that differences in ideology are moderated, negotiation is possible. The dynamics of the interplay between ideology and interests can be elucidated by a set of four propositions, developed from the literature on the sociology of conflict; those propositions serve to organize the discussion in this section, in the context of the Philippine case. The propositional format illustrates the utility of theory-based concepts for understanding particular cases of negotiations.[13]

PROPOSITION 1. *When contending positions are derived explicitly from opposed ideologies, the conflict will be more intense than when the link is not explicit.*

The National Democratic Front in the Philippines is a communist insurgency. It promotes radical social change by armed struggle; the avowed purpose is to overthrow the prevailing political order. Such an extreme stance renders negotiation highly improbable; indeed, the 1987 negotiations discussed in this chapter were the first to have occurred since the founding of the party in 1968. A change from a strategy of armed struggle to one of political struggle is a necessary, though not sufficient, condition for negotiation. Willingness by the NDF to achieve its goal of social change by working within the prevailing political structures was suggested by its stated desire to be represented in a coalition government. Such a change in orientation made negotiation possible, but did not remove the impact of ideological differences on the negotiation process. The National Democratic Front put forward an agenda calling for fundamental social change, to be achieved by political means within the context of a framework that would alter the existing political order. The government's agenda reflected a need for social change within the framework of a new draft constitution that would support the existing political order. Key points advanced by negotiating panels for each side on December 24, 1986 (see the chronology of events), were as follows. The government's agenda: short-run economic recovery designed to generate more jobs and increase purchasing power; social amelioration, including housing construction, agricultural assistance, and manpower training; economic and social reforms emphasizing land reform and industrialization; and an honorable amnesty for insurgents, as well as resolution of arms and settlement issues. The National Democratic Front's agenda: a complete dismantling of the remaining features of the Marcos regime, and release of all remaining political prisoners; comprehensive land reform aimed at ending the monopoly of land ownership by a few, and fair distribution of land to peasants; abrogation of all military treaties with foreign countries (especially the United States) and repudiation of unequal agreements with international financial institutions; and a political settlement and termination of armed hostilities to be monitored by a transitional coalition government (that would include NDF representatives) until a regular government could be chosen in free elections.

The types of changes advocated by the National Democratic Front on the one hand and the government on the other suggest a division along the lines of social change (the NDF) and system maintenance (the government). Defined in this way, the ideological division is similar to the contrasting ideologies used in a series of experiments on simulated political decisionmaking. The results of those experiments, which support Proposition 1, indicated that conflicting interests were more difficult to resolve when underlying ideological orientations were made explicit to negotiators.[14] The more polarized the ideologies, the more difficult it was to attain a negotiated agreement, and representatives who identified strongly with their role (and its obligations) were especially resistant to compromise.[15] Support for Proposition 1 is also provided by the Philippine talks between the NDF and the regime, wherein ideological differences were emphasized in arguments over the difference between fundamental and cosmetic changes, thus preventing the talks from advancing beyond the stage of agreement on an agenda. Without agreement on the meaning of those terms, or suppression of the underlying ideological differences during negotiations, the two parties could not address their conflicting interests over power-sharing, military reorganization, or land reform programs. (During the talks frequent references were made by both sides to ideologies or beliefs about society, indicating strong commitment.)

PROPOSITION 2. *Differences in ideological orientation among units within each organization or group will result in a less intense conflict between the groups than when units within each group are homogeneous in orientation.*

The intensifying effects on conflict of a link between ideological differences and negotiating positions, as stated by Proposition 1, are likely to be reduced by differences within the groups on ideological orientation or on strategic approaches to implementing plans or policies, especially when internal divisions are aired publicly. Referred to as the principle of dissent, Proposition 2 has been tested in experiments, which demonstrated that when there were divisions within each party, the moderates on both teams acted as mediators in attempting to bring their more extremist teammates together.[16] Divided teams produced more agreements and better terms of agreement than undivided teams; moreover, internal divisions within contending parties (bilateral dissensus) resulted in better agreements (a higher proportion of integrative rather than compromise agreements) than when there were no divisions, even when both teammates shared moderate positions (bilateral consensus, moderate).[17] Moderates within the contending parties may serve to depolarize ideological division by moving the parties' positions closer to the center, thereby reducing the intensity of the conflict (see Proposition 1). In the Philippine case, charting the intraparty divisions within the National Democratic Front from the time of the transition to the Aquino regime to the opening round of the talks on January 6, 1987 (see the chronology of events), indicates the growing role played by moderates in depolarizing the ideological division between the NDF and the government. (A similar division between government hard-liners led by Juan Ponce Enrile and soft-liners led by Aquino could be documented, showing that the Aquino position prevailed.)

The transition from the Marcos regime to the Aquino regime caused the party (CPP-NDF) to consider making significant adjustments in its strategy. For the first time the party questioned its strategy of a protracted people's war in which armed struggle against the regime and the military was necessary. According to Gareth Porter, "until 1986, it had been an unchallenged central tenet of the CPP's general line that the party would win power directly through a military victory."[18] Some cadres within the party argued that the party failed to appreciate the value of cooperation with the pro-Aquino forces, and claimed that the party's boycott was "a 'strategic' error rooted in the very line of 'protracted people's war'."[19] Lines were drawn within the party. Influenced by two papers written by a cadre under the name of Marty Villalobos, a significant intraparty debate occurred over the role of political versus armed struggle. Although the ruling executive committee reaffirmed the centrality of armed struggle, it modified its extreme position on this issue by adding that armed struggle must henceforth have "political impact." The debate intensified by the summer of 1986, with three issues being highlighted: the relative importance of armed and political struggle, the nature of the Aquino government, and the nature of the united front. Such questioning of strategic and ideological positions set the stage for policy shifts by the party.

Moderates within the party, referred to also as "rectificationists," served to move the NDF ideological position toward the center, resulting in turn in a depolarization of the differences between the government and the National Democratic Front as negotiations began. A more moderate NDF was the result of pressures from below. In contrast, a moderate government position was the result of pressures from above: a moderate Aquino wing prevailed over challenges by hard-liners led by former defense minister Enrile and by remaining Marcos loyalists.[20] By reducing the intensity of the conflict between the two sides, depolarized positions enabled both sides to consider a wide range of issues for peace talks, including a sixty-day cease-fire, which further reduced mutual suspicions about motives. Acceptance by both sides of a formal agenda on December 24, 1986, indicated common ground for discussions on substantive issues, which were to begin on January 7, 1987 (see the chronology of events). Cooperation was, however, short-lived. Although agreeing on the agenda, neither the government nor the National Democratic Front could develop an acceptable framework that would move the talks along by rendering the issues negotiable. Progress depended on third-party intervention; assuming the role of mediator, Philippine senator Diokno proposed a broad framework that was acceptable to both parties (see the discussion following Proposition 3).

PROPOSITION 3. *Vague principles that call attention to shared goals will provide a basis for further negotiation; they will also mask the substantive differences that must be resolved for a negotiated agreement.*

The need for a formula is emphasized in many discussions of international negotiation.[21] A formula provides a conceptual bridge between values that enables the parties to consider their differences in terms of a bargaining space, thus paving the way toward a transformed relationship.[22] The case study literature on international negotiation illustrates the advantages of early agreement on principles: agreement moves the negotiation to a next stage, at which details and technical issues can be discussed.[23] The literature also highlights the value of third parties in assisting in the development of formulas. According to Daniel Druckman, "to be effective, the intervention must occur before parties have committed themselves to courses of action."[24] The Philippine case illustrates the important role played by third parties as well as the importance of timing in offering assistance.

The Diokno proposal was accepted by the negotiating panels of both the National Democratic Front and the regime at the first round of substantive talks, held on January 6, 1986. The proposal consisted of three key points: "Despite ideological differences, we recognize the needs for food and freedom, jobs and justice for what they are, and that the answers to them . . . [will] enable every Filipino to live . . . proudly and with dignity; both panels accept that the solutions are as interrelated as the problems they address . . . and, that these problems are ours and ours alone to resolve in a manner that our people desire, and not as foreigners would want us to resolve them, for the good of the many who are poor, and not the few who are privileged."[25] In accepting the proposal, NDF negotiator Satur Ocampo noted that "the NDF cannot argue against food and freedom, jobs and justice, for the Filipino people."[26] The proposal served to encourage face-to-face discussions of the issues, but did not sustain the discussions at a level of give-and-take that would permit trade-offs and compromises; in Ocampo's words, "these are very broad principles and we have to flesh them out."[27]

A second round of talks began on January 13 in Quezon City, with the government negotiators responding to each point made in a ten-point proposal submitted by the National Democratic Front. Addressing the details in this way revealed fundamental differences between the parties that led them to conclude that there was no common ground found in the discussions. By January 16 the talks were at an impasse; no date was set for a third round. The inability to resolve their conflicting interests served to further polarize the parties.

PROPOSITION 4. *Through time and repeated encounters, factions (or cadres) within the contending parties converge on their ideological positions, producing further polarization between the parties which serves, in turn, to increase the intensity of the conflict.*

Negotiations between contending parties to resolve conflicts of interest may have polarizing or depolarizing effects on their differences in ideology.

Vilhelm Aubert claims that the nature of a confrontation to resolve the conflicting interests that derive from opposing ideological positions will influence the dissensus.[28] A resolution that satisfies both parties may lead to a meaningful dialogue on their ideologies and values, reducing the polarization; an unfavorable resolution may lead to further isolation between the parties, increasing the polarization. According to Druckman and Zechmeister, when the outcome of attempts to negotiate conflicts of interest leads to polarized ideological positions, future confrontations between the parties will be intensified (see Proposition 1).[29] Examples of the polarizing effects of repeated conflicts of interest can be found in the literature on the sociology of conflict as well as in writings on competition among academic disciplines in universities.[30] The dynamics of this interplay, having consequences both for the intensity of the conflict and for the polarization of the groups' ideologies, were evident in the Philippine case in the interactions between the National Democratic Front and the government both before and after the second round of discussions.

Within the National Democratic Front differences among cadres about strategy emerged after the first round of discussions with the regime. And the common ground between the NDF and the regime that was defined by the Diokno proposal was short lived, as noted earlier. The discussions in the second round, on January 13, 1987, resulted in an impasse because little common ground was found in the government's responses to the ten-point NDF proposal. National Democratic Front negotiators indicated that the government had failed to address the fundamental concerns of the party. In an attempt to save the talks, NDF negotiators proposed a deal to forgo armed struggle in return for inclusion of the National Democratic Front in a new coalition government. Although the NDF made it clear that this offer was not to be regarded as an ultimatum or precondition for further negotiation, the government negotiators, fearful of the implications of including the insurgency in a partnership arrangement, did not accept the offer (see the chronology of events). The NDF countered by rejecting the government's proposal to use the draft constitution as a framework for the talks, claiming that the document did not address the fundamental changes needed (see the chronology of events).

The inability of the two sides to negotiate their differences on the issues of power sharing, an integrated military, and land reform programs produced further polarization. The National Democratic Front leadership reversed course by deciding to resume the armed struggle when the cease-fire expired on February 8, 1987. National Democratic Front perceptions of recent government actions led the NDF to conclude that the regime was moving further to the right; the implicit alliance of moderates on both sides was eroding as the moderate wing within the government dramatically weakened. Contributing to those perceptions was United States support for the government's positions, as indicated by an offer by U.S. Representative Stephen Solarz of U.S. assistance to help the government defend itself should the cease-fire break down. Bolstering the NDF decision were renewed calculations indicating that as a weakened party it would continue to weaken if the negotiations continued and the cease-fire held. Weakness was particularly evident in regard to those aspects of the NDF's group assets and attributes that contributed to mobilization for collective action—namely, supporters and cohesion.[31]

With the resumption of armed struggle, the National Democratic Front leadership demanded a return to ideological unity and discipline within the party. Sanctions were imposed for deviation from the party line, thus moving the moderates in the direction of the more extreme leadership. The result was further polarization between the NDF and government, making negotiation unlikely in the near term. As Porter notes, "the lively intraparty debate that had flourished in 1986 was virtually dead by the summer of 1987 . . . [and those] who had supported the 'rectificationist' position, now toed the party line."[32] Just as the NDF moved further to the left, the government moved further to the right by accepting most of the military's recommendations for coping with the insurgency. According to Porter, Aquino "increased military pay and the military budget in general, requested more helicopters and other military assistance from abroad . . . and [gave] up investigations of human rights abuses by the Philippine military."[33] The increased polarization that resulted from the decisions and actions taken by both sides intensified the conflict and reduced the chance of resolving conflicting interests through negotiations. Without a mediating mechanism, the interplay between interests and ideologies through time and repeated encounters would lead to an increasing spiral of polarization and conflict intensity, as summarized by Proposition 4.[34]

The four propositions describe a negotiation process that alternates between cooperation and competition. In the language of game theory, this is a mixed-motive situation: the negotiator's dilemma is to cooperate or compromise in order to get an agreement and to compete or persuade in order to get a good agreement. Although the dilemma exists for all negotiators, the relative importance of cooperation (for an agreement) and competition (for winning) is likely to vary from one type of negotiation to another.

For example, the innovation agreements described by Fred Iklé are the result of cooperative problem-solving discussions, and the redistribution agreements he describes develop from terms largely imposed by one party on the other.[35] Conditioned by the context for group politics, these types of agreement reflect the relationship between the parties. In the case of insurgency-government interactions, that relationship is competitive, viewed often by the parties as zero-sum, and characterized by calculations of relative advantage (see table 12-1). Evaluations made with regard to the threefold choice—to continue negotiation, to reach an agreement, or to abandon talks—are conceived to be the result of a process of monitoring the indicators of relative advantage. An increasingly symmetrical relationship, as shown in cells 6A and 6B in table 12-1, is a condition that favors joint gains through negotiation. However, the situation is tenuous: if one side gains too much while the other loses too much (that is, if the relationship becomes more asymmetrical in favor of the government or "too" symmetrical in favor of the insurgents) the talks are likely to break down, as they did in the Philippines.

Of interest is what kind of negotiation was represented by the Philippine case. Iklé's typology, distinguishing among the negotiating agreement objectives of extension, normalization, redistribution, and innovation, can be usefully applied.[36] As they combined several of these objectives, the NDF-government talks could not be considered "pure." Their objective actually might have been closer to another type proposed by Iklé—negotiating for side effects rather than for agreements. For the National Democratic Front, political negotiations provided an opportunity to increase its legitimacy, which would in turn attract more supporters; the cease-fire would allow the NDF time to mobilize its troops for later offensives. For the government, negotiations provided an opportunity to reduce the insurgency threat through political co-optation, and to attract previously skeptical left-of-center supporters. Developments during the talks led the NDF to conclude that "further development of the NPA . . . required regular tactical offensives, which the ceasefire had brought to a standstill."[37] An expected victory in the constitutional plebiscite in February 1987 enabled the government to consolidate its power without achieving a negotiated agreement. In sum, these revised calculations of relative advantage combined with the increasing ideological polarization (resulting from lack of resolution on the issues) to doom the negotiation process, leading the insurgents to turn to armed struggle against a strengthened military.

The Situation since 1987

In the years since 1987 little has changed in regard to negotiations in the Philippines. There have been a few informal but no official contacts between the government and the New People's Army, and no attempts at negotiations. All reports indicate a stalemate between the two groups, but it has not been compellingly painful for either side. The NPA maintains strength in the less-populated rural areas, but has not been able to penetrate either well-populated rural areas or urban environments. The NPA has claimed an organized mass base of about 1 million supporters and an additional 10 million nominal followers—those influenced to some degree by the NPA and its political organization, the National Democratic Front. If those figures were anywhere near correct, the NDF should have had considerable electoral success in the 1987 elections. But even in many areas in which the government ceded control the insurgents failed to elect any of their candidates. This suggests that control over the population by the New People's Army is not as strong as claimed, and that the number of committed followers is probably far less than 1 million. The number of nominal followers must be revised downward in light of the election results. It would have been difficult for the insurgents to know their actual standing before the election and hard for them to believe or admit it afterward. Recent official estimates place New People's Army strength at levels somewhat below those attained in the mid-1980s.[38] An estimate by the *Asian Wall Street Journal* in 1990 indicated that the number of NPA rebels and party members decreased from a high of 24,000 in 1987 to 19,000 in early 1990.[39] The losses in legitimacy suffered by the insurgents during the early Aquino government had not been recovered.

Nor has the regime gained in strength. Successive attempts to destabilize the regime through military coups have called attention to the regime's inability to capitalize on the popularity acquired during its early years. Continued corruption, an economy that once again faltered in 1990, the failure of land reform programs, and a congress that has yet to implement the social-equality imperatives of the new constitution adopted in 1987 have all contributed to an apparent decline in the Aquino administration's legitimacy. Although Corazon Aquino remained personally popular, her regime did not achieve its goals.

It was thought that pressures from another direction might improve the situation. A national peace conference held in Tagaytay City in October 1990 brought together 175 leaders from the nongovernmental sectors of the country. By defining a broad-based constituency for peace, conference leaders were able to lobby the administration in support of their demands. The resulting "Vision of Peace" document stressed the need to address many of the concerns articulated by the National Democratic Front, including legalization of the Communist Party.[40] By moving the peace process from a bilateral to a multilateral track, the conference might have served to reduce the differences between the regime and the NDF. By reinforcing many of the demands made by the National Democratic Front, the conference could have encouraged potential NDF recruits to opt instead for the peace process.

Although the early days in 1992 of the Fidel Ramos regime seemed to hold promise for a reconciliation between insurgents and the government, events moved in the opposite direction.[41] Ramos's small electoral victory (a 25 percent plurality) limited his ability to act on issues central to National Democratic Front concerns. His broad-based legislative coalition has not made major reforms a priority. He also permitted many of the most prominent military leaders involved in earlier coup attempts to return to active duty. Those figures have opposed efforts to integrate the NDF into the mainstream of Philippine politics. Moreover, the military's success in capturing high-ranking leaders of the New People's Army, as reported in the *Daily Express* (Manila) and elsewhere, made it reluctant to risk losing its advantage in peace negotiations. However, the NDF had also lost strength. None of its candidates did well in the 1992 election. Furthermore, the downfall of world communism diminished the attraction of Marxism as a development ideology. Several intellectual leaders became discouraged and surrendered to authorities. Despite these losses, the movement remains sufficiently viable to resist dissolution; poverty grows, providing a fertile environment for continued insurgent activities.

What do these developments portend for the future? To date (mid-1995), the National Democratic Front has resisted another round of negotiations. For talks to occur it would seem that the NDF must either grow stronger or become weaker. It appears that the trend is in the direction of decreased strength: the military wing seems reluctant to engage in new campaigns, while the political leadership is increasingly drawn from peasant rather than intellectual cultures. To the extent that the movement continues to lose its strength and vitality, it appears to be moving toward the situation represented in cell 1A (decreasing power and legitimacy) in table 12-1. From this position, the insurgents can only hope to negotiate the terms of their surrender with a regime poised to accept such terms even under the extreme condition depicted in cell 9A, where their own legitimacy and relative power is seen to be decreasing. A reading of Philippine history and culture suggests that such an outcome would not result in a spate of sanctions, as Filipinos put behind them a twenty-five-year period of violent revolution.

Summary and Conclusions

The case presented in this chapter is an example of an attempt to superimpose general analytic frameworks on the details of a particular negotiation. Proposed as a research strategy by Druckman and Iaquinta, among others, this approach has gained popularity as a way of capturing richness without forfeiting rigor in the analysis of negotiation.[42] The details of interactions between the NPA-NDF and the Aquino government are captured in the chronology of events recorded in the daily reporting of newspapers in the Philippines during the period of the negotiations and in the interpretive essays of scholars and journalists appearing after that period. These details are understood in terms of two frameworks, one based on a model of competitive group politics (to explain the decision to negotiate), the other based on propositions from the literature on the sociology of conflict (to explain the negotiation process). As noted earlier, this approach illustrates the utility of theory-based concepts for understanding specific cases and the role played by cases in contributing data that demonstrates the relevance of theory.

Two concepts discussed in the literature on international negotiation are highlighted in the analysis in this chapter: the ripe moment for negotiating, and a formula for defining issues for bargaining. The group politics model provides an operational definition for ripeness—namely, the intersection of measurements (or group calculations) of each side's relative legitimacy and power. An elusive concept is thus translated into empirical indicators used for estimating regime stability. Some of the judgments in table 12-2 use the indicators for making rough calculations about the direction of legitimacy and power for both sides; support is given to the hypothesis that the 1986 decision to negotiate resulted from a combination of decreasing power and constant legitimacy for the regime and increasing power and constant legitimacy for the insurgents. Confirmation for these judgments awaits more precise measurements in the manner of the conclusions made in the Druckman and Green study.[43]

While monitoring these indicators during negotiations, the groups' representatives must address issues that reflect both ideologies and interests. The interplay between differences in ideology and conflicting interests through time produces cycles of cooperative and competitive interactions during the negotiations. Depolarized ideologies enable the parties to confront their differences on the issues; in the Philippine case moderate factions within the parties were shown to move their more extremist members toward the political center.[44] Progress depends, however, on the development of a formula that renders the issues negotiable; in the Philippines the mediator's proposed formula served to sustain the talks but did not produce an agreement on the fundamental differences that would enable the parties to address the issues. The resulting polarization intensified the conflict, leading first to an impasse in the substantive talks, and second to an end to the cease-fire agreement. Without a mediating mechanism, the interplay between interests and ideologies through time leads to an increasing spiral of polarization and conflict intensity.

Could the outcome in the Philippines have been different? Viewed from the perspective of competitive group politics, the answer is probably no, for two reasons. First, the parties' negotiating objectives were to achieve a competitive advantage—that is, to negotiate for the side effects of increased power and legitimacy in a continuing struggle for control of the political order. A negotiated coalition government would have led to reduced power for the regime and a loss of identity for the insurgents. Second, cross-cutting interests between the parties would have been necessary to offset the conflict-intensifying effects of polarized positions. Such shared interests on other issues were largely precluded by the structure of the parties' interactions; being outside a political system provides few, if any, opportunities for an insurgency to collude with a government on other issues. To provide such opportunities it would be necessary to negotiate a coalition government, which, in the Philippines, is unlikely to occur, for reasons stated above. This analysis suggests that efforts should be concentrated on discovering the conditions for acceptable power-sharing between insurgent groups and the governments they desire to replace. Those are likely to be the conditions for successful negotiation.

An alternative to power-sharing is a changed identity for the insurgent group. In the Philippines a new identity could emerge as part of the process of ideological convergence, whereby the government becomes more responsive to National Democratic Front concerns and the NDF gravitates toward a more moderate stance within the range of acceptable positions in the Philippine political system. Ultimately the National Democratic Front would become a partner that shares power rather than an antagonist. However, the political and economic difficulties facing the Ramos regime make convergence difficult. It is unlikely that a multitrack peace process will gain momentum and become instrumental in moving the parties to the negotiating table. At the same time, the National Democratic Front becomes weaker, presaging the end of the revolution.

Appendix—Chronology of Events

August 1986 — The Philippine government and the National Democratic Front insurgents agree to peace negotiations in two phases—talks on a cease-fire and talks on substantive issues.

December 9, 1986 — NDF negotiators demand removal of U.S. bases from the Philippines.

December 10, 1986 — A sixty-day nationwide cease-fire begins.

December 11, 1986 — The government proposes a four-point agenda (for talks) that includes amnesty for insurgents and economic and social reforms, but does not include a ruling coalition with the NDF.

December 14, 1986 — The National Democratic Front proposes a four-point agenda that includes removal of U.S. bases and nationalization of all strategic Philippine industries and businesses.

December 20, 1986 — The NDF demands that the new draft constitution not serve as a framework for talks (thus opposing the government's position) and accuses the government of being influenced by the United States.

December 21, 1986 — Agents of international communist organizations enter the country and are presumed to be establishing links with the National Democratic Front.

December 23, 1986 — The government rejects an NDF proposal for a coalition government and for integration of the forces of the New People's Army and the Armed Forces of the Philippines; Cardinal Sin supports the government position.

December 24, 1986 — Government and NDF negotiating panels exchange formal agendas for the substantive phase of the peace talks, scheduled to begin on January 6; each side submits four main points for discussion and expresses optimism about the prospects for a settlement.

December 25, 1986   The NDF demands the release of Rodolfo Salas, a CCP–NPA leader regarded as a key member of its negotiating team; the government rejects this demand.

December 27, 1986   The government rejects as nonnegotiable the NDF demands for power sharing, removal of American bases, integration of rebel forces into the armed forces, and lately the inclusion of Salas in the NDF negotiating panel; the NDF criticizes the government's negative posturing before the talks begin and defends its proposals as conditions for peace.

January 4, 1987   The NDF declares there is no common ground in the government's agenda and expresses concern over apparent U.S. influence on proposals.

January 5, 1987   U.S. Representative Stephen Solarz offers to help the government defend itself against the insurgents if the cease-fire breaks down as the peace talks begin.

January 6, 1987   The first round of substantive talks begins on a positive note as both panels declare finding common ground; the NDF softens its stance by accepting, in principle, former Philippine senator Jose W. Diokno's proposal, which was adopted as a framework for the talks.

January 13, 1987   The various NDF organizations debate extension of the cease-fire and the continuation of talks with the government.

January 13, 1987   The second round of peace talks commences with the government responding to each point of a ten-point proposal submitted by the NDF; no common ground is found in the discussions.

January 15, 1987   The NDF proposes to forgo armed struggle if the government agrees to the formation of a ruling coalition that includes the NDF; the NDF claimed that this was not to be viewed as a precondition for continuing the talks.

January 16, 1987   Talks are at an impasse as the negotiating panels disagree on the government's proposal to use the still-unratified constitution as a framework for negotiations; the NDF claims that this document does not address the fundamental changes in society that it seeks.

January 22, 1987   The NDF threatens to break off the talks, blaming the government for the lack of progress being made; it also defends the recent offensive of the Moro National Liberation Front (MNLF) against the government's military forces (the MNLF is a political and military Islamic organization).

January 23, 1987   The talks are suspended as both panels claim that the lives of the negotiators are being threatened; however, both sides agree to abide by the cease-fire, which is due to expire on February 8.

January 26, 1987   The NDF legal council rules out the possibility of resumption of the talks.

January 27, 1987   Government defense minister Rafael Ileto asks the NDF negotiators to return to the table, arguing that failure to do so would result in renewed armed hostilities; although agreeing to consider NDF demands, Ileto refuses to abandon the government position that the constitution serve as a framework for the talks.

January 31, 1987   The NDF formally withdraws from the negotiations, but indicates that it will continue to abide by the cease-fire.

February 7, 1987   NDF negotiators announce they will not renew the cease-fire when it expires the next day at noon.

February 8, 1987   NDF negotiators state preconditions for a return to the negotiating table, including a demand that Aquino reform and reorient the military.

Notes

1. See Daniel Druckman and Justin Green, *Political Stability in the Philippines: Framework and Analysis*, Monograph Series in World Affairs, vol. 22, book 3 (University of Denver, 1986).

2. See Sterling Seagrave, *The Marcos Dynasty* (Harper and Row, 1988).

3. Gareth Porter, "Philippine Communism after Marcos," *Problems of Communism*, vol. 36 (September–October, 1987), pp. 14–35.

4. On the growth of the NPA, see William Chapman, *Inside the Philippine Revolution* (W. W. Norton, 1987).

5. Employing a quantitative technique for estimating the NPA gains in arms, it was found that, even allowing for the most favorable conditions, the best estimate of the total number of weapons was about 12,000. See Druckman and Green, *Political Stability*. According to Porter, the CPP in 1984 admitted that "20,000 NPA guerrillas shared only 10,000 rifles," and the Armed Forces of the Philippines (AFP) claimed that the NPA had only 12,000 weapons in 1987. See Porter, "Philippine Communism After Marcos," p. 16. As Porter points out, ammunition is harder to obtain than guns. Just as true is that automatic weapons, used frequently and under jungle conditions, break down or become unreliable in relatively short periods of time. Replacing such weapons requires constant effort and consequent risk.

6. See Druckman and Green, *Political Stability*.

7. See Daniel Druckman and Justin Green, "Is Marcos Vulnerable? Analysis of Regime Stability in the Philippines," *Planning Review*, vol. 12 (November 1984), pp. 36–41); and Druckman and Green, *Political Stability*.

8. This relationship is depicted in the model in the form of instability curves. The curves are defined by the product of the difference in effective power (on the x axis) and the ratio of each group's legitimacy (on the y axis). Two properties of the curves have implications for instability: (1) the value of the curve (the size of the product), and (2) the slope of the curve. As the products decrease in value, instability increases, or, the closer the curve is to the axis, the more unstable the situation. Points located on the steep slopes of the curve are extremely sensitive to changes in effective power. Points located on the shallow parts of the curve are extremely sensitive to changes in legitimacy. For further details on the use of these curves, see Druckman and Green, *Political Stability*.

9. The levels are regarded in relative terms. "Constant" refers to relatively unchanging amounts of power or legitimacy during a particular period. Similarly, increasing or decreasing power or legitimacy refer to changing levels during a certain period.

10. These hypotheses can be tested. Support for the hypothesized relationships would make it possible to use the techniques to anticipate when negotiations would occur and perhaps whether they would be likely to succeed or fail. Measurement techniques can be used to chart changes in the variables over time. For details on data sources and measures, see Druckman and Green, *Political Stability*, pp. 31–79. It should be noted, however, that in that study the authors did not survey members of any of the groups used in the analysis about their own perceptions of differences among them in power and legitimacy. Because perceptions may not coincide with measured assets (for power estimates) or performances (for legitimacy estimates), it is possible

that decisionmakers may either miss opportunities to negotiate or may enter into negotiations that result in impasses.

11. See Druckman and Green, *Political Stability*.

12. See I. William Zartman, "Ripening Conflict, Ripe Moment, Formula, and Mediation," in Diane B. Bendahmane and John W. McDonald, Jr., eds., *Perspectives on Negotiation* (Washington: Center for the Study of Foreign Affairs, Foreign Service Institute, U.S. Department of State, 1986).

13. Theories of negotiation that discount the role of ideology, such as game theory, many social-psychological approaches, organizational frameworks, and power-structural analysis, are less relevant to this type of negotiation. Although it is difficult to define ideological differences in a rigorous way, the strength of ideological commitment can be inferred from statements made in a group's publications. In this analysis the content of ideologies is not examined. Attention is focused on whether contending groups (the regime and the NDF) are united or divided on ideologically derived positions and on their apparent commitment to those positions, as highlighted in the four propositions.

14. See Daniel Druckman and Kathleen Zechmeister, "Conflict of Interest and Value Dissensus," *Human Relations*, vol. 23 (October 1970), pp. 431–38; Daniel Druckman and Kathleen Zechmeister, "Conflict of Interest and Value Dissensus: Propositions in the Sociology of Conflict," *Human Relations*, vol. 26 (August 1973), pp. 449–66; Kathleen Zechmeister and Daniel Druckman, "Determinants of Resolving a Conflict of Interest: A Simulation of Political Decision Making," *Journal of Conflict Resolution*, vol. 17 (March 1973), pp. 63–88.

15. See Daniel Druckman, "Understanding the Operation of Complex Social Systems: Some Uses of Simulation Design," *Simulation and Games*, vol. 2 (June 1971), pp. 173–95; Daniel Druckman, Richard Rozelle, and Kathleen Zechmeister, "Conflict of Interest and Value Dissensus: Two Perspectives," in Daniel Druckman, ed., *Negotiations: Social-Psychological Perspectives* (Beverly Hills: Sage Publications, 1977), pp. 105–31.

16. See William M. Evan and John A. MacDougall, "Interorganizational Conflict: A Labor-Management Bargaining Experiment," *Journal of Conflict Resolution*, vol. 11 (December 1967), pp. 398–413; and Dan Jacobson, "Intraparty Dissensus and Interparty Conflict Resolution," *Journal of Conflict Resolution*, vol. 25 (September 1981), pp. 471–94.

17. See Jacobson, "Intraparty Dissensus." The results of comparisons among four experimental conditions can be summarized as follows: bilateral dissensus > bilateral consensus, moderate > bilateral consensus, extremist > unilateral dissensus (in terms of more and better agreements). Dissensus produces favorable results when both sides are divided. The worse results are produced when a divided team confronts a unified team. This effect is, however, time-specific. The process can work in the opposite direction. Through time and repeated encounters between opposed groups, the moderates in each group can gravitate toward their extremist teammates, serving to further polarize the differences between them. As the conflict intensifies, each group becomes more unified. See Proposition 4.

18. Porter, "Philippine Communism after Marcos," p. 28.

19. Porter, "Philippine Communism after Marcos," p. 29.

20. According to a 1986 report prepared by the Asia Society, Corazon Aquino was aware of divisions within the NDF. Her reconciliation strategy was based at least in part on her "[belief] that many members of the Party . . . might accept her challenge [of reconciliation] as an attractive alternative to remaining outside the political process." Furthermore, it was argued that "if the political center can hold, Mrs. Aquino might well be able to pursue this strategy to a successful conclusion." The Asia Society, "The Philippines: Facing the Future," *Asian Agenda Report 4* (New York: University Press of America, 1986), p. 23.

21. See I. William Zartman, "Negotiations: Theory and Reality," *Journal of International Affairs*, vol. 29 (Spring 1975), pp. 69–77; and Daniel Druckman, "Stages, Turning Points, and Crises: Negotiating Military Base Rights, Spain and the United States," *Journal of Conflict Resolution*, vol. 30 (June 1986), pp. 327–60.

22. See Daniel Druckman, "Social-Psychological Factors in Regional Politics," in Werner J. Feld and Gavin Boyd, eds., *Comparative Regional Systems: West and East Europe, North America, the Middle East, and Developing Countries* (Pergamon, 1980), pp. 18–55.

23. See Daniel Druckman, "Four Cases of Conflict Management: Lessons Learned," in Diane B. Bendahmane and John W. McDonald, Jr., eds., *Perspectives on Negotiation* (Washington: Center for the Study of Foreign Affairs, Foreign Service Institute, U.S. Department of State, 1986), pp. 263–88.

24. Druckman, "Four Cases of Conflict Management," p. 277.

25. Ibarra Mateo, "Panels Find Common Ground for Talks: Both Agree to Diokno Agenda," *Daily Express* (Manila), January 7, 1987, p. 6.

26. Mateo, "Panels Find Common Ground," p. 6.

27. Mateo, "Panels Find Common Ground," p. 6.

28. Vilhelm Aubert, "Competition and Dissensus: Two Types of Conflict and of Conflict Resolution," *Journal of Conflict Resolution*, vol. 7 (March 1963), pp. 26–42.

29. Druckman and Zechmeister, "Conflict of Interest and Value Dissensus."

30. See Lewis A. Coser, *Continuities in the Study of Social Conflict* (New York: Free Press, 1967); Donald T. Campbell, "Ethnocentrism of Disciplines and the Fishscale Model of Omniscience," in Muzafer Sherif and Carolyn W. Sherif, *Interdisciplinary Relationships in the Social Sciences* (Chicago: Aldine, 1969), pp. 328–48; and Charles Percy Snow, *The Two Cultures and the Scientific Revolution* (Cambridge University Press, 1959).

31. See Druckman and Green, *Political Stability*.

32. Porter, "Philippine Communism after Marcos," p. 34.

33. Porter, "Philippine Communism after Marcos," p. 34.

34. See Druckman and Zechmeister, "Conflict of Interest and Value Dissensus" (1973), p. 458.

35. Fred C. Iklé, *How Nations Negotiate* (Harper and Row, 1964).

36. See Iklé, *How Nations Negotiate*.

37. Porter, "Philippine Communism after Marcos," p. 32.

38. David F. Lambertson, statement by the Deputy Assistant Secretary for East Asian and Pacific Affairs before the House Foreign Affairs Committee, March 7, 1989, in "Future Prospects for the Philippines," in *Current Policy* 1157 (Washington: Department of State, Bureau of Public Affairs).

39. Matt Miller, "Party in Disarray: Communists Prove Unable to Capitalize on Crisis in Philippine Government," *Asian Wall Street Journal*, January 8, 1990, p. 4.

40. Sara Solis Castaneda, Orlando Guerrero, Edgar Rosero, and Antonió Da Costa Gasper, "The Peace Process in the Philippines, Guatemala, Nicaragua and Mozambique," in Göran Lindgran, Kjell-Ake Nordquist, and Peter Wallensteen, eds., *Peace Processes in the Third World* (Uppsala, Sweden: Department of Peace and Conflict Research, University of Uppsala, 1991), pp. 115–27.

41. William Brannigan, "Ramos to Filipinos: Sacrifice Lies Ahead," *International Herald Tribune*, July 1, 1992, p. 4.

42. See Daniel Druckman and Leonard E. Iaquinta, "Toward Bridging the International Negotiation/Mediation Gap," *International Studies Notes*, vol. 1 (1974), pp. 6–14; I. William Zartman, *The 50% Solution* (Anchor Press, 1976); Janice Gross Stein, *Getting to the Table: The Process of International Prenegotiation* (Johns Hopkins University Press, 1989); Druckman, "Stages, Turning Points, and Crises"; and Robert Mahoney and Daniel Druckman, "Simulation, Experimentation, and Context: Dimensions of Design and Inference," *Simulation and Games*, vol. 6 (September 1975), pp 235–70.

43. See Druckman and Green, *Political Stability*.

44. Ideological convergence or divergence is treated here as a cyclical process driven by other aspects of the conflict. Just where parties are located in the cycle—that is, the extent of convergence or divergence—is a measurement problem that entails the development of indicators. Development of indicators of ideological shifts remains a challenge for conflict analysts.

*This chapter is dedicated to the memory of
Kathleen Zechmeister.*

CHAPTER THIRTEEN

Conclusions: The Last Mile

I. William Zartman

As THE DOMINANT system of conflict and world order disintegrates, internal conflicts and their regional ramifications emerge as the primary challenge to international peace and security. Because of their inherent asymmetry, internal conflicts are condemned to escalate. Unlike the cold war system of conflict, they do not represent a cause and countercause that sweep the world and lock it in a global struggle. Rather internal conflicts are endemic infections in the body politic that demand attention and intervention—undulating fevers, old wounds, and running sores that do not heal, that result in neither victory nor defeat, have no common cause, and yet are merely the aberrational outgrowths of normal political processes gone bad.

In contrast to the kind of attention given to internal wars and rebellion during the cold war era (particularly in the 1960s),[1] the focus of this book is not on counterinsurgency or on the tactics of prevailing in conflict. The key to the new approach exemplified in these chapters is a basic acknowledgement of the legitimacy of internal dissidence, seen as the result of the breakdown of normal politics. This does not mean that in any of the internal conflicts studied the insurgents are assumed to be "right"; it only means that they are assumed to have a point and to represent legitimate grievances, even if they do not use legitimate means of pursuing them. The new focus of this study, made in the 1990s in the post–cold-war era, is on resolving rather than combating internal conflict.

Cold war studies of insurgency recognized the basic quality of asymmetry, captured in Henry Kissinger's famous judgment about when guerrillas win and conventional armies lose (see chapter 1). They did not focus on the counterbalancing element of commitment, seeing instead any commitment as merely a pathological aspect of communism, with which internal wars were associated. Nor did they see the internal dynamic of insurgency as a matter of rise and fall, with an influence on the possibilities for negotiations. Cold war studies of insurgency had their own set of stages of conflict, largely derived from the steps toward victory identified by Mao Tse-tung, Che Guevara, and Võ Nguyên Giáp.[2] Moreover, to both sides in the cold war (and hence to most scholars) insurgencies and counterinsurgency were not appropriate subjects for reconciliation and negotiation; rather, they were to be pursued to victory, for one side or the other. Stalemate as a solution was not to be desired and not to be pursued, nor was internal conflict thought of as something that could be traced back to its origins in the breakdown of normal politics.

The studies in this book begin by underscoring the difficulty of bringing internal conflict to any successful conclusion for anyone. It is hard to crush the rebels. At best, internal conflicts are simply subsumed back into normal politics; they are carried out by other means within accepted rules of political interaction, but never resolved in the sense of eliminating the parties or the causes. Even when the rebels "win," by achieving secession or overthrow of the government, many of the problems still remain, to reemerge at a later moment, as the conflicts in Chad, Angola, Mozambique, Colombia, Lebanon, and even South Africa suggest. As a result, negotiation rather than war appears to be the most appropriate means of managing internal conflict.

Yet negotiation is not an easy policy to carry out. Another theme of the cases analyzed here is the difficulty of finding appropriate conditions favoring negotiation. Stalemate is precluded by asymmetry, valid spokespersons are weakened by the internal dynamics of the insurgency on the one hand and the government on the other, and solutions are characteristically either too little or too early in terms of the evolution of the conflict. Similarly, negotiation is troubled by the difficulty of finding appropriate settlements. Nearly half of the conflicts here studied have ostensibly achieved some sort of solution. The new political systems set up in South Africa, Mozambique, and Colombia seem to embody the most durable type of settlement (discussed below). The secession of Eritrea solves some problems and poses others. The Ta'if agreement on Lebanon, which can only be called putting the fox in charge of the henhouse, poses more problems than it solves. Sudanese in the 1990s wonder whether the adequate solution toward which they should work lies in one or two Sudans. In three other conflicts a different sort of solution seems likely: in the Philippines, the Basque country, and the remaining rebellions in Colombia the insurgencies are running out of steam, often alienating potential followers by their tactics of violence. To the extent that in all three cases a new political system has been established, the loss of support for the rebellion may be a mark of solution, but events in the Philippines point to its fragility.[3]

This study examines many of the major protracted internal wars of the times, but other equally unresolved conflicts could also have been included; the case histories here cannot clearly indicate the way to bring all such conflicts to an end. However, the analyses all focus, precisely or broadly, on thematic keys and insights that are appropriate to understanding the path to solutions in each particular case. Thus the lessons of the past, which bring out the obstacles to negotiation, can be turned into insights for the future. There is no magic, but some features stand out over others.

Stalemate has been found to be as elusive as predicted. The lesson is straightforward; where both sides in a conflict perceived themselves to be in a stalemate that was painful to each of them and they saw a better alternative through negotiation (as in Sudan in 1972, Mozambique, South Africa, Colombia, and possibly Angola and Sri Lanka in the mid-1990s), they negotiated an agreement; and where the government (as in Spain, Sudan, and the Philippines) or the insurgency (as in Eritrea) felt it was winning, or where the pain of the stalemate was bearable or justified (as in Angola, Afghanistan, and Sri Lanka, and among the Colombian extremists), no settlement was negotiated. Stalemate was absent in cases where negotiations took place and then collapsed; in such cases parties often negotiated for other reasons, as in the Philippines, the Basque country, Afghanistan in the 1990s, and Eritrea. In some conflicts where stalemate did appear, as in Angola, Lebanon, and Sudan in the 1980s, it became a way of life that buried talks, not a deadlock that promoted them.

In chapter 12 Druckman and Green make it easier to conceive of the possibility of a stalemate conducive to negotiations by presenting stalemate as a dynamic, compound concept that combines power with commitment (legitimacy). They find three situations favorable to negotiation: when the insurgents' power and legitimacy are decreasing and the government's legitimacy is increasing, when the reverse obtains, and when the legitimacy of both is stable but the insurgents' power is increasing. In the first situation the insurgents are desperate and the government negotiates their surrender and integration by offering inducements to join the national team, as president and former guerrilla leader Hissene Habre did to the remaining guerrilla opposition throughout the 1980s in Chad (it did not prevent him from being overthrown by an alienated lieutenant in 1990) and as Druckman and Green suggest happened in the Philippines. In the second situation the government is on the ropes and the insurgency is on a roll, a situation leading to negotiations favorable to the rebellion, as happened in the case of the Eritreans and Ethiopians in 1989 with former President Carter (although the situation did not prevent the talks from breaking down), and as in Lebanon.

The third situation is more promising; characteristic power asymmetry is being overcome but both parties are strong and legitimate enough to come to an agreement satisfying to the minimal or reduced demands of both sides. The lesson reinforces other general findings: parties tend to negotiate in a dynamic situation of equality, when the underdog starts rising and the upper hand starts slipping.[4] In Druckman and Green's third situation it is the insurgency that is the underdog, but both sides must have legitimacy and strength to come to an agreement. It was under such conditions that the peace process got under way in Colombia under President Turbay, was reinvigorated under President Barco, and was brought closer to fruition under President Gaviria, although there were still some outliers to bring in. Under similar conditions, but with a slightly different twist, in South Africa it was the weakening not of government power per se but of its effective answers to the security and governance problem in general that led the government under de Klerk to turn to negotiation. In Mozambique, in yet another twist (not considered in Druckman and Green's typology), both government and insurgency were low in legitimacy, but the government was slipping in power vis-à-vis the insurgency, thus producing a stalemate that was made to hurt for both sides by a drought.

To turn stalemate into reconciliation requires a policy of recognition and dialogue. This means, first, that the insurgency has to be recognized as a legitimate actor—part of the problem and so part of the solution. Recognition of the rebels was the key to breaking the logjam in Mozambique and South Africa. It means, second, that government has to reaffirm dialogue and responsiveness as part of its normal business, not to be denied even to insurgents and to the populations they speak for, if not represent. Unconditional dialogue made solutions possible in South Africa and Colombia, and its absence long blocked a search for solutions in the Basque country and in Sri Lanka.

A policy of recognition and dialogue is not easy to achieve, nor are its effects automatic. Syria turned the Ta'if agreement to its own dominant designs, right-wing death squads assassinated left-wing Colombian rebels who turned legitimate, and morbid jostling for a place at the negotiating table between African National Congress and Inkatha Freedom Party followers (with the connivance of security forces) held up and nearly derailed the South African dialogue before it started. But recognition and dialogue are the first steps toward reconciliation.

Recognition and dialogue are simple principles with some very important fine print. The most significant concerns the relation between the conflict process and the reconciliation process, or between violence on one hand and recognition and dialogue on the other. The shift of the conflict from violent to political means does not happen in one move. After a long period marked by the absence of normal politics, there is suspicion of the newly promised effectiveness of those politics. There is the danger that reconciliation may be a trap; either the government or the rebellion might take advantage of the opportunity to rebuild its forces and to lure the other out into the open in ambush. Furthermore, violence is the only means the insurgents have to counter the power of government; without violence, the asymmetry is overwhelming, because government by definition retains the legitimate use of force.

For the government, a two-handed policy is indicated: engaging in dialogue to find common ground for both sides' reasonable demands, while combating the extremes. Unilateral disarmament by the government would be abdication from its duties, such as the protection of its citizens and the maintenance of law and order, and would be submission to the counterbalancing asymmetry of commitment. In South Africa, where internal conflict negotiations were among the most unprecedented and successful, the police and the judiciary never ceased to function, however badly, throughout the negotiations, sometimes with significant positive effect. In Colombia, where negotiations were also at least partially successful, the judiciary, police, and army continued to play important roles throughout the negotiations, and the battle for control of those forces was crucial, with the guerrillas intimidating the judiciary and antiguerrilla extremists infiltrating the police. The two hands of policy depend on each other for legitimacy and effectiveness: use of police powers is justified only when the state also shows itself open to dialogue, and dialogue is possible only as long as the state also maintains the means to defend itself.

Cease-fire, therefore, is an asymmetrical profession of faith during asymmetrical conflict. Because a cease-fire removes the dynamic relationship between force and negotiation and the possibility of last-minute adjustments in power relations, it is more likely to conclude than to open negotiations. Temporary, unilateral, tacit, and informal cease-fires can be trial balloons that help negotiations get started and can even turn into longer-term, more formal arrangements. However, to do so the conflict and the conflict resolution must be at such a point that the power relation between the two sides is no longer in doubt and force is no longer necessary to insure the support of both parties for a formal cease-fire. At that point refusal of a cease-fire is a sign of bad faith, but not before, as the analysis of the Basque conflict has shown. However, identification of that point is such a subjective matter that the signals are not always clear. Because the opening of direct talks can probably be considered a de-escalating step, a conflict event (such as an attack or arms delivery) during actual negotiations is almost certainly a negative signal, so a cease-fire represents a positive commitment. In Angola a cease-fire came only at the close of negotiations between the ruling MPLA and UNITA. (One must still be careful to discriminate between central control and local initiative in such cases, where part of the job of negotiations may be to protect an accommodating central organization from local challenges, as well as from poor communications.) A cease-fire is helpful as a prelude to negotiations, to create trust and initiate the process of commitment, but should not be a necessary precondition, and governments should not play into the hands of extremists by telling them that an incident would cause talks to collapse.

Commitment is a source of the insurgents' strength; the challenge is to turn commitment from solidarity making to problem solving and reconciliation. Because commitment can get in the way of these goals, it must be harnessed and put to work in outcomes that engage the representative responsibility of the insurgents in a new role involving participation, legitimation and allocation. The genius of the South African and Colombian solutions was to engage the former rebels in pursuit of their goals openly in a new political system. "Normalization" was the key word in Barco's round of the peace process in Colombia, meaning that insurgents could join the political process if they would stop fighting and government would stop fighting if the insurgents joined the political process.

The rebels' commitment is to a dream of full power in the future, however unattainable. In order to harness their commitment to solutions that manage conflict, insurgents must be given some power over their own affairs in the present and a stake in a new political system or new regime. The return to normal politics—a politics that handles grievances and demands—should be the basis of a new, inclusive polity that brings together those who feel deprived and discriminated against and those who have felt part of the old political system, now to share in power and benefits. The solution for regionalist conflicts must incorporate a high degree of regional autonomy and self-government; that for centralist conflicts, a high degree of representation and coalition. Characteristically, protracted internal conflict has gone on too long for the rebels to be satisfied merely with substantive responses to their initial grievances. The rebels no longer trust the government to provide the answers; they demand procedural involvement in a new system. Insurgents are understandably wary of government's empty promises, especially—as is so often the case—when a solution ending a previous round of the conflict has been sabotaged. Aborted experiments in regional autonomy in Sri Lanka and Sudan, in federation in Ethiopia, in power sharing in Angola, and in ethnic groups' management of their ''own affairs'' in South Africa permanently soured the prospects for such solutions in those countries. Because such formulas could have been salient answers to the conflicts in those countries, an important set of options has thus been rendered unavailable.

Of even more significance, many internal conflicts have broken out because an old pact that provided a previous solution either broke down or became outmoded by changing events. Sometimes a putative solution is abandoned: in Sudan, the 1972 Addis Ababa agreement was sabotaged by its author after it replaced the 1955 agreement, which was unsatisfactory to the South; in Sri Lanka, previous attempts to give the Tamils some self-rule in 1958 and 1969 were abandoned by the government; and in Ethiopia, the federation of 1952 was annulled by the emperor a decade later. In Angola, it was the UNITA rebels who rejected the electoral solution negotiated in 1990, after they lost the elections held in 1992. Sometimes a previous solution that worked for the same or different parties becomes outmoded by a new balance of forces. In Lebanon, the 1943 pact on governance was satisfactory to the parties at the time, but thirty years later its one-to-one parliamentary ratio, which had earlier given Christians a 6:5 advantage over the Muslims, was no longer an accurate reflection of the country's demographic proportions, given the high Muslim birthrate; in addition, the Cairo Agreement governing the Palestinian presence in Lebanon had been broken by Palestinian military and political activity. In Colombia, the National Front that ended thirty years of La Violencia in 1953 was a pact between rival factions of the political elite that solved the conflict of the moment, but because that pact excluded new social forces it set the stage for the internal conflict of the 1980s. Thus pacts broken (usually by government) and pacts outmoded sour the atmosphere, reduce trust, and eliminate possible solutions.

Insurgents must be assured of getting a real role in a new political system, with guarantees protecting that role, so that the agreement becomes not just the end of the war but the beginning of a new partnership that does not let the old neglect and discrimination happen again. Irrevocable, ironclad guarantees are difficult to produce, as the federated Eritreans and Sudanese, the decentralized Tamils, and both black and white parties in Zimbabwe can attest, and they ultimately depend on goodwill and proper functioning of the political system. Examples of new political arrangements that have worked are to be found elsewhere than in the cases studied in this book, although one might consider fifteen years of Basque autonomy in Spain and thirty years of National Front rule in Colombia and National Pact rule in Lebanon to be records as stable as one can find in the modern world. Where new political arrangements have worked it was because the formerly deprived groups still retained the potential for serious disruption if the new political system were set aside, and the government (unlike the Ethiopian emperor, the Sudanese Arabs, and the Singhalese) was wise enough to realize it.

The conditions for acceptable power sharing, in the phrase of the Philippine case study, are not preordained. Discovering these conditions is a process, and the final satisfactory formula is in part a result of a fair and constructive dialogue that builds confidence as an answer to specific needs. During negotiations a stepped process and short-term incentives can help to lead the parties toward final agreement on a new system, as was the practice over the four years of negotiation in South Africa. As the discussions on Angola, Mozambique, South Africa, and Colombia indicate, the process moves toward success when it shifts elections from being the mechanism to award a victory denied on the battlefield to being the means to admit all parties to legitimate and ongoing participation in the future political system. Again, the purpose is to break up the bilateral confrontation inherent in the conflict, but in such a way as to preserve the interests and access of the insurgent movement. Elections convey participation, legitimation, and allocation, the three elements necessary to the settlement of internal conflicts.

The purpose of negotiation is to construct an encompassing political system among a majority who can agree, isolating those who cannot. The parties do this by bringing together mainstream demands from each side into a coherent formula, and then bringing in as many outliers and extreme groups as possible by bargaining on the details.[5] It is permissible for the growing central coalition to leave out the spoilers, but is important for the centralists not to make spoilers by leaving out potential participants. Agreement with the rebellion is not achieved by coopting its irresolute edges, as happened in the internal settlement in Rhodesia; it means reaching deep into the rebellion with real concessions in order to carry the bulk of its followers into an agreement. The spokesperson or ''spokesgroup'' must represent the mainstream of each side if it is to produce a winning coalition. Dealing with a negotiator who speaks only for the willing fringe closest to the government will not produce agreements that will be obeyed and end the rebellion. Solutions negotiated with moderate leaders must provide real benefits for the rebels—benefits at least as great as those that would have been negotiated with a more radical leader. Yet the leader of a moderate solution will have a much harder time delivering followers' adherence to an agreement, without which the agreement is pointless. Governments sometimes confuse payoffs to the rebellion's representatives with payoffs to the rebellion; only in the rarer cases where there is an established patron-client structure and there are strong vertical divisions within the rebellion are such partial solutions conceivable.

Leadership and followership are prized political goods, so there will be serious infighting among the insurgents to capture the position of valid spokesperson for the rebellion during times of impending negotiation. This is neither a sign of immature instability nor the work of government agents, but a natural consequence of the struggle and a requisite for negotiation. Although negotiations require mainstream leaders, mainstream leaders may not be able to negotiate. In principle, negotiations are most difficult as long as a leadership struggle is going on, because an opponent can always tar a leader with claims of softness implied by negotiation, as happened in Ethiopia in the 1970s, Angola in the 1980s, and in South Africa in the late 1980s and even the 1990s.

Building a mainstream agreement also means entering into the complicated game, for each side, of helping the leader of the other side maintain domestic support for a joint agreement. In South Africa, de Klerk had to suggest negotiating alternatives and deliver messages that were attractive enough to the African National Congress rank-and-file to buttress the position of Mandela, while at the same time maintaining his own majority within the National Party; Mandela had to assure that same National Party majority so that it remained behind de Klerk, but do so without losing his own support within the ANC. Only by reaching deep into the other side can each party hope to resolve the conflict, thus isolating extremes too small to perpetuate the rebellion, and possibly drawing some of the extremes into the majoritarian settlement. This has been the successful policy in Colombia; but in Sri Lanka the inability to dismantle the extremists, who were resupplied by a new generation of radicals, has been the mark of failure.

Parties on the extremes seek to delegitimize agreement-building and upset the negotiations, either by trying to maintain the integrity of their extreme positions or by trying to discredit or eliminate the negotiating middle, usually by terrorist violence. Opponents of negotiation try to return the conflict to its dyadic nature, polarizing the sides; proponents of negotiation try to carve out a coalition in the middle. Extremists often find an ally in the government. Typically, government policy is to combat the insurgency, enhancing its unity by treating it as a monolith. Extremist leaders can raise commitment to total goals if even lesser demands face rejection by governments. Ethiopian government policies toward Eritreans, Sudanese government policies toward the South, P. W. Botha's policies toward the black majority in South Africa, among many others, made no effort to come to terms with the rebellions by meeting them part way. Any such move is treated as being soft on insurgency (in Ethiopia, "softness" was the reason for the assassination of every leader of the revolution before Mengistu Haile Mariam). The position of the extremists and spoilers is attractive in the long run only to the extent that the government is unresponsive to the underlying grievances and needs of the rebellion; the major tactic of the extremists is to provoke the government into hardening its position, thus reinforcing the appeal of the extremes. This is the dynamic that underlay the victory of the secessionist solution in Eritrea and the wrenching debate over solutions among the southern Sudanese, and it underlies the tactics of the Basque and Tamil extremists.

The discussion above assumes that at least one of the parties seeks to end the internal conflict through negotiation, and wants to entice the other into dialogue. Frequently this is not the case. In the end, progress in negotiation often depends on the presence of an external mediator. Although it is true that countries where most progress has occurred—South Africa and Colombia—have done it on their own, in the absence of any mediation, in all of the other cases examined except the Philippines mediation has already been attempted, and no progress appears to be likely without it. The failure of the experiments in those cases points to missing attributes of mediators and mediation, not to the inappropriateness of mediation itself.

Mediators must be important ("powerful"), multiple, and coordinated to succeed. Mediation must involve the highest external patrons of the parties, for reasons related as much to commitment as to power. In relation to power, the mediators have to insure that neither side is able to bolt the discussions and find ready matériel for renewed combat; the stalemate, such as it may be, must be enforced. In relation to commitment, mediators are needed to reassure the parties of their legitimacy and of their future role in a new political system. Mediators have to assure parties of their continued existence under an agreement, against a tendency—notable in third world experience—to turn a power majority into a power monopoly. No undefeated party in an internal rebellion will agree to commit certain suicide in a reconciliation.

Sometimes third parties can play an important role by defining legitimate outcomes, without actually becoming involved in the negotiations. The limits of reality can be marked by international declarations, which are most important for keeping internal conflict internal so that a new political system can be created. For example, a joint U.S.-Soviet declaration supporting the territorial integrity and political independence of Ethiopia and indicating that secession was not an option, combined with a reminder that sovereignty was a responsibility and not license, might have helped negotiations for Eritrean autonomy in the 1980s.[6] For Sudan, a similar joint declaration by the Organization of African Unity and the Arab League might be a useful, if more unwieldy, mechanism. In South Africa in 1994, the statement by an international mediation team that postponement of elections was not an option narrowed the choices for Buthelezi and eventually helped bring him to an agreement before the elections. Earlier, international consensus on the need for irreversible progress toward political equality before sanctions were lifted kept the pressure on the process in South Africa and underscored the goal. Such positions are not simply a priori predilections. The crucial ingredients of effective international declarations are their publicly binding nature and their sponsorship by potential supporters of the secessionist party. Moves to lower expectations are even more effective when accompanied by measures to limit real alternatives. Thus as negotiations move to the fore, an agreement among arms suppliers to both parties to suspend support can be very helpful. Previous moves toward negotiations with the Eritrean People's Liberation Front in Ethiopia in 1980–81, with UNITA and with the Popular Movement for the Liberation of Angola in 1989–90, with Renamo in Mozambique in 1984, and with various Lebanese groups throughout the 1980s were all derailed largely because external support for the war alternative was readily available.

Mediators must be able to change the mode of conflict and move it from violence to politics, rather than just enabling it to continue at a less costly level. Parties come to love their conflicts and use them as a justification for other policies; they tend to look for measures that make the stalemate bearable and the conflict continuable without demanding any of the compromises or reorientations necessary for resolution—which was the trap in the Namibian and Mozambican negotiations.[7] Mediators must keep up momentum, lest negotiations dissolve into the uncertain status quo that characterizes much internal rebellion, or break down into the recrimination that opens every meeting. Because internal rebellions are based on internal "family" quarrels, recriminations are a natural part of making sure the other side understands the depth of hurt, before turning to resolution. It is important for the parties not to be sidetracked by insults and incidents. Both are a natural part of the process and should not be seized on as a pretense for breaking off a reconciliation process. Often mediators must be present at all stages of the process to witness and testify to agreements; they must also ensure that agreements are executed and timetables are obeyed.

Although these are important counsels for mediators, none fully accounts for the breakdown of mediation in the cases studied in this book. Mediators were used in Ethiopia (where former U.S. president Carter mediated in 1989); Sudan (where the World Council of Churches and All-African Council of Churches, backed by the assistant secretary general of the Organization of African Unity and the emperor of Ethiopia, mediated successfully in 1972, but the Action Council of Heads of State and Government and the Inter-Governmental Authority on Drought and Development mediated unsuccessfully in 1989 and in 1993–94, respectively); Sri Lanka (where India mediated in 1986–88); Angola (Mobutu of Zaire in 1990, Portugal in 1991); Spain (Algeria in 1989); Afghanistan (Pakistan in 1992–93); and Lebanon (Syria in 1986–90). All of the mediators made some progress but they all failed, essentially for two successive reasons.

First, in each case, the moment was not ripe. In none of the cases did the parties feel themselves up against the wall, with only one exit through reconciliation. The absent condition—the ripe moment—is in part objective, in part subjective. Objectively, in the cases studied the military situation was such that the conflicting parties could continue the struggle, and even if the current phase was difficult for one side or the other, they could hang on in hope of a better turn of events. Subjectively, the conflicts had polarized to the point where the leaders in power could not see the situation as desperate, but rather saw it as worthy of their high commitment. This was true not only of the rebel leaders—militia militants in Lebanon, Renamo bandits in Mozambique, Islamic extremists in Afghanistan, Tamil Tiger fanatics in Sri Lanka, ideological revolutionaries of the Sudanese People's Liberation Movement, ETA plotters in Spain, peasant revolutionaries in the Philippines, FARC and ELN radicals in Colombia—but also of government leaders, among them the Islamic extremists in Sudan, heads of tribal factions in Afghanistan, and leftover Stalinists in Ethiopia and Angola. Polarization breeds polarization, because moderates are at risk when a conflict falls into the hands of the extremists. Conditions for negotiation did not obtain because both legitimate government and asymmetrical insurgents were weak (see chapter 12).

Yet there must be a way out of polarization. Situations where both parties are weak contain some of the elements of a hurting stalemate. Mediators are not simply hired hands of fate, passing by to pick the plums at the ripe moment. If mediators were only the midwives of propitiousness, they would be unnecessary, or at most epiphenomenal, and the parties could discover a way out all by themselves. In the cases studied something was missing in the mediators themselves; they were unable to transform the moment and overcome the obstacles to conciliation.

The second reason for failure of the mediators was that among the many incidentals that the mediators lacked, the most important was patronage as a source of leverage over the parties. More than resources for postreconciliation assistance or even arms to keep the parties in or out of the fight, the mediators lacked importance, prestige, weight, and a relationship with the parties that allowed them to guide the parties into agreement or to deliver the parties' compliance when an agreement had been made. In Sri Lanka, Spain, Eritrea, and Angola a partial mediator—one with special ties to one side—failed because it was unable to deliver the side to which it was partial.[8]

Maintenance or improvement of a close and ongoing relationship is the most important motivation for the acceptance of mediation, and that relationship has a greater chance than other elements of being used productively to favor results.[9] Someone is needed who can hold the coat of commitment for the parties when they enter into the chambers of conciliation and can bestow the blessings of legitimacy on the agreement when they come out. Even prestigious individuals such as former presidents Jimmy Carter of the United States and Olusegun Obasanjo of the Action Council of Heads of State and Government were not enough. Mediators must have an official ongoing relationship with the parties that is both material and ideological—a relationship that holds enough future promise that its denial could be used as a threat to keep the negotiating parties in line. In the cases studied incumbent presidents such as Arap Moi of Kenya and Mobutu of Zaire did not have enough integrity of their own, or enough patronage over the parties, to fill the mediator's role. Case studies suggest that only close cooperation between the United States and Russia would work in such conflicts as those in Ethiopia and Angola. In other conflicts an equivalent patron may not even be identifiable. The ultimate irony is that in cases where a proximate patron was available, the patron became so embroiled in the conflict as to become a party and hence part of the problem, even if against its will as happened with India in Sri Lanka, or according to its policy as happened with Syria in Lebanon.

Riding on that relationship, the mediator is in the best position to face its ultimate challenge—to turn the perception of losing into a perception of winning for parties opting for a second-best solution. The mediator must use its skills to get the parties to see that unattainable perfection is not worth the commitment, and that a partial solution that leaves both parties alive and able to pursue their own relations politically and productively is really a positive outcome, worthy of dedicated representatives of both the governors and the aggrieved.

Notes

1. See Special Operations Research Office, *Counterinsurgency*, in 3 vols. (Washington: American University, 1964,); Harry Eckstein, *Internal War: Problems and Approaches* (New York: Free Press of Glencoe, 1964); Franklin M. Osanka, *Modern Guerrilla Warfare: Fighting Communist Guerrilla Movements, 1941–1961* (New York: Free Press of Glencoe, 1962); Peter Paret and John W. Shy, *Guerrillas in the 1960s* (Praeger, 1962); and Kenneth W. Grundy, *Guerrilla Struggle in Africa: An Analysis and Preview* (New York: Grossman, 1971). On the Western social science basis of these studies, see Lewis A. Coser, *The Functions of Social Conflict* (Glencoe, Ill.: Free Press, 1956).

2. See Mao Tse-tung, *Selected Military Writings* (Beijing: Foreign Language Press, 1963); Mao Tse-tung, *Selected Works* (London: Lawrence and Wishart, 1954), especially vol. 1, *On the Rectification of Incorrect Ideas in the Party,* and vol. 2, *On Protracted War*; Che Guevera, *Guerrilla Warfare* (New York: Monthly Review Press, 1961); Võ Nguyên Giáp, *People's War, People's Army: The Viet Công Insurrection Manual for Underdeveloped Countries* (Hanoi: Foreign Languages Publishing House, 1961).

3. See William Branigan, "Philippine Rebels Show Violent Signs of Life," *Washington Post*, February 26, 1992, p. A19; William Branigan, "Feud Among Philippine

Guerrillas Heats Up," *Washington Post*, January 8, 1994, p. A22; and Keith Richburg, "Spoilers of the Peace," *Washington Post*, May 25, 1995, p. A33.

4. See I. William Zartman, *Ripe for Resolution: Conflict and Intervention in Africa* (Oxford University Press, 1989), p. 272.

5. On formula-details negotiation, see I. William Zartman and Maureen R. Berman, *The Practical Negotiator* (Yale University Press, 1982).

6. See Francis M. Deng, *Protecting the Dispossessed: A Challenge to the International Community* (Brookings, 1993).

7. See Zartman, *Ripe for Resolution*, pp. 170–254.

8. On partiality and delivery, see Saadia Touval and I. William Zartman, *International Mediation in Theory and Practice* (Boulder, Colo.: Westview Press, 1985); and I. William Zartman and Saadia Touval, "Mediation: The Role of Third Party Diplomacy and Informal Peacemaking," in Sheryl J. Brown and Kimber M. Schraub, eds., *Resolving Third World Conflict: Challenges for a New Era* (Washington: U.S. Institute of Peace Press, 1992), pp. 239–61.

9. The notion of relationship is based on work with Saadia Touval and Harold Saunders. See Saadia Touval, "Gaining Entry to Mediation in Communal Strife," in Manus I. Midlarsky, ed., *The Internationalization of Communal Strife* (New York: Routledge, 1993), pp. 255–73; and Saadia Touval and I. William Zartman, "Mediation in International Conflicts," in Kenneth Kressel, Dean G. Pruitt, and others, eds., *Mediation Research: The Process and Effectiveness of Third-Party Intervention* (San Francisco: Jossey-Bass, 1989), pp. 115–37; and Harold H. Saunders, *The Other Walls: The Arab-Israeli Peace Process in a Global Prospective,* 2d ed. (Princeton University Press, 1991).

Index